The Jamlady Cookbook

Calamondin Marmalade with Honey Bell Oranges—
Calamondins, Meyer lemons, clementines, pummelos,
Honey Bell oranges, and other citrus fruits can all be used
to make interesting marmalades. Calmondins, the smallest
citrus fruits shown in this picture,
are available in south
Florida in January.

The Jamlady Cookbook

By
Beverly Ellen Schoonmaker Alfeld

Foreword by Sherman Kaplan

Photography by Jim Smith

PELICAN PUBLISHING COMPANY
Gretna 2004

*The word "Pelican" and the depiction of a pelican are trademarks
of Pelican Publishing Company, Inc., and are registered
in the U.S. Patent and Trademark Office.*

Schoonmaker Alfeld, Beverly Ellen.
  The jamlady cookbook / by Beverly Ellen Schoonmaker Alfeld ;
foreword by Sherman Kaplan ; photography by Jim Smith.
      p. cm.
  Includes index.
  ISBN 1-58980-235-7 (hardcover : alk. paper)
  1. Jam. 2. Jelly. I. Title.

TX612.J3S36 2004
  641.8'52—dc22

2004005506

Photographic production assistance by Ryan Basten
Research assistance by Kim Alfeld
Technical administration by Tim Alfeld

The information in this book is accurate and complete to the best of our knowledge. All recommendations are made without guarantee on the part of the author or Pelican Publishing Company. The author and publisher disclaim any liability in connection with the use of this information and caution canners to always check the pH of their canned products and to educate themselves as to what constitutes unsafe storage, faulty sealing, or improper formulation of any hermetically sealed product.

If you have any problems not answered by this book, e-mail jamlady@jamlady.com, and Jamlady will attempt to answer questions if she can. She doesn't know how many will write, so she cannot promise to answer all. Also try your county extension agent.

Printed in Singapore
Published by Pelican Publishing Company, Inc.
1000 Burmaster Street, Gretna, Louisiana 70053

To Kimberly E. Alfeld, Timothy J. Alfeld, and Robert J. Alfeld, III

ତ୯

Contents

Foreword

I don't make jams, jellies, or preserves; I just eat them. But, for Bev Alfeld, making these wonderful spreads from raw fruits, nuts, and vegetables has become not just a hobby; it is almost a crusade. Forget any notion of jam only for your breakfast toast. It's a much bigger subject.

Within the pages of the book you are holding is a storehouse of information. There's some chemistry, some philosophy, some history, some common-sense ideas about living the good life. There is also more than a little bit of Love. And, along the way, there are recipes. Lots of recipes. As Jamlady rightly points out, cooking is as much an art as it is a science. She thanks Plato, in so many words, for that observation.

If you are looking for quick and easy, this book may not be for you. But, if you realize that rewards come from the time and effort needed for achievement, you and Jamlady are meant for each other. It may seem like a one-way conversation at times, maybe even a lecture here and there. But, Jamlady is at your side every step of the way, with history, cautions (that's where the chemistry comes in), and a sense of good taste.

Before you even begin to prepare any of Jamlady's recipes, I suggest you sit down in your most comfortable chair and read her book, cover to cover. That way, you'll get a sense of why this cookbook is really different from most others. If anything, it approaches the richness and knowledge of the original Fanny Farmer with a sense of the love of quality espoused by James Beard.

Herman Melville said it best in *Moby Dick:* "To produce a mighty book, you must choose a mighty theme. No great and enduring volume can ever be written on the flea, though many there be who have tried it."

Jams, jellies, and preserves may not seem like a mighty theme at first blush. But, consider the way Bev Alfeld presents her material, with such thoroughness, and you will come away eager to begin the journey with her.

SHERMAN KAPLAN

News Radio 780 WBBM restaurant critic

Miss Beverly Ellen Schoonmaker (right) with Mrs. Ruth Presbrey, Annual Easter Plant Show at Valley Gardens, Inc., Accord, New York, circa 1956 (Photo by Bob Presbrey)

Acknowledgments

Jamlady especially recognizes the culinary and canning practitioners of the Rondout Valley, specifically, her aunts Mrs. Frances Pine Basten, Mrs. Grace Gardner Schoonmaker, and Mrs. Gladys Marion Carle; her great-aunts Miss Gladys LeFevre Decker and Mrs. Luella Presbrey; her mother, Mrs. Doris Pine Schoonmaker; and her grandmothers, Mrs. Clara Ghear Pine and Mrs. Elizabeth Fitzgerald Schoonmaker and their "church lady" friends who taught Jamlady how to cook, work hard, and set goals. These women were Jamlady's inspiration.

Jamlady will be forever grateful to her father, Mr. Donald LeFevre Schoonmaker, for encouraging Jamlady to love and appreciate plants, for teaching Jamlady the knack of turning work into pleasure, and for modeling the perseverance necessary for doing any job well. Jamlady recognizes her grandfather Mr. Gross B. Schoonmaker, whose gardening business, Valley Gardens, Inc., survived the Depression despite his major disabilities. Gross B., or "Poppa," is best remembered for his strength, generosity, fairness, and integrity.

Special recognition goes to Mr. George Vicory, whose constant support and availability to discuss this book kept Jamlady on a straight and focused path. Jamlady thanks her cousin Dr. Kathleen Schoonmaker Linehan Grambling for being her best friend and supporter. Jamlady thanks her cousins Mr. Rodney Basten and Mr. Clifford Schoonmaker and her brother, Steve Schoonmaker, for having iron stomachs and the willingness to try and consume most anything Jamlady ever made from year one.

A word of thanks is extended to the staff at the Crystal Lake Library, whose names Jamlady will mention, so all can see the people behind the good works: Hugh Engleman, Elaine Falzone, Alice Hayes, John Hill, Cynthia Letteri, Cynthia Lopuszynski, Louise Nee, Jan Polep, Margeret Rals, Clare Schneider, and Nancy Weber. Jamlady especially wishes to thank Jan Polep and John Hill for their long friendship, as they both assisted and encouraged Jamlady to persevere with a book that started out as only an idea.

Special thanks to Ms. Cynthia Crawford-Oppenheimer, special collections librarian/archivist at Conrad N. Hilton Library, CIA, Hyde Park, New York, for the days she spent allowing Jamlady access to the Conrad N. Hilton Library's rare book collection and to Mr. Eric Roth, archivist/librarian at Huguenot Historical Society Library and Archives, New Paltz, New York, for his generous time and assistance. Jamlady thanks James Duke for his willingness to answer her various

Aerial view, Valley Gardens, Inc., 1960

Doris and Donald L. Schoonmaker, Valley Gardens, Inc., Accord, New York, 1975

questions. Jamlady thanks the many professors and staff at Purdue University who answered her frequent questions: Dr. Jules Janick, James Throop Distinguished Professor in Horticulture, and, most recently, Dr. James BeMiller and Ms. Susan Axel Bedsaul. Dr. ZoeAnn Holmes of Oregon State University is thanked and appreciated for her invaluable contributions and information on jelmeters, cellulose-tissue juice extraction, and ridgelimeters.

Jamlady appreciates the many people all over the world who answered her e-mails, even though they had no idea who she was. Thanks to Dr. B. Pickersgill of the University of Reading in Reading, England, and Mr. W. Hardy Eshbaugh for their expert opinions on the classification of peppers and to Mr. Michael Onken of www.MadSci.org. for his help on glycosides. Thanks to Dr. Kenneth N. Hall, emeritus professor at University of Connecticut, for the information he provided. Jamlady appreciates the help given to her by Mr. Thomas Watson; Ms. Jan Bilton; Dr. Elizabeth Andress; Mr. Jeff Rhodes; the Miller Family of Miller's Orchards in Nappanee, Indiana; Grandma Molasses/Mott, Inc.; the Nichols family in Marengo, Illinois; Mr. and Mrs. Dennis Windler; Mrs. Judy Garner; Mr. Bill Grimes *(CRFG)*; Ms. Katherine Long; Mr. and Mrs. Clarence Dey; Mrs. Margurite Sutton; Mr. Ovid Shiffras; and Mr. Robert Peterson. Jamlady thanks all the folks at Outdoor Resorts, especially Mr. and Mrs. Robert Young, Mr. and Mrs. Gary Collins, Mr. and Mrs. Delbert Honert, Mr. and Mrs. Gaston Giguere, and Mrs. Esther Schafer, for taste-testing Jamlady's recipes and for giving her the accolades and appreciation that kept her writing, testing, and cooking. Jamlady thanks all of you who wished to remain anonymous; you know who you are. Many thanks!

Jamlady thanks her publisher and editor for having confidence in her book. Jamlady thanks all the people behind the scenes who produced and promoted Jamlady's book. A special thanks to Ms. Jo Ann Denison, attorney at law, who has supported Jamlady in every way possible. To Mr. Jim Smith and Mr. Ryan Basten, thanks for your patience and artistic talent. Finally, Jamlady thanks all of her fans, neighboring vendors, and patrons at the various Chicagoland markets, who show up weekly to purchase and praise Jamlady's newly made products. Without the willing participation of these good people, this book would not have been written.

Introduction

Many books written on canning approach the subject economically, as a way to save money and preserve food. While Jamlady approves of saving money, she is primarily concerned with creating the "best-ever products" and doing so with ease. Jamlady is university schooled in art and science. She sees cooking and canning as an art, embracing Plato's idea of art as "techne," which presupposes knowing the end at which to be aimed and the best means for achieving the end. When a maker creates, he must judge the excellence of his product according to his insight into proportion and measure, for without the art of measure, there is no art at all. Yet, techne alone is not enough, one must use good judgment and inspiration as well. Jamlady hopes this book will inspire you to create "heavenly" foods, foods daring to imitate those of our divine maker.

If your product is to be heavenly, then you must always use quality ingredients. No one ever created a blue-ribbon preserve from overripe or moldy fruit. Of course, a large quantity of quality ingredients, such as gluts of tomatoes or hoards of cucumbers, should be used to make a lot of the best preserves, chutneys, or relishes. This book endeavors to guide the reader to new and innovative recipes without ignoring the tried-and-true classics.

Jamlady wants people to realize and acknowledge that not all people should eat in the same manner. There is growing support for the concept of eating according to your health problems, exercise regime, and the climate in which you live. Half the foods you eat should probably be raw, unless you have some specific health problem that prohibits raw food. Canned products, rather than supplying you with staple or subsistence foods, should be foods that complement or add flavor to the basic meal. For example, preserved bread and butter pickles should not be substituted for a fresh salad. They might well be eaten instead of an ice-cream dessert. And strawberry preserves, good as they are, should not be substituted for fresh fruits.

In perusing the literal hundreds and thousands of recipes in canning books, what strikes Jamlady as noteworthy is how little attention is paid to certain vegetables, fruits, and herbs. Equally amazing is how combinations of certain fruits and vegetables seem obvious to Jamlady but apparently have never been combined into a published recipe—at least not one that Jamlady has viewed. No recipes in this book require processing under pressure. Processing with a rolling water bath, the process known in this book as "RWB," is easier and faster than processing foods with high temperature and pressure.

A fault of many recipe books is that the quality control resides with the author or each individual submitting a recipe. If you've ever made a new recipe from a cookbook and no one liked it, you know what Jamlady means. Jamlady's recipes are popular recipes. The quality control resides in the taste buds of the consumers. Most all of Jamlady's canning recipes found in this book have been created many times for Chicagoland market patrons who have taste-tested them at open-air farmers' markets and favorably received them. Only experimental batches with tropical and other fruits not normally available in the Midwest represent the exceptions to this statement. Many of the recipes were born out of a discipline or method Jamlady learned in art school at Northern Illinois University while working on an M.A. in design (1972) and an M.F.A. (1974). A design teacher of Jamlady's, Dr. William Brown, once said, "The more limitations you place on yourself, the better the results will be." This premise holds true for cooking as well. Decisions are easier when you have fewer decisions to make. Working with limitations forces you to consider options that you might not otherwise have considered. The convent nuns of Puebla, Mexico, in an effort to create a special dish for a visiting viceroy, created Mole Poblano by improvising and cooking with the only things they had available: turkey, almonds, raisins, peanuts, tomatoes, onions, stale bread, a tortilla, lard, peppers, sesame seed, and, yes, chocolate! Would they have ever tried this combination if not for limitations?

If you have tomatoes, don't say, "Gee, I'd like to make strawberry jam." Think, "I am going to make something fantastic from tomatoes." Don't just think about using up the tomatoes. Seize the opportunity to create the best-ever tomato product. Tomato-dill jelly was such a creation. An overabundance of dill and tomatoes necessitated a recipe utilizing these two ingredients. Tomato-dill jelly evolved from one of many variations of a tomato-lemon jelly. One of the problems with

creative canning is the necessity of controlling sugar, salt, vinegar, and such ingredients to the extent that you do not create a medium in which harmful microorganisms can grow. Be mindful that you must learn the basics of canning and microbiology before venturing into the realm of recipe creation or modification of a hermetically sealed product.

Further, there are certification and licensing issues to be considered by the homemaker who wishes to sell her marvelous concoctions. The days of selling homemade products in an unlicensed kitchen, unfortunately, are gone. In addition to a licensed kitchen, you will need to prove your knowledge regarding safe canning. Courses available through the Better Process Control Schools, located in various United States universities, can be a good starting point for the homemaker who wishes to sell her wares. Better Process-affiliated schools teach courses of instructions as required by the Food and Drug Administration and are usually recognized by individual states' health departments.

The art of preserving foods in containers has many names. Some call it canning or preserving, others refer to jams and chutneys as "put-ups" or "putting things up." No matter what you call the art of home canning, its existence is in jeopardy. If the art of home canning is to survive the twenty-first century, those who love the art will have to embrace it and nurture its development and growth.

It would be a shame to lose the art of home canning that is so much apart of the American tradition. Legislators lobbied by large commercial food-processor associations, who would abolish the art of home canning in the name of safety, will need to be held in check by grass-roots home processors. Home canning can be safe, if not safer, compared to foods produced in large food-manufacturing plants. Courses in home canning and certification of home preservers could be the solution to those who would question the art learned mostly through apprenticeship, old to young, generation after generation.

Many would argue that there is no need to can anymore because commercially manufactured products are safer and cheaper. While commercially manufactured jams, jellies, chutneys, relishes, and pickles may be cheaper, they are not necessarily safer, and they certainly aren't superior in quality to the products made by the accomplished home preserver. Nothing can make up for the diminished taste and nutritional value caused by large industrial-batch preparation. The home canner's product is usually superior to a commercially produced product because small-batch preparation usually means shorter cooking times, fresher ingredients, organic ingredients, more careful preparation, and special recipes that cannot be produced by a larger food manufacturer profitably.

For those who still argue that the preparation time of canned foods is not worth the end product, consider the host of suspicious additives that are added to most commercial products. Does anyone's human anatomy really need five pounds a year of food additives in the forms of dyes and chemicals? The safety debate, when considering food additives, only strengthens the case of the home canner over the commercial canner and increases the need for people to eat lots of organic foods in a raw state. For this reason, more and more people are flocking to farmers' markets to purchase organic vegetables and home-canned products made in small commercial kitchens. The extra monetary cost may well outweigh the negative effects of chemical sprays and food additives, not to mention the improved taste and superior nutritional value!

Jamlady urges those interested in good health to pay special attention to herbs and spices and their historical, medicinal, and cultural use. Over time and without proper instruction regarding the benefits of certain plant products, many of us have forgotten or never knew the benefits of utilizing herbs and spices in our cooking. With new research on adaptogens and the body's natural anticancer system and the Nrf2 protein or switch (researchers at John Hopkins University in Baltimore and Tsukuba University in Japan have studied the system that disposes of toxic chemicals in our bodies), we need to revisit the use of handfuls of fresh herbs and spices instead of teaspoonfuls of dried, old spices.

America is a melting pot of diversified cultures and peoples. Jamlady was taught by her history teacher, Mr. Hal Ross, a decorated World War II veteran, that tolerance of differences and attempts to try new ideas are mainstays of our American tradition, troubled as we sometimes are with these concepts. Because of this tradition of accepting and trying ideas from other cultures, many international food recipes and techniques have been adapted and modified by Americans. Therein lies our strength. The "ability to adapt," said Lou Traversa, a past design professor of Jamlady's, "is the most valuable characteristic anyone can have . . . for in adapting one can handle any challenge or limitation." American cooks have adapted, modified, and embraced Indian chutneys, Mexican salsas, root jams, piccalillis, Italian *mostarda di cremona* (fruit relish), Indonesian vegetable pickles, sour Chinese cabbage relish, and English pickled green walnut, to name but a few unique, preserved foods found in American cupboards. Americans, because of their diversity, may well have been pushed to adapt. It is Jamlady's hope that Americans will continue adapting to new rules and regulations and not lose their wonderful tradition of home canning.

A Word to the Wise

Can wisely. Follow recipes carefully. Check the pH of recipes after you have made them and before you consume them, especially if you have never made a recipe before, and especially if the recipe is old and from an unknown source! Respect the 4.6 pH line and stay clear of recipes that hover in the 4.3-4.6 range or above. Remember, pH is a critical factor. When in doubt regarding a product's pH, refrigerate the product immediately and ask an expert for advice. Don't can products like baked bread ("bread in a jar"), for which the pH of the total ingredients is above 4.6!

Jamlady hopes that canners will encourage their local universities to establish better pH charts for all the fruits and berries that canners may wish to seal in a jar. The lack of easily available information is frustrating, to say the least. Farmers can find recommended soil pH for these plants, but try to find the pH of fruits like mamey, barberry, chestnuts, or jaboticaba. Of course, if you have the fruit and have a pH meter, there is no problem, as you can test the pH yourself, but if you do not have access to a pH meter, you might have no idea about what the pH might be.

First-time canners are advised to start with jam or preserves recipes, as the pH for most jam recipes is usually in a comfortable canning range! Please read current literature regarding the safe use of aspartame for sweetening jams or preserves. Aspartame is metabolized in the body into its components: aspartic acid, phenylalanine, and methanol. For more information, research these key words on the Internet. Many experts disagree on what constitutes safe use of aspartame.

The Alfeld Nomenclature System. Some new abbreviations and terms have been created by Jamlady as a form of shorthand or as a notation for the canner to go with the already established RWB. Jar, seal, and process in a rolling water bath (RWB) for 10 minutes means place the "jam" in a canning **jar,** attach the canning lid and tighten down the canning ring or **seal/close,** place the jar in a water bath of the same temperature as the jar and its contents, and **process** the jar in a **rolling water bath** for the **prescribed time,** to create a vacuum in the jar so that the jar is hermetically sealed. **The abbreviated form of this is JSP/RWB10. JSR means "jar, seal or close, and refrigerate." For pressure canning, the notation would be JSP/10PSI/75, meaning "jar, seal, process at 10 pounds per square inch for 75 minutes." Further specifics for jar size can be shown in parentheses after the times, such as JSP/RWB5(4OZ)10(8OZ)15(16OZ). If no jar size is shown, the jar size is**

assumed to be 4- to 8-ounce jars. The Switch Method of cooking down product is abbreviated SM or CD/SM or cook down, Switch Method.

Most recipes in this book may be cut in half, quartered, or even cut by $\frac{1}{10}$ or $\frac{1}{12}$, if you reduce the diameter of the cooking vessel proportionately. Two kiwis, for example, can be cooked into preserves in 15 minutes by using $\frac{1}{12}$ of the kiwi preserves recipe. For recipes calling for box pectin, please note that approximately 18 teaspoons of pectin are in a 1¾ ounce box of pectin. This means you "wannabe" canners with no real hobby time can maybe still eek out a little time to make a small personal stash of Kiwi Grand Preserves. So, joyful jamming, jammers!

The Jamlady Cookbook

Back: Yellow Champion juicing machine, cherry-pitting machine, pH meter, buffer solutions, and ridgelimeter. Front: M.C.P. Jelly-Making Set, one-half red prickly pear, and two glass jelmeters for testing the concentration of pectin in juice.

Chapter 1

಄಄

Processing Methods and Troubleshooting

There are several ways to hermetically seal a glass jar, but for the purposes of this book, the **rolling water bath or RWB** is the only type recommended for a shelf-stable product. Wax sealing or jar inversion is used for a couple of recipes for which the RWB method would cause the berries to bleed within the jar. For these products, inversion or wax sealing, combined with refrigeration, is recommended. Other methods, such as sealing by steam, sealing in a pressure cooker, sealing in the oven, sealing in the dishwasher, and jar inversion without refrigeration, are left out of this book on purpose, as they are not necessary or recommended for any recipes in this book.

There are pros and cons for all the different sealing methods, but the Jamlady and the USDA recommend the RWB for the type of recipes found in this book. Jamlady knows that some canners seal jam jars by inverting them after hot-filling the jars. While this will sometimes work, or seal the jar, it is not a recommended process for a shelf-stable product. The reason the inversion method is not recommended is that a jar can become unsealed with temperature fluctuations, because the vacuum in the jar is probably lower than it should be. Any inversion-sealed jar may become unsealed in a very warm location. **The inversion-sealed jar will usually unseal at a lower temperature more often than a RWB-sealed jar will. There are four primary factors that contribute to a proper vacuum seal on a jar. These are headspace, product-sealing temperature, air in the product, and capper vacuum efficiency.** Generally speaking, the headspace should not be less than 5 percent of the container volume at the sealing temperature. Insufficient headspace means not enough steam is trapped in the headspace area to form a sufficient vacuum and not enough space to allow for product expansion when processing in a RWB. Theoretically, **the higher the product temperature at the time of sealing, the higher the final package vacuum.** The air in the product and the processing temperature together also affect the resulting vacuum. **Vacuum is less where air trapped in the product is greater.** Capper vacuum efficiency is an indication of the ability of the top or cap to produce a proper seal and can be measured by a vacuum gauge.

Commercially, jars and cans are sealed in a variety of ways. Much of the time, they are sealed in a retort. Retorts vary in type. There are **still retorts, agitating retorts,** and **hydrostatic retorts.** A **retort** is a closed vessel used for thermal processing of foods. A **still retort,** a pressure vessel, accepts racks, crates, cars, baskets, or trays of jars to be sealed and is stationary or nonagitating. The pressure inside a still retort is great. The processing takes place at around 250 degrees F (121 degrees C) with fifteen pounds/square-inch pressure, or about ten tons of force. **A retort is a very big pressure cooker.**

A **hydrostatic retort** operates at a constant process temperature, and the product to be sealed is transported through the retort on a conveyor system, allowing for a constant flow of containers. Hydrostatic retorts are often built as high towers, with the conveyor belt carrying product up and down the tower's height several times in a continuous flow of product. **Agitating or rotary retorts** provide continuous container handling and additionally agitate the product intermittently. Agitating or rotary retorts are useful when processing thick products, as it allows for better heat distribution and even processing.

ROLLING WATER BATH (RWB)

Most recipes in this book can be sealed by a process called a rolling water bath or RWB. Any pot with a rack will work, but Jamlady recommends you outfit a tall cylindrical stockpot with a round perforated disc rack to serve as an elevation between the jars and the bottom of the pan. Jamlady is highly critical of the traditional canning pot, which is too short, in Jamlady's opinion, to cook quarts. When the tops of the jars are covered with water, as they should be, the water boils all over the stove because the pot is too short. Even with a taller pot, there will be some water finding its way to the stovetop. A taller pot is definitely recommended for quarts. For some of the modern home ranges, the short stocky canner is also too large in diameter, as many ranges have insufficient BTUs that do not properly heat up the pot. With a low BTU burner, it takes forever to bring a large and wide pot up to boil.

Look for at least 10,000 BTUs in a range burner; 12,000 or higher is better. If you have a 6,000 or 8,000 BTU burner, it will take too long to bring the jar of product up to temperature, and the contents will cook too long. This imprecision in the process time will not hurt most jellies or jams, but it will make a huge difference in pickles, which need to be cooked just enough to seal them safely. Many a mushy pickle can be traced to a low BTU burner.

Many home canners will find that some range salesmen have little information on the BTUs of the ranges they sell, and Jamlady cautions buyers to be informed by checking all of a model's specifications with consumer magazines and with the manufacturer directly. Many of the sheets distributed on a specific model do not even list this vital information. When buying a new range for a canning practitioner, consider that there will be water coming out of the pot and on to the top of the range. A sealed-burner gas range, with recesses to hold the water so it does not go all over the range (or range top and counter), is very desirable. Look to Magic Chef and Maytag, as well as other companies that might have new designs such as Jamlady describes. Special-order a range with hotter burners, if possible.

Commercial ranges have high BTUs, but many have trays to catch the water, and this means sticky water gets all over the range grates, in places that are not easily cleaned. A sealed-burner range can be sprayed with oven cleaner and wiped clean in five minutes. Take your time and ask the right questions when purchasing a new range. If you're stuck with a low BTU range, then can in smaller jars in a smaller canner.

Jamlady is frustrated to see all the ranges that cannot properly heat up a canner. If you don't have two, high-BTU burners next to one another, such that a huge canner can sit over the two burners, you may have a problem in making jardinieres in quarts, for example, unless you opt for a smaller pot, holding less jars but tall enough to take quarts. Since many home canners are canning unique products and are not production orientated, it may not be necessary to process twelve jars at a time. You can do two successive batches of six or use two canners on two burners, with six in each and using a taller stock pot with a rack and smaller diameter.

There are many books out there with illustrative pictures of how to use a **rolling-water-bath canner,** but Jamlady sees this as so much fuss over nothing. If you have ever made spaghetti in a spaghetti boiler or steamed a fish in a fish steamer, you can seal a jar using the RWB method. Take your spaghetti boiler or fish steamer (short jars only) with the rack inside. Place your filled 4-, 8-, or 16-ounce jars in the bottom. Fill the pan with water of the **same temperature** as the product to be processed, so that the jar tops are covered by at least 1" of water. Put the pot on the range. Heat the pot until the water starts to really boil. This does not just mean that bubbles are rising to the top of the pan, but that an actual rolling of the water is taking place on the surface. The process time is counted from the time the water starts to roll from boiling. When that time is up, remove the jars with canning tongs or lift the spaghetti rack out of the pan and set it on some pot holders to cool. You have just canned a jar of product. Make yourself a cup of tea and sit near the jars for the final proof positive. As you sit in the area of the jars, you will eventually hear a pop, a noise like the clicking of your tongue on the roof of your mouth. A little voice inside Jamlady usually shouts, "Success," and you will hear this voice too. This click or pop means your jar is vacuum sealed. Look at the top of the lid. You will see, hopefully, that it is sunken in. Push on it with your index finger. If it is down and does not timber up and down, it is properly sealed.

When cool enough, hold the supposedly sealed jar at eye level. You will see a depression in the lid if it is properly sealed. If it is not sealed, then put the jar in the refrigerator for immediate use or use a new lid and process again.

Caution: **Do not assume if a jar of product**

previously unsealed at room temperature seals in the refrigerator that you can take it out of the refrigerator again. More than likely, it will unseal with room temperature and reseal again when it cools. So, just keep that product in the refrigerator until you use it. Some products fail to seal on the first attempt. Jams can be reprocessed. Other products, such as pickles, will be ruined by being cooked for a second time.

You might wonder how sealing works. Basic science 101 teaches us that **hot things expand and cool things contract.** A hermetically sealed jar of jam is a perfect example of this principle. When you heat the jar, the contents expand and drive out the steam. When the jars are quickly taken out of the hot water, they cool quickly, and the contents contract, pulling the lid down and making a vacuum seal.

FILLING THE JAR

There are steps to follow in filling your jar of product that will be processed.

1. Inspect each jar, new or old, to make sure there are no cracks in the jar or nicks in the lip of the jar.
2. Make sure your jars are squeaky clean and sterilized. You can run your jars through the dishwasher or boil them in water to sterilize them. If you are hand-washing the jars, a little capful of household bleach in the wash water is recommended.
3. Make sure you have not overfilled the jars. The glass jar has a fill line on it, but basically fill to ¾ or ½" from the top. Jellies can be filled higher than pickles.
4. Check the rubber seals on the rings for imperfections. Use no bent or rusted lids or rings.
5. Place the rubber seal down on top of the jar rim. Make sure the jar rim is clean after filling the jar to the appropriate fill level. Do not overfill the jars. You cannot get a good vacuum seal with an overfilled jar.
6. Place the metal ring over the jar, with the lid

and screw on the ring. Do not screw it on tightly, but adjust to the first bit of resistance. Your jar is now ready for the RWB.

PROCESSING TIMES

Processing times vary according to the size of the jar and the thickness of the product. The typical bread-and-butter pickle would be processed 10 minutes for a quart and 5 minutes for a pint. A chutney or preserves could be processed 10-20 minutes, depending on the size of the jar, which could be a 4-, 8-, 12-, 16-, 22-, 24-, or 32-ounce jar. There are some 64-ounce jars out there, but Jamlady hardly believes anyone would use that much chutney at one time, but you never know. Maybe some of Jamlady's readers own restaurants. In any event, Jamlady would not recommend canning chutney or any other very dense and thick product in huge jars, as it is difficult for the heat to penetrate evenly into the center. The home canner has no agitating retort. Generally speaking, Jamlady would not can chutney in a jar larger than 24 ounces and usually seals chutney in a jar 16 ounces or smaller.

If the processing time is insufficient, a proper vacuum will not form to seal the jar. This can be disastrous for a jar of pickles. The best you can do is refrigerate the pickles immediately. Happily, many of the jars do seal when placed in the refrigerator and do not have to be consumed immediately. If the jar is sealed in the refrigerator, leave it there and use when you wish to open it. **Do not, Jamlady repeats, do not take the jar out of the refrigerator, believing it will stay sealed!** More than likely, the jar will become unsealed in a warm location, and it will reseal in a cooler environment. Needless to say, this is a potentially dangerous situation and one that you might not be aware of at the time. The jar may be sealed when you look at it on a cooler evening and may be unsealed during the hotter part of a day while you are not around.

Likewise, a rolling-water-bath-sealed jar,

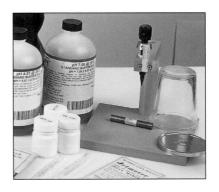

intended to be stored at room temperature, should not be subjected to higher temperatures like the front seat of a car on a hot, sunny day. On a hot day, the seal could pop and, when cooled again, seal again, and you would have no idea anything had occurred. With jams, this situation probably won't affect much and probably should not stop you from refrigerating the product and perhaps eating it, assuming the time in the car was only a very short time, but for other products without high sugar, this could be a major problem. **Just don't carry canned products in the car in the summer or dead of winter without keeping them at room temperature.** Freezing will also break a seal and ruin your product. Be smart! In the summer, transport your jams in a cooler or keep the car's air conditioning running at all times. In winter, keep canned products from freezing.

ALTITUDE CONVERSION

Unless you live on a mountain or in an airplane, you do not usually have to worry about altitude conversion. **Water-bath canner time does need to be increased as altitude increases.** This chart is for processing times of less than twenty minutes. *Note:* **If using a pressure canner, increase the pounds of pressure for processing as the altitude increases. Processing at ten pounds at sea level would need to be at thirteen pounds of pressure at 5,000 to 6,000 feet.**

For a RWB, it is sufficient to increase the processing times.

Altitude in Feet	Minutes Added to Processing Time
1,000	1
2,000	2
3,000	3
4,000	4
5,000	5
6,000	6
7,000	7
8,000	8
9,000	9
10,000	10

REACTIVE METALS

Please note that in canning, the canning practitioner is advised to avoid iron, aluminum, brass, copper, or zinc (galvanized) and opt for metals that cannot react chemically with acids and salts. Jamlady uses either enamelware, stainless steel, ceramic, or glass vessels or pots. Check with a good restaurant supply store for a tall pot. Racks from pressure cookers can be used in the bottom of cylindrical stainless-steel stockpots, or a makeshift rack can be made from heavy stainless-steel wire cut to fit the bottom of the pan and wooden slats or spacers attached to the wire. Alternately, very heavy wire mesh can be bent over to make a rack that will prevent jars from touching the bottom of the pot. Cooking pots for jelly making should have a heavy bottom core. Buy the best pots and pans you can afford. You will not be sorry. Again, go first to your local restaurant supply store for a quality pot or pan.

AVOIDING PROBLEMS

The best way to deal with any problem is to avoid it in the first place. Here are some suggestions for canning not only jams and preserves, but also other preserved products.

1. **Do not use homemade vinegar for canning.** Use only vinegar with a confirmed, 5 percent or higher acidity.
2. **Do not use hard water, especially for pickles.**
3. **Do not store canned goods in a warm or light spot.** Select a dark and cool location.
4. **Get the processing times right.** Cook on a range that takes the product to a rolling boil quickly.
5. **Use fresh products without sprays or other chemicals.** This directive includes not using really old spices. Some powdered spices may cause pickles or jellies to be murky, so try to use whole spices or fresh herbs when possible. Don't use hollow cucumbers in pickling. Discard any slimy or slippery pickles.
6. **Don't panic over pink pickled cauliflower or green garlic.** It isn't spoilage, but a chemical change that is okay. Jamlady often pickles cauliflower with beets, which naturally colors the cauliflower a beautiful fuchsia color and the problem is eliminated. Sometimes garlic or shallots turn green or blue in pickling. This too is not harmful. Immature and underdried garlic can turn blue or green in the presence of an acid because of the anthocyanin in the garlic. The green or blue color can also be due to sulfur compounds reacting with trace amounts of copper in the water. If the enzymes in the garlic cloves are not inactivated by heat, blue sulfate can form. Some people say that temperature-controlling the garlic cloves prior to use will eliminate the problem. Don't use immature garlic heads and store your garlic at room temperature for at least three weeks prior to using. Vegetables that turn brown were either overcooked or overripe to begin with, or the cook used iodized salt instead of canning salt.
7. **Don't pack vegetables tightly in a jardiniere or pickle jar, thinking you will get**

more in there. **Don't pack a jar with vegetables that block the neck of the jar.** A tightly packed jar cannot expand without forcing some of the juice out of the jar. If the jar seals, you can still use the product, but Jamlady always refrigerates these reduced-brine-level jars until opening day by laying them down in the refrigerator and rotating them often so the juice touches all surfaces of the vegetables. Use smaller pieces of vegetables toward the top of the jar so the liquid can freely flow around. Sometimes the liquid will travel out of the jar because of food trapped between the rubber of the seal and the jar's glass rim. Stray food pieces can lodge there due to the force of the steam leaving the jar. This is unavoidable in many cases and probably is not your fault. Just refrigerate the jar and use it up first. Liquid boiling out can often be traced to cracks in the jar rim or caps that were screwed on too tightly during the heating process.

8. **Discolored pickles are often traced to iron utensils, inappropriate cookware, metal-lid corrosion, use of iodized salt (use only pickling salt), too many or poor spices, and hard water.**

9. **Shriveled and tough pickles are often traceable to overcooking, too heavy a syrup, too-strong brine, unfresh fruits or diseased fruits, or fruits that have been cooked too harshly in brine or sugar syrup.**

10. **Cloudy jelly can be caused by insufficiently strained juice, use of overly green fruit, or allowing the jelly to sit for too long prior to being packed into jars.**

11. **Crystals in jelly** can be from using too much sugar, cooking too little and too slowly, or cooking for too long. Crystals in grape jelly can be **tartrate crystals** and can be avoided by letting the extracted juice sit in a cool place overnight. Then strain through two thicknesses of damp cheesecloths to remove the crystals.

12. **Jelly or jam can be too soft because the ratio of sugar to fruits or acid is insufficient.** Doubling and tripling recipes can cause soft jelly, as the measure of the surface area is reduced and the amount of evaporation is significantly reduced. Jellies made with no pectin can be cooked down further to affect a set. Other jellies can be cooked down, or some liquid pectin might be added.

13. **Syrupy jelly indicates too little pectin, acid, or sugar.** Sometimes syrupy jelly indicates way too much sugar.

14. **Weeping jelly often occurs with fluctuating storage temperatures.** Too much acid can cause weeping jelly. Jamlady doesn't worry about weeping jelly. Just stir it all back together.

15. **Stiff jelly is definitely a problem and is caused by too much pectin or by cooking the jam down too much.** To try to make the jam usable, thin it with hot water in a saucepan. Use for basting meats or whatever. A resourceful person might put some stiff jelly in their tea instead of sugar (Russian tea).

16. **Tough jelly indicates a mixture that had to be cooked too long to reach jell point because it had too little sugar.**

17. **Mold on jelly indicates an improper seal.** In the old days, people used to scrape the mold off and eat the jelly anyway. Today, it is suggested the product be discarded because of toxins produced by the molds. Molds can also grow on jars of jam that had no mold when they were opened. Some people, with their unsanitary jelly-dispensing habits, contaminate the jam. Don't expose a knife or spoon to the counter, the bread, and the jar of jam, back and forth. Jamlady suggests you use a clean, large tablespoon to take out what jam will be needed with one

scoop and then close the container. If a second dip is needed, use another, clean spoon or knife.

18. **Faded jelly is caused by improper storage or storage for too long a time.** Store canned products in a cool, dark place.

19. **Floating fruit in jam can indicate underripe fruits or fruits that are not properly crushed or not sufficiently cooked.** Jamlady does not see this as a big problem. Stir the jam after opening. To prevent fruit from floating in the jar, you might try lightly shaking the jars of jam as they cool or turning them upside down and back again as they cool and set. Some books recommend stirring the jam for 5 minutes before putting it in the jars, but Jamlady finds that this method makes it more difficult to load the sticky jam into the jars, and it usually increases the evaporation to the point that the jam could actually set up too hard. Using riper fruits is no answer either, because the pectin is then reduced as well.

20. **Cracks in jars can occur when you put hot jam in a jar and place it in cool water.** Any hot product in a jar needs to be placed in water of the same temperature. Even then, if you hermetically seal jars by canning frequently, you will eventually have a jar crack and destroy/lose all of the product. For this reason, really dear product may be best canned in new, smaller jars. If one breaks,

you won't have lost as much of your special creation.

21. **Fermented product usually means there probably is a break or leak in the seal somewhere, even though you may not be able to see it.**

HOW REGULAR PECTIN WORKS

Pectin is a fibrous carbohydrate containing entrapped water molecules. Some fruits have more pectin than others. Ripe apples, blackberries, crab apples, red currants, gooseberries, and cranberries all have a lot of pectin—unripe, even more. Citrus fruit, especially the rinds, contain a lot of pectin, as do raspberries and grapes. When the fruits containing pectin are cooked in the presence of acid, the pectin changes its molecular structure and physical properties so that it is less possessive of its water and more attracted to the other pectin molecules.

Sufficient acid is essential for fruits to gel or thicken. *Putting Food By* (Ruth Hertzberg, Beatrice Vaughan, and Janet Greene [New York: Bantam Books, Inc., 1976], 54-55) recommends a comparative taste test for judging the amount of acid in a substance. The tartness of the fruit is compared to 1 teaspoon lemon juice, 3 tablespoons water, and ½ teaspoon sugar. If your juice is not as tart, you need more acid for a gel to form. Jamlady recommends a pH meter or pH papers with testing ranges for 2.0 to 3.0, 3.0 to 4.0, and 4.0 to 5.0 as opposed to a pH paper that covers the entire range. In short, this will require 3 different sets of pH papers, which are relatively inexpensive. Jamlady believes any serious canner who is creating his or her own recipes should invest in a pH meter and use it.

When sugar is heated in the presence of an acid, it breaks down into simple sugars glucose and fructose. These sugars accept the water molecules from the pectin chains. The pectins then bind to one another, forming a web of pectin and a jell is formed. This jell

web holds the fruits together. **The amount of pectin in a fruit juice correlates to the viscosity of the fruit juice. The relative viscosity of a fruit juice can be measured with a viscometer, jelmeter (if you can find one), or homemade viscometer. (See Science-Projects.com for how to make one for seventy-five cents.)** LM pectin works differently and does not need added sugar for the chemical reactions or jelling process to take place.

HOW DID THEY SEAL JARS IN 1899?

Before jars were sealed with glass lids, "rubbers," or metal lids with rubber seals, other methods were used.

"For small families it is advisable to put the fruits into pint jars. If jellies are put into tumblers, fit a round piece of paper dipped in brandy over the jelly, then cut another piece of half an inch larger than the top of the tumbler, dip it in unbeaten white of egg and paste it over the tumbler; this will make it air-tight and will protect the jelly from molding. Another way is to pour melted white wax over the jelly, then put on a tight-fitting cover or paste paper over. The wax may be washed and laid aside when the jelly is served and used again. Still better way is to dissolve one tablespoonful of salicylic acid in half a cup of alcohol, dip round pieces of paper in this and fit it neatly over the jelly, then paste another piece of paper dipped in white of egg over the top. But the best and surest way is to put all jellies and marmalades in pint or half-pint glass jars which are perfectly air-tight, as fruit that is not air-tight will either ferment or mold" (Gesine Lemcke, *Preserving and Pickling* [New York: D. Appleton and Company, 1899], 1).

"Covering for Preserves. — White paper, cut to a suitable size, dipped in brandy, and put over the preserves when cold, and then a double paper tied over the top. All preserves should stand a night before they are covered. Instead of brandy, the white of eggs may be used to glaze the paper covering; the paper may be pasted round the edge of the pot, instead of tied— it will exclude the air better; and may be pasted and tied too" (Mrs. M. E. Peterson, *Peterson's Preserving, Pickling & Canning— Fruit Manual* [Philadelphia: G. Peterson and Company, 1869], 52).

Lemcke further states:

"How to put Fruit into Jars. — A good way to put hot fruits into jars without cracking is to dip a towel into cold water, wring it out half dry, fold double and lay it on the kitchen table. Have the jars clean and dry, set them on the wet towel, put a new rubber on each one, set the preserving kettle with the hot fruit near the jars and fill them to **overflowing.** As soon as one is filled put on cover (close tightly) and set the jar upside-down till cold. When all are filled wipe them off with a damp towel, examine each one if perfectly air-tight, put them in a cool, dry place; two days later examine again and see if air-tight. Sometimes it is difficult to get the jars tight. One or two extra rubbers put on will in most cases remedy the fault" (Gesine Lemcke, *Preserving and Pickling* [New York: D. Appleton and Company, 1899], 2).

Lemcke discusses the rolling-water-bath method, although she does not call it by name.

"How to can Fruit and Vegetables. — The best way for canning fruit and vegetables is to have a canner, and if not handy a boiler will have to answer the purpose, which is filled half full of water and placed on the side of the stove. Some put two or three layers of paper in the bottom of the kettle and lay something heavy on it to keep it in position; and others put hay or straw in. When the jars have been filled with fruit and sirup, they should be closed tightly, each wrapped separately in a towel, hay or straw, and placed in the kettle; the jars should be at least two inches under the water, and if bottles are boiled the water should reach one inch below the cork. The kettle is then placed over the fire to boil. The time for boiling depends entirely on the fruit. Peaches should boil from 20 to 30 minutes; apricots, 20 minutes; pineapple, 45 minutes; berries of all kinds, 5 minutes; cherries 5 to 10 minutes; and quince about 25 minutes. When the time for boiling is up, the jars should be removed and set upside down till cold. Care should be taken to put the jars when first taken from the water bath on a dry board or towel, and not on a wet table, for the least drop of cold water will crack the jars. In case the jars should not be quite full when taken from the bath, have ready some hot sirup, open the jars one at a time and quickly fill with the sirup, close at once. As soon as the jars are cold wipe them clean, examine each one if air- tight, and set in cool dry place" (Gesine Lemcke, *Preserving and Pickling* [New York: D. Appleton and Company, 1899], 2-3)

Any food historian can readily see that the canning concept is only partly understood by Lemcke, as she recommends the jars be filled to the very top, "overflowing." Through the over-filling of the jars, the rate of nonsealing jars and expiring jars increases. Present-day canning jars have a fill line, indicated by the protruding glass ridge approximately ¾" from the top of the jar, allowing for a proper vacuum to be achieved.

An 1869 citation in *Peterson's Preserving, Pickling & Canning Fruit Manual* suggests sealing-wax for fruit cans.

"Sealing-Wax for Fruit Cans — Take rosin, eight ounces; gum shellac, two ounces; bees'- wax, one-half ounce, and if you desire it colored, English vermilion, one and a half ounce. Melt the rosin, and stir in the vermilion, if used. Then add the shellac slowly, and afterwards the bees'-wax. This will make quite a quantity, and needs only to be melted to be ready at anytime."

Peterson also gives a recipe for cement for jars.

"To Make Cement for Jars. Common. — Take one-third bees'-wax and two-thirds rosin, according to the quantity of cement required. Pound the rosin fine, and put it with the wax to melt in any old vessel fit for the purpose. When it is melted, take it off the fire, and add powdered brick-dust, till it is as thick as melted sealing-wax. Then dip the bottle necks into the cement, and in a few minutes, the mixture will be dry" (Peterson, *Preserving, Pickling & Canning* [1869], 52).

As you can see, the history of canning is only about two hundred years old, yet many of the products canned now were still made prior to 1810. Many pickles, such as mango pickles, were kept in vinegar and lasted up to two years. Heavily salted, spiced, pickled, or dried foods, sugared syrups, or brandied fruits and fermented products were also quite common, as were minced-meat formulations. As the concept of vacuum-sealing and seal integrity was better understood, canning evolved to sealing glass jars with a metal lid and a rubber seal, the process now used in home canning. Likewise, commercial metal cans are traceable to Napoleon's era,

when the cans were sealed with lead, which subsequently caused lead poisoning in some of Napoleon's soldiers.

TWO SNIPPETS OF INFORMATION

Jamlady just had to include the two last snippets on canning techniques. Both are no longer done for one reason or the other, but Jamlady thought some of you younger people would like to know about them . . . just because lots of people get lots of ideas. Always make sure you check out the safety of any processing method you use before proceeding.

The first method is that of preserving rhubarb or other high-acid fruits in cold water, using a technique known as **cold-water canning.** Jamlady has never done this and has never seen it performed by someone who knew what they were doing but would really like to talk to someone who has practiced the technique successfully or who may still be practicing the technique. Of course, this method is not recognized as safe by the USDA, and Jamlady is not recommending its use, but it is interesting from a historical aspect. Despite the air left in some of the fruit tissues, this process apparently did work so long as the fruits were kept cool. Only high-acid fruits were being "cold-water canned," and the fruits were not expected to be canned for as long as heat-canned products. Fruits most generally canned in this manner were lemons, cranberries, green gooseberries, and rhubarb.

"**Rhubarb Canned Cold** — Wash and cut rhubarb in ½" pieces. Pack in cans. Place under cold water faucet and let the water run in and out for 20 minutes, filling the cans. Fasten cover on tight. — Mrs. C. H. Woolsey" (*De Ne Paltz Keuken Boek,* [New Paltz, New York: Committee of the Ladies of the Reformed Church, 1923], 59).

"**Canned Rhubarb** — Pare rhubarb and cut into small pieces. Pack in a jar, put under cold water faucet, and let water run 20 minutes, then screw on cover. Rhubarb canning in this way has often been known to keep a year" (*What to Cook and How to Cook It*—a booklet given out by the Kingston Savings Bank, 273 Wall Street, Kingston, New York, n.d. [value on top: 25 cents]).

The last snippet of information came to Jamlady's attention when a professor, Dr. ZoeAnn Holmes of Oregon State University, showed Jamlady a small 4" x 6" booklet entitled *The Romance of Jelly Making and How to Make Jam without Cooking or Boiling Using M.C.P. Jam and Jelly Pectin.* This booklet shows the **M.C.P. Jelly-Making Set and Process** and cites their patent numbers as 2231273 and 2235028. This kit contained a forked holder for holding a jelly bag, an M.C.P. jelly bag, a metal holder, a sample of a pure cellulose tissue, and the little romance book. What the jam maker was to do was to cook 10 sheets of pure cellulose (ordinary, white, unscented, cleansing tissues) in two quarts of water and to beat them up. After a couple of steps of beating, and cooking it with more water, the pulp was ready to put into the jelly bag with the fruit for extraction. Wild, right? This was the method of fruit-juice extraction. The bag was squeezed with the tool provided, and there was no twelve-hour wait for your extracted juice. The company touted their product as providing more juice per extraction: "The Extra Juice you get with the M. C. P. Jelly Set, more than pays for the Pectin."

"IMPORTANT NOTE—In preparing fruits, the finer you crush them before adding the cellulose pulp, and the more thoroughly you mix this pulp with the crushed fruit, the easier and more completely you can press out the juice (using the method described on pages 4 and 5)" (*The Romance of Jelly Making and How to Make Jam without Cooking or Boiling Using M.C.P. Jam and Jelly Pectin* [Anaheim, California: Mutual Citrus Products, Co., Inc., 1953], 5-6).

Again, Jamlady would love to talk to someone who has actually done this method. She can only assume that it is no longer practiced because (1) no one liked the idea, (2) the formulation of cellulose tissues changed, or (3) the company went out of business. Jamlady's mother, Doris, never heard of the process. Her first utterance upon hearing of the technique was "Disgusting!" Jamlady's Aunt Grace, upon hearing a description of the technique and being asked if she ever used the method, replied, "Never!" So, Jamlady doesn't think too many women liked the idea. Still, Jamlady is curious. Has anyone out there worked for the Mutual Citrus Products Company, Inc., in Anaheim, California, or used an M.C.P. Jelly-Making Kit? If so, Jamlady would like to talk to you.

Jars of Love—Apple Maple Preserves in
canning jars of different sizes

Chapter 2

Will the Real Jam Please Step Forward?

To many people, jellies, jams, preserves, conserves, spreads, and marmalades are all the same thing, and the word "butter" relates to the tasty yellow stick residing on their refrigerator door. For this reason, it is often difficult to respond to market patrons who come to the stand asking for a jelly but wanting something with very little sugar. Jamlady does not know if they really want jelly or if they want a preserve or a butter. Do they want a spread or an artificially sweetened jelly? Jamlady will explain.

Each one of these terms—**jelly, jam, preserve, butter, marmalade, conserve, spread, chutney**—is definable, but a specific product's name is not always so clear cut. **For example, "marmalade" usually, but not always, means there is citrus rind in the product.** However, a marmalade could be made with half fruit and half sugar, with rind, which would mean it is also a preserve. If the marmalade was made with added pectin and rind, as some of the pectin companies instruct jam makers to do, then the marmalade probably is a jam that is also a marmalade. **To confuse the issue further, in years past, marmalades were often so called without any rind or citrus fruit in the concoction.** For example, in *Mrs. Winslow's Domestic Receipt Book for 1871* (New York: Jeremiah Curtis & Sons and John I. Brown & Sons, 1870), there is a recipe for an **Apple Marmalade** with ¾ pound sugar to a pound peeled apples—no lemons or lemon rind.

Let us continue. **A jam, by definition, has more sugar than fruit and has chunks or fruit pieces.** If a product were made to be lower in sugar, such as a butter, but had chunks, then what do we call it? Butters are supposed to be smooth. So that would be either a low- or lower-sugar jam/preserve or a chunky butter. Low- or lower-sugar jam is an incorrect use of the word jam, as in that case there is not more sugar than fruit. Jamlady says this product has to be called a chunky butter, even though by definition a butter is smooth.

The term "chunky butter" at least relates the correct amount of sugar and the fact that it is chunky when most butters are smooth. If low- or lower-sugar jams should not be called jams at all, because they do not have more sugar than fruit, then what are they called? They are called spreads, butters, or chunky butters. **Butters are "jams" or "put-ups" with less sugar than fruit.** Notice Jamlady is using the word "jams" here to mean the whole category of sweet products including jellies, jams, preserves, butters, and spreads. For some reason, in English, many things can be called "jams," even if they are butters or preserves. Apple butter has

more apple purée than sugar. If you put an equal amount of sugar to apple purée or unsweetened applesauce, it would be a preserve, but it would be a smooth preserve, and most preserves are not necessarily smooth. Do you follow?

Many "jams" are really spreads, as they are not sweetened with added sugar but are sweetened with natural sugars in the form of fruit juices. A sugar-free jam is not a correct term then either, because the term "jam" implies the product has more sugar than fruit, which is totally untrue in the case of a "sugar-free" jam. Therefore, it cannot be a **true jam.** It would, therefore, be a sugar-free spread or a sugar-free "jam." So, in fact, the word "jam" is used as a catchall, for we have no word in the English language that lumps all of these products into one word, except for the word "jam." Perhaps, a real jam could be called "a true jam," and all other improper uses of the word "jam" could be allowed to go on their merry way, continually corrupting our English language. Jamlady considers "a true jam" to be a "proper jam," which means that the product is chunky and has more sugar than fruit. If no one likes the term "true jam," then, perhaps, "proper jam" or "real jam" would be equally fitting.

What about marmalades? **Usually, a marmalade is, by definition, a "jam" that has citrus rind.** This marmalade can be a "proper jam," or it can be a preserve, or it can be a chunky butter or a marmaladed butter. If the marmalade is made with added pectin, as the pectin companies would have you do, then it needs more sugar to spread out its natural pectin, so you need more pectin to set the product. This marmalade is a "true" or "proper jam," as it has more sugar than fruit. Marmalade, however, does not usually need added pectin to set the product, as it has plenty of its own. A marmalade made without added pectin usually is a preserve when it is completed, but because it has rind in it, it is also a marmalade. **A preserve has equal amounts of sugar and fruit.** Some marmalades will set with less sugar than half-and-half and would then be a butter or a marmaladed butter.

When Jamlady says a product is half sugar or half fruit, she is referring to the starting mixture before it is cooked. The ratio, of course, changes as the product cooks down. A butter would start out with perhaps $\frac{1}{3}$ sugar to $\frac{2}{3}$ fruit, but as the water cooks down, the ratio of sugar to the total remaining mixture is changed. The amount of sugar in comparison to the entire mixture increases because the water is decreasing. The water would evaporate from the product as it is cooked, and the product would become thicker.

If Jamlady has not confused you yet, then consider tomato "jam," which is made with a **preserve level of sugar (equal sugar and fruit)** and no added pectin but has raisins and vinegar added. **Since there is vinegar, technically that product would be a chutney.** However, Lillian Dickson's Tomato Jam has always been called a "jam" and is used like a regular jam. Technically, it is a chutney and could be used like a chutney. Just when Jamlady has indicated that **a chutney contains vinegar or a similar souring agent, like lemon or lime juice,** there is an exception. Sweet apple chutney has no vinegar, lemons, or limes. It is technically a conserve and not a chutney. Sweet apple chutney is a "jam" or preserve to which nuts, rinds, or dried fruits have been added, but no one calls it a conserve.

Technically, a marmalade that you add nuts

to is no longer a marmalade, but a conserve. Try explaining to somebody why you are handing them a jar of conserve when they requested a marmalade! In fact, the minute you add raisins to a marmalade, it is no longer a marmalade, but a conserve.

Another product that Jamlady does not make for the farmers' market is the **fruit curd,** good as it is. Fruit curds must be refrigerated or canned under pressure, as they contain eggs. All of Jamlady's products are canned and sealed in a **rolling water bath (RWB).** Fruit curds are smooth spreads made from acidic fruits such as lemons or limes. Fruit curds usually contain citric fruits, sugar, butter, and eggs. **Fruit pastes** and cheeses are similar to butters but contain more sugar and are much thicker.

From this point on, Jamlady will call anything she likes a "jam" but will refer to **"proper, true, pure, or real jams" as those products that have more sugar than fruit.** This whole topic is a can of worms, which is why most cookbook authors have had the good sense of mind to craftily skirt the issue entirely. Try to find a canning book with a full definition of these, well, "jams"!

One author states that jellies, jams, preserves, conserves, marmalades, and butters are related, and all have fruit and sugar in common but differ from one another in texture and form.

—A jelly, according to *Stocking Up* (Carol Hupping Stoner, ed. [Emmaus, PA: Rodale Press, Inc., 1977]), is "cooked twice." Other cookbook authors use jelly descriptors such as "clear," "tenderly firm," and "has great clarity."

—A jam, according to *The American Woman's Cookbook* (Ruth Berolzheimer, ed. [from the *Delineator Cook Book*, Delineator Institute, Martha Van Rensselaer, and Flora Rose, eds.]), Clara Pine's favorite cookbook, is made from mashed or cooked fruit pulp with sugar and is "soft, tender, and jellylike."

—Preserves are "whole fruits" or "pieces of fruit" in a thick syrup, maybe jellied.

—A conserve, according to *Pickles and Preserves* (Marion Brown [New York: Wilfred Funk, Inc., 1955]), is different from "preserves and jams in that it is a combination of fruits, sugar, and nuts."

—A marmalade is "a tender jelly" with "small pieces of citrus fruit" (Ruth Hertzberg, Beatrice Vaughan, and Janet Greene, *Putting Food By* [New York: Bantam Books, Inc., 1976]).

—A butter, according to *Young America's Cook Book* (Compiled by the Home Institute of the *New York Herald Tribune* [New York: Charles Scribner's Sons, 1940]), is made of "sieved, cooked fruit" with sugar.

Jamlady feels that while many cookbook authors' descriptors are usually true they normally do not fully sum up the differences between the terms or constitute a complete definition. For example, a jelly may be "twice cooked," but with juicing-machine-extracted juice, cooking twice is not always necessary. Jamlady admits to struggling with these terms for years and is sure others have likewise struggled.

The Food and Drug Administration has something to say about what is a jam, jelly, preserve, or butter. Here are some of their standards, found through a now-defunct FDA Web site.

Fruit Jams (Preserves), Jellies, Fruit Butters, Marmalades

"The **standard of identity for jams and jellies (21CFR 150)** requires that these products be prepared by mixing not less than **45 parts by weight** of certain specified fruits (or fruit juice in the case of jelly) and **47 parts by weight** of other designated fruits, to each **55 parts by weight** of sugar or other optional nutritive carbohydrate sweetening ingredient. Only sufficient pectin to compensate for a deficiency, if any, of the natural pectin content of the particular fruit may be added to jams and jellies. The standards also require that for both jams (preserves) and jellies, the finished product must be concentrated to not less than **65 percent soluble solids.** Standards of identity have also been established for artificially sweetened jams and jellies and for these products the fruit ingredients must be not less than **55 percent by weight** of the finished food product. Fruit butters are defined by the standard of identity as the smooth, semisolid foods made from not less than **five parts by weight** of fruit ingredient to each **two parts by weight** of nutritive carbohydrate sweetening agent. As is the case with jams and jellies, only sufficient pectin may be added to compensate for a deficiency, if any, of the natural pectin content of the particular fruit. The fruit butter standard requires that the finished product must be concentrated to not less than **43 percent soluble solids.** There is no formal standard of identity for marmalades. However, to avoid misbranding, a product labeled sweet orange marmalade should be prepared by mixing at least **30 pounds of fruit (peel and juice) to each 70 pounds sweetening ingredient.** Sour or bitter (Seville) orange marmalade, lemon marmalade, and lime marmalade should be prepared by mixing at least **25 pounds of fruit (peel and juice) to each 75 pounds** of sweetening ingredient. The amount of peel should not be in excess of the amounts normally associated with fruit. The product should be concentrated to not less than **65 percent soluble solids.** Jams, jellies, and similar fruit products should, of course, be prepared only from sound fruit. Decayed or decomposed fruits and insect-contaminated fruits should be sorted out and discarded."

Jamlady is the first to admit that her "jam" definitions may not stand up to standards set in all countries, but she feels quite certain her definitions, which include the amount of sugar in each product type, more closely approximates the FDA's idea of what a jelly, jam, preserve, butter, spread, or chutney is supposed to be. And if we still do not agree, then lets just eat the sweet stuff and not worry about how to define them. Your taste buds will tell you what "preserves" are good and what "preserves" are not.

The recipes that follow in the next few chapters represent fifteen years or more of cooking, experimenting, and documenting. **Most all of the recipes in these canning chapters have been made by Jamlady and have been sold at various Chicagoland farmers' markets. Many of the recipes have been made over and over in an attempt to improve or vary the recipes to suit requests for different combinations or to duplicate old family recipes.**

During one summer season, Jamlady concentrated on hot pepper "jams" and made every recipe that she could find, in an effort to obtain the best recipes. Each week there were samples for family, friends, and customers to compare. The resultant hot pepper jelly, jam, and preserve recipes are the very best of the very best, not in Jamlady's opinion, but in the opinions of all those who taste-tested the products.

Most all of the recipes included in this book have been fully tested. These are the recipes that folks ask for season after season. There are few recipes for which the ingredients are impossible or nearly impossible to find. This does not mean that everything used in these recipes is grown locally. Figs, for example, are available to Jamlady because of the large fruit market in Chicago, and with the assistance of Jamlady's established network of sources, she has been able to make products utilizing high-quality, nonlocal produce. Jamlady thinks it best to work only with fruits and vegetables that are of the highest quality and recommends not making product from older, less-than-"primo," or frozen vegetables and fruits.

The recipes in these chapters are made from ingredients that the average person can find, assuming they do not live in a rural area too far removed from a larger city. With the Internet at your fingertips, spices, pectins, unusual thickeners, vinegars, or even unusual tropical fruits may be available no matter where you live.

The following chapters are not intended to be an instruction book for someone learning to can. There are many books that display colorful pictures of the various processing steps. Jamlady's book is intended to present the results of her cooking experiments for the last fifteen years. She cooks most every day of the week, even the days she goes to market, because she is compelled to have something

going on the stove. She has long since stopped trying to figure out what drives this compulsion, but it has something to do with finding out how the next batch will turn out. It has to do with a never-ending curiosity. Once Jamlady gets to researching, there is always another combination to try and lending hands of those who want to learn by helping. Jamlady is thankful for all the people who have assisted her with testing various recipes—family, friends, and apprentices. Jamlady wants to thank all of her market patrons who have religiously shown up at market and thrown accolade after accolade in her direction. Because of your enthusiasm, Jamlady has been able to blossom and live a life in pursuit of a passion. She is not sure what drives the hard work and research, the desire to see how the next experiment will turn out or the actual reaction of the loyal patrons who show up each week expecting something spectacular. If nothing else, the exercise is both exciting and humbling, for no matter how much you know and no matter how much you learn, you are always reminded of how much you do not know.

Jamlady firmly believes that many recipes are not the best that they can be because there are no benchmarks. So many recipe books have recipes made by different people, but no one person has tried or compared them all. The more different recipes you have made, the better position you are in to judge what recipe is better. If there is any conclusive finding in this fifteen-year exercise, it is that in the combined knowledge learned Jamlady perceives how difficult it is to try to make everything and to experience a wide vista. Just when you think you've done everything you can do in a limited area, you think of something else or someone gives you a tidbit of information that points to another doorway. There is no end to learning. You can never get finished. You can only take a break or quit. Jamlady probably should have completed this book several years ago and started another on the advice of her mother, but she felt she was not finished. After another four years of experimentation, and two thousand pages of written material, Jamlady now sees that she will never be finished, so it is time to give you some of what Jamlady has now and see what will develop in the future. Jamlady has enough written material to fill many more resource cookbooks on many related subjects such as pickles, relishes, herbs, spices, chutney, winemaking, and natural dyeing.

So, *The Jamlady Cookbook* does not have all the "jam" recipes in the world, nor does it try to cover every fruit or classic. Some fruits Jamlady has been meaning to do but just hasn't gotten to them yet. Some recipes Jamlady does not like to make often. Quince, for example, is a hard-to-peel fruit, so Jamlady sometimes avoids making recipes using quince, opting for something easier to make.

Most all of the recipes presented here have been marketed with the recipes attached to the jar. Jamlady's reason for providing the recipe is to inform, educate, and inspire. Many patrons, relatives, and friends tell Jamlady the labels are the best part of the whole culinary experience. Many claim they read the recipe labels out loud when they serve the product and read how they are made, so the parties eating the product can imagine what goes into making the product. **Jamlady firmly believes that people want to know how their food is prepared and want to keep the art of jamming and canning alive, even if they never plan to can.**

Jamlady encourages canners to properly label their canned products and to attach, when possible, the canning recipes to their products. Nowadays, with the help of computers, it makes good sense to keep canning recipes in computer files and in a format that can easily be printed and attached to canned products. Labeling home-canned products reduces the validity of criticisms by those in the food industry and others who would argue that home canning is not an exact science and that safety measures and proper documentation are not practiced by home canners.

Jamlady hopes that this book, her Web site at Jamlady.com, her market presence, and her commercial kitchen will advance the art of canning and inspire more young people to take up the art of canning and jam making. While the art of home canning may not be needed for our actual subsistence, there is no doubt that it is needed for our holistic enlightenment, spiritual balance, intellectual pursuit, sense of family roots, and artistic expression.

Canning, jam making, and wildcrafting provide us with an appreciation of the beauty and bounty of the earth. One can hardly fail to reflect and think about our existence when plucking wild grapes from a tendrilled vine on a crisp and dewy September morning. Jamlady is awed by the fact that this earthy food is here, in the wild, given by the divine inventor to us, with no bill sent in the mail. It is Jamlady's belief that wild grape jam on the morning's toast can take a soul's mind to wandering with Jamlady as its label explains how to pick the grapes, how to process the grapes, and why the flavor is so intense. We all want to connect with what is real and wonderful, and canning provides us with that opportunity, either as a wildcrafter, master canner, or food critic.

To be inspired, one only needs to look at a batch of newly made preserves—or a meticulously stacked jar of jardiniere, to see the art of vibrant vegetable colors glistening against the umbered waters of tumbling spices and floating bay to know something special is in that jar. Whoever made this "put-up" made this jar with care and Love. Jamlady believes that love is actually transferred to the jar's recipient. Now, don't think Jamlady has become too sentimental, but think about it. It's just like getting that box of home-baked cookies at college from your grandmother. The cookies are good, maybe even great, but they are more. They represent Love. So, Jamlady leaves you with the idea that a jar of

Raspberry Jam with Grand Marnier is good, but it is more. It is Love! If you buy or make it for yourself or another person, it says, "Hi, I love you. You are a good person." If you doubt what Jamlady says, you need only to watch patrons shopping at market to see the time and energy they put into buying exactly the right food for someone they love.

Jamlady gives you these recipes so that you can give **jars of Love** to everyone who needs 8 ounces or more. If they do not need too much, there are 4-ounce jars out there. For the truly needy, there are 12-ounce, 16-ounce, and 32-ounce jars, and while hard to find, there are 64-ounce canning jars out there too.

Twenty crystal salt dishes of assorted jams, preserves, and butters. Top row: Sweet-potato butter with whole clove, boysenberry preserves, cranberry preserves, apricot preserves. Second row: Pear-ginger preserves, cactus jam, starfruit preserves, sweet green-pepper jelly. Third row: Carrot-apple preserves, strawberry gem(s), tango jam, quince with ginger preserves. Fourth row: Black Mission fig preserves, kiwi genie preserves, spiced tomato marmalade with raisins, persimmons marmalade. Bottom row: Orange-rhubarb preserves, currant jam, lemon marmalade, blueberry jam with coffee liqueur.

Chapter 3
❦

Jellies, Jams, and Preserves

Jamlady has made a lot of jams, preserves, and butters. She makes jellies too, but not more than she makes jams. This is mostly because of demand, time, and health factors. Jellies have the most sugar and are the least healthy of all the sweet "put-ups," at least for those individuals who need to cut down on sugar. From another perspective, when making jelly, much of the fruit from which the juice is extracted is thrown out or made into salvage jam when it could be eaten in its prime state. Lastly, jelly often requires a messy jelly bag and a long wait for the extract to drip completely from the jelly bag. There is no hurrying the process, as squeezing the bag only brings cloudiness to the extraction, and that means the jelly will not be as clear as it might have been. Still, there are those who love jelly, and crab-apple jelly, elderberry jelly, apple jelly scented with rose geranium, and wild-grape jelly are often requested.

Jam is very popular and is requested almost as often as preserves. Not everyone wants a sweet jam, but then, some people find preserves not sweet enough. Jamlady thinks one's choice of "jam" depends on how one will use the product. Many people love using sweet jam as a cookie or cake filling or on their morning toast, while other people prefer preserves because they are less sweet, fruitier tasting, and texturally thicker.

Many recipes have historical aspects that should add to the understanding of this art of jam making, and Jamlady will try to discuss jams and jellies representative of many different ethnic groups and cultures. Jamlady asks the reader to appreciate and ponder the interrelatedness of travel, immigration, religion, climate, geographical condition, culture, food, history, psychology, customs, free time, abundance, war, peace, scarcity, and their affect on food recipes. Foods, jams, and jellies are a far more complicated topic than Jamlady ever imagined. Just get into a discussion about beets or sour cherries at a farmers' market and see where it leads you.

We have the sour cherry lovers and the sour cherry haters. If they love the sour cherries, well good! But it doesn't end there. What about the almond problem? If you like almond flavor in sour-cherry jam, well good! But is it real almond extract, imitation almond extract, or crunchy nut parts in the jam? "It better not be that imitation stuff!" Of course, "many German Americans know it must be pure almond extract" that is put in that beautiful, bright, pinkish-red, sour cherry jam. So let us begin our adventure with sour cherries.

Jams and preserves aren't just for the morning toast. Bake with them and make interesting desserts, like layered noodle kugels. Sour cherry vinegar shown in the background.

CHERRIES AND PIES

Sour Cherry Jam

Bright-red sour cherries are market favorites! Seasonally available in late June or early July.

5 cups sugar
4 cups pitted, chopped sour cherries
1 1¾-ounce box powdered fruit pectin
½ teaspoon butter (optional, reduces foaming)
¼ teaspoon ascorbic acid crystals

Use the ascorbic acid crystals sparingly with the cherries to reduce oxidation as you pit them. A pinch of ascorbic acid is more than enough. Check for cherry pits by placing the cherries on a flat pan; visually scan for pits. Check further manually. Wear a thin plastic glove or a Ziploc bag and press your palm down over the pan's surface to check further for pits. Mix the pectin with the cherries and butter. Wait 10 minutes and then boil the mixture for 1 minute. Add the sugar and boil for 1 more minute. JSP/RWB10(8OZ).

Sour Cherry Jam does not always set. If the fruit is too ripe, the jam must be cooked longer or made with less sugar. Use the frozen-plate method to check the set and boil to 105 degrees C. If the jam does not set, try using it for ice-cream sauce. Jamlady recommends you label your Sour Cherry Jam with a warning to look for pits when spreading the jam and remind folks that once opened, jam should be refrigerated.

Sour Cherry Jam is best made from fresh fruits. Sour cherries can be frozen, but Jamlady finds "jams" from frozen fruits are never as good as freshly made jams or preserves. If you have access to sour cherry trees, you can make your own jam. **Remember, it is best to pick under-ripe cherries or a mixture of unripe cherries and ripe cherries, because as fruits ripen, the amount of pectin decreases.** If your sour cherry jam does not set, it is probably because you used too much sugar or you used overripe fruit. Jam that does not set can be cooked down more, or some liquid pectin can be added and the jam cooked down further.

Jamlady usually recommends that you use unset jam for ice-cream or dessert sauce and leave it in the jar as it is. It is preserved as it is, and you might better use your time to make a second attempt at getting it right in the first place. Practice makes perfect. There's no sense in trying to fix a jar of unset preserves when cherries are on the trees and will spoil if not picked and preserved. Trying to fix a botched batch is very discouraging, and Jamlady recommends you keep your progress on a positive path so that you don't get discouraged and give up. Learn to check your jam by placing it on a **freezer-frozen plate.** Count to sixty and push the side of the jam with your finger. If it wrinkles, it will set. If it does not wrinkle, keep cooking.

Sour cherries need to be pitted. Pitting can be done by hand or you can use a **#16T cherry stoner** made by Chop-Rite Two, Inc. Jamlady has tried other pitting machines and can tell you the #16T stoner works very well for sour cherries. This machine looks like it is old, as it is made in a style similar to the old silver-looking meat grinders that can be clamped on a table's edge. Chop-Rite's #16T cherry stoner may not work as well for some other kinds of cherries. Kids love to crank the #16T stoner, which has a flywheel with bumps on it that dispenses the pits out the front shoot and the cherry meats and juice out the bottom. Before pitting the cherries, wash them well in cold water dashed with a pinch of ascorbic acid crystals. Drain them. Jamlady usually removes the sour cherry stems before cranking, but the #16T stoner will work even if you do not remove the stems . . . it just will not work as smoothly.

Frugal folks may rationalize that sour cherries only come once a year, so it is rather expensive to spend seventy-five bucks or more on a pitting machine. Jamlady could not disagree more. A pitting machine is money well spent, and just wait until you see the enthusiasm on the part of children who are allowed to operate this machine. If allowed, the neighborhood kids come and volunteer to crank Jamlady's pitting machine. What's the value of free labor and love? Besides, husbands can crank while watching the football game. You just set it up next to the television, load the machine, empty the containers, and let them turn the crank. If the husband will not crank the pitting machine, Jamlady says keep the pitting machine and return the husband for a refund.

While pitting the cherries, Jamlady selects the best cherries for snacking and places them in a bowl in the refrigerator to chill. If one of the children will not eat the cherries with the pits inside, put some ascorbic-acid-dashed, pitted cherries in the refrigerator for them. During this entire pitting process, small pinches of vitamin C or pure, fine, ascorbic-acid-soluble crystals should be added to the pitted cherries to inhibit any oxidation. Jamlady does mean minute pinches of vitamin C. Too much vitamin C causes the color to be bleached from the cherries, and they will taste too tart. **Vitamin C crystals keep the sour cherries' brilliant, ruby-red color stabilized as it should be throughout the entire pitting process, refrigeration process, cooking process, and shelf-life.**

Health-food stores sell **vitamin C crystals.** Don't mistake vitamin C crystals for **vitamin C powder.** The vitamin C that Jamlady uses comes in a 1-kilogram or 2.2-pound container. This may seem like a lot, but you can use it on fruit cups, in baked fruit pies, in freshly juiced juices, and as a vitamin supplement.

Jamlady likes vitamin C for how it makes the food look. Everyone always comments about how beautiful Jamlady's apple and pear pies look. Jamlady buys the big kilo of vitamin C and ends up giving smaller containers of vitamin C to everyone who means to buy some but forgets. She has had such good success with Bronson Laboratories' brand that she has never changed. Jamlady is sure there are lots of good brands of vitamin C crystals out there, but when Jamlady is satisfied with a company and its product, she isn't likely to look elsewhere. Pitted cherries can be used for cooking jams and other "put-ups," but they are also wonderful in fruit cups, gelatin molds, pies, or fruit breads. Sour cherries can be cooked with just a little sugar and the sauce used for pancakes, ice cream, cakes, or cottage cheese. Sour cherries can be made into sour cherry vinegar and pickled sour cherries by merely placing them in vinegar and storing them in the refrigerator. Sour cherry vinegar may be sweetened with honey and the pickled cherries eaten with meats. The best sour cherry is washed, chilled, and eaten out-of-hand.

Many people want to know Jamlady's secret for light-colored applesauce for babies and white-meated apple pies. Vitamin C crystals are the secret. Jamlady's apple pies are made with processor-sliced apples that have been peeled and bobbed in water treated with a little vitamin C. While they are slicing, a minute pinch of vitamin C crystals is put in the processor's hopper.

Green Tomato Pie or Apple Pie

If you don't have any apples, just use the green tomatoes from your garden instead. They will make a grand pie. Don't think about it too much. Really, it will be fine. Just slice up those garden green tomatoes, peeled (best) or unpeeled, in your processing machine and bake a few pies. Take one to a church supper or to a baby shower and say nothing. This pie will be gone in a lick. Most folks like green tomato pies, but then there are those few unadaptable types!

Freeze a few dozen green tomato pies—made, "crust and all,"—and use them in the winter as hostess gifts. You can even make a **Dutch Green Tomato Pie** by adding in some dark or golden raisins. Serve your tart, green tomato pie warm with vanilla ice cream, just as you would for apple pie. You may need a little flour in the filling, depending on how juicy you like your pie. A fifty-fifty pie can be made from equal parts of apples and green tomatoes. This is an old-fashioned trick for those who grow tomatoes but have to buy apples. There are few good excuses for not using up those green tomatoes in your garden. If you don't want to eat them all yourself, donate some to a food pantry. You can quickly processor-slice the green tomatoes for a pie. Add 1 cup sugar, lemon rind or 2 tablespoons vinegar, 1 tablespoon flour, and spices. Nutmeg is a good spice to use (or use oil of cinnamon for a **Green Genie Pie**). Freeze the pie without a crust. The pie can be constructed and baked later.

Jamlady Tip: One other Jamlady trick for a tasty apple pie is to toss all of the pie-filling ingredients with 1 tablespoon of your best bourbon or whiskey. You'll notice the difference. Grand Marnier or maple syrup in place of some sugar is excellent too. For another variation, add in some "jam," instead of sugar. Apricot preserves are excellent in apple pie. What the heck, use both the brandy and the preserves! One very nice food writer and Jamlady customer uses Apple-Maple Preserves in her apple pie.

Green Tomato Pie or Apple Pie

½ to ¾ cup sugar for **apple** (alternately, rose geranium sugar and no spices) or 1-1¼ cup sugar for **green tomato pie**

¾ teaspoon true cinnamon (light, not dark, cinnamon spice or oil of cinnamon for an **Apple Genie Pie** or **Green Tomato Genie Pie**)

¼ teaspoon freshly grated nutmeg (optional)

½ teaspoon salt for the **green tomato pie** and optional for **apple pie**

1 teaspoon grated lemon or lime rind, or lemon or lime juice, or 2 tablespoons vinegar (optional for **green tomato pie**) (not needed for **apple pie**, use ascorbic acid crystals instead)

6-7 cups processor-sliced **apples**—kept creamy white with a pinch or two of vitamin C crystals on the apples—or 6-7 cups processor-sliced **green tomatoes**, or 3½ cups of both

1 tablespoon butter (Distribute little pieces of butter on top of the pie before adding the crust.)

0-2 teaspoons flour, arrowroot, or other thickener for **apple pie** and 1-2 tablespoons flour for **green tomato pie**. (The amount of thickener necessary depends on how juicy the fruits are.)

To make either pie, select your ingredients, toss all the ingredients together in a mixing bowl, and place the mixture in a prepared pie crust or into a pie pan (for a no-bottom-crust pie). Bake at 425 degrees F for 50 to 60 minutes.

Jamlady usually uses a French crust on the top of her apple pies. Pie or "Betty" can be made with no bottom crust and only a top crumb crust.

Regular Pie Crust or Bottom Crust—Two 9" one-crust pies or 1 pie with two crusts

2 cups flour
½ teaspoon salt
4 tablespoons ice-cold water
⅔ cup shortening

Mix the ingredients by hand or in the processor, but do not overprocess. **Roll out the crust between two pieces of flour-dusted plastic wrap, waxed paper, or no-stick foil. Put the crust in the freezer for 40 to 60 seconds.** Quickly peel back the plastic wrap and put the crust into the pie pan. Do not leave the crust in the freezer for too long, or it will crack, and you will have to start all over and re-roll it out. Makes two 9" one-crust pies or 1 pie with two crusts. If you use a regular bottom crust but want to be a little fancier for the top, try Jamlady's Nutty Topping.

Jamlady's Nutty Topping

½ cup cut-up butter
½ cup brown sugar
¾ cup flour or ¼ cup oatmeal and ½ cup flour
¼ cup small pieces of pecan or pecan dust, walnut, almonds, or other nuts
¼ teaspoon ground cinnamon

Mix the ingredients in the food processor, but not too much. The topping should just crumble. Don't overwork the mixture, or you will have dough. Put the crumb topping on the pie and bake the pie as usual.

Of course, this topping can be used on many different kinds of pies. This topping is great on peach pie, with almonds instead of the pecans, and it is equally good on sour cherry, pear, or green tomato pie. Jamlady calls this pie a "Betty" if she makes it with no bottom crust and only a crumb topping. Either way, it is deliciously crunchy. If you have lots of cherries and need to get them processed, you can freeze the cherry pie filling in a pie pan with no bottom crust. Jamlady either freezes it with nothing and makes the crust later or freezes it with no bottom crust and uses a plain crumb or nutty topping. A pie filling, frozen in an aluminum pie pan, can be turned over frozen and removed such that it can be set right back into a slightly larger pie pan after the pie pan is prepared with a bottom crust. Having a sour cherry pie in the winter is downright homey! Remember, it takes longer to cook a frozen pie. Bake the pie until its filling is bubbling out of the docked pie crust.

Jamlady's Sour Cherry Pie Filling—9"

¾-1¼ cups sugar

4-5 tablespoons flour, arrowroot, or other thickener, such as tapioca

½ teaspoon cinnamon (optional)

4 cups pitted sour cherries, with a pinch of vitamin C crystals worked into the cherries

1 tablespoon butter (distribute on the top)

1 tablespoon pure almond extract (optional, highly recommended)

Use large whole almonds around the entire crust's edge. If using a regular crust for the top, cut leaves from the crust in the center (dock) and decorate with leaves and almonds around the edge. Alternately, a crumb topping with pecans or almonds can be used for this pie. This same recipe can be used for raspberries, black raspberries, loganberries, blackberries, wineberries, strawberries, blueberries, or boysenberries. Bake at 425 degrees F for 35 to 50 minutes. You may wish to reduce the temperature toward the end.

*Note: If you are lucky enough to find **wild black raspberries,** **Rubus occidentalis,** what a fantastic pie you can make, and if you find **wild wine raspberries** or **wineberries,** **Rubus phoenicolasius,** in Pennsylvania, you should sit right down and eat a bowl with thick whipped cream!*

*Note: **Arrowroot** is a tasteless, edible starch derived from the rhizomes of **scitamineaeous plants (Order Scitamineae)** such as **Bermuda Arrowroot,** **Maranta arundinacea** (useful for those with allergies to wheat and corn), and **East Indian Arrowroot,** **Curcuma angustifolia.** Unfortunately, some arrowroot is not specifically labeled as to the plant from which it was derived. In past years, arrowroot was used to make jellies (some medicinal and for the weak intestines) like this Arrow-root Wine Jelly of 1 cup boiling water plus 2 teaspoons arrowroot, 2 teaspoons sugar, and 1 tablespoon brandy or 3 tablespoons wine—from Miss E. Neil's* Everyday Cookbook, *1872.*

ᎶᏇᏰ

Sugar-Free Sour Cherry Jam

4 cups pitted sour cherries

1 1¾-ounce box lite or "no-sugar" pectin

34 packets aspartame

Use a pinch of ascorbic acid crystals on the cherries while pitting them. Mix the pectin with the cherries; wait 10 minutes. Boil 1 minute, add the aspartame, and boil 1 minute more. JSP/RWB10.

Several companies make **"sugar-free" pectin** or **lite pectin,** formulated as a **one-step process.** A few years back, when Jamlady first started research for this book, some jam makers were using a more complicated process for sugar-free jams. This process (Carol Hupping Stoner, *Stocking Up,* [Emmanus, PA: Organic Gardening and Farming, 1977], 208) involved using honey or sugar, dry LM pectin, and a dicalcium phosphate solution (calcium salts). Most people now exercise the easy-to-use, one-step process.

LM, or low-methoxyl, pectin requires no sugar to "jell" to "gel" (short for gelatin), unlike Home Jell® or other brands of regular pectin. Jamlady likes and uses Mrs. Wages' brand, Lite Home-Jell®. Jamlady has used **Lite Home-Jell® successfully with honey, maple syrup, sugar, no sugar, concentrated licorice tea, or less than the usual amounts of sweetener because it does not use the sweetener to bind the jam together or affect the set. The**

flip side, sugar is part of the chemical reaction that causes a regular fruit pectin jam to set.

Mr. Fred Edwards, a retired chemist who previously was employed by **Precision Foods,** has spoken with Jamlady on several occasions and has responded to questions regarding Home Jell® (regular pectin) and Lite Home Jell® ("sugar-free" pectin). You will find recipes here that approximate commercial pectin product instructions and other recipes that go beyond the scope of these directions. Pay particular attention to some of Jamlady's butter recipes that are made with "no-sugar" or lite LM pectin. A normal, traditional butter gets cooked down until it is thick. Some of the flavor is diminished and the color often darkens excessively. Jamlady has used "no-sugar" pectin or lite pectin to improve the taste, color, and cooking time for butters she calls Heavenly Butters.

Jamlady is aware that several other companies make pectins. Jamlady has used some of them and found them satisfactory. Most brands with equivalent products should work just as well. Just make sure the weight equals 1¾ ounces, as product weights often get changed with new packaging. For quite a few years, however, the standard box size for powdered fruit pectin has been 1¾ ounces, or approximately 18 teaspoons, of pectin per box.

Jamlady usually uses pectin manufactured by Precision Foods. One reason for Jamlady's loyalty to Precision Foods is that, as a company, they willingly sold to Jamlady's small company when other big giants wanted Jamlady to buy her canning staples at discount marts instead of purchasing them at wholesale prices. It is a sad but true commentary that jam makers who make jams for a living sometimes cannot buy their ingredients any cheaper wholesale than they can buy them at a discount store. This is particularly true of canning jars. Canning jars and lids for the larger manufacturers are usually purchased separately. To buy the lids and jars together, it is very difficult to purchase at a lower price, unless you are willing to buy skids of jars, and then the jar price may not be as low as if you purchased the lids and jars separately.

Jamlady Tip: Pay attention to the jars in the stores that can be reused as canning jars, as they are canning jars. Specifically, some of the spaghetti-sauce jars with canning-ring tops are really worth at least 50 cents each to the canner. Consider that fact when price-comparing spaghetti sauces and other items. Jamlady is not referring to the thinner glass, one-trip-type jar.

Ask your friends to save all canning jars for you. Jamlady has been receiving these jars from folks for years. When you get some for free, it doesn't hurt so much when other people don't return your jars. For relatives and friends who do not return your canning jars, Jamlady has a few suggestions. Jamlady does not give homemade wine or cordials to relatives and friends who do not return canning jars. This modus operandi has improved the jar return rate. Indeed, the empty wine bottles come back as well.

Seriously, many canners have been taken for granted over the years. Jamlady has often heard market patrons comment that they never realized how much home-canned products were worth until their grandmother, mother, grandfather, or resident canner passed on. When any patron, friend, or relative tells Jamlady "homemade" (homemade batch size, but made in a licensed commercial kitchen) farmers' market food prices are too high because they "used to get this stuff for nothing," Jamlady reminds them of how underappreciated their canning or baking friend or relative must have been. Homemaker skills have value, and it is high time the contributions of women and men who stay at home and take care of children, clean the house, and make homemade foods are appreciated and praised for their efforts. In today's world, the issue goes beyond labor and cost and extends to availability, health, food-additive issues, and love.

Sour Cherry-Almond Jam

These two flavors have been married for a long time.

5 cups sugar
4 cups pitted, chopped sour cherries
1 1¾-ounce box powdered fruit pectin
1 tablespoon pure almond extract (optional, not imitation almond flavoring)
½ teaspoon butter (optional, reduces foaming)
¼ teaspoon ascorbic acid crystals

Use a pinch of ascorbic acid crystals on the cherries as you pit them, but do not feel compelled to use the entire ¼ teaspoon. Mix the pectin with the cherries and butter. Wait 10 minutes and boil for 1 minute. Add the sugar and boil for 1 minute. Add the extract and boil for 1 minute more. JSP/RWB10.

Rhubarb-Sour Cherry Preserves

This combination is not usually seen. How can anything with sour cherries or rhubarb not be great?

3 cups white sugar
2½ cups (1¼ pounds) well-washed, finely chopped, unpeeled, pink rhubarb
1½ cups hand-pitted sour cherries
1 cup water
3 tablespoons freshly squeezed lemon juice (add in at the end)
1-2 pinches ascorbic acid crystals

Use the ascorbic acid crystals, one pinch at a time, on the sour cherries as you pit them. Cook the water with the rhubarb and sour cherries until plump and tender (5 minutes). Add the sugar and boil. Add the lemon juice and boil until thick. Check the set point with a frozen plate. JSP/RWB10.

Most fruits with sufficient pectin can be made into preserves with just fruit and sugar. Some need, as with peaches, to be cooked with a little water first to plump them, and then the sugar is added. No water is needed with this next recipe, but it is helpful, in making preserves, to let the sugar sit mixed with the fruits for at least 30 minutes before beginning to cook. For strawberry preserves, Jamlady recommends "weeping the fruit in sugar" for at least 8 hours.

Classic Sour Cherry Preserves with No Added Pectin

Great on ice cream, bread, or cheesecake!

4 cups washed, pitted sour cherries
3 cups sugar
1-2 pinches ascorbic acid crystals

Use a pinch of ascorbic acid crystals on the cherries as you pit them. After removing the pits with your trusty, "crank-type," stoner (pitting machine), lay the cherries out on a tray and with a plastic bag or plastic glove over your hand, push down on the thin layer of cherries to feel for any stray pits, and visually check carefully. It is very easy to miss cherry pits that are the same color as some of the flesh. Cook all ingredients slowly until transparent and thick when cool. JSP/RWB10.

*Variations: These classic preserves can be flavored with 1 tablespoon pure almond extract per batch to make **Sour Cherry-Almond Preserves.** **Sour Cherry "Genie" Preserves** can be made by adding 1-2 drops oil of cinnamon. Other liqueurs such as crème de cassis can be used too. These preserves do not have to be cooked down all the way if you plan to use them for ice-cream sauce. You may even want to use a little less sugar, but that is up to your taste buds! Too little sugar would not be good either, if you are planning on canning the ice-cream sauce, as sugar is a preservative. If you will always refrigerate the sauce, then go ahead and use the amount of sugar you desire for the ice-cream sauce. Too little sugar will also remove the gloss or sheen from the sauce, and this may not be desirable either, so you can always start with a little sugar and add more as you go.*

***Jamlady Tip:** Always label your sour cherry jams and preserves with a notice to the consumer to visually check for pits while spreading the product. If you don't have a source for sour cherries, consider putting in a couple of standard or dwarf sour cherry trees. They aren't all that difficult to grow and the rewards are worth it.*

Jamlady hand-pits sweet Bing cherries. Many of you may consider this a desuete activity, but trust Jamlady, this is the very sort of sport or hobby that many people need. Think of it as one less visit to the psychiatrist. Do not classify this activity as work, because once you have done that, you have created a mindset that dismisses half the rewarding fun activities that balance your spiritual self. If you cannot go as far as to sit on the deck in the sun . . . and pit cherries and . . . think about your life . . . and plan, then set up the activity on a big tray in front of the television. Have a large towel handy to wipe your arms, which will get wet with cherry juice. Select light-red cherries and no dark-red cherries, as you want the unripe fruits with the most pectin. If you are buying the Bing cherries as opposed to picking your own, this may mean handpicking each cherry you purchase. For the onlookers, simply ignore them or announce, "I am making homemade cherry preserves." Hopefully, they will smile! Wash the cherries well before you **pit** them. This is an interesting term. We **destem,** but we do not depit; we **pit** the cherries, meaning we remove the stones or pits.

Classic Sweet Bing Cherry Preserves with No Added Pectin

Select underripe fruits for the best preserves.

10 cups pitted dark or sweet cherries
6 cups sugar
½ teaspoon butter or margarine (optional)

Double-check for stray pits. Layer the pitted cherries with sugar. Let the sugar and cherries weep for about 2 to 6 hours. Add ½ teaspoon butter or margarine. Cook the mixture until transparent and jell point is achieved (105 degrees C). To be sure of the final consistency, you might want to chill the preserves in the refrigerator. JSP/RWB10.

Variations: Cherry Almond Preserves, Cherry Vanilla Preserves, or Cherry Genie Preserves—Use 1 tablespoon pure almond extract, 1 tablespoon pure vanilla extract or flavoring, or 1-2 drops oil of cinnamon as the last step and boil for 1 more minute. Other liqueurs, such as crème de cassis or brandy, can be added too. If you will use this preserve as ice-cream sauce, then cook it less and, perhaps, reduce the sugar a little.

Jamlady Tip: You can buy and use either vanilla extract or vanilla flavoring, because vanilla extract and vanilla flavoring can be of the same strength. Vanilla extract has 35 percent alcohol or more and vanilla flavoring has less than 35 percent alcohol. If both are full strength, they have 13.5 percent vanilla bean extractive per gallon. Vanilla pods come from a climbing orchid plant, Vanilla planifolia Andr., **which is picked yellow or unripe and cured by repeated sweating and drying until the vanillin crystallizes on the outside of the "bean," well, actually, pod.**

Jamlady Tip: Jamlady always sorts out the *best cherries for out-of-hand snack fruits and chills them in the refrigerator for children who come looking for that after-school snack.*

"**Genie Jams**" or "**Genie Preserves**" are Jamlady's creations, and they were named "Genies" because they are magical. When first introduced to oil of cinnamon, Jamlady was amazed at how wonderful it was for making pickles. A mother of one of Jamlady's students, a Woodstock, Illinois, resident and excellent pickle maker, first introduced Jamlady to oil of cinnamon. In those early days, oil of cinnamon was almost impossible to find, and it had to be ordered through a pharmacist at the drugstore. Today, if you need such a product, you can jump on a Web site and just order it. How times have changed!

Jamlady calls all jams with oil of cinnamon **"Genie Jams"** because, after tasting them, Jamlady's genie jumps out and says, "Ta dah!" Jamlady's genie is always around, whispering in her ear and giving her suggestions. You probably have a private genie as well, for Jamlady believes everyone is equipped with a genie. It is just a matter of getting in touch with your genie and allowing him or her to talk to you. All genies are great cooks.

You will notice that most newly created jams worthy of special attention get named by Jamlady. "Jams" without good names, like good nameless recipes, are often forgotten. A good name is essential for the "movie star" jam!

Jamlady's Original Sour Cherry Genie Jam

5 cups sugar
4 cups pitted, chopped, underripe sour cherries
1 1¾-ounce box powdered fruit pectin
½ teaspoon butter (optional, reduces foaming)
1-2 drops oil of cinnamon
¼ teaspoon or less ascorbic acid crystals

Add a pinch or two ascorbic acid crystals on the cherries as you pit them. Mix the pectin with the cherries and butter; wait 10 minutes. Boil for 1 minute, add the sugar, and boil for another minute. Add 1-2 drops oil of cinnamon and boil 1 minute more. JSP/RWB10. This jam does not always set. If the cherries are too ripe, the jam must be cooked longer or made with less sugar. Use a frozen plate to check for set and boil to 105 degrees C. If the jam does not set, use it for ice-cream or dessert sauce.

Sour Cherry-Strawberry or Cherryberry Jam

Try a cherryberry and peanut-butter sandwich!

6 cups sugar
2½ cups washed, hulled, and processor sliced strawberries
2 cups washed, pitted sour cherries
1 1¾-ounce box regular powdered fruit pectin
⅛ cup water
¼-½ teaspoon ascorbic acid crystals (on fruit during fruit preparation)
½ teaspoon butter

Mix the water, cherries, and strawberries, and butter with the pectin. Wait 10 minutes. Boil 1 minute, add the sugar, boil to 105 degrees C, and check the set. JSP/RWB5-10.

❧❧

Lite Sour Cherry Jam

Half the sugar of regular jam.

5 cups washed, pitted, chopped sour cherries
3 cups sugar
1 1¾-ounce box lite or "no-sugar" pectin
1 teaspoon butter
½ teaspoon ascorbic acid crystals (on fruit during preparation)

Mix the cherries, butter, and pectin; wait 10 minutes. Boil 1 minute, add the sugar, and boil 1 minute more. JSP/RWB10(16OZ).

Sour Cherry-Apple Almond Jam

A nice, tart jam for your morning toast.

5 cups sugar
2 cups pitted, chopped sour cherries
2 cups peeled, chopped, tart apples
1 1¾-ounce box powdered fruit pectin
1 tablespoon pure almond extract
½ teaspoon butter (optional, reduces foaming)
¼ teaspoon ascorbic acid crystals (on cherries as you pit them)

Mix the cherries, apples, butter, and pectin. Wait 10 minutes. Boil the mixture for 1 minute, add the sugar, and boil for 1 minute more. Add pure almond extract and boil for 1 minute. JSP/RWB10.

☙❧

Sweet Cherry Jam

Excellent in thumbprint cookies!
Cherries go well with vanilla-flavored baked goods.

5 cups sugar
4 cups pitted, chopped sweet cherries
1 1¾-ounce box regular powdered fruit pectin
¼ cup lemon juice
½ teaspoon butter (optional, antifoaming agent)
¼ teaspoon ascorbic acid crystals

Wash, pit, and chop the cherries, with a pinch of ascorbic acid crystal. Mix together the cherries, lemon juice, butter, and pectin. Wait 10 minutes; boil for 1 minute. Add the sugar; boil 1 more minute. JSP/RWB10.

Variation: Cherry Vanilla Jam—Cook the jam with a vanilla pod ("vanilla bean").

If you ever took a science class and grew bacteria in a petri dish, you have probably encountered agar-agar. **Agar-agar flakes can be used to make jam.** You can purchase them from most Asian markets, health food stores, or some on-line sources. Jamlady recommends you make a no-cook jam with sour cherries, *Prunus cerasus,* and agar-agar flakes.

The sour cherry tree, "pie-cherry," 'Morello,' *Prunus cerasus* Linn., is a tree or thicket-forming shrub with a short trunk. Its crown is broad and rounded and its branches spread wide and droop. A sour cherry tree's bark is scaly and rough. The fruits are ⅝"-¾" (15-19 mm) in diameter, bright red in color, soft, juicy, and sour and possess an edible pulp surrounding a round stone. Sour cherries start to mature in Crystal Lake, Illinois, around late June but may mature at slightly different times depending on the tree variety and climatic conditions.

Jamlady picks sour cherries from very old trees where several major branches form a V, where one can sit while picking. Years ago, Jamlady and her Polish friend would race to see who could pick cherries the fastest. In the end a tie was declared and Jamlady and her friend snickered about the poor city girls who have no idea what fun they are missing. Jamlady misses the days when most people used to enjoy simple pleasures. Jamlady recommends that all suburbanites or rural folks with a couple of sunny land spaces put in some dwarf sour cherry trees. If you have space and ladders and are able to climb, consider full-sized trees.

Jamlady Tip: Jamlady doesn't use ladders; she just drives her old van under the limbs or alongside the sour cherry trees and picks like crazy. Use a vehicle with a sturdy roof, or lose weight.

Uncooked Adaptogenic Sour Cherry Jam with Agar Agar

A union of the rainforests', oceans', and lands' bounty!

Uncooked cherries with herbs and no added sugar.

> 1 tablespoon lemon juice
> 3 cups pitted sour cherries, processor chopped
> ½ cup cold water or adaptogenic tea/infusion such as suma or Cat's Claw
> 3½ tablespoons agar-agar flakes
> ½ cup honey or other alternative sweetener

Use 1 tiny pinch of ascorbic acid crystals (not ascorbic acid powder) on the fruit to inhibit oxidation. Check very carefully for pits by spreading the pitted cherries out on a tray and, with a plastic glove or plastic bag on your hand, push down on the surface to feel for pits. It is easier to see or feel the pits if the cherries are spread out very thinly. To make a batch of jam, cook the agar-agar in the water, tea, or infusion. Add the honey or sweetener, and fully dissolve. Add the lemon juice to the fruit. Then add the agar-agar solution to the fruit and not the other way around. Stir constantly and completely. Refrigerate or freeze.

This basic recipe with uncooked fruits can be made with other fruits. For the sour cherries, just substitute mashed raspberries, blackberries, blueberries, or strawberries. Similarly, uncooked freezer jams can be made with regular powdered fruit pectin or lite fruit pectin. The insert sheets inside these products usually have recipes for **"freezer jams,"** which call for: 1) mixing the crushed fruits with the sugar or sweetener and waiting 20 minutes, 2) adding the pectin (which has been precooked with 1 cup of water for 1 minute) into the fruit and sugar mixture, 3) plac-

ing the completed freezer jam in sealed freezer containers and allowing them to sit at room temperature for 24 hours, after which time they can be refrigerated or frozen.

Jamlady Tip: Jamlady suggests that the water in these recipes might well be an adaptogenic or herbal tea or infusion. Strawberry-Mint Freezer Jam could easily be made by substituting a mint infusion for the water. It is possible to avoid using sugar or artificial sweeteners, if you mix a strong, adaptogenic, naturally sweet licorice tea or licorice spice tea with a complementary fruit such as blueberries to make a "no-sugar" pectin or agar-agar "Fruitnic Jam." Jamlady coins fruit, vegetable, or herbal "jams" that are also tonics or medicines as "Fruitnic Jams" or "Vegnic Jams."

The glycyrrhizin ($C_{42}H_{62}O_{16}$) found in licorice root, *Glycyrrhiza glabra,* **is 50 times sweeter than sugar.** Licorice is effective in combating viral infections such as a cold and helpful for arthritis, female disorders, herpes, eczema, psoriasis, bursitis, TB, and a host of other maladies. **Glycyrrhizin exhibits adaptogenic properties by stimulating cortisol production or reducing it when necessary, thus aiding the adrenal glands and reducing inflammation.** Also read about other adaptogens like **Eleuthero** or **Siberian Ginseng,** *Eleutherococcus senticosus,* **Schizandra Berries,** *Schizandra chinensis,* **Reishi Mushroom,** *Ganoderma lucidum,* **Ashwagandha** or **Indian Ginseng,** *Withania somnifera,* **Gotukola, Centella,** or **Indian Pennywort,** *Centella asiatica,* **Astragalus,** *Astragalus membranaceus,* **Fo-ti Root** or **Ho Shou Wu,** *Polygonum multiflorum,* **Burdock,** *Arctium lappa,* and **suma,** *Pfaffia paniculata.*

Suma, Pfaffia, or **Brazilian Ginseng,** *Pfaffia paniculata* Martius, is an adaptogenic Brazilian plant that can inhibit the growth of cultured tumor-cell melanomas (T. Takemoto, et al [six other authors]: *Tetrahedon Letters* 24: 1,057-60,

1963; S. Nakai, et al [six other authors]: *Phytochemistry* 23: 1,703-5, 1984; and N. Nishimoto, et al [six other authors]: *Tennen Yuki Kagobutsu Toronkai Koen Yoshishu* 30: 17-24, 1988). According to *Prescription for Nutritional Healing*, page 109, suma is of benefit for inflammation, anemia, fatigue, stress, AIDS, arthritis, cancer, liver disease, menopausal symptoms, high blood pressure, Epstein-Barr virus, and a weakened immune system. **Many scientist believe that we may need adaptogens, with their steroidlike compounds, just as we need minerals and vitamins, and the lack of them may be responsible for certain chronic illnesses.** Jamlady suggest you try using some suma infusions in your medicinal jellies. Knowing Americans, someone will put suma tea in their "Jell-O®shots" and call them "suma shots!" Jamlady suggests that suma infusions might well be put in "Fruitnic Jams."

Years ago, the Ojibwa Indian medicine men used Essiac tea of burdock root, sheep sorrel, Turkish rhubarb root, red clover, watercress, blessed thistle, kelp, and slippery elm bark to treat cancer, arthritis, circulatory problems, urinary tract infections, prostate irregularities, and asthma. Today, medicinal jellies or preserves can be made with teas and infusions of herbs now known to be medicinal (research the German *Commission E Monographs*, J. Duke's *The Green Pharmacy*, A. Chevallier's *The Encyclopedia of Medicinal Plants*, and others).

𖠰

SUGAR FREE

Lots of health-concerned people have asked Jamlady about **sugarless jams.** Actually, there is no such thing. There are jams that have no table sugar (sucrose) or no added sugar, but since jams are usually made from fruits or vegetables that contain natural sugars, there are sugars present. Even some artificial sugars have sugars, but they are in a form the body cannot assimilate. The term "sugar free" may imply no calories to some people when, in fact, it may mean the product is sweetened with honey, corn syrup, high fructose, dextrose, glucose, or molasses. These other sugars are just as high in calories as table (castor) sugar. We can find reduced-calorie or low-calorie jams, usually meaning one-half lower calories or, in reference to low-calorie jams, less than 40 calories per serving. A typical recipe for "sugar-free jam" or "no-sugar-added jam" might look like this.

"Sugar-Free" Jam

A cooked jam made with gelatin.

1½ cups unsweetened juice
¼ ounce unflavored gelatin
4 cups mashed fruit or 2 cups each of two fruits
1 tablespoon lemon juice
1 teaspoon butter
¼ teaspoon spice such as ginger, nutmeg, or cinnamon

Combine the juice with the gelatin and let it stand for 2 minutes. Cook, stirring constantly, until the gelatin is dissolved. Stir in the rest of the ingredients and cook for 10 minutes, stirring constantly. Refrigerate. As you can see, this is gelatin, but it is a solution!

In the old days, **isinglass,** a gelatin obtained from the swim bladders of certain fish like sturgeons, was used to thicken jams. Today, some cooks and chefs, especially Amish cooks and larger manufacturers, use modified food starches to thicken pies and other things like jams. **Instant CLEARJEL® is a modified food starch that thickens food instantly without cooking.** CLEARJEL® resembles cornstarch and reduces the amount of sugar needed in certain recipes. Modified food starch products may be used as a replacement for cornstarch, flour, and tapioca. **One tablespoon cornstarch equals 1½ tablespoons CLEARJEL®; 2 tablespoons flour or tapioca equals 1 tablespoon CLEAR-JEL®.**

No-Sugar Freezer Jam with Modified Food Starch (CLEARJEL®) can be made with 2 cups mashed fruit (fresh, frozen, or canned), ¾ cup sweetener/sugar or other (not referring to aspartame or packet sweeteners, although their equivalent to sugar might be tried), and 1½ tablespoons Instant CLEARJEL® starch. CLEARJEL® comes in two versions, instant or cooked. **CLEARJEL® is a maize starch that is crosslinked and stabilized.** This starch has high viscosity, good stability, clarity, and sheen. CLEARJEL® is made by the National Starch and Chemical Co., which also makes **Novation Starch®,** a clean-label starch that is not chemically modified. Some manufacturers of spaghetti sauces prefer to use these kinds of thickeners in their products as they do not mask flavors and because of how they may list ingredients. Most, if not all, suppliers of food starches have similar products. CLEARJEL® in #2.5 containers can be purchased from waltonfeed.com and some restaurant supply stores. **Many starches, as well as table sugar, do not impact pH very much, if at all, so you can often use them in your canned products with fewer pH concerns.** Some manufacturers of these types of products, however, do list a pH that is higher than 4.6 on their product specifi-

cation sheets, so to be safe, always check the pH of your completed product. To understand more about why some ingredients you might add to your product may not influence the pH as much as you think they should or vice versa, please read up on molarity or talk to a chemist.

❧ "Sugar-Free" "Jam"

No added sugar, honey, corn syrup, dextrose, molasses, high fructose, fructose, or glucose.

To make a "sugar-free" "jam," meaning no added sugar or sugar substitute with any appreciable calories that can be used by the body for energy, **there are at least seven choices:**

1. a gelatin-based "jam" sweetened with fruit juice or fruit concentrate. A fruit juice or a fruit concentrate is a natural sugar. This natural sugar can contain calories.

2. a gelatin-based "jam" sweetened with no calorie sweeteners (synthetic or glycoside) or not sweetened at all (plain fruit with gelatin).

3. a "jam" made with "no-sugar" pectin, fruit and fruit juice or concentrate, and nothing else. This jam will not be sweet except for the sweetness imparted by fruit.

4. a "jam" made with "no-sugar" pectin and sweetened with a no-calorie sweetener (artificial or glycoside).

5. a "jam" made with agar-agar or another thickener such as CLEARJEL® and sweetened with fruit and fruit juice or concentrate.

6. a "jam" made with agar-agar or another thickener such as CLEARJEL® and sweetened with a no-calorie sweetener (artificial sweetener or glycoside).

7. a "jam" made by cooking fruits with dried fruits and fruit concentrates only. This mixture

will not, in most cases, be very sweet or, if it is, it will probably have more calories. This dried-fruit jam could also be sweetened further with an artificial sweetener or glycoside.

If there are other ways, Jamlady is not aware of them. Perhaps, sago or other thickeners can be used. Sweetening any one of these recipes may also be done with a naturally sweet tea or infusion like licorice, but that is pretty much the same thing as using the sweetening substances that have been extracted from these fruits or herbal plant parts.

All of these concoctions are technically not jams either, as we discussed before, because by definition, a jam requires more sugar than fruit, and clearly none of these recipes fits that description. Of course, jams can be sweetened with alternate sugars, but these are not helpful for the diabetic, who must reduce sugar. In fact, cooked-down fruits with a lot of fruit concentrate may result in lots of natural sugars and may not be appropriate for many diabetics. The recipe below is for an experimental batch of "no-sugar jam," made to translate a "with-sugar," apple-raspberry jam into a jam that is appropriate for some people seeking to reduce sugar. While some people may object to using aspartame in hermetically sealed jam, it is still, in Jamlady's opinion, a possible solution for a "sugar-free, no-substantial-calorie jam" that will be hermetically sealed. It is possible to add aspartame after cooking the jam, when the jam has cooled some. Seal the jar with paraffin wax and refrigerate, or just refrigerate.

Note: It is not possible to adequately seal a canning jar without boiling, so if you are concerned about possible changes in aspartame due to high heat, then you will need to refrigerate your jams, adding the aspartame or other "sugar-free" sweeteners to the hot or warm, but not boiling-hot, product. Depending on the viscosity of the completed "no-sugar" jam, it may be possible to can it and add liquid sweetener after opening.

Sugar-Free Apple-Raspberry Jam

This jam copies the with-sugar, apple-raspberry jam as a "sugar-free" version.

3 cups sliced tart apples
1 cup juiced seedless raspberry pulp
¾ cup water
1 1¾-ounce box lite or "no-sugar" powdered pectin
1 tablespoon lemon juice
28 packets aspartame
¼ teaspoon ground cinnamon
1-2 pinch ascorbic acid crystals

Use the ascorbic acid, sparingly, by the pinchful, on the fruit and in the prep water. Mix the water, raspberry pulp, lemon juice, cinnamon, and apples with the pectin. Let the mixture sit for 10 minutes. Boil the mixture for 1 minute to cook the apples. Add the sweetener; boil 1 minute more. JSP/RWB20(4-8OZ). Do not shorten this processing time. The challenge with this jam is to have enough moisture, because apples are somewhat dry. Another method would be to cook the apples with the water first. Of course, this jam could be made with juiced apples, but then there would be no chunks in the "jam" and a chunky jam was the desired effect. The shelf life from the date of manufacture is 3 months. Refrigeration may extend the shelf life of this jam and, when possible, refrigeration is always recommended for "no-sugar" jams.

Jamlady has been told there are only three FDA-approved synthetic sweeteners. Synthetic (artificial sweeteners) may be nutritive or non-nutritive. Synthetic sweeteners must be approved by the FDA before they can be marketed in the U.S. **The three synthetic sweeteners with FDA approval are: aspartame, saccharin, and acesulfame K. Aspartame is a nutritive sweetener (has calories); saccharin and acesulfame K are non-nutritive (no calories). Nutritive sweeteners provide 4 calories per gram.**

There are natural sweeteners that are taken from fruit concentrates. A *glycoside* is a group of compounds derived from *monosaccharides* or any organic compound that yields a sugar and one more nonsugar substance on hydrolysis. "In the case of some plant-derived sweeteners, these are non-hydrolyzable *disaccharides* composed of glucose linked to some modified hexose. **The glycoside's sweetness is caused when the glucose binds to the sugar receptor on the tongue. At the same time, the nature of the disaccharide linkage or nature of the modification prevents the glycoside from being ingested"** (MadSci Network). Therefore, there is no caloric intake. The major sweetening agent in Lo Han Kuo (Luo Han Guo) is *mongroside,* a glycoside in which the terpenoid group is covalently bound to one of the two sugars of the disaccharide such that it inhibits hydrolysis. **Mongroside is about 250 times as sweet as sucrose.** One sweetener is made from kiwi fruit, and *Stevia rebaundiana* extracts contain *stevioside,* which is 200 or more times sweeter than regular sugar. Another "no-sugar" sweetener has been made from Lo Han Kuo fruit and crystalline fructose.

※

BLUEBERRIES AND CRANBERRIES

If Jamlady asked you what you thought was the most popular jam in taste tests, what jam would be your answer? Perhaps you would guess strawberry, raspberry, or blackberry. You'd be wrong. Strawberry isn't even in the top three. Perhaps you think grape jelly? Wrong again. The most selected "jams" in taste tests at Chicagoland farmers' market are Blueberry-Almond Jam and Peach-Almond Preserves. This fact or finding holds true to **Jamlady's Tenet: Changing just one variable a little is the impetus for culinary greatness!**

Note: Jamlady has learned there are limits on substitutions beyond which no one should go. Jamlady's aunt Frances Basten, a great pickle maker, strawberry-tart maker, and all-around great American cook, was trying to accommodate Jamlady and her cousin Rodney's demands for a pizza. She had no pizza dough, so she used English muffins; she had no pizza sauce, so she used ketchup; she had no oregano, so she used parsley flakes; she had no sausage, so she used hot dogs . . . need Jamlady go on? The spices were cloves and Jamlady forgot the rest, but Frances's coup d'essai was a disaster! It just goes to show you even the best cooks can make errors in judgment, especially when they are substituting or cooking in foreign territory.

There is no crunch in this next jam. The almond flavor is provided by the pure almond extract. Blueberry-Almond Jam is made with the addition of one ingredient, pure almond extract, to an already fabulous blueberry preserve or jam. Shazam! The whole is greater than the sum of its parts. Form kisses function.

Blueberry-Almond Jam on almond biscotti is
indescribably delicious. Just one extra ingredient is added to classic blueberry jam . . .
pure almond extract!

Jamlady's Original Blueberry-Almond Jam

This big favorite could be called a preserve as the berry-to-sugar ratio is equal.

Blueberries are low in natural pectin . . . so pectin is needed!

4 cups chopped blueberries
4 cups sugar
1 1¾-ounce box regular powdered pectin
2 tablespoons lemon juice
½ teaspoon butter (optional)
1 tablespoon pure almond extract

Boil the blueberries, lemon juice, butter, and pectin for 1 minute. Add the sugar; boil for 1 minute more. Add the almond extract and boil for 1 more minute.
JSP/RWB5(4OZ)10(8OZ)15(16OZ).

*Variations: Blue Rummy Jam—Add 1 table-spoon rum or rum extract instead of the pure almond extract. **Blueberry Jam with Pectin—** Leave out the almond extract. **Blueberry Jam with Crème de Cassis—**Instead of the almond extract add ¼-½ cup Crème de Cassis at the end and boil for 1 more minute. **Blueberry Sambuca Jam or Preserves—**Instead of the almond extract add ¼ cup Romana Sambuca, Luxardo Sambuca, or similar liqueur and boil for 1 more minute. **Blueberry Preserves—**See fact on blueberries.*

*Fact: Blueberries are low in acid. It is necessary to add acid to the blueberries in order for the jam to thicken or set. This product, blueberry jam or blueberry preserve, is often referred to as a "jam" because added pectin is used to set the product. Preserves often require no pectin, as many fruits, given half sugar and half fruits, will set with no added pectin. **Equal blueberries and sugar will not set without added pectin.** More berries than sugar are necessary for blueberries to set without*

*pectin. Blueberries will set with less sugar, more fruit, more lemon juice (acid) and/or vinegar. **Try 4 cups blueberries with ½ cup 5 percent acidity herbal vinegar (perhaps vinegar infused with adaptogenic or especially flavorful herbs or spices like anise or ginger) and 3 cups sugar for Blueberry Preserve without Added Pectin.** If you like, spice the jam directly with pure almond extract, cinnamon, nutmeg, or cloves. Lemon or lemon rind with blueberries increases the pectin and acid levels. In any given recipe, never change a high-acid ingredient like lemon, lemon rind, or lime except for a pH like-in-kind exchange. For example, you can add grated lemon rind to blueberry preserves and reduce the lemon juice by the same amount (up to half the called-for amount) or you could substitute lime juice for lemon juice.*

Jamlady has seen recipes for blueberry "jam" that are made with whole coffee beans, 1 extra tablespoon grated lemon rind, and coffee liqueur. Supposedly, the coffee beans can be nibbled.

Caution: Be careful not to chomp down on a coffee bean and break a tooth. *Most of the coffee beans will soften up in jam, given time to soften, but there always is the possibility that one well-roasted bean won't soften up, so nibble carefully. Jamlady sees coffee beans in jam as more of a novelty than any great flavor enhancer, as the coffee flavor is adequately imparted by the liqueur.*

Jelly, of sorts, can even be made from coffee itself. Jamlady found a copy of *The Cook's Manual*, Ulster Co., NY: The Ladies Aid Society, Esopus Methodist Episcopal Church, 1891. This manual was "circulated at their bazar (*sic*)—Wednesday, Thursday and Friday, Dec. 16, 17 and 18, 1891" and gives a recipe for coffee jelly and molasses candy: "**Coffee Jelly:** 2 ounces gelatine, water to cover, soak 15 minutes, add one qt. boiling water, 2 cups sugar and 1½ cups very strong coffee" and **Molasses Candy:** boil 1 quart molasses with "piece of butter the size of ½ an egg" until it "breaks short between the teeth." And you know these are small-town recipes when you see the Methodist and Episcopal congregations apparently sharing the same building.

Jamlady's blueberry jam recipe uses less sugar than the liquid-pectin jam recipes found on manufacturers' insert sheets for liquid pectin, so Jamlady has always used powdered-pectin recipes with blueberries. Of course, blueberry jam recipes using liquid pectin might be reformulated by increasing the blueberries and decreasing the measure of sugar.

ᴐᴄ

Blueberry-Almond Jam Sweetened with Aspartame

Appropriate for some individuals whose diets allow the use of aspartame!

4 cups chopped blueberries
1 1¾-ounce box lite or "no-sugar" powdered pectin
2 tablespoons lemon juice
25 packets aspartame (18-30 may be used)
1 tablespoon pure almond extract

Mix blueberries, lemon juice, and pectin; wait 5-10 minutes. Boil for 1 minute and add the sweetener and pure almond extract. Boil for 1 minute; skim. JSP/RWB5(4OZ)10(8OZ). The shelf life of this product is 3-4 months but may be extended with refrigeration.

The blueberry, *Vaccinium* spp.; **huckleberry,** *V. canadensis* and *V. pennsylvanicum;* whortleberry or bilberry, *V. myrtillus* and *V. corymbosum* Linn.; and **high bush blueberry,** *V. corymbosum,* are all deciduous shrubs bearing white or pink flowers and small, edible, purplish-black berries. Blueberries are native to North America and

Europe. Both the berries and the leaves of the blueberry shrub are used for food or tea. Many people are confused by the various names for blueberries, and the terms whortleberry or bilberry aren't often used in everyday conversation. Many market patrons rebuke the offer of any other blueberry jam when they request huckleberry jam. In the Midwest, the term **huckleberry** refers to the low-growing species *V. canadensis* and *V. pennsylvanicum,* and in New England a "huckleberry" refers to a species of *Gaylussacia* while "blueberry" is reserved for the low-growing species cited above. A decoction of the dried blueberry fruit is supposedly antibacterial and is used for diarrhea in children. Ripe blueberries are natural laxatives. Blueberries may be of some benefit to those with MS, ulcers, a bladder infection, or early-stage cataracts.

ᴐᴄ

Jamlady's Original Blueberry-Plum Jam with Cinnamon

Delicious!
No sugar—it's sweetened with aspartame.

3 cups cooked-down plums (see below)
1 cup chopped blueberries
1 1¾-ounce box lite or "no-sugar" powdered pectin
2 teaspoons lemon juice
25 packets aspartame
1 teaspoon ground cinnamon

Processor chop the pitted plums and cook them down for 10 minutes. Measure out 3 cups plums. Boil the plums, blueberries, lemon juice, and pectin for 1 minute. Add the cinnamon and aspartame and boil for 1 more minute. JSP/RWB5(4OZ)10(8OZ).

Cinnamony Blueberry-Plum Jam

Blueberries and plums with sugar and cinnamon!

6 cups sugar
3 cups prepared plums (see below)
2 cups chopped blueberries
1 1¾-ounce box regular powdered pectin
1 tablespoon lemon juice
1 teaspoon ground cinnamon

Cook down stoned and processor-chopped plums for 5 minutes; measure out 3 cups. Boil the plums, blueberries, lemon juice, and pectin for 1 minute. Add the sugar and cinnamon; boil 1 minute more. JSP/RWB5(4OZ)10(8OZ).

☙❧

Jamlady's Original Blueberries in Snow

A lite jam with wonderful color contrast! Only ⅓ cup sugar per jar.

5 cups peeled, chopped pears
2 cups sugar
½ cup dried blueberries or dried cranberries
½ cup chopped or whole macadamia nuts
¼ cup lemon juice
1 1¾-ounce box "no-sugar" pectin

Mix the pectin with the pears and lemon juice; boil for 1 minute. Add the sugar; boil for 1 minute. Mix in the macadamia nuts and place the jam in the jar alternatively with the dried blueberries—so as to reduce bleeding. JSR or this jar can be sealed by a RWB, but there will be some bleeding of the blueberries into the snow.

Variation: Cranberries in Snow with Sugar—*To make this jam with regular pectin, follow the recipe for pear jam and add in the macadamia nuts and dried cranberries. Seal in the same manner as* ***Jamlady's Original Blueberries in Snow.***

Cranberry or **craneberry** plants are low vines in the Heath or Ericaceae family. They are known for their small, red, sour fruits. The cranberry plant belongs to the *Vaccinium* genus, the same genus as the blueberry. Cultivated for about 100 years, cranberry plants require an acidic soil. The small or **European cranberry,** *Vaccinium oxycoccos,* grows wild in the marshlands of Europe and North America (Massachusetts, New Jersey, Wisconsin, Washington, Oregon, and Nova Scotia). The large or **American cranberry,** *Vaccinium macrocarpon,* is cultivated in the northeastern United States in regulated bogs that can be drained or flooded as necessary. Flooding is used to prevent freezing and to destroy insect pests. The **cowberry** or **mountain cranberry,** *Vaccinium vitis-idaea,* usually gathered from the wild and rarely cultivated, is found in Europe and North America. The **high bush cranberry** is from the Honeysuckle family and its red fruits are sometimes substituted for real cranberries. Cranberry jam or preserves is not often requested in the summer months, but when fall comes around, everyone is looking for something cranberry. This recipe is so easy and requires no added pectin. **Cranberry Preserves** is on Jamlady's **Beginner's List** and it makes a great Thanksgiving or Christmas gift. **Some other beginner "jams" are pineapple, basil pineapple, pina colada, and apple maple.**

Cranberry Preserves with Grand Marnier

A beginner's preserve!
Equally delicious on turkey or a turkey sandwich.

24 ounces fresh cranberries
⅝ cup water
3½ cups white sugar
½ cup Grand Marnier (optional)
½ teaspoon butter

Wash the cranberries. Cook the cranberries and butter in water until tender. Add the sugar and cook to 104-105 degrees C. Add Grand Marnier (orange-flavored liqueur). Cook 1 more minute. JSP/RWB10(8OZ). Makes 5½-6 eight-ounce jars.

Variations: Cranberry Marmalade—To transform this preserve into a marmalade, add some grated orange or lemon rind (and/or orange or lemon juice, a little more water, and rind). Alternately, make half an orange or lemon marmalade recipe together with half a cranberry recipe, or make them separately and mix some together for the third product. **Strawberry-Cranberry Preserves—***Layer 6 cups hulled, quartered strawberries with 6 cups sugar and leave overnight. Add the strawberry mixture to the Cranberry Preserves with Grand Marnier recipe when the sugar is added to the cooked cranberries. The Grand Marnier is optional.*

Strawberry and Cranberry Jam

Can be sweetened several ways!

4 cups processor-sliced strawberries
1½ cups fresh cranberries
1½ cups water
1 1¾-ounce box lite or "no-sugar" pectin
¼ cup water
23-30 packets aspartame, alternate sweetener, or
   1-2 cups sugar
½ teaspoon or less ascorbic acid crystals

Use the ascorbic acid crystals in the prep water and while processor-slicing the strawberries. Use a pinch at a time. Cook cranberries in 1½ cups water until tender and almost all of the water is gone. Add sliced strawberries with a small pinch of ascorbic acid crystals. Add pectin and ¼ cup water and let the mixture sit for 10 minutes. Boil for 1 minute. Add aspartame or sugar and boil for 1 minute. JSP/RWB5(4OZ)10(8OZ).

FIGS AND STRAWBERRIES

The fig tree, *Ficus carica,* native to southwestern Asia, is grown for commercial production. Most U.S. figs grow in tropical and subtropical regions such as California and Texas. Some figs, especially if covered in the winter, have grown as far north as Michigan. The fig tree is a low, deciduous tree, averaging about 20 feet tall with downy, greenish bark on its branches. Small flowers of the fig plant grow on the inside of a hollow organ called a "receptacle." As the receptacle grows it becomes the fruit of the fig tree. Fruit development relies upon fertile pollen, and many commercial fig varieties produce no pollen, so the pollen of the wild fig tree is used. A method of juxtaposing flowering wild-fig branches and cultivated fig trees is called ***caprification.*** Caprification is crucial to proper fertilization of the cash crop called figs. New fig trees are usually produced by the propagation of cuttings. Figs that growers intend to dry are left on the trees until they shrivel and fall. The fallen figs are then dunked in salt water and put in a sunny location to dry.

For many years Jamlady heard how wonderful homemade fig preserves were but never could afford to make the preserve due to the high cost of the figs and having no homegrown source. In Chicagoland, since 2002, it has been possible to buy figs from California at reasonable prices. Jamlady has noted that, in season, Eurofresh Market in Palatine, Illinois, and one other local fruit market carry fresh figs at reasonable prices.

No doubt many of you who live in the South have your own fig trees. Lucky you! If you have more figs than you can eat or process, cover them with wine and keep them in the refrigerator. This is a quick method of preservation and will buy you about two weeks' time. Give some **drunken figs** as hostess gifts

Jamlady values figs for their exquisite taste, low fat, and high food value. However, if you are on a low-carbohydrate diet, then figs are not the fruit for you, as they are almost three-quarters carbohydrates with about 4.3 percent protein, 2.4 percent ash, and 18.8 percent water.

If you've never tasted fig preserves, then you have missed one of mother nature's true gifts to man. The market master at Jamlady's Wilmette Market, Illinois, was addicted to Jamlady's fig preserves and would often tell Jamlady how quickly the jar got consumed at her house. Many people are amazed at how quickly good "jam" disappears. Some comment that they thought their family did not like "jam," as jars of store jam would sit in the refrigerator for months. There is no better way to say I love you than a jar of fig preserves.

If you've never tasted fresh figs before, they actually taste very similar to strawberries or the soft filling in fig fruit bars. Figs have been eaten by people at least since 2900 B.C. If you'd like to try filling a cakelike cookie dough with fig preserves or another special "jam" like Raspberry Genie Jam (**Raspberry Genie-Accordion Cookies**), Cactus Jelly, Lemon-Ginger Marmalade, Seedless Berry Preserves, Strawberry Genie Preserves, Apple and Maple Preserves, Apricot Preserves, Strawberry-Fig Preserves, Sour Cherry-Almond Preserves, or Orange-Rhubarb Marmalade, try **Accordion Cookie Dough Recipe #1**—½ cup butter, ½ cup margarine, ½ cup sugar, ½ cup honey, 2 large eggs, 4½ cups self-rising flour (or **homemade self-rising flour: 1-1¼ teaspoon baking powder to 1 cup flour plus a pinch salt**). Chill the dough, construct the cookie bar, and bake at 400 degrees F (190 degrees C) for about 15-20 minutes, depending on the thickness of the dough, which is initially rolled out to about ¼" thick, filled with preserves, and folded over to make a jelly-dough sandwich. Cut in rectangles with a pizza wheel after it is baked. Or try **Accordion Cookie**

'Black Mission' Fig Preserves—All you need to make this delicious and easy-to-make preserves is 'Black Mission' figs, lemon, sugar, and water. Take a taste and dream a little dream . . . maybe all the way to Cockaigne.

Dough Recipe #2—½ cup shortening, 1 cup sugar, 1 egg, ½ cup milk, 1 teaspoon vanilla (pure almond extract, some cinnamon, or a drop of oil of cinnamon for **Accordion Genie Cookies**), ½ teaspoon salt, 3 cups flour, and 1 tablespoon baking powder. Chill the dough, construct the cookie bar, and bake at 400 degrees F for about 15-20 minutes, depending on the thickness of the dough, which is initially rolled out to about ¼" thick, filled with preserves, and folded over to make a jelly-dough sandwich. Cut in rectangles with a pizza wheel after it is baked. Display the cookies stacked sideways like an accordion, but then know the cookie, with all its magical fillings, is really named after Jamlady's hometown. The cookie dough can also be constructed like an accordion and baked with jam in the recesses of the folds. Serve for the kids with "oompah and squeezebox" music.

♒

'Black Mission' Fig Preserves

Made from fresh figs and lemons with no added pectin.
Lower sugar than jam!

> 4 pounds fresh 'Black Mission' figs
> 1 lemon
> 4 cups sugar
> 1 cup water

Chop the outer rind of the lemon, discarding the white pith, remove the seeds, and chop the lemon pulp. Wash the figs and removed each hard stem end. Cook the sugar and water with the very finely chopped lemon peel and chopped lemon pulp to make a clear syrup. Add half the figs (processor chopped) and cook for 1 minute. Add the rest of the figs (cut into ½" slices). Cook until thick. JSP/RWB5(4OZ)10(8OZ).

Note: *In Roden's* Middle Eastern Food, *there is a recipe for* **Dried Fig Jam** *that is made with dried*

figs, sugar, water, lemon juice, ground aniseeds, pine nuts, walnuts, and a little pulverized mastic—the resinous gum of **Pistacia lentiscus.** *Those wanting to experiment might try some of these spices and nuts in the recipe above or in other preserve recipes. Also in Roden's book is a coconut jam recipe.*

♒

Fig and Rhubarb Preserves

Maybe try some of this preserve baked in some Accordion Cookie Dough!
Jamlady usually makes seven times this recipe.

> 1 pound chopped, unpeeled rhubarb
> 1 pound sugar
> ¼ pound destemmed, chopped, fresh figs
> 3 tablespoons lemon juice

Mix all the ingredients and let them sit in the refrigerator or a cool place for 24 hours. Simmer the pot slowly until thick. Check the sample for thickness by cooling some in the refrigerator. JSP/RWB10(8OZ).

This next fig jam recipe is provided to illustrate a point. It is not the very best recipe for a fig product. It is a jam recipe made with added pectin. **As you can see, the figs are stretched out with sugar so that pectin is needed to jell the jam.** This is a jam because there is more sugar than fruit, 7½ cups sugar to 5 cups fig fruit and ½ cup lemon juice. Additionally there is ½ cup water. Compare this recipe to one that has 4 pounds figs (8 cups—"a pint's a pound") plus a lemon to 4 cups sugar and 1 cup water. **The ratio of the first recipe is 1.5 parts sugar to 1 part fruits and the second recipe is 1 part sugar to 2 parts fruits.** The differences are greater than exact opposites and the Black Mission Fig Preserves, in Jamlady's opinion, are more than twice as good as the Fig Jam.

Fig Jam

Made with fresh, ripe figs.
This fig jam is good but never as good as Black Mission Fig Preserves!

7½ cups sugar
5 cups destemmed, processor-chopped figs
½ cup lemon juice
½ cup water
1 1¾-ounce box regular powdered pectin

Mix the pectin, water, figs, and lemon juice together; boil 1 minute. Add the sugar; boil 1 minute. JSP/RWB10.

The problem comes in trying to convince cooks who have been making these sorts of fig jam recipes that they are not making the "best stuff"! They will say, "I make the best homemade jams and preserves," and this is the type of recipe they show Jamlady. Granted, these recipes will produce jams that are better than the store jams, but we cooks want the very best and healthiest "jams" we can make. Don't we? Having said all of that, there are people who prefer the sweeter jams to the preserves. Jamlady herself prefers the less-sweet "jam" or butter but knows that many people do not. Consider also that some fruits have an intense flavor and can be tastily and successfully stretched out. Others, like figs, do not have enough flavor when stretched out to make a star-worthy product. Some sweeter, more successful jams are strawberry, peach, and figberry jam.

Figberry Jam

This combination is not often seen!
Rich luscious strawberries complementing figs.

7½ cups sugar
3 cups hulled, processor-sliced strawberries
2 cups destemmed, chopped, unpeeled figs
½ cup lemon juice
½ cup water
1 1¾-ounce box regular powdered pectin
¼ teaspoon or less ascorbic acid crystals
½ teaspoon butter for anti-foaming (optional)

Use 1 pinch ascorbic acid crystals on the fruits during preparation. Mix the strawberries, figs, lemon juice, water, butter, and pectin. Stir; let sit for 10 minutes. Boil the mixture for 1 minute. Add the sugar and boil for 1 minute more. JSP/RWB5(4OZ)10(8OZ).

Variation: Figberry Preserves—Combine half a fig preserves recipe with half a strawberry preserves recipe, or make the full recipes of both and mix some of each completed preserves to make Figberry Preserves. Retain some strawberry and fig preserves too. There are people who prefer strawberry or figberry jam over strawberry or figberry preserves, stating they like that sweet stuff. So, there is a jam formulation that is right for everyone. Jamlady sees her job as that of an expository cook or food scientist. Beyond that, customers and readers are on their own to choose what jam or preserve they will consume.

Folk Jam is another jam made with more sugar than fruits. It is basically a strawberry-peach jam to which a folk liqueur is added. Folk Jam is requested so often that Jamlady is not sure if the market patrons truly love it that much more than strawberry-peach jam or if they just like the name and the idea of the unusual liqueur. For whatever reason, Folk Jam is hugely popular! This again brings up **Jamlady's Tenet:**

Changing just one variable a little is the impetus for culinary greatness.

Thanks to the Jamlady's mother, who visited Sint Maarten, Jamlady has discovered the **Wild Sint Maarten Guavaberry Liqueur!** Nothing tastes quite like this liqueur. The bottle says, "Guavaberry is the legendary folk liqueur of Sint Maarten. It was first made here hundreds of years ago in private homes." This woody flavor is not the taste of guavas but **guavaberries**, *Myrciaria floribunda*. This liqueur is made from rum and berries that are found high in the warm hills in the center of the island. Next time you are in the Caribbean Islands be sure to buy some of this wonderful liqueur!

ꙮ

Jamlady's Original Folk Jam

Strawberries, peaches, and Guavaberry Liqueur!

> 6 cups sugar
> 2½ cups processor-sliced strawberries
> 1⅞ cups peeled, diced peaches
> ¼ cup Guavaberry Liqueur
> ⅛ cup water
> 1 1¾-ounce box regular powdered pectin
> 1 tablespoon lemon juice
> ½ teaspoon butter

Mix the fruit, water, lemon juice, butter, and pectin. Wait 10 minutes; boil for 1 minute. Add the sugar; boil for 1 minute. Add the Guavaberry Liqueur and boil for another minute. JSP/RWB5(4OZ)10(8OZ).

Variations: Strawberry-Peach Preserves—Use half a peach preserves recipe and half a strawberry preserves recipe. Peach-Plum Preserves—Use 4 cups peaches, 5 cups red pitted plums, 8 cups sugar, and 1 tablespoon finely grated lemon rind.

The next jam is an interesting sugar-free jam made with the artificial sweetener called aspartame. It could also be made with any one of several glycoside sweeteners or with 1-3 cups sugar or 1 cup honey.

ꙮ

Strawberry Genie Jam #1

Sweetened with aspartame, alternate sweetener, or 1-3 cups sugar.

> 5 cups washed, hulled, processor-sliced strawberries
> 1 1¾-ounce box "no-sugar" powdered pectin
> ¼ cup water
> 25 packets aspartame
> 1 teaspoon oil of cinnamon or ground cinnamon (optional)

Mix the strawberries, cinnamon, and water with the pectin; wait 10 minutes. Boil for 1 minute. Add the aspartame, alternate sweetener, or sugar and boil for 1 minute. JSP/RWB5(4OZ) 10(8OZ). This jam's shelf-life is 3 months. Refrigeration is recommended for low-sugar or "no-sugar" jams but is not necessary.

To make strawberry "jam," you do not need pectin. If you do not add pectin you have more fruit than sugar, as strawberries have sufficient pectin to make a "jam" or preserved product by themselves. Many people prefer the brightly colored strawberry jam with powdered pectin that is Jamlady's specialty. This is a true jam with more sugar than fruit and has added pectin. Many people tell Jamlady they have never tasted such delicious and good-looking jam. The color is the actual color of strawberries. Most jam patrons have seen strawberry jam elsewhere that is darker and less appetizing to the eye. **Jamlady's secret**

ingredient is ascorbic acid crystals or vitamin C crystals, not powdered vitamin C.

Jamlady uses "oh so little" or trace amounts of ascorbic acid crystals when slicing the strawberries, in the water the strawberries are washed with, and in the final product. Ascorbic acid prevents the strawberries from oxidizing or browning, which darkens the beautiful bright red color of natural strawberries. Jamlady also uses under-ripe and ripe strawberries and avoids the very dark, dead-ripe strawberries, which have less pectin and could spoil the set of the jam. Half of this basic recipe can be used with half of another recipe like plain peach, mango, nectarine, plum, fig, etc. This basic or classic strawberry jam recipe with oil of cinnamon makes one of Jamlady's well-known "Genie Jams." Of course, Genie Jam can be made with double-fruit jams as well. **Strawberry-Peach Genie Jam,** for example: half a peach jam recipe and half a strawberry genie recipe.

Strawberry Genie Jam #2

A light-red strawberry jam with oil of cinnamon.
The kids keep coming back for more!

7 cups sugar
5 cups hulled, processor-sliced strawberries
$\frac{1}{4}$ cup water
1 1$\frac{3}{4}$-ounce box regular powdered pectin
$\frac{1}{2}$ teaspoon butter
$\frac{1}{4}$ teaspoon or less ascorbic acid crystals
1-2 drops oil of cinnamon

Place a very small pinch of ascorbic acid crystals on the strawberries while washing, hulling, and slicing them. Do not use too much ascorbic acid crystals or the jam will become too tart. Mix the sliced strawberries, ascorbic acid crystals, water, butter, and pectin. Let the mixture sit for 10 minutes. Boil the mixture for 1 minute, stirring very well. Add the sugar and boil for 1 more minute. Add the oil of cinnamon; stir. JSP/RWB10(8OZ)

Strawberry Genie Jam should not need to be checked for jell point, but if you are inexperienced with jam making and might have done something wrong, then this step should be included so you can tell **what a jam looks like that does set on a frozen plate.** Drop a drop of jam on a frozen plate; wait 60 seconds. Push the side of the drop with your finger. If it wrinkles, the jam should set.

This same base recipe can be used with many spices or liqueurs. Instead of oil of cinnamon you can add ground cinnamon, cinnamon and nutmeg, oil of orange, banana extract, Grand Marnier, and so on. This basic jam can be turned into **Strawberry Conserve** by adding in golden raisins, nuts like slivered blanched almonds or pecans, currants, candied peels, or pieces of dried apricots. Just don't overdo the addition of high-pH ingredients.

CURRANTS AND GOOSEBERRIES

The common currant, *Ribes sativum,* the **northern red currant,** *Ribes rubrum* Linn., and the **European black currant,** *Ribes nigrum* Linn., are all in the Saxifragaceae or saxifrage family. *Ribes rubrum* has been crossed with many other currant cultivars because it is such a hardy variety. Many black currant bushes have been pulled and destroyed in the U.S. because they are a common host of the **white-pine blister rust.** This is unfortunate for jam makers wanting the currant fruits for preserves.

The **American black currant,** *Ribes americanum,* is more resistant to the white-pine blister rust than many of the other varieties of black currant. The red currant varieties are more resistant than the black and 'Viking' is completely immune. A liqueur, **crème de cassis** or **cassis,** is made from black currants and is wonderful in gourmet preserves, especially blueberry jam or preserves. If you have a source for freshly picked black, red, or white currants, Jamlady highly suggests you take the time to make some exquisite, tart preserves. Currants are high in acid and need no additional pectin, assuming you do not try to stretch the currants out too much with unnecessary sugar.

Some pectin makers do not provide a currant recipe on their insert sheet, for which Jamlady commends them, as their product is not needed for the best currant "jam" or preserves. Other companies do list recipes with pectin for currants. One insert-sheet recipe for currant jelly calls for 5 cups prepared juice to 7 cups sugar to 1 pouch liquid pectin. Jamlady hardly thinks most cooks want to make a product with more sugar than is needed so that they need to buy pectin to make the jelly set. To be fair, that jelly recipe does make more jelly from the same poundage of currants, but Jamlady knows it will not make better-tasting jelly.

Standard **Currant Jelly** can be made with about 6 to 7 pounds of red currants to about 4½ cups of sugar. Jamlady has seen several successful methods of juice extraction for currants and knows that some people used to extract currant juice with cellulose pulp made from facial tissues (M.C.P.'s method). For one method, the currants are puréed and hung in a jelly bag overnight (Mme. Brassard's technique, Cordon Bleu Cooking School in Paris, described in Carey's *Perfect Preserves,* p. 96), and a second method calls for cooking 4 quarts of mashed currants with stems with 1½ cups of water in a pan (*The Settlement Cookbook,* p. 553) or in a steam juicer and then hanging the fruit in a jelly bag. A third method utilizes a Champion juicing machine or press to extract the juice from cooked or uncooked currants. The juice is then hung from a jelly bag or not. The clarity of the completed jelly is greatly impacted by the method and care used to extract the juice. To cook the jelly, combine 2 cups currant juice to 1½ cups sugar or equal parts currant juice to sugar. To complete the currant jelly, the jelly mixture is cooked to jell point. Jamlady likes to determine set with a frozen plate. **Place the jelly on a frozen plate. Count slowly to 60 and push the side of a dime-sized drop to the side. If it wrinkles, the jelly will set.** With some experience, you can use the spoon in the jelly to determine when the jelly is done. Basically, the drop that does not drop off, but "kinda" looks like a tiny hourglass, is an indication that the jelly will set. This takes a lot of experience to visually determine, but please do check the drops after you have tried the frozen-plate method. A jelly thermometer reading around 105 degrees C is also a good indicator.

Beginners, or those unsure about a jam's jell point, could, to be safe, refrigerate the jelly until it is cold. If a set has been achieved, it will be visible when the jelly is chilled. Then, with the assurance of a set, the jelly can be put into canning jars, topped, and sealed in a rolling water bath (RWB). Make sure to start the processing water bath ice cold if the jars are ice cold, or you could reheat the jelly to warm, load the jelly into the jars, and process in a warm water bath.

Jamlady Tip: *If there is a substantial differential between the temperature of the jar and its contents and the RWB temperature, the jar may crack, and its contents would then be lost. Equalization of temperatures between the water bath and the jar temperature is essential to a successful RWB process.*

For **Currant Butter** or smooth preserves, 2 quarts of currants can be cooked with ½ cup of water and juiced through a juicing machine. Add ¾ cup of sugar to 1 cup of purée. This method is quick, requires no added pectin, and results in about 36 ounces of completed butter. Jamlady often combines red and white currants when she does not have enough of either, for a **Blushing Currant Butter** or jelly. Blushing Currant Butter will not be a clear product and, while good, is not, in Jamlady's opinion, superior in taste to a clear currant jelly.

Bar-le-Duc Preserves can be made with or without seeds. If you're looking for a challenge, make some seedless Bar-le-Duc, and you will really have made something truly dear! Plan on taking about 3 hours' time to remove the pips from 2 pounds of currants.

Take yourself back to fourteenth-century northeastern France, when Bar-le-Duc preserves were made for Bar-le-Duc's royalty in Lorraine. Often, the seeds of each currant were removed with the needlelike end of a goose feather before cooking the preserves. The French term for this technique of removing the pips, or "without pips," is ***épépinée.*** Bar-le-Duc can be made with black, red, or white currants. This gastronomical specialty of Bar-le-Duc is considered to be the most expensive preserves in the world. Some artisan jam makers are charging as much as

thirty-five dollars for an 8-ounce jar of seedless Bar-le-Duc preserves, the white version pricier than the red. **Bar-le-Duc Spread** can be made by mixing 4 parts cream cheese, 3 parts Bar-le-Duc Preserves, and 2 parts rich cream. Serve on Melba toast.

✑✒

Bar-Le-Duc (bar-luh-DOOK, "Duke's Fortress")

Black, Red, or White Currant Preserves with No Added Pectin

> 1 quart destemmed currants
> 2 cups sugar
> 1 cup water

Allow 1 hour of time for destemming each quart of currants. Measure the currants after destemming and after seed removal. For the seedless version of Bar-le-duc, remove each currant seed with a needle. Boil the sugar and water for 1 minute. Add the currants and cook for about 15 minutes. Check the jell point with a frozen plate. JSP/RWB5(4OZ)10(8OZ). Yields four 8-ounce jars.

In Mrs. Victor's *The Dime Cookbook*, (Irwin P. Beadle Publishers, n.d., 69), there is an interesting recipe for **Green Currant Jam:** "Weight equal portions of unripe red currants and sugar; set the fruit over the fire, at some distance, with a small part of the sugar, breaking the fruit a little, that the juice may prevent it burning; stir it continually and let it remain for a quarter of an hour, then add the rest of the sugar, and boil up for a quarter of an hour longer." (This dimebook recipe is old, because within this same book, Prince & Company were advertising

Improved Melodeons with Divided Swell for $45-$350.) Some of you adventurous "jammers" may like to try this recipe or experiment with green and underripe jostaberries. The **jostaberry**, *R. nigrum x hirtellum* and/or *Ribus nidigrolaria*, is a cross between the black currant and the gooseberry. These hybrid fruits are larger than a currant, look like a gooseberry except for the darker color, and taste like a black currant.

Gooseberries, like currants, belong to the *Ribes* genus. The **European gooseberry,** *Ribes uva-crispi*, has large fruits but does not grow well in the United States due to problems with hot, dry summers and mildew. Hybridized varieties, such as *Ribes hirtellum*, are available in the United States. Gooseberries are acidic, have a high pectin content, and do not need powdered or liquid pectin to jell. Jamlady has seen green or red gooseberries in the local markets, but they are sold in those little plastic cartons and cost a small fortune to make a batch of preserves. Still, consider that you could make a very small batch and splurge. Additionally, there are u-picks for gooseberries; check the u-pick farms and markets on the Internet. Again, if the price of the berries is high, make a half or quarter recipe in a very small sauce pan. Don't miss this flavor. You don't have to be a canner to be a "jammer."

A German fellow who knew and loved gooseberries often frequented Jamlady's stand at the Sunday Mount Prospect, Illinois Farmers' Market. The following recipe is the one Jamlady made for him, to keep him coming back for more. It is hard to top these preserves in tartness and flavor. This recipe works equally well for green or red gooseberries or jostaberries. Jamlady likes red gooseberries the best, but Jamlady's German patron determined green gooseberries to be the best. Take your pick!

Classic Red or Green Gooseberry Preserves

Gooseberries have stems and bloom ends, which must be removed.

Allow about 1 hour per quart for deblooming.

A good recipe for the beginner.

1 quart ripe, red or green gooseberries or jostaberries
3 cups sugar
1 cup water

Wash the gooseberries. Remove the stem and bloom end ("head and tail") by hand. Add the water and cook until tender. Add the sugar and cook quickly until the preserves thicken. JSP/RWB10(8OZ)15(16OZ).

ELDERBERRIES

Elderberry, Bourtree, European Elder, or **Pipe Tree,** *Sambucus nigra* Linn., is a deciduous tree with oval leaves, creamish-colored flowers, and purplish-black berries—seen hanging on umbrella-shaped stems. The **elderberry tree or bush,** of the Caprifoliaceae or Honeysuckle family, grows wild around Crystal Lake, Illinois. Jamlady used to have more time to go looking for elderberries, but with markets going all summer, there is less and less time for wildcrafting. With the new housing developments going up everywhere, bushes are being eradicated left and right. Still, elderberries can be found. **It is best to look for elderberries in June, when the white elderflowers can easily be seen.** Mark your elderberry plant locations on a map, so you can remember where to return for the tiny berries in early to mid-August and avoid wildcrafting on protected lands or where plants might have been sprayed. The berries and flowering tops can be used fresh or dried. Elderflower tea is good for colds, coughs, flu, allergies, ear infections, candidiasis, and arthritis. Elderberry blooms can be batter fried or made into lemonade. The **American or common elder,** *Sambucus canadensis,* is similar to the escaped *Sambucus nigra* and can be used for the same purposes.

The recipe below uses pectin. Since elderberries are low in pectin, either a commercially boxed pectin or a natural fruit that is high in pectin, such as apple juice. needs to be used to assure a good set. Jamlady's grandmother always called labor-intensive products "dear," and so they are!

To make elderberry jelly, you must find and pick the wild elderberries that are, on average, $\frac{3}{16}$" of an inch in diameter. Elderberries grow on umbrella-shaped stems with their berries positioned at the ends of the many small, sprawling stems. These umbrellas or flat-topped clusters of flowers are called **corymbs.** The center flowers of these corymbs bloom last. This opening of the outer flowers first is called **corymbose inflorescence** and can be seen in elderberry, cherry, and candytuft blossoms.

After picking the main umbrella stems, one must remove the berries from the smaller stems. If you do not do this carefully, you will get small stem pieces with the berries, and the stem pieces will cause the jelly to be bitter and cloudy. For two batches of this jam ($4\frac{3}{4}$ cups per batch), allow about 2 hours for finding and picking the elderberries and about 4 to 6 hours for destemming, longer for the novice. Some people use a fork to assist with destemming, but fingers work well too. Remove the pieces of stems that do break off into the berries. Jamlady usually picks and destems in one day and refrigerate the berries for the next morning when she makes the jelly. Jam can also be made by juicing the berries, but it is not the same clear product known as elderberry jelly, nor is the product made from elderberries and apples, which requires only half as many elderberries. There may be a few seeds in the jelly, as smaller seeds may go through a regular strainer or jelly bag. Try running the juice through one of those gold coffee filters that Braun makes, or use a very fine strainer to remove the straggler seeds.

"Dear" Elderberry Jelly

This small purple berry grows on umbrella-like stems.

3½ pound crushed elderberries (not too ripe)
4½ cups sugar
½ cup water
¼ cup freshly squeezed lemon juice
1 1¾-ounce box regular powdered pectin

Cook, uncovered, elderberries with water for 15 minutes. Strain or hang the elderberries in a jelly bag for 6-12 hours. Measure 3 cups elderberry juice and add lemon juice. Boil the juices with the powdered pectin for 75 seconds. Add the sugar and boil for 60-90 seconds. Boil to 105 degrees C, to jell point. JSP/RWB5(4OZ)10(8OZ).

Variations: Jamlady makes **Elderberry-Lemon Jelly** *without added pectin or apples. To every pound of berries add about ½ cup water, the juice of 2 lemons, and a pound of sugar. Boil for 30-45 minutes until jell point is achieved. As you can see from this recipe, something has to be added to the elderberries to increase the pectin. For this reason, Jamlady usually uses the "dear," powdered-pectin recipe, because the elderberry jelly then tastes more like elderberries and not so much like apples or lemons. For* **Elderberry-Apple Jelly,** *equal quantities of extracted elderberry juice and freshly extracted apple juice will require about 1½ pounds sugar to 2 cups extracted elderberry juice and 2 cups freshly extracted apple juice.*

A **Spiced "No-Sugar" Elderberry Jelly** *can be made with 3¾ cups extracted elderberry juice, ¼ cup freshly squeezed lemon juice, ¹/₁₆-⅛ teaspoon cinnamon, 35 packages aspartame, and "no-sugar" pectin. Jamlady found a slight bitterness to this jelly when it was left plain or without spice, and Jamlady plans to experiment further with ½ apple and ½ elderberry as, perhaps, a better solution to a plain, "no-sugar" elderberry jelly. Using 1 cup honey or only 1 cup sugar for a lite elderberry jelly or jam might also be tried.* **A Champion juicing machine will remove the seeds from elderberries, just as it does for raspberries and blackberries. So, elderberry jams, as opposed to jelly, can now be explored further.**

Elderberry pulp is not as clear as extracted juice, but in double or triple fruit preserves, multifruit sauces, baked items—such as fruit breads or cakes—or gourmet meat dishes, it may prove to be a very desirable culinary and medicinal ingredient. Besides making jelly, jam, sauce, juice, or tea from elderberries, some people still **pickle elderberry buds** as **false capers.** Jamlady hopes to inspire all of you budding chefs and home cooks to experiment with fruit pulps obtained by juicing with a Champion juicing machine or a comparable machine. Let us move canning and gourmet cookery into the twenty-first century with some new recipes, innovations, and techniques.

☙❧

The Plummed Elder or Jamlady's Elder-Plum Jam

A good way to get the elderberry taste without a lot of elderberries!
Combine elderberries with plums.

6¼ cups sugar
1½ cups extracted elderberry juice or pulp (2 pounds crushed elderberries)
3 cups cooked-down plums (from 4-5 cups processor-chopped plums)
1 1¾-ounce box powdered pectin
½ cup water
⅛ cup freshly squeezed lemon juice

For the clearest flavor, use the extracted juice of the elderberry, as opposed to the juiced pulp.

Cook, uncovered, elderberries with water for 15 minutes. Strain for speed or hang the berries in a jelly bag for 6-12 hours. Measure 1½ cups elderberry juice; add lemon juice and plums (measure the plums after cooking for 15-20 minutes first). Boil the fruits with the powdered pectin for 75 seconds. Add the sugar and boil to 105 degrees C. Check the set. JSP/RWB5(4OZ)10(8OZ).

PLUMS

'Damson' plums, *Prunus domestica* Linn., are a special type of summer plum with bluish-black fruits, 1-2" (25-50 mm) in diameter, with a thick, juicy, sweetish, edible pulp and a smooth stone when freed from the pulp. 'Damson' plums are native to Western Asia and Europe but, luckily, have been naturalized in Southeastern Canada and many northern states in the United States. The **prune,** a dried plum, is derived from this species. Michigan fruit vendors often have 'Damson' plums at the Evanston, LaGrange, and Mt. Prospect, Illinois markets. In August, check with the J. W. Morlock folks, all dressed in red T-shirts, for 'Damson' plums. 'Damson' plums are clingstone fruits, and each plum's meat has to be cut off its stone for this recipe. The extra work will be worth the results, as you never will taste a more wonderful and tart conserve—short of gooseberry or currant.

'Damson' Plum Conserve

A lemony plum conserve with walnuts and raisins!

8 cups 'Damson' plum pieces
Reserved plum pits in a spice bag
6 cups sugar
1 cup raisins
1 cup walnuts (or other type of nuts)
1 lemon
1 teaspoon ground cinnamon
1 pinch salt

Finely chop the lemon rind, remove the seeds, and chop the lemon pulp. Mix the plums, lemon, and salt; cook, with the pits (in a spice bag), until soft. Add the sugar, raisins, and cinnamon and boil to jell point. Check the set by chilling. Heat slowly, adding the walnuts. Stir constantly. Be careful not to burn the conserve.
JSP/RWB10(8OZ).

Jamlady has observed that "tastier than normal" plum jam can be made by cooking down the plums before making plum jam with liquid pectin. Start with 18-20 round black, Italian prune or red plums. 'Damson' plums might also be used, but they are so good in preserves that one might reserve them for 'Damson' plum preserves. 'Damson' plum preserves are made with lemons, and the completed preserves have a lemony flavor. Spiced plum jam has a more true plum flavor, so you will have to try both to decide which one you like the best. Cut the plums from the pits and run the plum pieces through the juicing machine. Use both the juice and the pulp (both outputs from the juicing machine) to make the jam. Both the juice and the pulp are then cooked down to make the necessary 4 cups plum purée for this next recipe.

Spiced Plum Jam

Plum-delicious jam with cinnamon and all-spice!

6½ cups sugar
4 cups cooked-down, Italian prune or red plum
   purée (from 6-7 cups chopped plums)
1 3-ounce pouch liquid pectin
½ teaspoon butter
½ teaspoon ground cinnamon
⅛ teaspoon ground allspice

Remove the pits from the plums and processor-chop the plums or juice the plums and retain both outputs. Cook down the chopped plums for about 15 minutes. Boil the sugar, plum purée, butter, cinnamon, and allspice for 1 minute. Add the liquid pectin and boil for 1 minute more. Check the set. JSP/RWB10(8OZ).

Variation: For **Spiced Plum Ice Cream Sauce,** *double the recipe for Spiced Plum Jam and don't cook the mixture so long, or make the regular recipe, but add two extra cups of plums. Use on pancakes and other desserts, like pound cake.*

Cinnamon Plum Jam

Sweetened with aspartame or alternate sweetener!

4 cups pitted, chopped plums (5 cups with sugar
   formulation)
1 1¾-ounce package lite or "no-sugar" pectin
29 packets aspartame (or 1-3 cups sugar)
½ teaspoon cinnamon (optional or alternate
   spice/flavoring)

Mix the chopped plums with the pectin and cinnamon; let sit for 10 minutes. Boil the mixture for at least 1 minute. Add the aspartame; boil for 1-2 minutes. If you prefer, use 1-3 cups sugar instead of the aspartame and increase the plums to 5 cups. Jamlady has not tried maple syrup or honey instead of the sugar, but this is a possibility. See Bee Peachy Jam. Make sure you check the pH of your final product, as some sweeteners are above 4.6—molasses (4.90-5.40), for example. JSP/RWB10(8OZ). The unrefrigerated, 3-month-long shelf life of this jam may be extended with refrigeration. **Jamlady recommends refrigeration for all sugar-free jams.**

'Damson' plums can be made into luscious 'Damson' Plum Preserves with only two ingredients, or you can make your own 'Damson' Plum Cordial in less than ten minutes and a couple of months' waiting time. The orange persimmon is ready to cut and eat with a spoon, or you can make it into a small batch of preserves.

Plummed Strawberry Jam

Sweetened with aspartame, alternate sweetener, or low sugar!

3¾ cups hulled, sliced strawberries (4¼ cups with sugar formulation)
1 cup cooked-down plums (1½ cups with sugar formulation)
1 1¾-ounce box lite or "no-sugar" powdered pectin
¼ cup water
25 packets aspartame (or 1-3 cups sugar)
¼ teaspoon or less ascorbic acid crystals

Use ascorbic acid crystals in the wash water and on the fruit during preparation. Mix the fruit with the pectin; wait 10 minutes. Boil the mixture for 1-2 minutes; add the aspartame. Boil 1 minute. If adding sugar instead of aspartame, boil 1 minute, add the sugar, and boil for 1 more minute. JSP/RWB10(8OZ). The shelf life of the aspartame-sweetened jam is 3 months.

Since plums are high in pectin, there is no need for added pectin. Plum recipes that call for added pectin use a lot more sugar than preserves recipes. The effect is to dilute the flavor, reduce the nutrition, and add unneeded calories to the "jam." A plum jam with added pectin normally has approximately 6 cups fruit to 8 cups sugar (unless the fruit was cooked down some to begin with—see Jamlady's version of Spiced Plum Butter), as opposed to the ratio of 6 cups fruit to 4 cups sugar for no-added-pectin preserves. That represents a reduction in sugar by one-half. Especially good plum preserves can be made with only 'Damson' plums and sugar. **'Damson' Plum Preserves:** Cook down 10 cups pitted 'Damson' plums with 7 cups sugar. To halve or quarter the recipe, use a smaller pan with a proportionally smaller surface area. JSP/RWB10(8OZ).

Old-Fashioned Black Plum Preserves with XO Brandy

An easy set is the sign of good homemade preserves!

20 black plums
2 cups water
⅔ cup sugar for each cup of fruit
¼ cup XO brandy

Wash the plums. Remove their stems. Cook with water until tender. Allow the mixture to cool and remove the pits. Count the pits to make sure you have removed all of them. Measure the fruit and add the sugar accordingly. Cook the mixture until thick or until 102-104 degrees C is reached. Add the brandy and cook to 102-104 degrees C. again. Check the set on a frozen plate. JSP/RWB5(4OZ)10(8OZ).

Note: This preserves may appear runny or thin at room temperature, but it gets thicker when refrigerated.

There are other types of plums, such as **'Greengage' plums** or *Prunus domestica*. 'Greengage' plums have a light-green skin and pulp and are named after Sir William Gage, who introduced this plum from France into England circa 1725. **Cook 'Greengage' plums in a nonreactive pan.** Mrs. Victor's *The Dime Cookbook* instructs, on page 69: "Peel the fruit and divide; take out the stones, and blanch the kernels if you wish them added to the jam; boil the broken stones and paring in a little water till the water is half reduced, and add a little spinach juice to color it; then strain it and put in the preserving pan with the fruit; simmer a quarter of an hour; then add equal weight of sugar; boil and skim for twenty minutes longer."

Miss Neil, in her *The Every-Day Cook Book* (1892, page 222), shows a similar recipe for **Preserved 'Greengages' in Syrup**— "To every pound of fruit allow one pound of loaf-sugar, one-quarter pint of water. Boil the sugar and water together for about ten minutes; divide the 'Greengages', take out the stones, put the fruit into the syrup, and let it simmer gently until nearly tender. Take it off the fire, put it into a large pan, and the next day, boil it up again for about ten minutes with the kernels from the stones, which should be blanched. Put the fruit carefully into jars, pour over it the syrup, and when cold, cover

down, so that the air is quite excluded. Let the syrup be well skimmed both the first and second day of the boiling, otherwise it will not be clear." Some of Jamlady's old-timer friends "hot-water plunge" the plums and peel them prior to making **'Greengage' Preserves** with 4 pounds 'Greengage' plums to 3 cups sugar. Weep the plums with sugar overnight, drain off the sugar syrup, cook down some, and add the plums back in and cook until thick enough. JSP/RWB10(8OZ).

༺ༀ༻

GRAPES

'Concord' and wild grapes both make good jellies, jams, and butters. The more the grape juice is cooked down, the more intense the jelly will be. Jamlady does not often make regular 'Concord' grape jam, jelly, or conserve, for not very many patrons ask for them. Patrons are looking for wild grape jelly, herbal grape jams, or tasty grape butter.

Grapes belong to the Vitaceae family or Vine Grape family. The **European grape,** classified as *Vitis vinifera,* accounts for over 90 percent of world grape production. The '**Concord' grape,** *Vitis labrusca* Linn. syn. *Vitis labruscana* Bailey, is also called the **American bunch grape** or **fox grape.** There are thought to be about 65 genuine species of grapes, but over 100 species are discussed in literature. Other varieties, such as the **Muscadine,** *Vitis rotundifolia,* are called **Southern Fox Grape, Bullit, Bull Grape,** or **Bullace.** The **Summer, Bunch,** or **Pigeon Grapes,** or *Vitis aestivalis,* when seen, can be distinguished by reddish fuzz on the underside of their leaves. *Vitis* is split into two subgenera, *Euvitis,* or **"True Grapes",** and *Muscadinia,* or **Muscadine** grapes, which are characterized by small fruit clusters, thick-skinned fruits, simple tendrils, and berries that detach one by one as they mature. "True Grapes" are characterized by

elongated clusters of fruit, forked tendrils, and berries that adhere to the stems at maturity.

In Illinois, people can wildcraft for wild grapes, which Jamlady believes are usually **Riverbank** or **Frost Grape,** *Vitis vulpina* Linn. Riverbank grapes are the commonest grape in the northern states west of New England and are abundant along streams or near moist roadside ditches. The berries are very small, less than ½" in diameter, and are purple-black, ripening just before or even after frost. The best wine is made from wild grapes just after the lightest frost.

Jamlady makes wild grape jelly, wild grape combined with domestic grape jam, wild grape wine, and wild grape wine jelly. Jamlady normally makes classic wild grape jelly if she has enough grapes for an entire batch. If not, ½ of a wild grape recipe can be combined with ½ of a domestic grape recipe.

Look for wild grapes by old fences and farm roads, where the grapes have not been sprayed or disturbed. **Make sure you pick only from vines with tendrils.** Other poisonous vines and berries resemble grapes, but do not have tendrils. Expect wild grapes to stain your fingers during the destemming process. To extract the wild grape juice, cover the grapes with water and cook or possibly use a steam juicer to obtain the juice. Strain and allow the grapes to hang in a jelly bag for a few hours. The pH of the extracted grape juice should be in the vicinity of 3.14—at least it is here in northern Illinois. Besides making a wonderful jelly, wild grapes provide an opportunity to take children hiking around farmlands and wilderness areas while gathering wild grapes. Make sure you are allowed to take vegetation from the areas where you wildcraft. Any leftover extracted juice can be drunk as fruit juice or canned as grape juice. Sweeten wild grape juice with sugar or honey. Sweetened wild grape juice can also be made into a gelatin with unflavored gelatin or used to make sorbet.

ᏰᎧ

Classic Wild Grape Jelly

Rich, luscious, and great in peanut-butter-and-jelly sandwiches!

7 cups sugar
4 cups extracted, cooked-down, wild grape juice (10 pounds wild grapes)
1 3-ounce pouch liquid pectin
½ teaspoon butter

Destem 10 pounds of wild grapes. Cover the grapes with water and simmer for about 1 hour. Strain and cook down to 8-12 cups of juice or drip in a jelly bag for the clearest jelly. Boil the juice with the sugar and butter, add the pectin, and boil for 1 minute. JSP/RWB10(8OZ).

Grape Jelly can also be made with powdered fruit pectin. Use 5 cups extracted juice to 7 cups sugar to 1 box regular powdered fruit pectin. Boil the juice with the pectin for 1 minute, add the sugar, and boil for 1 minute or until the jelly sets on a frozen plate.

Note: Grape jelly recipes are formulated differently when using bottled grape juice. See the pectin insert sheets for jelly recipes using bottled juice.

To make **grape jelly without added pectin,** you need to use underripe fruits: 1 cup extracted juice to ¾-1 cup sugar. **Grape-Apple Jelly** can be made using half-extracted grape juice and half-extracted apple juice with ¾ cup sugar to each cup of 50-50 apple-and-grape-juice mixture. It is best if you use underripe grapes, but it is not absolutely essential. Boil until the jelly sets on a frozen plate. Wild grape juice can be flavored with herbs such as thyme, basil, or sage and then used to make jelly, jam, or exotic beverages. Medicinal juices can be made with grape juice that has been infused with herbs, such as 3 parts thyme, 1 part rosemary, and 1 part spearmint. This herbal combination might be effective for hangovers or nightmares. Jamlady suggests that **"hangover jelly"** might be made with some of that thyme-, rosemary-, and spearmint-infused grape juice for the "morning-after" breakfast toast.

Wild Grape Party Meatballs—You've all probably seen small ground-beef meatballs simmering in a crockpot full of grape jelly, chili sauce, and a little water. Try the same combination with the wild grape jelly instead of regular grape jelly and watch the accolades fly your way. Alternatively, try ½ cup currant jelly and ½ cup grape jelly with 1-2 cups chili sauce and ¼ cup water. Simmer for 45 minutes.

This tasty conserve is very labor intensive. According to Jamlady, grape butter and wild grape jelly are the Rolls Royces and Bentleys of the jam world, grape conserve—the Jaguar.

Grape Conserve

**Lots of work, but worth the effort!
Without the walnuts, it's a preserve.**

2 quarts destemmed grapes
5 cups sugar
1 cup chopped walnuts
Water

Separate the grape skins from the pulp by hand. Cook the skins and the pulp separately, the skins with some water. Add a little water at a time to keep the bottom from burning and to keep the skins cooking or stewing in minimal amounts of water. Remove the seeds from the pulp using a sieve. Add the two batches together and cook with the sugar until thick, at about 105 degrees C. Stir in the nuts.
JSP/RWB5(4OZ)10(8OZ).

Variation: Green Grape Conserve—8 cups sugar, 6 cups seeded green grapes, 1 pound raisins, 1 cup white grape juice (or juice some grapes to get the juice or use water), 2 oranges or 3 chopped Clementines, and ½ pound hickory nuts. Cook all ingredients except the nuts; add the nuts last. If you wish to minimize any bitter taste, then remove all the white pith and use only the citrus pulp and finely chopped outer rind.

The recipe included here for herbed grape jelly can be made with any kind of grapes, including light-green-colored grapes, ruby grapes, concords, and wild grapes. The spice can be varied. Jamlady can vouch for thyme, basil, and sage. Grape herbal jellies can be placed on deli-sliced roast beef and rolled up for hors d'oeuvres. This jelly is also great on a hamburger or warmed and used as a dip for cooked meatballs.

Thyme and Grape Jelly

**Serve with a ham or beef meal.
Good on dark breads!**

7 cups sugar
4 cups concentrated 'Concord' grape juice (4 pounds grapes to 1 pint water) (heat extracted and dripped or use steam juicer)
2 cups chopped fresh or 1+ tablespoon dried thyme, basil, or sage
1 1¾-ounce box regular powdered pectin
½ teaspoon butter

Boil the thyme leaves with the grape juice and butter for 10 minutes. Strain. Add the pectin to the juice. Wait 10 minutes; boil 1 minute. Add the sugar; boil 1 minute more.
JSP/RWB10(8OZ).

GROUND CHERRIES

The **ground cherry, Chinese Lantern, bladder cherry, strawberry tomato,** or **winter cherry,** *Physalis alkekengi* Linn., isn't often found. Preserves made from ground cherries are out of this world. One reason many people shy away from this plant is that the unripe fruits are toxic, and large quantities of the ripe fruit can cause diarrhea. Ground cherries are an edible member of the Chinese Lantern/Nightshade family. The ground cherries that Jamlady obtained were greenish-yellow, somewhat firm, and tasted nutty and "pineappley." Don't miss this culinary delight, even if it means you have to grow ground cherries yourself.

There are three ground cherry recipes that Jamlady made in the 1999 season: one with ground cherries and lemon juice, one with ground cherries and apples, and a third with ground cherries and lemon rind. Ground cherries are not easily found, so Jamlady was thrilled with having enough ground cherries to try all three recipes. The ground cherry with lemon rind recipe is an old one. It is on the Internet and in many old recipe files, but as you can see, it is a standard, low-sugar, preserves recipe with grated lemon to assist the set. Indeed, ground cherries are mentioned in Willa Cather's *O Pioneers!* (1913) as being made into preserves with lemon peel, although she evidently didn't think much of the fruit.

"She made a yellow jam of the insipid ground cherries that grew on the prairie, flavoring it with lemon peel; . . ."

⚬⚬

Ground Cherry Preserves with Lemon Zest

An edible member of the Chinese Lantern/Nightshade family.

1 pound husked ground cherries
½ pound sugar
Grated rind of 1 lemon

Cook the ground cherries and sugar for about 20 minutes and then add the finely grated lemon rind. JSP/RWB10(8OZ).

Jamlady takes this view: if you are making ground cherry preserves, it is to experience the flavor of the ground cherries. While all three of these ground cherry recipes make acceptable preserves, in Jamlady's opinion, the recipe with the apple is the best, as it showplaces the distinctive ground cherry flavor. The second-best recipe is the lemon rind recipe.

It is clear that the ground cherries need more pectin to set the preserves than they themselves possess. Both the apples and the whole lemon or lemon peels can do the job, but the preserves made with lemon juice and or lemon peels taste completely like lemons, and Jamlady is of the view that the lemons mask the very special taste of the ground cherries, which you want to shine. The ground cherry with apple recipe is indicative of the age-old practice of using apples for their natural pectin, as is done in the elderberry jelly formulation and other low-pectin fruit preserves. Further research needs to be done with ground cherries (pH 4.25-4.35) combined with other high pectin and high acid fruits. Little is seen in literature regarding ground cherries, and more should be done. Perhaps, a formulation with citric acid instead of the lemon juice or apple would be even more distinctive. Just make sure you check the pH of your new formulation.

Ground Cherry Preserves with Apples

The true flavor of ground cherries shines through.

Nutty and "pineappley!"

¾ pound ground cherries
1 cup water
½ pound sugar
¼ pound peeled, very thinly sliced, small pieces of apple (or, perhaps, quince)

Boil the sugar, apples, and water for 1 minute. Simmer for 2 minutes; add the washed and hulled ground cherries. Simmer until thick enough to set on a frozen plate. JSP/RWB10. Makes two 8-ounce jars. Check the completed pH when substituting other fruits for apples.

Caution: If you grow ground cherries, make sure no one ingests them before they are ripe. Unripe ground cherries are toxic.

Ground Cherry Preserves or Sauce with Lemon Juice

Beginners, make this and use on pound cake or ice cream.

Similar ingredients are found in many ground cherry pie recipes.

3 pounds ground cherries without husks
4½ cups water
2¼ cups sugar
Juice of 3 lemons

Cook the water, sugar, and lemon juice. Add the ground cherries; cook until thick. Check the set with a frozen plate. JSP/RWB10.

Jamlady has noticed other ground cherry jam recipes with added pectin. Jamlady feels recipes using 6 cups sugar to 2 pounds ground cherries and a ½ cup lemon juice are really stretching out the ground cherries and adding a lot of competing lemon flavor. The same can be true of pies using only 2 cups ground cherries instead of 4 cups. Jamlady does not need to make this recipe to know that it will be "less fruity than" a recipe calling for 3 pounds ground cherries to 2¼ cups sugar. Furthermore, Jamlady would prefer to pay for more ground cherries, use more ground cherries, and not have to buy any pectin. If you have wildcrafted the ground cherries or grown them, so much the better.

Some Amish women and chefs make pies with modified food starches. For those of you unfamiliar with modified food starch, it comes in an instant form and cook form and can be purchased in Amish stores or from on-line stores. The **cook type of modified food starch** can be used for canned pie fillings. **CLEARJEL® Instant,** for example, and **Novation®** starch, for another, can be used for cooked jam, puddings, creamed soups, syrups, pie fillings, and frozen jams. **One of the advantages of instant modified food starch is that it thickens without heat.** Jamlady notes that pie recipes with modified food starches enable the pie maker to stretch out the fruit. Jamlady prefers more fruit in her pies and less thickener, but this starch product may be useful for those desiring to sell pies at a profit, for those teaching children to cook, or for those with limited supplies of fruits. **Some pie recipes with modified food starch use only 1-2 cups of fruit, instead of the usual 4 cups.** Small amounts of modified food starch may be used as any thickener for regular pies needing thickening.

Jamlady's old-fashioned method of pie construction uses approximately the same ingredients for ground cherry pie as green tomato or apple pie. Indeed, a pie could be made with apples and ground cherries. Just go easy on the lemon in any ground cherry pie recipe.

☙❧

Old-Fashioned Ground Cherry Pie

4 cups husked ground cherries
½ cup sugar
1 tablespoon flour or ½ tablespoon tapioca plus ½ tablespoon flour
1 tablespoon of lemon juice or grated lemon rind or some sliced apples
1-2 tablespoons butter

Dot the top of the pie filling with 1-2 tablespoons butter. Place the filling in a two-crust pie. Bake at 450 degrees F for 10 minutes, then decrease to 350 degrees F for 40 minutes or until golden brown.

Canned Pie Filling with Modified Food Starch

2 cups modified food starch, cook type (CLEAR-JEL®)
2 cups cold water
7 cups sugar
1 teaspoon salt
6 cups water
Food coloring (optional)
4-6 quarts fruit (under 4.3 pH fruits)
Flavoring (optional, to taste)

Mix the modified food starch (cook type) and 2 cups water. In another pot, mix the sugar, salt, 6 cups water*, and food coloring; boil. Add to the modified food starch mixture slowly and stir. Boil, cooking 1 minute until thick. Add the fruit and flavoring, if used. JSP/RWB20(32OZ).

An herbal infusion (like mint with apple-pie filling) could be used here.

Some fruits may require less sugar and water. Pie filling can be canned with flour or thickeners too. Jamlady has heated up many regular filling recipes and canned them in a RWB. Just make sure your pH is comfortably under 4.6. Actually, there is no need to can the filling with the thickener, as the thickener can be added when making the pie. By not adding the thickener, it is still possible to use the canned fruit as plain fruit or in a fruit cup.

Jamlady Tip: Skip canning the fillings altogether if you have a freezer. Just make the pies and freeze them or freeze the filling separately. Freezing is faster! If canning the pie filling, make sure the pH of all the ingredients is well under 4.6. Most fruit pies with lemon juice are well under the 4.6 pH, but pumpkin is not and must be canned in a pressure cooker or acidified.

Ground Cherry Pie with Modified Food Starch

2 cups ripe ground cherries
2 cups water
1³/₄ cups sugar
3¹/₂ tablespoons modified food starch, cook type (CLEARJEL®)
2 tablespoons butter

Cook ground cherries in half of the water until soft. Mix the sugar, other half of the water, and modified food starch. Boil for a little and add the butter and cooked ground cherries. Use this filling in your homemade pie crusts and bake at 450 degrees F until golden brown.

HOT JAMS

Hot jams are extremely popular. Jamlady started making various hot jams ten years ago, when she saw how popular the hot chutneys were. Different varieties of peppers produce "jams" of varying degrees of hotness; their relative hotness can be measured by the *Scoville-Organoleptic Test.*

Note: **The Scoville-Organoleptic Test** *is a test devised by Wilber Scoville for empirically measuring the hotness or pungency of a hot pepper by using the human tongue as the tester of diluted volumes of sweetened water and pepper extract. Scoville Heat Units were the unit of measure. For example: Japanese chilies = 20,000-30,000 Scoville Heat Units, 'Zanzibar' chilies = 40,000-50,000, and Mombasa chilies = 50,000-100,000. The capsicum, cayenne, or chili pepper,* **Capsicum annuum,** *is an annual or biennial in warmer climates. The chili pepper is known for its hot podlike berries.* **Capsicum frutéscens** *Linn. also produces chilies of commercial value.*

Mango chutney or jam can be made with any of the various varieties of **mangoes,** *Mangifera indica,* found at your local market. In India, unripe mangos are even dried and used as a spice, **amchoor powder.** Incidentally, the term "mango" can also denote a pepper, a brined pepper, or a stuffed pickle made from peppers, cantaloupes, cucumbers, or peaches. Look for more discussion on the mango-pickle topic in future Jamlady books.

Jamlady's Original Hot Mango Jam

A light-green-colored jam from mangoes and jalapeño peppers.

Serve on top of heated Brie or with cream cheese and crackers!

5 cups sugar
2¾ cups peeled, chopped mangoes
1 cup seeded or unseeded chopped jalapeño peppers
¼ cup white wine vinegar
1 1¾-ounce box regular powdered pectin
2½ tablespoons lemon juice or lime juice or ⅓ teaspoon citric acid
½ teaspoon butter

"Blenderize" the peppers and white wine vinegar. Mix the lemon juice, butter, chopped mangoes, pepper mixture, and pectin in a pan and boil for 1 minute. Add the sugar; boil for 1 minute more. Check the set. JSP/RWB10(8OZ).

Variation: Hot Picante Peach Jam—Use peaches (instead of mangoes) and ripe, red jalapeño peppers. The resulting jam will be an orange-colored jam.

Note: Unsealed hot jam can last up to a year in the refrigerator because of the hot peppers' capsaicin, *which has some preserving qualities.*

Hot Pepper Jelly

Great with cream cheese and crackers!

4 cups sugar
1½ cups seeded, chopped, sweet green peppers (or other sweet peppers, such as banana peppers)
1 cup unseeded, chopped jalapeño peppers
1 cup white wine vinegar
½ cup lemon juice
2 3-ounce pouches liquid pectin (6 ounces)
1 slice onion
Green food coloring

You may vary the ratio of hot peppers to mild peppers, but just make sure the total cups of peppers remains the same. Liquefy the peppers, vinegar, lemon juice, and onion in the blender. Add the sugar; boil for 1 minute. Add the pectin; boil for 1-2 minutes. Skim if necessary. Add the food coloring. JSP/RWB10(8OZ).

Note: Hot pepper jelly can sometimes fail to set, even for the experienced jam maker. Allow a few days for it to set up. If it does not set up, pour it over cream cheese and eat it anyway, or paint it on broiled pork chops or ribs.

Jamlady's Original Hot Pepper-Olive Jelly

Serve crackers and this hot pepper jelly at your next martini party!

Try this jelly blended with cream cheese on celery.

4 cups sugar
1 cup seeded, chopped, sweet green peppers
1 cup unseeded, chopped jalapeño peppers
1 cup white wine vinegar
½ cup lemon juice
½ cup diced Spanish olives
2 3-ounce pouches liquid pectin (6 ounces)
1 thin slice of onion
Green food coloring (optional)

Liquefy the peppers, olives, vinegar, lemon juice, and onion in the blender. Add the sugar; boil for 1 minute. Add the pectin; boil for 1-2 minutes. Skim if necessary. JSP/RWB10(8OZ). This jelly may take awhile to set up. Approximate pH = 3.49.

Variation: Jamlady's Original Hot Pepper-Olive-Garlic Jelly—Use garlic instead of onion. You may reduce the olives a little and add in a few more garlic cloves.

Hot 3-Pepper Jelly

No food coloring is necessary.

4 cups sugar
1 cup chopped, seeded, sweet green peppers
1 cup chopped, unseeded jalapeño peppers
1 cup white wine vinegar
½ cup chopped, fresh, seeded problano peppers
½ cup lemon juice
2 3-ounce pouches liquid pectin (6 ounces)
1 slice onion (or equivalent amount of chopped garlic cloves)
½ teaspoon butter (optional, reduces foaming)

"Blenderize" the peppers and onion slice with the wine vinegar and lemon juice. Boil the liquified pepper mixture with the sugar and butter for 1 minute. Add the pectin and boil 1 minute more. Check the set. JSP/RWB10(8OZ).

Jamlady's Original "Hotsa" Pepper Jelly

A hotter pepper jelly that's made with red wine vinegar.

4 cups sugar
1 cup chopped, seeded, sweet banana peppers
  or red sweet peppers
1½ cups chopped, unseeded, jalapeño peppers
  or hotter peppers
1 cup red wine vinegar
½ cup lemon juice
2 3-ounce pouches liquid pectin (6 ounces)
1 small slice of onion
1 teaspoon butter (optional, inhibits foaming)
Green food coloring (or use only red and yellow
  peppers)

Liquefy the peppers, vinegar, lemon juice, and onion in a blender. Add the sugar and butter to the mixture; boil for 1 minute. Add the pectin; boil for 1-2 minutes. Skim if necessary. Add food coloring. JSP/RWB5(4OZ)10(8OZ). This jelly may take several days to set up.

Jamlady's Original Hot Plum Jam

A popular, homemade hostess gift!

9½ cups sugar
5 cups plums, cooked down to 4 cups
1¼ cups unseeded, chopped jalapeño peppers
½ cup red wine vinegar
¼ cup lemon juice
2 3-ounce pouches liquid pectin (6 ounces)

Cut slightly underripe plums from their pits. Allow 15 minutes to cook 5 cups of processor-chopped plums, with skins, down to 4 cups. Cool the plums. "Blenderize" the peppers, vinegar, and lemon juice. Add the pepper mixture to the sugar and plums. Boil for 1 minute. Add the pectin; boil until the jam sets on a frozen plate. Skim, if necessary. JSP/RWB10(8OZ).

Jamlady's Original Hot Seedless Raspberry Jam

Especially good with cream cheese and crackers.

10½ cups sugar
4 cups seedless raspberry pulp
2¼ cups unseeded or seeded, chopped jalapeño peppers
1 cup fine red or white wine vinegar
½ cup lemon juice
4 3-ounce pouches liquid pectin (12 ounces)
1 teaspoon butter (optional)

Run the raspberries through a Champion juicing machine or similar machine. Repeat this process at least 10 times to get all of the purée. Only the raspberry seeds will be left, and they will be warm from the friction. Discard the seeds and reserve the raspberry pulp. Chop the jalapeño peppers in the food processor and measure. Put the peppers, lemon juice, and vinegar in a blender and liquefy. Cook the sugar with the raspberry pulp, butter, and "blenderized" mixture. Boil 1 minute. Add the pectin; boil 1 more minute. Check the jam on a frozen plate for set. JSP/RWB10(8OZ). Approximate pH of the jam = 3.66.

Jamlady's Original Hot Cranberry Jam

Try tortilla wraps with deli turkey, cream cheese, and hot cranberry jam.

7½ cups sugar
24 ounces cranberries (2 bags)
2½ cups chopped, unseeded or seeded jalapeño peppers
1 cup good, red wine vinegar (Marconi brand recommended)
⅝ cup water
½ cup fresh lemon juice
1 large slice onion
6 ounces liquid pectin (2 3-ounce pouches)
1 teaspoon butter

"Blenderize" the peppers, onion, wine vinegar, and lemon juice. Cook the cranberries with the water until soft. For jelly, juice the cranberries first and use the cranberry juice instead of the whole cranberries. Add the sugar, cranberry mixture or juice, butter, and liquefied mixture together and boil. Add the pectin and boil to 105 degrees C. Check the set.
JSP/RWB10(8OZ).

Jamlady Tip: If you wish to make a recipe for hot pepper jelly from some fruit Jamlady has not included in this book, simply do a math calculation. Take half the ingredients in each recipe (the pepper jelly recipe and the fruit "jam" recipe) and combine them together. It's best to use recipes with the same kind of pectin.

Jamlady's Original Hot Orange Pepper Jelly

Ripe jalapeños and red sweet peppers naturally produce this orange-colored jelly.

4 cups sugar
2 cups chopped, seeded, red sweet peppers
1 cup red wine vinegar (5 percent acidity)
½ cup freshly squeezed lemon juice
½ cup chopped, unseeded, red jalapeño peppers
  or red serrano peppers
1 very thin slice of red onion
2 3-ounce pouches liquid pectin (6 ounces)

Liquefy the peppers and onion with the red wine vinegar and lemon juice. Boil the pepper mixture with the sugar for 1 minute. Add the liquid pectin; boil for 1 minute. Check the set. JSP/RWB10. Approximate pH = 3.65.

Note: If the peppers are orange when ripe, Jamlady calls this jelly Hot Orange Pepper Jelly. If all dark-red peppers, both the sweet and jalapeños, are used, Jamlady calls the jelly Red Fire Engine Jelly. This jam is hot! For a less hot version, seed the jalapeños and measure the peppers after seeding.

Jamlady's Original Hot Grape Jam

Good as a dipping sauce for meatballs!

9 cups sugar
4 cups concentrated, freshly extracted grape juice
  (not bottled juice)(10 pounds grapes)
1⅛ cups seeded, partially seeded, or unseeded,
  chopped jalapeño peppers
½ cup fine red wine vinegar (5 percent acidity)
¼ cup lemon juice
2 3-ounce pouches liquid pectin (6 ounces)
½ teaspoon butter

Destem 10 pounds 'Concord' grapes. Cover the grapes with water and cook until soft. Put the cooked grapes in a jelly bag to collect the juice. Reduce the juice's volume to 4 cups by boiling further. "Blenderize" the lemon juice, vinegar, butter, and peppers. Add the blended ingredients to the sugar and grape juice. Boil for 1 minute; skim. Add the pectin; boil for 1-2 minutes. Check the set. JSP/RWB10(8OZ). Makes twelve 8-ounce jars. Approximate pH = 3.77.

Jamlady's Original Hot Nectarine Jam

Unseeded peppers, so it's hot, folks!

5¼ cups sugar
2 cups chopped nectarines and juiced skins
1⅛ cups unseeded or seeded jalapeño peppers
½ cup white wine vinegar (5 percent acidity)
⅜ cup lemon juice
½ teaspoon butter
2 3-ounce pouches liquid pectin (6 ounces)

"Blenderize" the peppers, white wine vinegar, and lemon juice. Cook the pepper mixture with the sugar, nectarines, and butter. Don't worry about the color. It clears up as the jam gets translucent. Juicing the skins enhances the color of this jelly. The discharge from both hoppers of the juicing machine or only the juice section may be used with the peeled, chopped fruit to make up the required measure of fruit and skins. Boil for 1 minute. Add the pectin; boil for 1 more minute. JSP/RWB10(8OZ). Approximate pH = 3.8.

Caution: Make sure you always use 5 percent acidity vinegar or higher in your canning recipes. Do not use 4 percent vinegar or homemade vinegar unless you have a pH meter and check the vinegar's pH, compensate the recipe accordingly, and test your completed product several times.

Jamlady's Original Rhubarb-Pepper Jelly

Delicate and slightly hot!
Cook more than enough rhubarb and chill the rest.

5½ cups sugar
1¾ cups fresh rhubarb juice*
1¾ cups chopped, seeded problano peppers
½ cup white wine vinegar
¼ cup lemon juice
2 3-ounce liquid pectin (6 ounces)
½ teaspoon butter (optional)
Red or green food coloring (optional)

"Blenderize" the peppers, white wine vinegar, and lemon juice. Cook the blended mixture with the sugar, rhubarb juice, and butter. Boil for 1 minute. Add the pectin; boil for 1 more minute. JSP/RWB10(8OZ). Add the food coloring, if used. Approximate pH = 3.52.

** The Rhubarb juice used for this recipe may be raw juice that has been juiced in a juicing machine, or it may be heat-extracted juice that has been obtained by cooking a quantity of rhubarb with minimal amounts of water. This cooked rhubarb is then hung from a jelly bag to collect the juice. Also, fully cooked rhubarb, instead of just rhubarb juice, could be used to make a **Rhubarb-Pepper Jam,** as opposed to a jelly.*

Jamlady's Original Hot Pineapple Jelly

Quick to make and delicious.

4 cups sugar
1 20-ounce can crushed pineapple in its own juice
1 cup white wine vinegar
$\frac{1}{2}$ cup freshly squeezed lemon juice
2 3-ounce pouches liquid pectin (6 ounces)
12 serrano peppers
$\frac{1}{2}$ teaspoon butter

"Blenderize" the vinegar, peppers, and lemon juice. Combine the pepper mixture, sugar, pineapple, and butter; cook for 1 minute. Add the pectin; boil to 104-105 degrees C. Check the set. JSP/RWB5(4OZ)10(8OZ).

Jamlady's Original Hot Tomato Jam or "Hot Burger Jam"

Try this hot jam on a lambburger or hamburger!

$6\frac{1}{2}$ cups sugar
$1\frac{1}{2}$ cups freshly cooked down tomato sauce
$1\frac{1}{2}$ cups seedless, skinless tomato meats
$1\frac{1}{8}$ cups seeded jalapeño peppers
$\frac{1}{2}$ cup lemon juice
$\frac{1}{2}$ cup red wine vinegar
2 3-ounce pouches liquid pectin (6 ounces)
1 tablespoon minced onion
1 chopped garlic clove
1 tablespoon Chinese five-spice powder
$\frac{1}{2}$ teaspoon butter

Place the lemon juice, peppers, wine vinegar, onion, and garlic in a blender and liquefy. Add the liquefied mixture to the rest of the ingredients, except the pectin, and boil for 1 minute. Add the pectin and boil to 105 degrees C. Check the set. JSP/RWB10(8OZ).

Note: Chinese five-spice is a spice mixture containing spices like anise, cinnamon, star anise, cloves, and ginger. Formulations vary.

FRENCH PLUNGE METHOD

Preserves can be made by the **French Plunge Method.** This method requires the fruits to be put into the hot sugar water or syrup and then be removed. The remaining syrup is cooked down further and the fruits are again put into the hot syrup. Cooking the preserves by this method maintains the integrity of the fruit.

Thick, whole-fruit, or chunky preserves are very desirable and can be made from all sorts of fruits. Seasonally, many fruits are available at reasonable prices. One such fruit is the kiwi. For some reason, few people are making kiwifruit preserves. Jamlady has no idea why, because in Illinois kiwis are often sold in the stores for ten cents each. This makes **kiwi a best buy!** The kiwi's flavor is similar to that of the strawberry, and Jamlady encourages **beginners** to start with **Grand Kiwi Preserves** and then move on to try half-kiwi, half-strawberry preserves or an all-kiwi preserves. There is no pectin to buy, and the preserves can be refrigerated for a couple of hours to check the set. This is an **easy preserve recipe,** one that will embolden the beginner to attempt more difficult recipes.

❧❧

Jamlady's Original Kiwifruit and Strawberry Preserves

No pectin added—French Plunge Method. A preserve, by definition, is about ½ fruit and ½ sugar or even less sugar!

9 cups sugar
3 pounds halved strawberries (about 7 cups)
4 cups peeled, diced kiwifruits (about 18-20 kiwis)
½ teaspoon crystalline citric acid

The fruits in this recipe are kept intact by removing them during the boiling process and then adding them back into the hot mixture! Cook the kiwis with the citric acid for 1 minute. Add the sugar and the strawberries. Turn the heat off. Let the sugar weep out the fruit juices. Heat up the mixture again. Remove the fruits with a slotted stainless-steel spoon. Cook down the syrup. Add in the fruits once or twice and remove them right away. Boil the syrup to 105 degrees C. Add the fruits back in and check the thickness on a frozen plate. Repeat removing and plunging the fruits and then boil down the preserves until the jell point is reached. JSP/RWB10(8OZ). Cook a ½ or ¼ recipe in a smaller pan.

UNUSUAL JAMS

Sometimes it is difficult to know what to call a product that "sorta" fits into two categories. The recipe below is one of those interesting "cross-cat" types. **Lilian Dickinson's Tomato Jam** (from *Pride of the Kitchen*) is not a jam because it does not have more sugar than fruits. It has twice the fruits to sugar or 6 pounds of tomatoes to 3 pounds of sugar. Further, it has a pound of raisins. Technically, because there are 2 cups of vinegar in this recipe, it is a chutney recipe. When the tomatoes cook down, lots of water is removed, and the resulting "jam" is probably close to the amount of sugar in a preserve(s) or butter. Certainly, Lilian Dickinson's Tomato Jam never approaches the sugar levels of a "true" or "proper" jam. The spices of cinnamon, cloves, nutmeg, pepper, and salt are an unusual combination for a jam or conserve. Lilian Dickinson's Tomato Jam recipe has been reprinted in several other books, and Jamlady considers it a classic chutney recipe that is used like a jam, preserve, or conserve. Here again, this is a "jam" few pay attention to until they taste it. If you like mincemeat, you will love this "jam." It is perfect for the biscuit with a traditional roast beef dinner, or it may be used as chutney on fried vegetables or braised meats. **If you have lots of tomatoes and want to make a "jam" at which you just can't fail—unless you burn it—this is the recipe.**

Lilian Dickinson's Tomato Jam*

No lemons or lemon rinds.
Easy to make!

6 pounds ripe tomatoes, scalded and peeled*
3 pounds brown sugar
1 pound raisins
1 pint vinegar
2 tablespoons ground cinnamon
1 tablespoon ground cloves
1 tablespoon salt
1 grated nutmeg
½ teaspoon black pepper

Cook all of the ingredients except the raisins for about 2-3 hours or until nearly thick. Add the raisins and stir continually until thick. Be careful not to burn this "jam." Stir very frequently, as the tomato pieces can fall to the bottom of the pan, stick, and burn. JSP/RWB10(8OZ).

* *Jamlady removes all tomato seeds for this recipe, but the original recipe did not call for seed removal.* **(Pride of the Kitchen, *a small-sized publication of the Clarksville Literary Club, Scotland Neck, North Carolina, n.d. This club was formed in 1917 and still exists today. The literary club's current members have graciously granted Jamlady permission to reprint Ms. Dickinson's wonderful recipe.*)**

Mango products are very popular. To make good mango jam or preserves, it is important to scrape the peels to collect the entire mango pulp, which is close to the peel. The pit should be scraped clean, a job that requires some skill, as mango pits are very slippery. Don't give up at first try. Experiment with the different types of knife blades. Sometimes a serrated blade is needed, and other times a good carving knife works best. Soon, you will have your own favorite knife for the different types of cutting and peeling jobs.

This mango and blueberry jam can be made either light (red) or dark (blue). Jamlady also

calls this formulation **"Blue Mango Jam," "Red Mango Jam," "Tango Jam," "Red Tango Jam,"** or **"Blue Tango Jam,"** because it takes two to tango and the mangoes and blueberries in this jam certainly dance well together. **This seedless mango and blueberry jam can be made into two different jams or preserves, depending on the technique used!** Red Mango Jam could just as well become Blue Mango Jam, as the color can be red or dark blue. The color of the resulting jam depends on the pigment of the blueberries and the number of times the skins are juiced. For a lighter jam (red), run the blueberries through the juicing machine only once. (Use leftover blueberry skins in a gelatin mold or in salvage jam or preserves.) Jamlady prefers the look of Red Mango Jam or Preserves. Mango Preserves could be made as **Red Tango Preserves** by using ¼ of the **Blueberry Jam** recipe (with the blueberries juiced only once) with ¾ of the **Mango Preserves with Pectin** recipe.

Having never seen the combination of blueberries and mangoes in a jam or preserves, Jamlady decided to try it! What a delightful combination it is! Historically, many combinations of fruits have not been made or tried because the fruits considered for use do not grow in the same geographic area. However, with fruits being flown in from all over the world, this combination of mangoes and blueberries is now possible—and the Champion juicing machine, as a tool, enables the jam maker to experiment with all sorts of new or modified recipes.

Jamlady's Original Tango Jam*

This recipe is a perfect example of "having the recipe, but not being able to make the jam."

4½ cups sugar
1⅞ cups juiced blueberries (without the skins and seeds)
2 cups peeled, chopped mangoes ('Tommy Atkins' variety or other)
1 1¾-ounce box regular powdered pectin
2 tablespoons lemon juice

The key to making this jam correctly: How many times do you run the blueberries through the juicing machine to get a red-colored jam instead of a blue-colored jam? Mix all of the fruit and lemon juice with the pectin. Wait 10 minutes; boil for 1 minute. Add the sugar; boil for 1 minute more. Check the set. JSP/RWB10(8OZ).

Both mangoes and blueberries are low in acid. Mangoes are low in pectin.

If you're a mango lover, this next jam is for you. What could be more tropical and luscious than mango jam or preserves? The cinnamon stick adds just enough cinnamon taste without any ground spice affecting the beauty and delicate color of the mangoes. Make sure you use a pinch of ascorbic acid (Vitamin C crystals) when you are preparing the mangoes. Jamlady chops the peeled mangoes in the food processor with just a pinch of ascorbic acid crystals. The addition of ascorbic acid makes all the difference in the appearance and freshness of the end product. Jamlady also makes **Mango Butter** using lite or "low-sugar" pectin. **Mango Preserves with Pectin** can be made with pectin, using the Peach Preserves recipe.

As you can see, Jamlady measured the pH of this jam to show you the effects of the pinch of ascorbic acid crystals and lemon juice on the pH of the entire batch. Mangoes are low in acid, with a pH reading of 4.28 for the plain fruit. The completed jam measured 3.52 or higher in acid. If you remember, from your high-school science class, **acids are low numbers on the scale and bases are the higher numbers.** In order to can safely, you should be well under the 4.6 reading on the pH scale. A reading of 3.52 is well below the 4.6 "botulism line." Plain mangoes could be canned without added acid or lemon juice, but the pH is in a safer range with these acidic ingredients. Some raisins or nuts can easily be added to a jam to make a conserve. Besides, without the addition of ascorbic acid crystals, the fruit would begin to brown or oxidize. And remember, for jams, acid is necessary for the breakdown of sugars, which then allows those sugars to accept water, freeing the pectin to form the pectin chains. See how regular pectin works in the "Processing Methods and Troubleshooting" chapter. **Having enough pectin is important for a set, but having enough pectin without enough acid means there will be no set.**

Canners have to be careful they do not decide to dump in small pieces of dates or some similarly high pH ingredient, which will turn a jam into a conserve and, at the same time, raise the pH to a level that is not safe to can. There probably is not much danger of this happening with most fruit jams, as jam has a lot of sugar and most fruits are fairly acidic. However, adding high pH ingredients (basic) in the preparation of chutneys, pumpkin preserves, or pickles could be especially dangerous, as the amount of sugar is often reduced from that of a jam and low-acid vegetables (high pH) that may be contained in the formulation increase the overall pH of the product. Of course, with pickles there is usually salt, but if you reduce the salt or sugar and raise the pH in a canned product (making it more basic as opposed to acidic), you may be creating an unsafe situation.

❧❧

MANGOES, APRICOTS, NECTARINES, AND PEACHES

Mango Jam with Cinnamon Stick

If you love mangoes, you'll love this jam! One nonedible cinnamon stick per jar.

5 cups sugar
3¾ cups peeled, chopped mangoes
1 1¾-ounce box regular powdered pectin
2 tablespoons freshly squeezed lemon juice
1 true cinnamon stick per jar
A very small pinch of ascorbic acid crystals

In this recipe, lime juice or crystalline citric acid may be substituted for the lemon juice (⅛ teaspoon citric acid equals 1 tablespoon of lemon juice). Additional acid and pectin are needed, as mangoes are low in both. Use ascorbic acid crystals on the mangoes in preparation. Mix the juice, fruit, and pectin and wait 10 minutes. Boil 1 minute; add the sugar and cinnamon sticks. Use a true cinnamon stick, ***Cinnamomum zeylanicum*** **Nees** (tan, not brown in color), and not *Cinnamomum cassia* Blume, **Cassia,** or **Chinese Cinnamon,** which tastes somewhat bitter. Boil 1 minute more. JSP/RWB10(8OZ). The pH of plain mangoes tested around 4.28 and the approximate pH of this mango jam recipe equals 3.52. Makes approximately seven 8-ounce jars.

***Variation: Mango Preserves Without Pectin**—2 quarts peeled, diced mangoes, 5 cups sugar, ½ cup lime or lemon juice. Weep the fruits with*

Mango Jam or Mango Preserves with Cinnamon Stick—
Stacked, oval cinnamon-swirl bread cutouts with luscious
layers of flavored mango jam or preserves.

the sugar and cook down slowly or use the French Plunge Method. Mangoes may be substituted for peaches, nectarines, or apricots in most any "jam" recipe. (Also see the recommended mango preserves recipe: **Mango Preserves with Pectin** or **Peach Preserves with Pectin**.)

Lots of wonderful variations can be made by adding a liqueur to most "jam" formulations. These liqueur "jams" are special. Liqueurs are often added to peach, apricot, and mango jams, preserves, and butters. For **Frangelico Mango Jam**, add ⅓ to ½ cup of Frangelico Liqueur (at the end) and boil for 1 more minute. Grand Marnier, Liqueur 43, Curaçao Orange Liquor, or a blend of Rumraisin and Curaçao Liqueur may also be used. Shop around the liqueur shelves of your local or foreign liquor store in search of the new liqueur to make a new special "jam."

'Ataulfo' Mangoes, *Mangifera indica,* Indonesian-type mangoes with lighter flesh inside, are not easy to find, but they are available in the local grocery stores sometimes during the early summer months. This variety of mango makes spectacular mango jam and is one of Jamlady's personal favorites. There is a tremendous difference in the jam's taste, depending on the type of citrus fruit used in this mango recipe.

Variation: 'Ataulfo' Mango Jam—Follow the recipe for mango jam, but use Ataulfo mangoes and substitute freshly squeezed lime juice for the lemon juice.

A standard mango jam, spiked with a liqueur, can be transformed into a jam worthy to top a picnic pound cake or party cheesecake. Jamlady uses an entire 8-ounce jar of her Mango Marnier Jam or Mango Marnier Preserves between the layers of a torte cake or regular layer cake. Frost the cake with white icing and top with grated orange peels or candied orange peels.

Variations: Mango Marnier Jam, Mango 43 Jam, Mango Marnier Preserves, or Mango 43 Preserves—Use the mango jam recipe minus the cinnamon stick or use the mango preserves recipe. *Add ¼ cup French Grand Marnier Liqueur or Cuarenta Y Tres Liqueur at the end and boil 1 more minute or to set point (105 degrees C).*

Let's assume you have a recipe for mango jam and a recipe for peach jam. You can take one half the ingredients in the mango recipe and half the ingredients in the peach recipe and make mango-peach jam in one pan. Look over the plain mango recipe and the plain peach recipe and see what Jamlady has done. You can do this with most any recipe for jam, assuming they both are using the same type and quantity of pectin. It is advisable to use the whole box of pectin, thereby avoiding apportionment of the pectin.

☙❧

Marnier Mango-Peach Jam

Created by Jamlady for the Grand Marnier lover!

5 cups sugar
2 cups peeled, chopped, slightly underripe 'Ataulfo' mangoes
1¾ cups peeled, chopped, slightly underripe peaches
1 1¾-ounce box regular pectin
⅓ cup Grand Marnier
2 tablespoons lemon juice
1 teaspoon butter or margarine (optional, antifoaming agent)

Boil the pectin with the fruit, lemon juice, and butter for 1 full minute. Add the sugar; boil for 1 minute. Add the Grand Marnier; boil for 1 minute. JSP/RWB10(8OZ).

Variation: Mango-Peach Jam with Cinnamon Stick—Substitute the Grand Marnier for 1 true cinnamon stick per jar.

Marnier Strawberry-Peach Jam

A delightful jam for a tea party or shower.

6 cups sugar
2½ cups processor-sliced strawberries
1⅞ cups peeled, sliced, slightly underripe peaches
⅓ cup Grand Marnier Liqueur
⅛ cup water
1 1¾-ounce box regular powdered pectin
1 tablespoon freshly squeezed lemon juice
½ teaspoon butter (optional, antifoaming agent)
¼ teaspoon ascorbic acid crystals

Use the ascorbic acid crystals, a small pinch at a time, as needed, on the fruit during preparation and in the prep water. Mix the pectin with the fruits, water, lemon juice, and butter. Wait 10 minutes; boil the fruit mixture for 1 minute. Add the sugar; boil for 1 minute more. Add the Grand Marnier and boil until the temperature reaches 104-105 degrees C. Check the set. JSP/RWB10(8OZ).

Variations: Strawberry-Peach Preserves with Grand Marnier—Combine half of the ingredients in strawberry preserves with half the ingredients in peach preserves; add ¼ to ⅓ cup of Grand Marnier. Mangoes are interchangeable with the peaches for **Strawberry-Mango Preserves.** *In a previous recipe, oil of cinnamon was used to make Sour Cherry Genie Jam. You can use the same oil of cinnamon in strawberry-peach preserves or strawberry-peach jam for* **Strawberry-Peach Genie Jam** *or* **Strawberry-Peach Genie Preserves.**

Apricots are stone fruits. The stone-fruit classification includes plums, cherries, peaches, nectarines, apricots, and almonds. **Apricots,** *Prunus,* are of three species, all thought to be native to China or Japan. The **European** or **American common apricot,** *Prunus armeniaca* Linn., has red or yellow flesh and a smooth, large, flat stone. The **Russian apricot,** *Prunus armeniaca* var. *pendula,* is a smaller and hardy version of the common apricot. It is thought to have been native to Armenia. The **Japanese apricot,** *Prunus mume,* has small, hard fruits and is grown mostly for its beautiful flowers and not its fruits.

Jamlady has noticed several newcomers to the market, the plumcot, aprium®, and pluot®. The **plumcot** is a cross between an apricot and a plum (*Prunus armeniaca x Prunus domestica*). Besides the obvious plum and apricot derivation of the word, Jamlady notes the similarity of the word plumcot to the term poult eggs or poulett, meaning poultry eggs. Hence, perhaps, the use of the term **dinosaur eggs** for plumcot or other such crosses, as they are larger than eggs from young chickens or poults, poullets, poulets, or pullets? Who knows? More crosses have produced the **aprium®,** a cross between a plumcot and an apricot (*P. armeniaca x P. domestica x P. armeniaca*), and the **pluot®** is a cross between a plumcot and a plum (*P. armeniaca x P. domestica x P. domestica*).

Jamlady noticed the National Arbor Day Foundation was featuring, in 2001, the 'Moorpark' apricot, *Prunus armeniaca,* as a large yellow variety of apricot that bears fruits in early July. The 'Moorpark' apricot is hardy in zones 5-8, which includes most of the United States except for the extreme north such as Minnesota and the Dakotas and the extreme south and California. For this variety, you need to plant two trees to guarantee cross-pollination and fruiting. Some sources do report the 'Moorpark' is self-fertile, but two trees will guarantee a better yielding crop. Any spot with full sun and adequate drainage (sandy soil preferable) is appropriate for the 'Moorpark' apricot tree, but the 'Moorpark' apricot will still need to be watered during dry spells as it is not drought resistant. Keep in mind, the best fruit quality of apricots come from cultivars that are up to or only hardy, perhaps, to a 3B zone. The *Prunus armeniaca* var. *mandshurica* is one such 15-20-foot tree with lovely white to pink spring flowers. This variety produces delicious, juicy fruits of high quality and makes excellent preserves. Cultivars like 'Moongold' or 'Sungold' are hardier, but their fruits are less desirable for preserves.

Caution: Do not consume the wilted leaves, twigs, stems, and seeds of the apricot, **Prunus armeniaca**, *as they are poisonous.* **Laetrile** *is found in the apricot seed. The leaves, twigs, stems, and seeds of the common apricot contain known toxins such as* cyanogenic glycosides *and* amygdalin *and may be fatal if eaten.*

☙❧

Marnier Mango-Apricot Jam

If you love apricots and mangoes, you will love this jam!

6 cups sugar
2½ cups peeled, finely chopped apricots
1⅞ cups peeled, chopped mangoes
4 tablespoons freshly juiced lemon juice
1 1¾-ounce box powdered pectin
⅓ cup Grand Marnier

Mix the lemon juice, apricots, and mangoes with the pectin. Let the mixture sit for 10 minutes. Boil for 1 minute. Add the sugar; boil for 1 minute more. Add the Grand Marnier; boil 1 minute. Test the set on a frozen plate. JSP/RWB10(8OZ).

Note: Apricots are interchangeable with mangoes, peaches, and nectarines in most jam or preserve recipes. **Nectarines** are one of those fruits not too many people know very much about. The family Rosacea includes both nectarines and peaches. Both nectarines, *Prunus persica* var. *nucipersica* Schneid, and peaches, *P. persica,* are in Jamlady's old, outdated copy of L. H. Bailey's *The Standard Cyclopedia,* 1930, which lists two types of nectarines, **clingstones** or **brugnons** (*Persica laevis* Risso) and **freestones** (*Persica violacea* Risso). **Current-day experts state there is no scientific name distinction for freestone or clingstone anymore and that most nurseries list the cultivar name and not a variety name anyway.** So look for cultivars like 'Easternglo' (dark red skin, yellow-fleshed freestone), 'Dwarf Nectarine' (dark red and yellow skin, yellow-fleshed freestone), 'Honeykist' (yellow flesh), and 'Fantasia' (yellow-fleshed freestone) or for the Latin name form, *Prunus persica* 'Fantasia.'

Note: The word **cultivar** *is derived from culti(vated) and var(iety) and is an agricultural or horticultural variety that is found under cultivation or as an escaped plant. It is a variation of a species that has been produced by breeding and deliberate selection. Cultivar names are usually capitalized and are surrounded by single quote marks, but they also may be denoted by bolding their non-Latin name name or by using the word* cultivar *or* cv. *before the capitalized cultivar name. Unlike genus and species names, which are usually written in italics and Latin, cultivar names are not written in italics and are written in English or a foreign language, excluding Latin. A variety is ranked below a subspecies and before a forma, the narrowest taxon.*

A nectarine is a special type or kind of peach. A peach pit or seed planted may give rise to a tree that may bear either peaches or nectarines and a nectarine pit may give rise to a tree that may bear either peaches or nectarines, but peaches only if it is not self-pollinated. Nectarines are smooth skinned as opposed to the peach's fuzzy skin. The fuzzy condition of a peach is a dominant characteristic and the smooth-skin characteristic of a nectarine is a recessive trait. To have a nectarine, you must have a double-recessive combination. If self-pollinated, the nectarine tree will grow into a nectarine tree. Not very many nectarines are cultivated in the United States. Some are grown in California. Jamlady finds it curious that more people don't ask for nectarine "jams," for when they are offered nectarine jams or butters, they readily try them.

❦

Nectarine-Almond Conserve

Nectarine jam with pure almond extract, almonds, and golden raisins!

5½ cups sugar
4 cups chopped nectarines and juiced skins
½ cup sliced, skinless almonds
½ cup golden raisins
1 1¾-ounce box powdered pectin
2 tablespoons lemon juice
1 tablespoon pure almond extract
½ teaspoon butter
¼ teaspoon ascorbic acid crystals

Use ascorbic acid in the prep water and when chopping or juicing the fruit. Combine the pectin, nectarines, and lemon juice. Wait 5 minutes; boil for 1 minute. Add the sugar and butter; boil for 1 minute. Add the almond extract, nuts, and raisins. Boil for 1 minute.

JSP/RWB10(8OZ).

Nellie Melba was an Australian opera star who was fond of good food. The dessert **Peach Melba,** raspberry purée poured over peaches, was named in her honor. With the invention of ice cream, Peach Melba evolved into ice cream and fresh peaches with raspberry purée on top. If you have a Champion juicing machine or similar piece of equipment, you can run raspberries through 10-15 times and remove all the seeds, reserving all of the fine purée or pulp. With a juicing machine, Peach Melba is actually a quick dessert. Or better yet, substitute Jamlady's **Lemony Raspberry Sauce** for the raspberry purée. You'll be able to enjoy Peach Melba all year long.

Jamlady, inspired by the Nellie Melba story and voice (see www.bassocantante.com), has created several renditions of the original dessert, in jam form. One is made with nectarines, others with peaches or mangoes. And, of course, the proper hostess might well play opera music while serving Peach Melba Jam or dessert. How about a little Charlotte Church, Joan Sutherland, Marilyn Horne on *Coloratura Spectacular* (Decca), Renee Fleming on *Great Opera Scenes* (Decca), Kathleen Battle on *Baroque Duet* (Sony), or Nellie Melba?

Peach Melba, the well-known dessert, can also be made with nectarines or mangoes. This Nectarine Melba Jam is a culinary aria substituting nectarines for the peaches of the traditional dessert. Peaches, mangoes, or apricots could also be used instead of nectarines in this jam. These Melba jams could also be made with less sugar, but then they would be called preserves or butters and not jams. Another formulation for Peach Melba Jam with powdered pectin uses less sugar than this formulation with liquid pectin.

Nectarine Melba Jam, Peach Melba Jam, Mango Melba Jam, or Apricot Melba Jam

Made with liquid pectin.

6 cups sugar
4 cups nectarines (unpeeled or peeled), peaches (peeled), mangoes (peeled), or apricots (unpeeled or peeled)
2 cups juiced, seedless raspberry purée
1 3-ounce pouch liquid pectin
2 tablespoons lemon juice
½ teaspoon butter

Peel and chop the peaches and mangoes. The apricots are best juiced many times and the small amount of skin discharged from the juicing machine discarded. Alternately, the apricots may be chopped whole after stoning or peeled and the fruits chopped. The nectarines are best juiced and the outputs from both hoppers used, but they may be used chopped with their skins or peeled and chopped, skins discarded. Add the processed fruits, sugar, lemon juice, purée, and butter and boil for 1 minute. Add the pectin; boil to 104-105 degrees C. Check the set. JSP/RWB5(4OZ)10(8OZ).

Peach Melba Jam #2

Sugar free—sweetened with aspartame.

4⅖ cups peeled, chopped peaches
½ cup seedless raspberry pulp
⅕ cup lemon juice
1 1¾-ounce box lite or "no-sugar" pectin
30 packets aspartame or 1-3 cups sugar

Mix peaches, raspberry pulp, lemon juice, and pectin. Wait 10 minutes; boil for 1 minute. Add aspartame or sugar; boil for 1 minute more. JSP/RWB5(4OZ)10(8OZ).

♋♋

Sunshine Jam

Nectarines and peaches—sweetened with aspartame or sugar.

3 cups unpeeled, puréed peaches (see below)
2 cups unpeeled, puréed nectarines
¼ cup lemon juice
30 packets aspartame or 1-3 cups sugar
1 1¾-ounce box lite or "no-sugar" pectin

Juice the unpeeled peaches and nectarines to obtain the purée. If you have no juicing machine, peel the fruits and purée the fruits in the food processor. Mix the fruit purée and juice with the pectin. After 10 minutes, boil for 1 minute. Add the aspartame or sugar and boil for 1 minute more. JSP/RWB10(8OZ).

Note: *Do not attempt to make this jam with regular pectin. Lite or "no-sugar" pectin must be used. The shelf life of this jam is 3 months, but it may be extended by refrigeration.*

Nectarine Jam

The juiced nectarine skins give this jam extra flavor and color!

5½ cups sugar
4 cups peeled, pitted, processor-chopped nectarines
Juiced nectarine skins (see below)
1 1¾-ounce box powdered pectin
2 tablespoons lemon juice
¼ teaspoon ascorbic acid crystals
½ teaspoon butter

Use the ascorbic acid when working with the nectarines. Juice the nectarine skins many times and use the skins' juice along with the peeled nectarines, or alternatively, use both outputs from the juicing machine—the juice section and the pulp-extraction section—with the peeled, chopped fruit. **The Champion juicing machine or similar machine is a wonderful tool for the jam maker as it pulverizes skins and rinds so they can be used in a recipe—without concerns over textural inconsistencies.** Boil the nectarines, lemon juice, and butter with the pectin for 1 minute. Add the sugar; boil for 1 minute more. Check the jam for set on a frozen plate. JSP/RWB5(4OZ)10(8OZ).

Variation: Nectarine-Almond Jam—Add 1 tablespoon pure almond extract; boil for 1 more minute.

Suppose you want to take this nectarine jam recipe and turn it into a mango and nectarine jam recipe. Both the plain mango recipe and nectarine recipe normally use 1 box of pectin. So, all you need to do is divide the nectarine ingredients in half. That would be 2¾ cups sugar, 2 cups chopped nectarines, 1 tablespoon lemon juice, ⅛ teaspoon ascorbic acid, ¼ teaspoon butter, and a ½ box of pectin. Add that to one-half the recipe for mango jam or 2 ½ cups sugar, 1⅞

cups chopped mango, 1 tablespoon lemon juice, a pinch of ascorbic acid crystals (for use when working with the mangoes), and a ½ box of pectin. The completed nectarine-mango jam formulation is shown here.

⌘

Nectarine-Mango Jam

5¼ cups sugar
2 cups peeled, pitted, chopped nectarines
Juiced nectarine skins (see below)
1⅞ cups peeled, chopped mangoes
2 tablespoons lemon juice
⅛-¼ teaspoon ascorbic acid crystals
1 1¾-ounce box powdered pectin
½ teaspoon butter (optional)
1 cinnamon stick (optional)

Use the ascorbic acid when working with the fruits. Juice the nectarine skins many times and use the skins' juice along with the peeled nectarines, or alternatively, use both outputs from the juicing machine—the juice section and the pulp-extraction section—with the peeled, chopped nectarines. Add the cinnamon. Boil the nectarines and mangoes, lemon juice, and butter with the pectin for 1 minute. Add the sugar; boil for 1 minute more. Check the jam for set on a frozen plate. JSP/RWB5(4OZ)10(8OZ).

*Variations: Nectarine-Strawberry Jam— Can be made with half a strawberry recipe and half a nectarine recipe. Nectarine-Strawberry Jam can be spiced with 1 teaspoon ground cinnamon or 1-2 drops oil of cinnamon for a **Nectarine-Strawberry Genie Jam.***

Peach Melba Jam #3

Made with powdered pectin.

6 cups sugar
2½ cups seedless raspberry pulp (see below)
1⅞ cups peeled, chopped peaches
1 1¾-ounce box regular powdered pectin
1 tablespoon lemon juice
½ teaspoon butter
¼ teaspoon ascorbic acid crystals

This jam has a little more raspberries than peaches and is made with powdered pectin. Alternatively, this jam can be made with more peaches than raspberries. When raspberries predominate, the recipe is more expensive and time consuming to make because the seeds must be removed from the raspberries and raspberries usually cost more than peaches. Use the ascorbic acid when working with the fruits. To begin, juice the raspberries in a Champion juicing machine many times until you have all the juice and pulp. Discard the seeds. Add the chopped peaches, pectin, butter, and lemon juice to a pan; wait 10 minutes. Boil the mixture for 1 minute. Add the sugar; boil for 1 more minute or to jell point. JSP/RWB5(4OZ)10(8OZ).

Some jams turn out quite differently with a predominance of one fruit over the other. Jam makers of today should take a longer look at this idea of formulating with varying ratios and modified ingredients. This Peach Melba Jam is a perfect example. The color of the jam is redder depending on the quantity of raspberries added. However, a perfectly tasty jam can be made with a predominance of peaches. For the jam maker who must buy pricey raspberries, using a predominance of peaches may be more economical. Use ¼ of a raspberry recipe with ¾ of a peach recipe. Both versions of raspberry and peach jams or preserves are wonderful and attract a lot of attention. Indeed, both jams and preserves are great in fresh-fruit crepes with whipped cream! Another, less successful way to try to imitate the flavor of Peach Melba Jam is to use a raspberry liqueur with a peach jam, but Jamlady was not impressed with any she has tried in jam.

Probably the most versatile liqueur to use in "jams" is **Grand Marnier.** This liqueur is 40 percent alcohol by volume, or 80 proof. Grand Marnier's advertising says it is "made with Orange and Fine Old Cognac Brandy the Origin of which is Certified by the French Excise." For those of you worried about the alcoholic content of the completed jam, don't worry too much. Some of the alcohol burns off when boiling the jam, but the wonderful orange flavor remains. Jamlady has put Grand Marnier in mango, peach, red raspberry, nectarine, cantaloupe, strawberry, strawberry-raspberry, and many other combinational "jams" with equally good results. If you desire the alcohol to stay, mix the liqueur into the cooled jam, paraffin seal, and refrigerate the jars. Please see wine jelly.

ॐ

Marnier Peach Jam

The full flavor of peaches with Grand Marnier!

5 cups sugar
3¾ cups peeled, chopped, tree-ripened or
    slightly underripe peaches
1 1¾-ounce box regular powdered pectin
2 tablespoons lemon juice
¼ cup Grand Marnier
¼ teaspoon ascorbic acid crystals

Use pinches of ascorbic acid in the prep water and on the fruit while chopping. Combine the pectin, fruit, and lemon juice and boil for 1 full minute. Add the sugar and boil for 1 minute more. Add the Grand Marnier; boil for 1 minute. JSP/RWB5(4OZ)10(8OZ).

Peach-Almond Jam and Blueberry-Almond Jam are two super jams. When these are given as hostess gifts, accolades are soon to follow. Peach-Almond Jam or Peach-Almond Preserves are relatively easy to make, but do not attempt to make them with dead-ripe peaches, as they will not set properly. **If you must make Peach-Almond Jam or Peach-Almond Preserves with fully ripe peaches, then reduce the sugar by ¼ or ½ cup.** Ripe peaches have the advantage that their skins will slip off after they are plunged in boiling water, while unripe peaches usually must be peeled. However, the best peach "jam" is made with slightly underripe peaches.

Peach-Almond Jam or Peach-Almond Preserves is wonderful in a multijam torte cake. Try a jar of Peach-Almond Jam or Peach-Almond Preserves between the layers of a lemon cake. Frost and then decorate the jam-filled lemon cake with blanched, slivered almonds. Peach-Almond Jam or Peach-Almond Preserves is especially good in spritz cookies, as is Peach Melba Jam or **Peach Melba Preserves** (half a recipe of peach preserves plus half a recipe of raspberry jam or preserves).

One difference between preserves and jam is the amount of sugar used. Peach preserves can be made without pectin, but Jamlady prefers peach preserves with added pectin to a traditional peach preserves, as the taste and color is better. **Those individuals preferring a less sweet "jam" product will probably prefer preserves over jam.** Almond extract can be used or not used in either peach jam or peach preserves.

Peach-Almond Jam

Incredibly delicious—the full flavor of peaches and almonds without the nut texture!

5 cups sugar
3¾ cups peeled, chopped, slightly underripe peaches
1 1¾-ounce box regular powdered pectin
2 tablespoons lemon juice
1 tablespoon pure almond extract (not imitation)
¼ teaspoon or less ascorbic acid crystals
½ teaspoon butter (optional)

Use a pinch of ascorbic acid crystals in the prep water and a pinch in the processor as you prepare the peaches. Add the butter. Boil the pectin with the fruit and lemon juice for 1 full minute. Add the sugar; boil for 1 minute. Add the extract; boil for 1 minute. JSP/RWB5(4OZ)10(8OZ).

Variations: Deluxe Peach Jam—Can be made by eliminating the pure almond extract from the recipe. Other jams can be created by the addition of liqueurs or other flavorings.

Jamlady has made **Peach Preserves** by the classic method of cooking 4 pounds peaches (peeled and sliced or chopped) with 3 cups water and 6 cups sugar. The water is first cooked with the peaches to plump them. The sugar is added after the peaches are sufficiently plumped. By this method, if you cook the peaches down to be thick, as opposed to syrupy, the peaches tend to darken and caramelize. Some people claim they like this caramelized taste, but Jamlady prefers her peaches to remain a true peach color and taste. Adding a pinch of ascorbic acid crystals while working with the peaches and adding a pinch of ascorbic acid crystals in the preparation water will also help retard oxidation. Most taste testers also like Jamlady's new formulation for peach butter, which is in the butters chapter.

Some cooks use 5 pounds peaches to 3½ pounds (5⅓ cups) sugar plus ½ cup fresh lemon juice, cooked together, to make peach preserves or butter. Other cooks, like Jamlady, use 4 cups peaches and 4 cups sugar, adding enough liquid or powdered pectin to make a set quickly, before the sugar caramelizes.

⌒⌒⌒⌒

Peach-Almond Preserves with Added Pectin

This preserve uses a regular 50-50 fruit-to-sugar ratio, and the added pectin helps it to set more quickly.

- 4 cups pitted, peeled, hand-sliced peaches (or mangoes, nectarines, or apricots)
- 4 cups sugar
- 1 1¾-ounce box regular powdered pectin
- 2 tablespoons freshly juiced lemon juice
- 1 tablespoon pure almond extract (optional)

Do not pack the peaches too tightly when measuring them. Add the pectin and lemon juice to the peaches, wait 10 minutes, and boil 1 minute. Add the sugar, begin to boil for 1 minute, and add the pure almond extract near the end of the cooking time. Check the set on a frozen plate. Cook more, if necessary. If making this preserve for the first time, cover the jars with plastic wrap and refrigerate to make sure the set is correct. If

the product is not thick enough—does not set on a frozen plate in 60 seconds—cook it down further. Alternately, very finely grated lemon rind can be added and cooked to hasten the set. If the set is good, then JSP/RWB10(8OZ). Overly ripe peaches are not recommended for this recipe. Getting the right set is tricky and, remember, the preserves, when refrigerated, will be stiffer. Do not overcook! This preserve is better on the soft side of set so it will spread more easily.

*Variations: **Peach Preserves with Pectin** or **Mango Preserves with Pectin**—Eliminate the almond extract. Many different preserves can be made with the addition of different flavorings, such as a few drops of oil of cinnamon, for **Jamlady's Original Peach Genie Preserves** or **Jamlady's Mango Genie Preserves**. Small amounts of other fruits can be added with equal sugar for interesting changes in flavor. Good brandy and peaches are a wonderful combination. Peach Jam with VSOP Brandy is a favorite comfort food. Most peach buffs vary their weekly stash between the Grand Marnier, VSOP, Peach Genie, and Peach-Almond versions. To make **Peach Jam with VSOP Brandy** or **Peach Preserves with VSOP Brandy,** follow the recipes for peach preserves or peach jam. Add 2 ounces VSOP Brandy near the end and boil for 1 more minute. Jamlady uses **VSOP Brandy** in her pickled peaches too. Jamlady saw a recipe in another book on award-winning preserves. Jamlady does not understand how the recipe, as shown in this book, could possibly work as it calls for mixing sugar with peaches and then adding powdered pectin. This ordering of steps does not allow the powdered pectin to bind with the fruit first. **Normally, powdered pectin is cooked with the fruits to bind the pectin to the fruits and then the sugar is added. Jamlady cautions jam makers to always add powdered pectin to the fruits first, then boil, and then add the sugar.***

Liquid pectin may be used to thicken peach preserves or jams. By opting to use liquid pectin, which can be added after the sugar is combined with the fruits, the pectin can be added little by little until a set is achieved. With the Liquid Pectin Method there is more control than having to add all the pectin up front.

Jamlady prefers the **Peach-Clementine Marmalade** or **'Valencia' Orange Marmalade** (see **Oh My Darling Marmalade**) to all of the regular peach preserves and produces more jars of peach marmalade than classic peach preserves. Peaches are low in both acid and pectin and the citrus fruits are a natural way to provide both of what the peaches are lacking. Of course, Grand Marnier, VSOP Brandy, or other liqueurs can be added to any of these recipes too.

Pricey feijoas are oval, range in size from about ¾"-4½" long, emit a wonderful perfume, produce edible flowers, and have a somewhat granular consistency or texture like some pears. Jamlady decided to splurge and create a new recipe using peaches and feijoas, as peaches are extremely popular and who doesn't want to try a market newcomer? The **feijoa, guavasteen, or pineapple guava tree,** *Feijoa sellowiana,* is native to subtropical Paraguay, Uruguay, northern Argentina, and southern Brazil but is also grown in New Zealand and California. If you live in a subtropical climate, put two feijoa trees in your backyard! Then you can afford to make an entire batch of jam from just feijoas.

🐝

Feijoa and Peach Preserves

Feijoas taste somewhat like pineapple and spearmint!

4 cups sugar
2 cups peeled, chopped feijoas (approximately 15)
1¼ cups peeled, chopped underripe peaches (3)
4 tablespoons lemon juice

Layer the fruits with the sugar; wait 1 hour.

Cook all of ingredients until thick and translucent, to about 105 degrees C. Test the set. JSP/RWB10(8OZ). Alternately, fruits may be plumped in water first. See Feijoa Preserves (below).

Variation: Feijoa Preserves—Use 2 pounds feijoas to ½ cup water and 4 cups sugar. Start making the preserves by plumping (cooking) the feijoas in water for 15 minutes. Then add the sugar and cook until thick. A combination of feijoas and apples can also be made into preserves. Jamlady has seen commercial products with apples and feijoas together. Try half an apple recipe with half a feijoa preserves recipe, or make a feijoa and apple chutney.

Apricots are very popular. Jamlady formulated this apricot jam recipe utilizing a combination of apricots and crabapples with added pectin. A recipe for apricot preserves with crabapples, **Crabby Apricot Preserves,** would work too; use equal fruits to sugar. Also, please check out the deliciously smooth and zesty apricot butter recipe in the butters chapter.

🐝

Crabby Apricot Jam

Quick to make if you have a juicing machine.

6¼ cups sugar
4 cups juiced apricot purée
1½ cups juiced, cooked, strained crabapple juice or juiced crabapple juice
1 1¾-ounce box regular powdered pectin

Crabapples can be juiced in the Champion juicing machine, but it may not be good for the machine. Crabapples are tough. Put the apricot pulp through the juicing machine several times. Hard boil the apricot purée, crabapple juice, and pectin for 1 minute. Add the sugar and boil for 2 minutes. JSP/RWB5(4OZ)10(8OZ).

OLD TIMERS: CHOKECHERRIES, QUINCE, AND ROWANBERRIES

Chokecherry or **wild cherry**, *Prunus virginiana* Linn., is a wild fruit often used by old-timers to make jelly, jam, or syrup. Each year about three or four individuals ask Jamlady about chokecherry jam or jelly. Many people do not like chokecherry jam, finding it too tart, but for the chokecherry maven, there is no substitute.

To make **Chokecherry Jam,** destem, wash the fruits, and drain. Use 1 cup water to every 4 cups fruit. Cook the chokecherries until tender and rub them through a sieve to obtain the pulp. Proceed as for preserves, using equal parts sugar and fruit pulp. Cook to 104-105 degrees C or about 220 degrees F. JSP/RWB5(4OZ)10(8OZ).

For a **No-Pectin-Added Chokecherry Jelly,** use 4 cups extracted juice to 3-4 cups sugar and 4 tablespoons lemon juice. If you wish to use pectin or if you are having trouble getting a jelly to set, you can always slowly add some liquid pectin. Always check the completed product for set on a frozen plate.

To make **Chokecherry Syrup,** use 8 cups extracted chokecherry juice, 8-10 cups sugar, ½ cup freshly squeezed lemon juice, and 1 1¾-ounce box powdered pectin. Remember to cook the powdered pectin with the juice before adding the sugar. Some folks thicken the syrup by using corn syrup instead of some or all of the sugar, and others use liquid pectin.

Chokecherry and Crabapple Jelly can be made by cooking 4 cups extracted chokecherry juice to 4 cups extracted crabapple juice and 6 cups sugar. For a **Chokecherry and Crabapple Jam,** use 4 cups chokecherry pulp, 2 cups crabapple or apple pulp, and 4 cups sugar.

Quince, *Cydonia oblonga,* is a highly ornamental tree with large, cupped, pink and white flowers and woolly, dark-green leaves. The yellow fruits of the quince can weigh up to a pound. The quince tree has a gnarled appearance and can grow to 20 feet in height. Organic farmers like quince, as they are not often bothered by pests or diseases.

There are different cultivars of quince. Orange quince is known for its large fruit with orange flesh that turns red when cooked, and pineapple quince tastes like pineapple. The coating on quince seeds, **mucilage of quince seed,** is used in hairdressing products and as a demulcent.

The Greek name for this fruit is **"Cydonian apple."** Thomas Jefferson's first orchard at Monticello included quince. According to Kimball in *The Martha Washington Cookbook,* Martha Washington made quince pie with sugar-sweetened, stewed quince. Quince can be made into quince conserve, quince honey, quince jelly, quince marmalade, quince and ginger marmalade, quince syrup, and many more concoctions, but quince are extremely troublesome fruits to peel due to their hardness. Some books report that the word marmalade is derived from *marmelo,* the Portuguese name for quince.

Quince Conserve can be made with 4 cups each of quince pulp, cranberry pulp, and apple pulp to 8 cups sugar and the juice from 2 oranges or 3 lemons and their grated rinds. Add in ¼ to ½ cup walnuts or pecans at the end, when the marmalade is thick. Once you've added in the nuts, this "jam" is now a conserve.

Quince Honey requires 5 cups quince to be peeled, chopped, and cooked with 4 cups sugar and 2 tablespoons lemon juice. For **Quince Jelly,** cut up 4 pounds quince (6 large including the skins), and tie the cores and pips in a pip bag. Cook the quince, covered with water, until they are easily pierced with a fork. Drain out the liquid and cook it down some with the pip bag. Take 6½ cups extracted quince liquid and cook it with 8¾ cups sugar. Add 2 tablespoons lemon juice, if necessary, for a set. For **Paradise Jelly,** use the extracted liquid from 20 quince, 10 apples, and 4 cups cranberries with equal parts sugar.

Jamlady Tip: One tablespoon peeled and finely grated ginger root can be cooked with quince to flavor jellies, conserves, or honey.

For **Quince and Ginger Marmalade,** peel 18 quince (11-12 pounds) and cut in small pieces. Cover with about 1-1¼ cups water, 1-2 tablespoons grated fresh grated ginger, and 2 lemons (juice and grated rind). Cook to obtain the measurable pulp and proceed as with preserves with equal parts fruits to sugar. JSP/RWB10(8OZ). Quince and Ginger Marmalade is excellent in **Iced Snowballs**—baked pastry-covered apples that have been first hollowed and filled with orange or quince marmalade. See Hayes' *Mackenzie's Five Thousand Receipts*, 1860, p. 182.

The **rowanberry** or **mountain ash tree,** *Sorbus scopulina,* is a member of the rose family and is commonly found in the Midwest. Wine, resembling the taste of some brand names, dry sherry, lemonade, and jam can be made from rowanberries. To make lemonade, soak seeded rowanberries in water for several hours, 1 part berries to 3 parts water. A mountain ash infusion can be sweetened and drunk or used for intestinal problems. The fruits and seeds of the mountain ash tree have been used as an antiscurvy. According to some sources, **the mountain ash seed contains cyanogenic glycosides that combine with water to make poisonous prussic acid.**

Chevallier, in *Encyclopedia of Medicinal Plants,* suggests removing the mountain ash seeds before using the fruits. Considering the size of the fruits, this is most impractical, and these berries have long been used to make jelly and alcoholic drinks. Jamlady believes that the amount of contact with the seed is very minimal if the berries are soaked, without cooking. To be on the safe side, cook or boil the lemonade, if the seeds are not removed prior to soaking.

Jamlady consulted with several experts. One was kind enough to reply to Jamlady's e-mail requesting further information on rowanberries. He said he would not be afraid of cooked rowanberries but was wary of uncooked or frozen product. Freezing apparently doesn't get rid of the *cyanide* or the **amygdalin,** which can produce **cyanide.** Unseeded, frozen berries, for that reason, are not a good idea unless they would first be cooked. So, Jamlady is not going to stop making rowanberry jelly. It's cooked! As for wine, the seeds are separated from the juice extract partway through the winemaking process, so might be ok, but to be safe, seed the fruit first. The experts Jamlady consulted all stated they'd drink Jamlady's rowanberry wine, so it looks as though her friends will keep sipping away on homemade Mountain Ash Berry Wine.

Caution: Jamlady does not and cannot recommend the consumption of uncooked and unseeded rowanberry fruits. See above.

☙❧

Rowanberry or Mountain Ash Berry Jelly

Use this jelly with meats or on biscuits.

1½ pounds mountain ash berries (rowanberries)
1½ pounds crabapples
3 cups water
3 cups sugar

Simmer the berries and crabapples with the water until soft. Place the cooked and mashed fruit in a jelly bag and hang it overnight. Use 4 cups of the juice, keeping the rest of the juice for drinking, sweetened, or in tea. Add the sugar; boil to jell point. JSP/RWB10(8OZ).

Iced Snowball with Orange Marmalade—Top off a fine meal with this luscious, icing-drizzled, apple dessert. This old and forgotten snowball recipe has been re-created by Jamlady using an orange-marmalade-stuffed 'Granny Smith' apple in a flaky, tart-pastry jacket. Roll out the Grand Marnier and hot Gold-Tipped Darjeeling tea for this elegant dessert.

ACID AND PECTIN

The amount of acid and pectin in a fruit affects what must be combined with that fruit to make a jelly, jam, preserve, butter, or conserve. For your information, there are four lists here that should prove useful. Some fruits have a wide range of possible pH measurements depending on their ripeness and other factors, so it is difficult to place them correctly on such a chart or group of lists. Jamlady attempted to find some relative viscosity or relative pectin charts already in existence but was unable to locate any, despite a large effort in contacting food-science professors at major universities, viscometer manufacturers, and companies selling pectin commercially. Viscosity or concentrations of pectin can vary a lot, even for one specific fruit, so keep in mind that these are only generalized classifications. While this chart may not be perfect and it is generalized, it still should be of some help to the home canner when used with the **pH table in the back of this book.**

Home canners trying to buy a jelmeter may be just as frustrated. Jamlady has her jelmeter because it was given to her by someone who already had one. Jamlady could not find any source where jelmeters were offered for sale, but there are directions on-line for making viscometers for less than a dollar.

A jelmeter is a graduated glass tube with an opening at each end. This tube is used to determine the amount of pectin in fruit juice. The rate of flow of juice through this tube correlates with the jelling power of the juice. A jelmeter measures the relative viscosity of the fruit being extracted by determining the rate of flow of the juice. **Viscosity is directly related to pectin content.** Pectin molecules are large and the more of them there are, the slower the juice moves through the tube of the jelmeter. A jelmeter is marked to indicate how many cups of sugar should be added per cup of extraction for making jellied products. Since viscosity varies with temperature, all products must be measured at room temperature to get an accurate measurement. **Fruit juices lose their viscosity if they are allowed to sit,** so measurement must be taken right after extraction.

To use a jelmeter, hold your finger over the bottom of the jelmeter tube. Pour in the extracted juice. Then take your finger away and let the juice run for 1 minute. Replace your finger over the bottom and note the level in the glass tube, which indicates the amount of sugar needed to make a jelly, jam, or marmalade that will set. Inaccurate timing of rate of flow or squeezing the jelly bag during extraction of the juice are other variables that can cause an inaccurate reading. **The optimum pH range for a good jelling of the pectin molecules is between 3.2 and 3.4.**

Note: At some time in the past, jelmeters were made by Jelmeter Div. D, Delaware Motor Sales Co., 1606 Pennsylvania Avenue, Wilmington 6, Delaware.

Acid and Pectin in Fruits and Jam Vegetables

Approximate categories. The acid and pectin values for different fruits are very variable. Unripe fruits usually have more pectin than fully ripe fruits.

High Acid and High Pectin	Low Pectin and Low Acid	High Acid and Low Pectin	High Pectin and Low Acid
Apple, tart	Apricots	Cherries, Sour	Apples, sweet
Blackberries, unripe	Bananas	Pineapple	Blackberries, ripe
Citron	Beets	Rhubarb	Cherries, sweet, unripe
Cranberries	Blueberries	Strawberries	Feijoa
Currants, black	Cactus		Guavas, ripe
Currants, red	Carambolas		Kiwifruit
Gooseberries, green or red	Elderberries, ripe		Kumquat
Grapefruit	Mango, ripe		Oranges, sweet
Grapes, domestic	Mulberries		Papaya, almost ripe
Grapes, wild	Nectarines		Pummelos
Guavas, almost ripe	Papaya, ripe		Quince, ripe
Lemons	Peaches		Tangerines/Clementines
Limes	Pears		
Limes, Key	Pears, Asian		
Oranges, Seville	Pumpkins		
Oranges, Sour	Radishes		
Plums	Raspberries		
Quince, unripe	Squash		
	Tomatillos		
	Tomatoes		

Pectin and acid are necessary substances in jam making. Pectin, which is found naturally in many fruits, combines with sugar and acid to make a gel. **Pectin and acid contents are variable.** Depending on the growing condition, degree of ripeness, and diseases of the plant, the amount of pectin and acid can vary considerably.

The pH of any given fruit can be checked with a pH meter or rustically tested with pH papers. The major problem with the pH papers is that it is almost impossible to tell between 4.3 and 4.7 and you absolutely need to know.

Jamlady Tip: Papers are available for 2.0-7.0 range on one strip. You do not want those pH papers for canning. You really want a pH meter, but if that is not available, at least use the pH paper strips with a range between 4.0 and 5.0 only or 3.0-4.0 only (per strip).

Canned products that will be processed in a RWB need to be safely less than 4.6. Otherwise you must process using a pressure cooker. Pressure cooking cooks at higher temperatures and under pressure. Not only does the high heat diminish some vitamins, but a pressure cooker in action can be dangerous. If using a pressure cooker, read the instruction booklet carefully and replace the rubber seal as recommended by the manufacturer.

Note: A bad seal in a pressure cooker can cause a destructive incident. Equipment doesn't have to be old or mistreated to cause an accident.

ALCOHOL TEST FOR PECTIN

Fruits can be checked for pectin by testing some of the cooked fruit juice. The fruit juice must be cooked for more than 5 minutes and cooled to get an accurate reading on the test. Mix 1 teaspoon of the juice with 1 teaspoon of rubbing alcohol (70 percent isopropyl alcohol) in a small jar with a lid. Shake the jar and pour the contents onto a plate. If a solid mass forms, the pectin level is high and a cup of sugar to juice, or juice with fruit, will be sufficient to cook down to a jellied product. If only some gelatin forms, 1 cup of juice will need ½ to ¾ cup of sugar. If no gel forms, you will need to add pectin from another source or, perhaps, cook the juice down further and re-test.

Caution: Do not taste the sample with the rubbing alcohol. Rubbing alcohol is for external use only and can cause serious gastric disturbances if ingested.

NATURAL PECTIN FROM APPLES

Not many people cook down apples anymore to make extracted pectin, but it can be done, if you have time, apples, or no desire to buy pectin. Cook washed and sliced tart apples in a ratio of 2 pounds to 1 quart of water for about 20-25 minutes. Strain and cook down the liquid to about 3 cups. Jamlady sometimes juices crab apples or very tart apples in her juicing machine. Juicing tough crab apples probably is not good for the machine nor recommended by the manufacturer, but Jamlady's has never broken. Add this juice into fruits that have low pectin. This method is a whole lot faster. This juice can also be cooked down, as Jamlady often does with plums, for a better set and a more intense flavor. Besides tart apples, lemons and some other citrus fruits are high in pectin and acid and are often added to fruits to assist the jelling process.

FAILURE

Even after doing what appears to be the right steps, some "jams" do not set right away. Don't panic! Wait at least 3 days to see if they eventually set. Jamlady once put hot pepper jelly away in disgust, returning three weeks later to find the jelly was still unset. Jamlady closed up the jelly case and forgot about it. Several months later, she looked in the case only to find that the jelly did indeed set. For this reason, Jamlady does not re-do batches. Just use the completed product as is and move on. Even unset hot pepper jelly can be used as a meat glaze, poured over a cottage cheese, or mixed with vinegar and use as a salad dressing. Failed jellies and preserves can be drizzled over pancakes or ice cream.

Jamlady has often found that if you don't tell anyone, they will never know you failed. Just present the product as ice-cream sauce, and it will be devoured. There is, however, one failure from which there is no return, the **scorched butter, jam, chutney,** or **preserves.** Minimize the tears and just throw it out fast. Try everything in your power to avoid burning butters and chutneys. Consider turning off the gas stove's burner or removing the pan from the electric range's burner if you have a ringing doorbell or telephone call. Set an alarm clock or timer for every so many minutes so you do not forget to stir the butter, chutney, or preserves. If you are the forgetful type, never preserve alone. As one of Jamlady's patrons told her, "My four year old reminds me to stir the strawberry preserves because she doesn't want them to burn, having had some of that slightly burned preserves just once!" Just in case some of you are imagining how you can cover up that burned taste—give it up! Even cinnamon doesn't work, but go ahead, try and cry!

ALTERNATIVE SUGARS

Many individuals ask for recipes using alternative sugars. Jamlady made this next jam with lite or low-sugar pectin. There is no added sugar or aspartame in this jam, but there is honey. The amount of honey is small, only ⅛ cup or 2 tablespoons per 8-ounce jar. This honey-sweetened jam is best kept in the refrigerator after being made, as it may weep some if left in the sunlight. Any weeping can be remedied by stirring up the jam before use.

Bee Peachy Jam

Only ⅛ cup of honey per 8-ounce jar.

5 cups peeled, chopped peaches
1 cup clover-ginseng or clover honey
¼ teaspoon ascorbic acid crystals or less
¼ cup lemon juice
1 1¾-ounce box "no-sugar" pectin

Use ascorbic acid in the prep water. Mix the pectin with the lemon juice and peaches; let the mixture sit for 2 minutes. Boil the mixture for 1 minute, stirring constantly. Add the honey; boil for 1 minute more. JSP/RWB5(4OZ)10(8OZ).

Note: The shelf life of this canned jam is 3-4 months. Refrigeration is recommended.

Another alternative to a jam with no added sugar, artificial sweetener, or honey is to use a small amount of maple syrup. This original Jamlady "jam," envisioned at midnight on July 12, 1998, combines maple syrup and peaches. Again, the shelf life of this canned product is 3-4 months, and Jamlady recommends storing it in the refrigerator.

Vermont Marries Georgia Jam

Great on waffles!
Only ⅛ cup of maple syrup per 8-ounce jar or ¹⁄₁₆ cup per 4-ounce jar.

5 cups peeled, chopped peaches
1 cup pure maple syrup
¼ teaspoon ascorbic acid crystals
¼ cup lemon juice
1 1¾-ounce box lite or "no-sugar" pectin

Use the ascorbic acid crystals on the peaches during their preparation and use a pinch in the prep or wash water. Mix the pectin with the lemon juice and peaches; let the mixture sit for 2 minutes. Boil the mixture for 1 minute, stirring constantly. Add the maple syrup and boil for 1 minute more. JSP/RWB5(4OZ)10(8OZ).

Lemon and Honey Jelly can be made with ¾ cup freshly juiced lemon juice; 1 tablespoon grated, outer, lemon rind; 2½ cups honey; and one 3-ounce pouch liquid pectin. Boil the lemon juice and rind with the honey, add the pectin and boil again for 1 minute. Remove from the heat and stir some more. JSP/RWB5(4OZ)10(8OZ). In the same recipe, other citrus juices could be tried instead of the lemon juice or in combination with the lemon juice. Just use the same ratios of honey to pectin to citrus juice. Ginger is optional, for **Gingered Lemon and Honey Jelly.**

Again, we are back to the aspartame as a sweetener. This Vermont Marries Georgia recipe, a peach jam made with lite or "no-sugar" pectin, could be made with a glycoside sweetener, but the cost would be higher. Jamlady thinks the most sensible solution to lower-sugar "jams" is to use LM pectin, lite, or "no-sugar" pectin, with only 1 cup of honey, maple syrup, or sugar per batch of jam. Still, if you can really have no sugar at all, then you will have to weigh your options.

Peachy Almond Sugar-Free Jam

Sweetened with aspartame.

5 cups peeled, chopped peaches
1 1¾-ounce box lite or "no-sugar" powdered pectin
¼ cup lemon juice
25 packets aspartame (or 1-3 cups sugar)
1 tablespoon pure almond extract
2 pinches ascorbic acid crystals

Use a pinch of ascorbic acid in the prep water and on the peaches while chopping them. Mix the peaches and lemon juice with the pectin. Wait 10 minutes and boil the mixture for 1 minute, stirring completely. Add the aspartame or sugar; boil for 1 minute more. Add the extract and boil for 30 seconds. JSP/RWB5(4OZ)10(8OZ).

It is possible to make a conserve with no added table or castor sugar.

Note: Castor sugar is table or granulated sugar. Many British or Australian books use the term "castor sugar," and it is sometimes confusing to young American cooks.

Conserve with No Added Sugar

A basic recipe—vary the choices given!

1 cup dried apricots or dried figs
2 cups water
2½ cups drained, shredded pineapple; peeled, sliced nectarines; peeled, sliced peaches; sliced rhubarb; or peeled, diced pears
Juice of 1 lemon
2 tablespoons sweetener equaling the sweetness of 1 cup sugar (or 1 cup sugar)
1 cup nuts or raisins (or ½ cup both)

Boil the apricots (or figs) in the water; then purée the apricots (or figs) in the blender. Cook the apricots (or figs) with the pineapple or alternate choice. Add the lemon juice; continue to cook until the right thickness is achieved. Add the sweetener, nuts, and/or raisins at the end. Figs go well with rhubarb. JSP/RWB5(4OZ)10(OZ).

Lite or " no-sugar" pectin (LM pectin) can be used to make "jams" with no sugar, low sugar, honey, maple syrup, or other sweeteners. **When using "no-sugar" pectin, 1-3 cups of sugar can be used for most all the recipes.** Most of the insert sheets for no-sugar jams list only single-fruit jams. Multifruit "jams" or "jams" made with juice and/or chopped fruits can be made just as easily.

Apricot-Orange Jam

Made with "no-sugar" pectin and sweetened with aspartame.

5 cups apricot pulp
⅛ teaspoon ascorbic acid or less
1 1¾-ounce box "no-sugar" pectin
1 grated orange peel
Juice of 1 'Valencia' orange
32 packets aspartame, alternate sweetener, nothing, or 1-3 cups of sugar
½ teaspoon ground cinnamon

Use a pinch of ascorbic acid crystal on the fruit during preparation and/or in the wash water. Juice the apricots or alternate fruit in a Champion juicing machine or equivalent machine. If you have no juicing machine, peel the fruits and chop them in the food processor. Mix the pectin with the apricots, orange peel, and orange juice. Let the mixture sit for 10 minutes. Stir and boil the mixture for 1 minute. Add the aspartame and cinnamon; boil for 1 minute more. JSP/RWB5(4OZ)10(8OZ).

Note: For those people who object to the process of boiling aspartame, this jam can be made without any sweetener, or the aspartame may be stirred in after the spread ("jam") cools some. The jar could then be sealed with hot paraffin and refrigerated.

*Variations: **Plain Apricot Jam**—Make without the grated orange peel or orange juice. Use 5 cups apricot pulp for 0-1 cup sugar or 6 cups apricot pulp for 2-3 cups sugar. For **Mango-Orange Jam, Peach-Orange Jam,** or **Nectarine-Orange Jam,** substitute mango, peach or nectarine, respectively, for the apricot.*

Peachy Cinnamon Sugar-Free Jam

Sweetened with aspartame or not sweetened.

5 cups peeled, chopped peaches
1 1¾-ounce box "no-sugar" powdered pectin
¼ cup lemon juice
25-30 packets aspartame, no sweetener, or 1-3 cups sugar
½ teaspoon ground cinnamon or 1 drop oil of cinnamon for a Genie Jam (both optional)

Mix the peaches, lemon juice, and cinnamon with the pectin. Let the mixture sit for 10 minutes. Boil 1 minute, stirring completely. Add the aspartame; boil 1 minute more or add the aspartame after the jam has cooled some. JSP/RWB5(4OZ)10(8OZ) or JSR (jar, seal, and refrigerate).

CITRUS FRUITS

This new recipe was made in the summer of 2000 and was the first time Jamlady used the **Clementine** or **mandarin orange,** *Citrus reticulata* (cultivar not identified), from Spanish cultivars, instead of Florida tangerines. Not to be unpatriotic, but Jamlady can tell you emphatically that the Spanish Clementines make the best **Oh My Darling Marmalade.** Henceforth, Jamlady pledges to pay more attention to Clementines and mandarins and to read more about the different cultivars. One citrus grower's Web site showed **17 cultivars of mandarins,** *Citrus reticulata.* There is no doubt that the diminutive, thin-skinned, orange Clementines from Spanish cultivars are more strongly flavored than many of the domestic varieties. It appears that some of these strains are grown in Australia as well as in Spain. In Spain, the bright-orange Clementine is grown in the Castellon-Valencia region of Spain's eastern seacoast, where a unique climate and just the right soil make conditions optimum for growing them. Domestically grown calamondins will work as well as Clementines, except that they fruit in January and there are not a lot of reasonably priced peaches available in January.

One **Australian grower** listed **8 cultivars of Clementines**—clone Spain—that, evidently, are available commercially. These are 'Marisol,' 'Oroval,' 'Nules,' 'Fina,' 'Clementard,' 'Fortune,' 'Fallglo,' and 'Nova'. According to several sources, the 'Marisol' and the 'Oroval' are about the same, but the 'Marisol' is harvested in late March and the 'Oroval' in April. 'Nules' is noted to be one of the most popular and is harvested in May. The 'Fina,' harvested in May, has a smooth rind, high juice content, and are very tender and sweet. The 'Clementard' matures in mid-July and August. Popular in Spain, the 'Fortune' cultivar has fruit of a good size, thin rind, and high acid. The 'Fallglo' matures at the end of April and in May and has a good size, flavor, and peeling ability, but has a lot of seeds. Interestingly enough, 'Fallglo' is a complex hybrid mix of ⅝ mandarin, ⅜ orange, and ⅛ grapefruit. The 'Nova' has a thin rind, medium size, high-quality flavor, and a reddish-orange color to its rind.

Jamlady assumes these harvest dates are for Australia and that harvest dates for Spain-grown Clementines start in November with 'Marisol' and 'Oronul' and continue with 'Oroval' and 'Clemenules' from November to January, and with 'Finas' from December to February. **With Australian and Spanish growing seasons exactly opposite to one another, it is possible to buy Clementines in the summer or the winter.**

Clementines seem to have a rating scale for the size with 'Oronuls,' being mostly 36s, 40s, and 45s and 'Finas' mostly 36s, 40s, 45s, with only a few 32s and 28s. These numbers correspond with the number of fruits in a 2.3-kilogram or 5-pound wooden gift box. A size #1, the larger size, has about 26-29 Clementines with diameters of 62-68 millimeters. A size #2 has about 30-33 Clementines with diameters of 58-66 millimeters, a size #3, has a count of 35-39 Clementines with diameters of 54-64 millimeters, and a size #4, the smallest size, has a count of 42-46 Clementines or a diameter of 50-60 millimeters. Jamlady's Clementines, which she purchased around July 20, were very thin skinned and especially flavorful and juicy. Jamlady paid no attention to the size rating or place of origin but will be sure to do so the next time she sees a crate of Clementines.

The Clementine from Spain is small, virtually seedless, and has a loose, "zipper" skin. Opinions vary regarding the origination of the Clementine. Some say it's a cross between an orange and a mandarin. Some say it is an accidental hybrid, discovered by a clergyman by the name of Pierre Clement Rodier in the garden of his orphanage in Misserghin, near Oran, Algeria, thus the name Clementine. Others say it's a Chinese variety that's been here a long time.

A single Clementine is the perfect snack fruit, because it only contains about 50 calories and provides half of an individual's vitamin C requirement for the day. Clementines have a lovely scent. Stack some in the center of your table as a scented display. Juice the fresh fruits for morning breakfast and don't toss out those peels. There is very little bitter, white part on them. Chop them in the processor, smell the aroma, and lift your spirits with instant aromatherapy. Lay some peels out to use in tea, or place some in a bottle of brandy, or use some in a beef-and-broccoli stir-fry. If concerned about unknown sprays, use a fruit wash on the fruit before eating or buy organic fruits.

This next Clementine marmalade recipe is easy to make and **appropriate for beginners!** This recipe has no added pectin, so this marmalade is inexpensive to make. Cook until you think the marmalade is thick enough. Beginners: refrigerate this marmalade to gauge its set. If the marmalade is not stiff enough, warm it up again, but very slowly. Stir the marmalade completely, scraping the bottom of the pan. It is easy to burn marmalade if the product is cold and one tries to quickly heat it up again. If afraid of burning the product, simply reheat it with a double boiler set up and then return it to the stove.

Oh My Darling Marmalade

A peach marmalade made with Clementines and no added pectin.

This marmalade is worthy of its own special name and has equal sugar to fruit.

6 cups sugar
5 cups peeled, chopped peaches
1 cup chopped pulp and juice of 3 Clementines
Finely chopped peel of 2 Clementines
2 tablespoons lemon juice
½ teaspoon butter

Cook all ingredients to set point. JSP/RWB5(4OZ)10(8OZ).

Variation: Peach-Valencia Marmalade—6 cups sugar, 5 cups peeled, chopped peaches, 1 cup chopped pulp and juice of 2 'Valencia' oranges, finely chopped peel of 1 'Valencia' orange, 2 tablespoons lemon juice, and ½ teaspoon butter.

The quality of these marmalade recipes all depends on the sweetness and flavor of the **Clementines, Valencias, Sevilles, blood oranges, kumquats, calamondins** (*X citrofortunella mitis* J. Ingram and H. E. Moore, or *Citrus mitis* Blanco), or other citrus fruits available for use. A marmalade can be no better than the flavor and freshness of the fruits used. Marmalades can be made from any citrus fruit. Jamlady has made marmalade from grapefruit, limes, kumquats, ugly fruits, tangerine, calamondins, Clementines, lemons, key limes, and other citrus fruits, alone and in combination with each other.

Amber Marmalade can be made with 1 grapefruit, orange, and lemon plus 6 cups water, and 7 cups sugar (added last). Use the whole fruit without removing the pith, or if you wish to remove the pith, add more grated rind or cook longer to achieve a set. **Kumquat Preserves or Marmalade** can be made with 4 pounds of thinly sliced kumquats and 8 cups of sugar. Cook the kumquats slowly without the sugar and then add in the sugar and cook or bake in the oven until done. Or, for **Kumquat Conserve,** add raisins,

nuts, or other ingredients of choice. Consider substituting kumquats or calamondins for the oranges in carrot marmalade. Check the pH, because kumquats are not as acidic as lemons, so you would need to use more kumquats and less carrots or acidify further with citric acid.

Lemon Marmalade can be made with a pound and a quarter of sugar to a pound of fruit, but use only half the peel. Add some grated gingerroot for a **Gingered Lemon Marmalade.** **Calamondin Marmalade** can be made with 2 cups puréed, seedless whole calamondin, 3 cups sugar, 1 cup fresh orange juice, and **Calamondin Preserves** can be made with equal parts of seedless purée of whole fruit and sugar.

Many Americans, unlike the average European, do not like a **bitter marmalade.** To the marmalade connoisseur, the bitterness is what makes the marmalade, marmalade. It is an acquired taste. One time, Jamlady made some lime marmalade without removing the pith. It took all season to sell it. One British fellow bought a jar and returned the next week for the remaining jars, stating it was the best lime marmalade he had ever eaten. Jamlady had had the lime marmalade out on sampling for three weeks running and had not sold one jar to an American. So, there are differences in cultures and acquired tastes. The next recipe is for pink grapefruit marmalade.

Pink Grapefruit Marmalade

A wonderful marmalade for a plain scone and tea!

5 cups, approximately 2 pink grapefruits (2½-3 pounds)
1 lemon
Water (sufficient to cover and a little more)

Wash the fruits carefully and completely. Cut the peels from the grapefruits and the lemon. Remove the white bitter parts from the rind and sliver the rind into small splinterlike pieces. Boil or microwave the rind pieces in water to remove some of the bitterness (5 minutes on the stove, 3 minutes in the microwave). Jamlady uses a bowl with a plate as a lid for the microwaving container, but a saucepan on top of the stove will work too. Discard the water and repeat process with fresh water. Discard the water and reserve the cooked rinds. Seed and pith the fruit. Finely chop the fruit pulps and reserve the juices. Either discard the seeds or put them in a spice bag and cook them with the marmalade. Some cooks cook them for a minute in the juice and strain, reserving the juice and disposing of the seeds. Place the cooked rind, grapefruit pulp, and juice in a saucepan and add about 2 cups of water. Bring the mixture to a boil and cook uncovered for about 10-12 minutes. Cool the mixture in the refrigerator overnight. In the morning, measure out equal sugar to cooled mixture of rind, pulp, and water; the water should have largely been boiled away. The overnight sit should have allowed the fruits and rinds to be plumped and made ready to accept the sugar. Basically, you are making a grapefruit preserve, as the ratio of sugar to fruits is equal. This "jam," according to Jamlady's definition, is called a marmalade because it contains rinds and also is a preserve because it is made with equal fruits to sugar. Cook the sugar and cooled mixture to 105 degrees C or 220-225 degrees F. Skim any foam. Test the set on a frozen plate. JSP/RWB10(8OZ).

The type of orange that is selected for any given batch of orange marmalade dramatically changes the flavor and color of the resulting marmalade. The **orange** belongs to the Rutaceae or Rue family. There are several varieties of oranges. The **bitter orange** or **Seville orange,** *Citrus aurantium* Linn. or *Citrus bigaradia* Risso (older name), is not easily obtained in the United States but is used to make the world-famous **Oxford Marmalade** or **Seville Marmalade.** Grand Marnier liqueur is made from *Citrus bigaradia,* Risso. The **sweet orange,** *Citrus sinensis* Osbeck, commonly grown in California and Florida, is used to make jellies, jams, and marmalades and can even be pickled. **Bitter-orange peel** is made from the rinds of unripe bitter oranges and **sweet-orange peel** is made from the ripe orange peel.

Jamlady Tip: To save the peel as spice, slice thin pieces of the peel without the white part from the orange. Chop the peels in a blender and dry. You can also grate the peel from the orange or sliver orange-peel pieces for use in tea or alcohol—like gin, rum, sherry, vodka, whiskey, or wine.

Orange peel derives its orange flavor from oil of orange. **Oil of orange** contains *limonene, citral,* and *terpineol* (all three lemon scents),

methyl anthranilate or *neroli oil* (orange-blossom flavor), and *linalool* (lavender scent). **Orange flower water,** a byproduct of the distillation processs, is used as flavoring for candy and baked goods, and it also is used in perfumes. Bitter oranges are similar, but they also contain *naringen* (bitter tasting). Both orange peels are colored with *hesperidin* (vitamin P), as are lemons. The **Mandarin orange,** *Citrus reticulata,* makes tasty marmalade, and the peel is used by Chinese herbalists to treat chest pain, congestion, and malaria. Medicinally, the Seville orange is the most valuable, but all orange peels are diuretics and digestive aids and provide a sedative effect on the digestive organs. Oranges are high in vitamins A, B, and C and contain antioxidants.

Jamlady Tip: Do not include the bitter, white part from any citrus peel, except when you want a more bitter taste.

Caution: Oil of orange or lemon can cause contact dermatitis in some individuals.

⁤

Orange Marmalade

The proper preserve for the toasted English muffin or an iced snowball!

Make this marmalade with blood oranges or Seville oranges, if you can find them.

7 cups sugar, approximately
8 oranges (sliced)
2 lemons
Water

Always begin by washing the citrus fruits well. If possible, use organic fruits or use a fruit wash. Since the peel will be consumed, Jamlady is very

sensitive to the issue of harmful sprays, dyes, and other substances that might be on these citrus fruits. Cut thin slices of peel from the oranges and lemons. Cut any white parts from the backside of the peels and discard the white parts. Slice the peels into small slivers. Cover the peels with water and cook for about 5 minutes. Strain and discard the water; reserve the slivered peel. Recover the peels with water and boil for another 5 minutes. Discard the water. **This process removes some of the bitterness.** Remove the white parts from the oranges and lemons and discard. Thinly slice the oranges and lemons and remove the seeds. Place the seeds in a spice or pip bag. Remove the core and discard. If you have a juicing machine and do not want any fibrous partitions in the marmalade, run the pulp through the juicing machine and use both outputs in the marmalade. Add the peel to the pulp and measure. Add 3 cups of water for every cup of pulp and slivered peel mixture. Add the **pip bag** and let the mixture sit overnight. In the morning, cook the mixture for about 35-40 minutes to plump the fruits and peel so they can receive the sugar. No sugar has been added to this point. Continue making the marmalade as a preserve, using 1 cup of pulp mixture to each cup of sugar. Boil rapidly until jell point is achieved. Test on a frozen plate. JSP/RWB10(8OZ).

Variations: This same recipe can be used to make other combinations of citrus marmalades. Jamlady has noticed so many new, citrus-hybrid names, like cit- range, citrandarin, citremon, citrumelo, citrangedin, citrangeremo, eremoradia, orangequat, ichandarin, lemandarin, limequat, siamelo, tangelolo, and tangor. There is no end to the number of combinations that can be used to make new marmalade formulations.

Jamlady has made another marmalade that is technically a butter, as it has lower sugar. The lower-sugar marmalade will not be clear and shiny, but it tastes great! View this lower-sugar marmalade recipe in the butter chapter. For **Whiskey Marmalade, Caribbean Marmalade, or Marnier Marmalade,** *¼ cup whiskey, rum, or Grand Marnier, respectively, can be added to marmalade, and some people cook marmalade with 2 tablespoons of molasses to enrich the flavor.* **Pineapple-Orange Marmalade** *can be made by adding equal parts of canned pineapple, in its juice, and sugar to the basic orange marmalade recipe. For another variation, try substituting 1 cup sugar with ¾ cup honey for* **Beekeeper's Marmalade,** *which is a honeyed orange marmalade.* **The substitution of just 1 cup sugar for ¾ cup honey can be done with most all of the citrus marmalades that have been made without added pectin.** *Honey can be added to recipes using "no-sugar" pectin, but you should not substitute honey for most or all the sugar in regular-pectin recipes.*

A small batch of orange marmalade can be made in the microwave. Mrs. Grace Schoonmaker provided Jamlady with this quick recipe. Make some for a couple of snowballs or can it in 4-ounce jars for a couple of small gifts.

Microwaved Orange Marmalade

A small-batch marmalade with no added pectin.

A good, quick-to-make recipe for the beginner.

2 or 3 well-washed, unpeeled large navel
  oranges* (cut into chunks)
2½ cups granulated sugar
Whole cloves

Wash the oranges and cut them into 1" chunks; remove all seeds. Processor-chop the orange pieces into ¼" x ¼" pieces and measure out 2½ cups. Place the sugar and the oranges in a microwave-safe bowl and mix. Microwave on high for 4-5 minutes; stir once. Microwave on high 4-5 minutes longer, until syrupy. Let the hot mixture stand in the microwave with the door open for 15 minutes. Add a clove or two to each jar. JSP/RWB10(4OZ) or JSR. Makes about 3¼ cups of marmalade. As with other marmalades, liqueurs, 1 tablespoon of molasses, flavorings, a rose-geranium leaf, nuts, currants, or raisins may be added.

The original recipe called for naval oranges, but other orange or citrus varieties, such as blood oranges or Clementines, can be used.

Caution: This is a good beginner recipe, but be careful not to burn yourself or allow the marmalade to explode on you. Microwaved foods can get superheated and can explode. When microwaving, wear eye protection.

Orange Jelly

A delicate jelly that can be subtlely flavored with different spices or spirits!

¾ cup lemon juice
2¼ cups water
6-7 whole oranges, sliced with peel on
Sugar
Liqueur (optional, to taste)

Combine the water and lemon juice and pour over the sliced oranges; let the mixture stand overnight. In the morning, boil the mixture until soft. Strain or hang the mixture from a jelly bag. Add 1¾ cups of sugar to each 2 cups of juice. Boil until the set point is reached. Check the set. If you desire extra flavorings for this jelly, consider a liqueur or, perhaps, an apricot brandy, apple brandy, or Jamaican rum. Make sure to recheck the set with the frozen plate. JSP/RWB10(8OZ).

*Variation: If you will flavor the jelly with rose geranium, for **Rose Geranium-Orange Jelly,** add the leaf during the last minute of boiling and then remove it. If you wish for a leaf to remain in the RWB-sealed jar, use a fresh leaf. Label the jar so the consumer knows the leaf is not supposed to be eaten.*

*Variation: As with the microwaved orange marmalade, a clove could be added to a jar of Orange Jelly. For a unique, cocktail-inspired jelly, add some grenadine syrup or passionfruit juice in place of some sugar and juice for **Jamlady's Orange Smiley Jelly.** Check out a bartender's book to see what flavors go well together in alcoholic drinks. This often gives you ideas for interesting "jam" combinations.*

*Variation: Substitute lime juice for lemon juice and add Grand Marnier or substitute limes, equaling the volume of 6-7 oranges, and add Grand Marnier for **Margarita Marmalade.***

*Variation: Infuse an herb, such as rosemary, in the water prior to making the orange jelly for **Orange-Rosemary Jelly.***

Variation: Jamlady has had several **Orange Jam** inquiries, one from as far away as England. This is not marmalade, as there are no rinds, and it is not jelly, for which all the solids are removed. To make this product, follow the recipe above but remove the rinds and place them in a spice bag, so they can be cooked with the orange pulp but removed when the juice/pulp is measured. Orange jam could also be made with no rinds at all, but it would take longer to cook or would require the addition of some pectin.

⟪⟫

SPIRITS IN JAMS

Some of the interesting alcoholic brandies or liqueurs that might be considered by the jam maker have been listed here. This is by no means an exhaustive list, and Jamlady has not tried even most of them, alone or in preserves, but has successfully used those marked with an **asterisk** in preserves. Jamlady has compiled this list of interesting spirits as a short course for those who are interested in trying different liqueurs and spirits, finding them when traveling in the countries in which the liqueurs originated, and utilizing them in all types of cooking, including canned "put-ups."

Some of you may even like to make your own liqueurs, which is very easy to do. Many manufactured liqueurs are regional products and are not distributed in the United States. When traveling, buy things you cannot get in the United States and then cry when they are gone. Some great wines from elderberries and other unusual berries are available in the state of Washington, for example, but are not even sold in neighboring Oregon.

This list further illustrates the ingenuity of man in utilizing plants, herbs, spices, roots, nuts, pits, and other indigenous materials to create unique liqueurs and other alcoholic and non-alcoholic drinks. Many of these secret formulas, made by families or monks, have been handed down generation after generation, some since medieval times. Look for minature sample bottles of quality liqueurs in stores and on the Internet. Jamlady spoke with a salesman from a British site called Just Minatures who stated they carry a quince liqueur made from 'Vranga' quince. So check around and experiment with new and different liqueurs in your jellies, jams, preserves, and butters, or just serve some for tasting.

Just as herbal vinegar can be homemade, herbal spirits can also be homemade. Many of these herbal spirits are known as *ratafias.* Originally the name *ratafia* was given to any liqueur offered at the ratification of a treaty. The word **tafia** in Creole means *rum.* Today, **a ratafia is any liqueur made by infusing fruits, herbs, or nut kernels in spirits of wine.** The liqueur is often sweetened and additional flavors may be added.

According to W. B. Dick's *Encyclopedia of Practical Receipts and Processes,* (1872): "Ratafia, may be made with the juice of any fruit." Dick cites a basic ratafia recipe for fruit juice: "Take 3 gallons cherry juice, 4 pounds sugar, dissolve in the cherry juice. Steep in 2½ gallons brandy 10 days 2 drachms [1 British fluid *drachm* = 0.961 United States fluid dram = ⅛ ounce United States] cinnamon, 24 cloves, 16 ounces peach . . ., 8 ounces bruised cherry kernels. Filter; mix both liquors, and filter again." Jamlady has not written the peach ingredient in this recipe (marked with an ellipsis) because it is peach leaves, and peach leaves, like the seeds of the mountain ash tree, contain the glycoside **amygdalin,** which quickly breaks down by hydrolysis from bruising, wilting, and frost damage into the highly toxic compound **hydrocyanic** (prussic) **acid** (or cyanide). While fresh peach leaves may be potentially less toxic than dried ones, and leaves generally have less of the amygdalin than the roots or pits, Jamlady says skip the peach leaves in any old recipes you find—like cordials recipes. Peach leaves as an ingredient can also be seen in pudding recipes (Miss Leslie of Philadelphia, *Seventy Five Receipts for Pastry Cakes*. Fine Custard—flavored with "a large handful of peach leaves.") Of course, the custard recipe is cooked, but the cordial recipe is not. See the discussion in the rowanberry/mountain ash berry section. One other point to consider on this issue of *amygdalin* in peach leaves and its use in ratafia is that low amounts of many substances like *amygdalin* were used medicinally for conditions like fever, dysentery, and nausea, when in higher doses it might have been toxic.

Jamlady often soaks pricked 'Damson' plums in vodka—the mixture of which can be sweetened—initially or later, and flavors with other herbs. **As a rule of thumb, a pound of any fruit or berries can be put with 3 cups of vodka or equal parts of grain alcohol and water plus 1-1¼ cups sugar to make a fruit liqueur.** Gin and other spirits can be used too. Try 4 cups sugar, 4 cups gin, 3 pounds plums, and spices for **Plum Cordial;** 2 cups ripe chokecherries, 1½ cups sugar, and 3 cups vodka or gin for **Chokecherry Cordial;** 2 cups currants or raspberries, 1 cup sugar, 1 cup vodka in a quart canning jar for 24 hours, strain, mix 1 pound sugar to 2 quarts of strained liquid and spices, such as ginger for **Currant Cordial;** or 1¼-1½ cups sour cherries, 1 cup sugar, 2 cups vodka, and spices like cinnamon stick, cloves, or vanilla pod (vanilla bean) for **Cherry Cordial.** Homemade cordials can be used to flavor your "jams," as can commercial brands. Experiment and imitate some of the commercial cordials.

Rum raisins are raisins that are first covered with rum or other spirits and then stored in a sealed jar. These drained raisins, or rum raisins, can be used in bread puddings, muffins, and other recipes. The entire product can be served over ice cream or thickened with cornstarch, instant CLEARJEL®, or arrowroot and used as a sauce for cakes or steamed puddings.

Jamlady Tip: Drained rum raisins can be stirred into a cold and completed jam or marmalade to make an alcoholic conserve, or they can be put into tomato marmalade.

QUICK REFERENCE TO SPIRITS AND LIQUEURS

For Flavoring Jellies, Jams, Preserves, Butters, Relishes, Pickles, Baked Goods, and Other Foods, or Just to Drink

The terms *liqueur* and *cordial* are often used synonymously. Webster's dictionary lists them as synonyms, but some people believe cordials are made from fruit pulps or juices and liqueurs are flavored with herbs, nuts, seeds, roots, spices, chocolates, flowers, and other plant parts. **These liqueurs or cordials can be homemade, generic, or proprietary. Famous proprietary liqueurs include Grand Marnier®, Kahlua®, Romana Sambuca®, Courvoisier®, and Galliano®.** A liqueur can be made by percolation, maceration, distillation, or by a combination of these methods.

The following list includes cordials and liqueurs that are commercially made and some that are no longer commercially made but have been included because homemade versions are always possible. There are many liqueur and cordial enthusiasts who have posted their knowledge on the Internet for others who are similarly motivated to make these wonderful elixirs and drinks. Some of these enthusiasts concentrate on reviving liqueurs, cordials, tonics, and elixirs that are no longer commercially manufactured, and others create new libations!

Absinthe—An anise seed or licorice-flavored alcoholic drink that contains harmful wormwood. Absinthe is illegal in the United States, but some countries still allow the production and sale of absinthe.

Absinthe substitutes—Abisante, Abson, Anisette, Mistra, Ojen, Oxygene, and Pernod.

Advocaat® or Egg Liqueur—A thick, creamy liqueur made with yolks and pure spirits. Dutch, English, Polish, and German manufacturers. Warninks Advocaat and Advocaat Gdanski. Make a "snowball" with 1½ ounces advocaat and 10 ounces lemonade.

Afrikoko—A coconut and chocolate liqueur, Sierra Leone.

Aiguebelle—A spicy, green or yellow, Trappist liqueur known for its restorative properties. Available at Abbaye Notre-Dame d' Aigebelle (www.abbaye-aiguebelle.com), France.

Alkermes—A traditional red liqueur from pure spirits, with flavors of cinnamon, coriander, nutmeg, orris root, vanilla, extract of roses, and jasmine. Made by the Carthusian monks in Italy. A dessert liqueur.

Alizé Gold Passion®—A blend of French Cognac and natural passionfruit juices. Also Alizé Red Passion and Wild Passion.

Alpestre—An Alpine herbal liqueur. (See www.monasteri.it.)

Amaretto*—An almond liqueur that is good in jams, macaroons, and cheesecake. Amaretto di Sarrono, Italy, Luxardo Amaretto.

Amer Picon®—A bitter, orange-flavored cordial of oranges, cinchona bark, and gentian. A drink, Picon Limon, is made with Crème de Cassis, lime juice, and Amer Picon, so this apéritif might go well in a currant, lemon, or lime preserve or marmalade.

Angelica Liqueur—A Basque liqueur flavored with angelica and other plants. A German variety includes violet extracts.

Anisetta Stellata—An Italian aniseed liqueur that is made in Pescara, Italy.

Anisette*—An anise seed, licorice-flavored liqueur. **Anis del Mono,** Barcelona, Spain.

Anthemis—A pale-green, herbal-mint

liqueur made by Benedictine monks. *Anthemis nobilis* is chamomile.

Apéritif—A general term for a predinner alcoholic drink, like vermouth, which is taken to stimulate the appetite.

Armagnac*—A type of dry brandy, drier than Cognac, which is from the Armagnac region of France.

Atholl Brose—An old Scottish drink made from Highland malt whiskey, uncooked oatmeal, honey, cream, and secret ingredients.

Baerenfang—A honey liqueur with extra flavor from lime flowers and mullein flowers, Germany.

Bahia—A coffee liqueur, Brazil.

B&B®—A mixture of Benedictine and French Cognac, drier than Benedictine.

Benedictine® D.O.M. (*Deo Optimo Maximo* or "To God most good, most great")*—A secret, twenty-seven-herb and spice formula first produced by Benedictine monks. Superb!

Ben Shalom—An Israeli liqueur from **'Jaffa' oranges.** 'Jaffa' oranges are a cultivar derived from *Citrus sinensis* (L.) Osbeck. There are many common names for the 'Jaffa' orange, such as Shamouti, Florida Jaffa, Palestine Jaffa, Yafa, and others—not all of them are actually 'Jaffa,' but 'Shamouti' and other cultivars, which are very similar to 'Jaffa.' For further inquiry, search the key word *Beledi*. According to James Saunt's *Citrus Varieties of the World* (Norwich, England: Sinclair International, 1990), the 'Jaffa' is an 1844 bud mutation of a local Israeli common orange. Sabrà is another Israeli liqueur and is made with chocolate and 'Jaffa' oranges. Jamlady could not find Ben Shalom to buy, but you can make homemade liqueurs from all sorts of oranges.

Bilberry (*Blaubeere*)—A full-bodied liqueur from the fermentation of Black Forest bilberries.

Bitters (several types)—Orange bitters made from the peel of the Seville orange, the orange of choice for marmalade.

Black Walnut—Domaine Charbay's Nostalgie™ Black Walnut Liqueur, United States. Tastes of egg cream, nutmeg, coffee bean, walnut, and other flavors. This liqueur is highly rated by experts! Use in all sorts of recipes.

Brandy* or **V.S.O.P.** Brandy*—Distilled from the fermented mash of grapes or other fruits. Brandy is aged in oak casks and can be fruit flavored with blackberries, peaches, apricots, cherries, ginger, and other ingredients.

Brontë—A brandy-based liqueur with honey and herbs, pottery container.

Cacao mit Nuss—A white liqueur with chocolate and hazelnut flavors, German.

Café Bénédictine®—A liqueur that blends coffee and Bénédictine.

Calisay®—A Spanish liqueur flavored with cinchona and other bark. See China.

Calvados,* Apple Brandy,* or **Applejack***—Distilled from apple cider. Good with sautéed chicken and apples.

Campari Aperitivo or **Campari Bitters***—An herbal apéritif with 25 percent alcohol. This spirit is not a bitter like most Americans think of bar bitters. Campari was founded by **Gaspare Campari** and has been in operation for many years. Serve Campari on ice or experiment with it in cooking. Campari is good on grapefruits and with oranges, and a tablespoon is good in a batch of marmalade. A little Campari is excellent in fig preserves, poached figs, or other fig dishes.

Can-y-Delyn—An herbal whisky-and-honey liqueur, Wales.

Capricornia®—An Australian liqueur made from tropical fruits.

Carlsbad Becherovka Becher Liqueur®—A bitter-herbal liqueur from Czechoslovakia or Germany.

Chambord®*—A liqueur made from small black raspberries, other fruits, herbs, and honey. Royal Chambord Liqueur de France.

Chartreuse® Green or **Yellow**—A green or yellow herbal liqueur formulated by Carthusian monks. Chartreuse® is made with 130 different herbs and is aged in oak barrels. French. Highly rated.

Cheri-Suisse®—A liqueur with the flavor of cherry-filled chocolates.

Cherry Blossom Liqueur—A pink liqueur from cherry blossoms, Japan.

Cherry Liqueur—Taam Pree Cherry Kosher Liqueur® (United States), Wisniowka Cherry Cordial® or Wisniak (*Wisniak* translated means *Polish cherry cordial*), Luxardo Morlacco® Cherry Liqueur, Cherry Grand Marnier® (France), Maraska Maraschino (Yugoslavia), Cherry Heering® (Danish), and a cherry-flavored beer or *kriek*—Lindemans Kriek Cherry Lambic Beer® or Book Krick Lambic Berry. Krieks are Belgian fruit beers or fruit beers of other countries. The fruit or juice is added to young Lambic, fermented, filtered, and bottled, according to www.euro-beer.co.uk.

China Elixir or **China Liqueur**—An old Chinese digestive liqueur. China Martini, a China liqueur, is described as made from *"China calissaia* (Italian) or Chinaroot, a tree originating high in the Andes mountains of Peru and Bolivia"* (www.yndella.com). Similarly, the same spelling is shown—"Liqueur of china calissaia"(Italian)—on the *"La bottega del Parco"* site. Jamlady found **Cinchona calsaya,** or **Yellow Cinchona,** to be the Latin name for other versions or spellings seen on Italian language sites—*Cinchona calissaia* Wedd. or *Quina Calissaia,* or *China Calissaia.* Anyone confused? Jamlady was. Turns out *China Calissaia* is the Italian name for *Cinchona calsaya* (quinine)—may be the cultivar name, as Jamlady did see it once as 'China Calissaia.' And do not even confuse yourself more with another China root, Galangal, *Alpinia officinarum* Hance., which also has been used to flavor liqueurs. Jamlady thinks she has just made her case for using Latin names and using them correctly. Cinchona Bark is also known as Peruvian Bark or Jesuits' Bark. China

liqueur is good for muscle aches and pains, and quinine is still used for malaria. Might be just the right liqueur for a "Fruitnic" preserve. See www.geoities./com/farmaciaguidetti/elixir.htm.

Coconut—Kamasutra Ginseng Coconut, Kalani Coconut Liqueur, and Marie Brizard Pineapple-Coconut Liqueur. See Malibu®.

Cognac*—A fine brandy from the Cognac region of France. **VS** or Three Star has to be 2.5 years old but usually is 4-7 years aged; **VSOP, VO,** legally has to be aged to 4.5 years but usually is 5-13 years aged; and **XO** Extra, Napoleon, Vieille Reserve or Hors d'Age legally must age for 6 years but usually is 4-40 years aged. It takes so little Cognac to flavor "jams" that Jamlady recommends you use the best you can afford. Jamlady uses **Courvoisier® Napoleon** in "jams" and pickled peaches or the upgrades from there. Look for sampler bottles, which contain enough for one batch of preserves or jam. Even if you pay $4-5 for the sampler, you have not spent that much per jar of jam. Pickled peaches, for example, need only 1 tablespoon of Cognac per quart jar. Remy Martin XO Special Cognac Fine Champagne is great but pricey, as is A. E. Dor Hors d'Age No. (various) Cognac Grande Champagne.

Cointreau®*—An orange-flavored liqueur, France. Highly rated.

Cream Liqueur, Key Lime—KeKe Beach Key Lime Cream Liqueur, taste of Key lime pie, Netherlands.

Crème d'Amandes—An almond liqueur (usually sweet).

Crème d'Ananas—A pineapple liqueur made with pineapple brandy and vanilla.

Crème de Banane—A banana liqueur, Australian and Turkish. Sometimes called Mus. Bols Crème de Banana.

Crème de Cacao* and **Crème de Cacao a la Vanille**—A liqueur from cacao and vanilla beans, colorless or brown.

Crème de Café—Coffee liqueur.

Crème de Cassis*—A liqueur from black currants. Great in blueberry preserves, chocolate recipes, and with fruit.

Crème de Cerise—A sweet cherry liqueur.

Crème de Fraises—A strawberry liqueur.

Crème de Framboise—A raspberry liqueur.

Crème de Genève—A juniper berry liqueur. Good with pears.

Crème de Mandarine—A liqueur made with dried tangerine peels.

Crème de Menthe—A peppermint liqueur, colorless or green.

Crème de Mure—A blackberry-flavored liqueur.

Crème de Noisettes*—A hazelnut liqueur (with floating hazelnuts). Meyer's brand is famous.

Crème de Noix—A liqueur from walnuts, southwestern France.

Crème de Noyau—A liqueur of almonds.

Crème de Prunella—French and Dutch liqueurs made from plums.

Crème de Vanille—A liqueur made from vanilla pods.

Crème de Yvette—A violet-flavored liqueur.

Cuaranta-y-Tres,* Quarenta Tres, or **Licor 43**—A gold-colored, nutty-flavored liqueur from Spain. Contains 43 herbs.

Curacao*—An excellent orange-flavored liqueur made of dried orange peel, Curaçao.

Cynar®—An artichoke-flavored apéritif, Italy.

Damina®—A light, herbal-based liqueur made from Damina, *Turnera aphrodisiaca.* Historically, this herbal tonic was used by the Guaycura Indians, and it is still used today for headaches or digestive complaints.

Danzig Goldwasser—A sweet, water-white aniseed and caraway liqueur with **gold flakes.** Produced since 1598, German. Gold flakes, or ***varak,*** are common in special-occasion Indian foods, and for that reason, this liqueur has gained popularity in India. Also made as **Danzig Silberwasser,** or **silver flakes.**

Date Cordial—See recipes for homemade date cordials (Meilach) or try Tamara (Israel).

Drambuie®*—A fine, aged scotch, delicate herbs plus honey.

Dubonnet®—A French apéritif, aromatic.

Eaux-de-Vie ('Waters of Life')—Fruit brandies from Germany and Switzerland, some distilled and some macerated production to preserve the flavor, which would be destroyed by distillation. Flavors of macerated ones: *Framboise* (raspberry), *Fraises* (strawberry), *Fraises de Bois* (wild strawberry), *mûre* (mulberry), *sureau* (elderberry), *sorbier* (rowan-berry-mountain ash tree berry), *gratte-cul* (holly-berry), fig (Morocco), and *baix de houx* (hips). Distilled ones: Quetsch, Kirsch, Mirabelle, Cassis, Apricot, Poire 'Williams', Prunelle, Vogelbeer. Some are made into liqueur with the addition of sugar (Poire 'Williams' & Framboise).

Eaux-de-Vie-de-Cidre (dePoire)—Fruit brandies made by distillation of cider: apple wine or perry (pear wine). Quince Eau de Vie is also produced.

Elixir d'Anvers—A green-yellow, 32-herb and seed liqueur with a bittersweet flavor, Belgian national liqueur. Made since 1863.

Elixir Dr. Roux—Aromatic herbal liqueur, France.

Elixir de Spa—An herbal liqueur formulated by the Capuchin Friars, historically recommended as a tonic and digestive aid (www.fx-debeukelaer.be). Very old formulation.

Enzian Liqueurs—A liqueur made from gentian plants in Bavaria (www.erniesdeli.com).

Escarchado—Sugar crystals are found in this Portuguese liqueur. An escarchado (frozen) liqueur is a liqueur that has more than 250 grams of sugar per litre or is supersaturated with sugar.

Ettaler Elixir—A yellow or green herbal liqueur made in Germany by monks. For more information, search www.google.com for *Ettaler cloister;* open ausflug.eng.

Farigoule—A green-golden liqueur of wild thyme.

Fig Liqueurs—The *eau-de-vie,* **Boukha**

Bokobsa (Tunisia), and the herb- and licorice-flavored fig liqueur, Thitarine, from North Africa. The owning family has been vinifying Boukha since 1870.

Filfar—An excellent, Cyproit, apéritif/liqueur of citrus and herbs; sixteen to eighteen oranges of different types are required to make one bottle of Filfar. Filfar's closely guarded secret recipe originated with the monks of Kantara and was passed down within the family of the current owner. Try this liqueur in jams or preserves.

Fior d'Alpi (Flower of the Alps)—An herbal liqueur with flower extracts from 1,000 flowers. This liqueur has a **"Christmas tree"** twig in the bottle on which the sugar crystallizes as it cools. Jamlady could not find a place to buy this liqueur, but she did find pictures of a bottle of it (www.hovard.org/vines/images/00097.jpg). (Go to Web site and select *liquori,* page 2, www.cosevecchie.com.) According to Jamlady's e-mail buddy who lives in Italy, Millefiori Cucchi, with a Christmas tree inside, has not been produced since 1965. He says he still has some because he bought some years ago in an old wine shop that does not exist anymore. There are many other flower-flavored liqueurs.

Forbidden Fruit Liqueur—A red liqueur that used to be made from oranges, brandy, and the citrus fruit **shaddock,** *Citrus maxima* (Burm.) Merr. (synonyms—*C. aurantium* var. *grandis, Aurantium maximum, C. decumana,* or *C. grandis*). According to barnonedrinks.com, this liqueur is currently not available commercially. Many experts agree that today's grapefruit is a cross between a sweet orange and *C. grandis,* the **"forbidden fruit."** The "forbidden fruit" was first identified in 1750 by Griffith Hughes and was likely transported around by English sea captain Phillip Shaddock circa 1649. Shaddocks, pummelos, and pomelos all fall within the classification of *Citrus maxima* (Burm.) Merr.

Frangelica*—A nutty liqueur made with hazelnuts. Good in cheesecakes, mousses, "jams," and peach recipes.

Galliano®—A pale, amber liqueur made with herbs, roots, and flowers and sold in a long, tapered bottle. The **Harvey Wallbanger** is purportedly named after an intoxicated, walking-into-the-wall surfer named Harvey who put Galliano in his orange juice and vodka, but the true story is utterly dependant on the storyteller.

Gilka Kaiser Kümmel*—A sweet, colorless liqueur that is flavored with caraway seed, cumin, and fennel. Kümmel was first distilled in Holland in the late sixteenth century but is now produced in Russia and Berlin, the Berlin kümmel being slightly smoother due to the longer distillation process. Kümmel is good in blueberry preserves.

Gin*—Flavored with orange, lemon, or mint.

Ginger Liqueurs—One spicy, Dutch, ginger liqueur is **"the King's Ginger Liqueur."** Another is an old formulation from the Quing dynasty: **Canton Ginger Liqueur,** which is made with six varieties of ginger and ginseng. Homemade ginger liqueurs can be made with macerated ginger root in pure spirits. **Just as homemade herbal vinegar can be made, so can homemade herbal spirits be made.** Barbados islanders put chilies in their rum. Try sherry with chilies, black pepper, cloves, allspice, and cinnamon or orange peel, like is done in Spain.

Giovanni Buton Gran Caffe Expresso—An Italian coffee liqueur, excellent.

Glayva—An herb and spice liqueur, Scotland. Similiar to Drambuie.

Godet Belgian White Chocolate Liqueur—Excellent in tiramisu ("Tuscan Trifle"), France.

Godiva*—A chocolate liqueur.

Goldschläger—A clear, cinnamon, schnapps liqueur with 24-karat, gold-leaf flakes; Switzerland.

Gorny Doubnyak—A bitter liqueur from Russia that is made from oil of ginger, galingale, angelica root, cloves, acorns, and oak shavings. Sounds interesting, but Jamlady couldn't find any to buy.

Grand Marnier®*—An orange-flavored brandy that is used extensively in jam making. Good with duck and in fancy desserts. **A liqueur similar to Grand Marnier can be made by combining a very finely chopped mixture of ⅓ cup orange zest and ½ cup sugar with 2 cups French brandy and ½ teaspoon glycerine.** Age all together and seal in a cool place for about 3 months. Shake several times during the process, then strain, and rebottle. Seville oranges have the best flavor for a liqueur seeking to approximate the quality of top, brand-name, orange liqueurs. **For more information, consult books like Cheryl Long's *Classic Liqueurs: The Art of Making and Cooking with Liqueurs.*** When traveling to the West Indies or countries like Spain, Italy, France, Curaçao, and Japan, pay attention to liqueurs and other spirits that are available there but difficult to find here in the United States.

Grappa—An Italian brandy made from the distillation of grape pomace (residue of grapes after pressing). There are four categories of grappa: new grappa, aged grappa, aromatic grappa, and flavored grappa. Grappa of Amarone Barrique, Venetian area, Italy; Torre di Luna Grappa; or Tignanello Grappa.

Grenadine Syrup*—A strong-flavored, red syrup made from pomegranates.

Guavaberry Liqueur*—A liqueur made from island guavaberries, Sint Maarten.

Hazelnut Liqueur*—Nutty-flavored liqueur. See Frangelica, Kamora, and Cacao mit Nuss.

Hiram Walker Rock and Rye—Citrus and other fruits in rye whiskey.

Honey Liqueurs—Liqueurs made with different kinds of honey. Wild Turkey is an excellent, bourbon-based honey liqueur.

Irish Mist*—A whisky liqueur with herbs and honey, excellent.

Izarra® (Basque for "Star")—A green or yellow herbal liqueur (Armagnac base).

Jägermeister—A dark-red herbal liqueur that is flavored with gentian, Germany.

Jamaican Pimento—An allspice berry liqueur (Meilach). Wray and Nephew Pimento Liqueur and Monte Aguila Liqueur, Jamaica.

Kahlúa® Lico de Café*—A Mexican coffee-flavored liqueur. Quite different from Tia Maria®. Good in preserves and tiramisu recipes. Kahlua Royal Cream Liqueur, Dutch, excellent. Godiva Tiramisu is similar.

Kakshe—A fruit brandy from Nepal.

Kamora*—A French vanilla-coffee liqueur and a hazelnut liqueur, Mexico. Recommended.

Karpi—A fine Finnish liqueur made from cranberries and other bittersweet, wild-growing berries from Finland's marshlands.

Keglevich*—A melon-flavored vodka and liqueur. Can be used in banana or peach jam.

Kenya Gold Liqueur—A fine coffee liqueur, Kenya.

Kirsch Mit Mokka—A coffee and cherry liqueur.

Kirsh,* **Quetsch**—A stone-fruit brandy such as *Eau-de-vie de Kirsh* (cherry), prune, *quetsch* (Switzen plum), and Mirabelle (Mirabelle plum). Good in raspberry, loganberry, and other berry preserves. Also good in strawberry-kiwi formulations.

Kiwi Liqueur—A kiwi-flavored liqueur, Wonder Bois Liqueur, Germany. Other companies: Teichenné and Campeny.

Kola Liqueurs—Liqueurs made from these: kolanuts, citrus peel, tonka beans, vanilla, and spices.

Krupnick—A honey liqueur, Poland.

Kümmel*—A liqueur of caraway and anise seeds with other herb flavors, a digestive tonic, Crème de Cumin. See Gilka.

Kumquat Liqueur—A liqueur of kumquats, Corfu, Greece. Try locating this liqueur and others on sites selling miniature bottles of liqueur (Morten's).

L' Angélique de Niort— The angelica, *Angelica archangelica,* of the town of Niort, France, is candied and made into a green herbal liqueur.

La Senancole—A yellow, aromatic, and spicy herbal liqueur made by monks. Marseilles, France.

La Vielle Cure®—An herbal liqueur with 50+ herbal ingredients in Armagnac and Cognac. A secret formula that has been made since medieval times. Do not confuse it with Chateau la Vielle Cure, a good wine.

Lemon Liqueurs—Crema di Limoncello, Rosolio, Agrumino, Kitron (Greek). Luxardo Limoncello, very good. Villa Massa Liquore di Limoni, Italy, and Caprinatura Lemon Liqueur, Italy, recommended.

Liqueur d'Or—The French and Dutch versions of goldwater, Danzig Goldwasser.

Madeira*—A kind of fortified wine made on the island of Madeira, Portugal.

Malibu®*—A coconut liqueur. Jamlady has used Malibu but does not recommend it for jam making. **San Tropique*** is a recommended brand of coconut liqueur, but it is often hard to find. **Captain Morgan's*** coconut rum is good in Pina Colada "jams."

Mango Liqueur—Many mango liqueurs are homemade (Meilach). Cruzan Mango Rum, St. Croix.

Maple Liqueur—A unique liqueur made in Canada.

Maraschino—A cherry liqueur. Luxardo Maraschino®, (clear, not red in color) a marasca cherry liqueur with many culinary uses, has been produced since 1821. Recommended. See cherry.

Mastic, Masticha, Mastika—A licorice liqueur from aniseed and the gum of a cashew-family tree, *Pistacia lentiscus.*. Look to buy this popular Levantine liqueur on the island of Chios, Greece. See fig preserves.

Melocoton—A peach liqueur, Licor De Melocoton, Malaga, Spain; and Artic Vodka and Peach, Italy. Nectarine versions are often homemade.

Mesimarja Liqueur®—A smooth liqueur that is made from *mesimarja* berries (Finnish word), literally *honey-berry*. **Arctic-stone bramble berries,** *Rubus arcticus* Linn., L and P also make Mesimarja-Vadelma (raspberry) Liqueur, and a Lakka Light Liqueur from **cloudberries,** *Rubus chamaemorus.* Lignell and Piispanen, has manufactured liqueur since 1882. L and P e-mailed Jamlady a list of their various mesimarja products; they come in several versions and colors.

Milk Liqueur—Milk and cream liqueurs were introduced in the 1970s. Example: "Aberdeen Cows," Old Boston.

Millefiori—A liqueur flavored with flower petals and plants. See Fior d'Alpi.

Mint, Roman Mint, *Mentuccia* (Italian), *Calamintha officinalis*—Italians in the Abruzzi mountain area produce a bitter mint and multi-herbal, after-dinner liqueur known as **Centerbe.** This liqueur dates back to the fifteenth and sixteenth centuries and is similar to **"Terriaca Universale,"** which contained over ninety-nine medical ingredients. See Jamlady's source, *La Nostra Storia* (www.nonasteri.it/en/order/products.doc). Also see Bénéfort Centerbe Liqueur at yndella.com.

Murtaberry Liqueurs from *Myrtus communis* or myrtle berries—Tremontis Liquore di Mirto is made with no preservatives from an infusion of myrtle berries in alcohol and sugar, Sardinia. Also, Mirto San Martino Liqueur—**Murtaberry Syrup** is made from the murta or murtaberries in Puerto Rico and Brazil, with equal parts juice to sugar, and Caribbean islanders make **Murtaberry Cordial** from murtaberries, sugar, and brandy.

Nocino—Pure spirits infused with tender, green walnuts. Italian. Nocino Falad is seen at yndella.com. This liqueur is often used to flavor ice cream. Try some with preserves.

Noyau—An almond-flavored liqueur made from extracts of peach and apricot kernels. Some water-white, some pink. French producer Vve Champion.

Nut liqueurs—Hazelnut Liqueur; Praline Liqueur; Peanut Liqueur; Marron Chestnut Liqueur, Italy; Frangelico Hazelnut, Italy; Domaine des Chestnut Liqueur; and others. See pine nut, Nocino, Noyau, black walnut, and Crème de versions, listed above.

Okhotnichya, "Hunter's Brandy"—A brandy infused with citrus peel, ginger, galingale, clove, pepper, juniper, coffee, and aniseed, Russian. Stoli Vodka Okhotnichya.

Old Jamaica Blue Mountain Coffee Liqueur—A rum and coffee liqueur. Look for Sangster's Old Jamaica Liqueurs while at the Appleton Estates in Jamaica.

Oran-Pear—An orange-pear liqueur. **Oran-Pear Liqueur** can be made at home with ½ pound pears, 1¼ cups sugar, ½ pound orange peels and 1 cup grain alcohol. Many liqueurs can easily be made at home—easier than making wines and just as good for holiday or hostess gifts. Peeling the pears is recommended for some varieties of pears.

Ouzo*—A licorice-flavored apéritif from Greece and Cyprus. Turns white on ice. Made with aniseed or by an alternative distillation method. Try Ouzo No. 12, Greece.

Pamplemousse—A citrus liqueur, Spain. *Pamplemousse* is French for *pummelo*. See "Forbidden Fruit."

Papaya rum—Papaya or papaya and flower petals.

Parfait Amour (perfect love)—A citrus and violet liqueur, sometimes lemon peel and vanilla. Wyand-Fockink Parfait Amour, Holland. Similar to Crème de Violettes.

Passion Fruit—A sweet citrus-flavored Australian liqueur. Bantu: a German passion-fruit-citrus liqueur. Passoa. See Alizé.

Peppermint Schnapps*—A peppermint spirit, usually with a higher alcohol content than Crème de Menthe.

Pernod*—A French anise-flavored liqueur made with special anise seeds from the "star aniseed" (*anis étoilé*). Turns green in water.

Pimm's Cup No. 1®—An old-English, gin-based drink that is infused with aromatics. Pimm's Cup No. 1 has been around for over 150 years. Other versions, No. 2 scotch, No. 3 brandy, No. 4 rum, No. 5 rye, and No. 6 vodka, have been introduced over the years, but only the original No. 1 and vodka-based No. 7 have continued to be made. Try some at Wimbledon; they serve a lot of it there.

Pimpeltjens—A Dutch citrus liqueur, has been made for three centuries. Delft design bottle.

Pineapple Liqueur—Dekuyper Pineapple Liqueur or homemade pineapple liqueur from 2 cups pineapple, ½ teaspoon vanilla, 2½ cups vodka, and ½ cup simple syrup. See various Internet sites on homemade liqueurs.

Pine Nut—A homemade liquor made with vodka, toasted pine nuts, vanilla, and simple syrup (McMorran). **A simple syrup can be made with 4 cups sugar simmered with 4 cups water.**

Pisco—A distilled spirit made from wine in South America. Usually made from the highly aromatic and orange-like muscat grape. Pisco Capal or Pisco Control.

Pistachia—A liqueur made from walnuts or pistachio nuts (Meilach).

Poire Williams—An eau-de-vie produced from 'William' pears. Especially famous for the fruit brandy's presentation in a pear-shaped bottle—**a full-sized pear in the bottle,** the pear having been grown within the bottle by attaching a bottle to a pear tree's individual blossom. Subtle flavor of pears. ***Note: Eau-de-vie or eaux-de-vie (denotes singular and plural respectively).***

Ponche—A brown Spanish liqueur, tasting somewhat like sherry. See Spanish "Ponche Liqueur Sherry" at wwwoutback.co.uk/winelist.htm. Ponche Crema (www.pinkpages.bm).

Poncio—An Italian citrus and vanilla liqueur. Poncio is a typical liqueur of the Molise region of Italy (www.agricolturaoggi.com).

Port*—A strong, sweet wine, either dark red, tawny, or occasionally white; originally from

Portugal. Port makes good wine jelly. Styles of port: white port, ruby port, tawny port, aged tawny port, colheita port, late-bottled vintage port, crusted port, vintage-character port, vintage port, and single quinta.

Pulque—A Mexican drink made of fermented maguey juice.

Quince—A liqueur of quince is made by Bramley & Gage (Devon, England). Another, Emil Scheibel Black Forest Quitten-Liqueur. See homemade recipes (www.guntheranderson.com).

Raki—A Turkish, aniseed-flavored liqueur that is often served on the rocks with water. The term *raki* is now generic. Raki tastes something like Pernod.

Raspail—A yellow, herbal, and medicinal liqueur containing angelica, calamus, and myrrh. French. Interestingly enough, in 1847, François Vincent Raspail made a medicinal liqueur for the purpose of destroying parasites in humans (www.pinkieonline.com/cordials.htm). Raspail was a very colorful figure.

Reserva de Señor Almendrado (Height of the Almond)—Tequila and almonds, Mexico.

Rhubarb Liqueur—A homemade liqueur made from rhubarb, sugar, and vodka (Long).

Rompope—96-proof alcohol with milk, sugar, egg yolks, and vanilla, Mexico. Santa Clara Rompope.

Root Beer Schnapps*—A root-beer-flavored liqueur.

Rowanberry or Mountain Ash—A liqueur of rowanberries. The Russian factory of Petrovskyi, label: Spirit of the Northland of Karelia, makes vodka that is flavored with rowanberries, or *ryabinovaya,* as well as vodkas that are flavored with other wild berries. Additionally, they produce **Karelian Balm,** a liqueur of thirty cure grasses, berries, and roots (aurinko.karelia.ru/u/petrovski/pricee_e.html). See rowanberry discussions in other parts of this book.

Rums*—Light and dark, which has richer molasses flavor. Flavored rum such as Captain Morgan Coconut Rum or St. Tropique (coconut).

Sambuca*—A white or dark-colored liqueur made with elderberries and aniseed. The terms white sambuca or black sambuca are used to delineate between the clear or dark product. Try Romana Della Notte Black Sambuca, Luxardo Sambuca, or Opal Nera Black Sambuca, Italy. Sambuca is good in blueberry preserves.

Sève d' Or—A sweet and smooth fruit liqueur that is based on Cognac.

Sherry*—A strong wine originally made in the south of Spain. Many styles of sherry: Manzanilla, Fino, Amontillado, Palo Cortado, Oloroso, Cream, Pedro Ximenez, Moscatel, Old East India, and Almacenista. Look for names like Domecq, Lustau, Argueso. Harvey's Rare Oloroso Sherry is well rated.

Slivovitz—A distilled plum brandy. Jamlady brought some Slivovitz back from a Russian trip and can attest to its "high octane."

Sloe Gin*—Sloe berries of the wild European plum, **blackthorn bush,** *Prunus spinosa,* are purple-skinned and tart. The liqueur does little for jams, at least the brands Jamlady has tried. It is best to make the jam directly from the berries, after the first frost. **Blackthorn Jelly**—cook the berries and crab apples, extract the juice, and make as preserves with equal sugar to juice. Spice with cinnamon and allspice and use brown or white sugar.

St. Hallvard—A yellow herbal liqueur made from a potato-based spirit with many herbs and spices. This Norwegian liqueur is aged in oak barrels.

Stonsdorfer—A dark, bitter, herbal, and bilberry liqueur, Germany.

Strega—An Italian yellow/green-hued herbal liqueur with over 70 herbs and barks. Tradition says those who drink it together are united forever. Liquore Strega.

St. Rémy Fontainebleau*—A liqueur with brandy and coffee.

Tamara—A date liqueur, Israel.

Tangerine Liqueur—Tangerine peel or fruit in brandy. Manderine Napoleon, aged Cognac with tangerine flavor, Belgium.

Tapio—A clear herb-and-juniper liqueur, Finland.

Tea Liqueurs—See recipes on the Internet for homemade, but basically tea leaves in vodka for twenty-four hours, strain, then add simple syrup.

Tequila*—A colorless Mexican liquor made from the mescal plant. Not the same as Pulque, but made from the same plant.

Tia Maria*—A Jamaican rum liqueur with the essence of Blue mountain coffee beans, spices, and other ingredients.

Trimbach Liqueur de Framboise—A French raspberry liqueur. Very good with fruit salad and ice cream.

Triple Sec*—A colorless liqueur like Curacao, but less sweet.

Tuaca—An amber, brandy liqueur with flavors of vanilla and orange—the secret formula of Lorenzo the Magnificent, ruler of Florence.

Van der Hum—A deep-amber, brandy-based liqueur to which wine distillates, tangerine peels, herbs, and spices have been added. Named after Admiral Van der Hum of the Dutch East India Company, this South African, naartjie-peel (Afrikaans) liqueur can be homemade. Soak for one month: 6 cloves, 1 cinnamon stick, ½ grated nutmeg, 750 millileter brandy, ¼ cup rum, and 1-2 ounces naartjie, *Citrus reticulata;* tangerine; mandarin; or calmondin peel; strain and add a sugar syrup of 1 cup water to 9-10 ounces of sugar. Some recipes eliminate the water and rum and add the sugar to the whole mix initially, and some recipes additionally flavor with 1-2 extra green cardamom seeds. Shake the mixture daily. Hum: put some in preserves or marmalade? To buy, look for KWV Van der Hum Cream Liqueur.

Vandermint—A minted chocolate liqueur, Dutch. Delft bottle.

Verveine du Velay Elixir—This herbal liqueur of thirty-two plants, one version green and one yellow, has been made in the south of France since 1859.

Vodka or **Zubrovka**—Flavored vodkas such as orange, lemon, mint, grape, or buffalo grass.

Whiskey or **Bourbon**—Flavored whiskey, like CC Citrus, lemon; Glen Mist; or Irish Mist Liqueur, honey, orange, and spices.

Wines and **Champagnes***—Fermented juice of fruits. Many kinds of wines and champagnes are used in cooking and pickling. Wine itself can be made into both wine or herbal-wine jellies. Homemade wines from unusual fruits can be used to make very interesting jellies.

Unicum Zwack—A bitter liqueur of 40 herbs.

ASIAN AND EUROPEAN PEARS

Asian pears (see p. 203) are not the same as regular **European pears,** *Pyrus communis.* Asian pears are genetically different. Although the fruit is called a **pear apple** or an **apple pear,** it is not a cross between an apple and a pear. Asian pears have been around for at least three thousand years; they just haven't been grown much in the United States—even though Chinese immigrants brought them to the American West Coast in the 1800s.

Asian pears are either **Ussuri pears,** *Pyrus ussuriensis,* or **Japanese sand pears,** *Pyrus pyrifolia,* or a complex hybrid of the two. The Japanese types are round as an apple, and the Chinese varieties, which produce more fruit, are pear shaped. The Japanese varieties are further divided into the **smooth**, with colors of green to greenish-yellow, or the **russetish**-skin texture, with colors of brownish-green to copper. A 'Chojuro' pear might well be mistaken for a 'Golden Russet' Apple.

Unlike European pears, which can be picked prior to ripening, Asian pears must ripen on the tree and then be picked, as they will not ripen after being picked. European pears are soft and melt in your mouth, and Asian pears are crispy, juicy, and very sweet, as they are low acid. Nichols Farm and Orchard in Marengo, Illinois, a vendor at some of Jamlady's Chicagoland markets, supplies Jamlady with 'Chojuro' pears, and they are wonderful!

European pears

'Chojuro' Pear Jam

Delicious 'Chojuro' pears are shaped like apples.

5 cups sugar
4 cups peeled, chopped 'Chojuro' pears (or any pear apple or European pear)
¼ teaspoon or less ascorbic acid crystals
1 1¾-ounce box regular powdered pectin
2 tablespoons lemon juice

To minimize the oxidation, use ascorbic acid crystals, one small pinch at a time, while preparing and washing the fruit. Mix the chopped 'Chojuro' pears with pectin and lemon juice. Wait 10 minutes; boil for 1 minute. Add the sugar; boil 1 minute more. JSP/RWB5(4OZ)10(8OZ).

Several sources state that the 'Housi' has the best flavor and ripens in August, but the 'Chojuro', an older variety, ripens in mid-August, keeps for five months' time, and is fireblight resistant and good tasting. While the skins may be faulted for being somewhat astringent, this factor does not come into play when they are peeled for jam. Fresh 'Chujoros' have good, full-bodied flavor, which is essential for tasty jam.

The Lloyd Nichols family has had good luck growing the 'Chojuro' cultivar, and this cultivar is the only Asian pear cultivar in quantity, with which Jamlady has had to work. 'Chojuro' pears make very acceptable jam. Jamlady loves freshly picked 'Chojuro' pears as hand fruits. The 'Chojuro' pear's white flesh and mild sweetness contrasted with its firm texture is a culinary delight. A variation of the basic 'Chojuro' pear recipe can be seen in this next Jamlady recipe utilizing dried currants.

Jamlady's Original Violet 'Chojuro' Pear Jam

These very crisp and tasty Asian pears are good with dried currants.

Currants add the lavender color and complementary flavor!

5 cups sugar
4 cups peeled, chopped Asian pears (or European pears)
¼ teaspoon or less ascorbic acid crystals
1 1¾-ounce box regular powdered pectin
½ cup dried currants
2 tablespoons freshly squeezed lemon juice

Use small pinches of ascorbic acid crystals on the newly cut fruit and in the prep water. Mix the chopped Asian pears with the pectin and lemon juice. Wait 10 minutes. Add the currants; boil for 1 minute. Add the sugar; boil 1 minute more. JSP/RWB5(4OZ)10(8OZ) or JSR. **Variation in technique: To reduce bleeding of colors, add the currants as you ladle the jam into the jars, and seal with hot paraffin wax or cap when very hot (JSR).**

Classic Victorian Pear Preserves

This preserve is the perfect topping for scones at high tea!
No added pectin or lemon rind is used.

8 cups peeled, sliced pears
2 cups sugar
1 cup water
Juice of ½-1 lemon
⅛ teaspoon ascorbic acid crystals

Use the ascorbic acid sparingly in the prep water and on the newly sliced pears. Cook the pears, water, sugar, and lemon juice until thick! JSP/RWB10. To cook down the pear preserves more quickly, use a ¼ recipe and a smaller pan with a smaller diameter. (See the next recipe.)

Classically, pear preserves were made with lemons and sometimes gingerroot. This original Jamlady recipe substitutes oranges for lemons and doubles the quantity of citrus fruit. Additionally, no rind is used, which is usually seen in pear honey, a sweeter version of pear preserves.

Look for plump, healthy rhizomes of **gingerroot,** *Zingiber officinale* Rose. Peel the gingerroot prior to putting it into "jams." Gingerroot may also be candied. Ginger is used for nausea, flatulence, and as a febrifuge. **The *gingerols, zingerone, paradols,* and *shogaols* are responsible for ginger's nippy or biting taste and possible antifungal qualities** (Christine E. Flicker et al., "Inhibition of Human Pathogenic Fungi by Ethnobotanically Selected Plant Extracts," *Mycoses* 43, nos. 1-2 [2003]).

Gingered Pear Preserves d'Orange

Not a quick recipe, but well worth the effort and the wait.
Mete out some, but keep a stash for yourself!

16 cups peeled, sliced pears (4 pounds)
4 cups sugar
2 cups water
Juice from 2 large or 3 small oranges (no white pith or rind used)
2 ounces peeled, finely grated gingerroot

The fruits in this recipe may be cooked first with water. Or, cook the fruits with all of the ingredients—very slowly and with very low heat—until thick. Cook the water with the fruits to plump them, so the sugar can enter the fruits more easily. To avoid burning the preserves, stir constantly. Refrigerate the preserves overnight to check the thickness. If the preserves are not thick enough, reheat them, stirring constantly. These preserves must be carefully watched at all times. One little burn and you have spoiled the entire batch! JSP/RWB5(4OZ)10(8OZ).

Variation: Gingered Pear and Apple Preserves d'Orange or Classic Victorian Pear and Apple Preserves can be made with the recipes above by using 60 percent pears and 40 percent apples.

Note: For faster results, half or quarter these pear recipes. Usually, smaller batches of preserves turn out better and cook down much faster. Indeed, very small batches of some preserves might even be considered convenience foods, as they can be made so quickly!

During the nineteenth century, **pear honey** and other similar **"fruit honeys"** were known as **"spoon sweets"** because they were put on the table in small silver or crystal bowls with small spoons resembling the baby spoons of today. Pear honey has 6 cups water and 6 cups sugar to 16 cups of pears (4 pounds), whereas pear preserves has 4 cups sugar and 2 cups of water to 16 cups of pears. Still, pear honey is low in sugar when compared to many other jams or jellies. **Classically, no pectin is added to either pear honey or pear preserves.** Pear preserves are great on pancakes, pudding, dessert, yogurt, ice cream, bread pudding, cake, or muffins. Jamlady prefers pear preserves to pear honey and Gingered Pear Preserves d'Orange to Classic Pear Preserves. Pear lovers like all three, with most people asking for the Classic Pear Preserves.

The Greeks make sour cherry or **'Morello' preserves,** *Vissino Glyko,* which they mix into iced water or mineral water to make a cherry drink known as *Vissinada.* If ever served a bowl of cherry preserves with a glass of water and a spoon, do not eat the preserves from the spoon, but place a spoonful of the **"spoon sweets"** into the glass, stir, and drink.

ᘒᘓ

Pear Honey

A spoon sweet.

A jam fitly named is "like apples of gold in pictures of silver" (Prov. 25:11)!

16 cups peeled, finely grated pears (4 pounds)
6 cups sugar
6 cups water (to plump the preserves)
3 tablespoons freshly squeezed lemon juice
Grated zest of 1 lemon in some water

Parboil the grated lemon zest in water (enough to cover the lemon zest twice over); strain. Reserve the grated rind; discard the water.

Cook the first four ingredients plus the prepared lemon zest together, very slowly, until thick. Chill; check the thickness. If the pear honey is not done, continue to cook, but be very careful not to burn it. Stir constantly and use a spatula to get the settled "honey" off the bottom of the pan, while slowly heating it. Expect to cook this full-sized recipe all day or longer. Cook some and allow the preserves to cool some (Switch Method or SM). Use evaporation to your advantage. This recipe may be halved or quartered to lessen the cooking time. A smaller batch size will maintain the integrity of the fruit best. JSP/RWB10(8OZ).

One year Jamlady made a jar of this next pear jam without the oil of cinnamon, especially for some elementary-school students who were reading a book about eating pear jelly! Jamlady's pears grow on two, young, European pear, *Pyrus communis,* trees that yearly produce only about 50 pears each. There are two pear trees, because two are necessary for cross-pollination. Both trees were purchased, half dead, at a closeout sale for three dollars each. Each year as the trees get larger, there are more pears, but they must be picked quickly, as the squirrels also love pears! These small trees are never sprayed, and the pears are still perfect! What luck! Jamlady coined the term "Genie Jam" because of oil of cinnamon's tongue-tingling effect! Make Raspberry Genie, Kiwi Genie, and other wonderful Genie Jams! Each bite is a sensory sensation!

Pear Genie Jam

As with all Genie Jams, the genie says "ta-dah"!

5 cups sugar
4 cups peeled, chopped pears (Asian pears or apples)
¼ teaspoon or less ascorbic acid crystals
1 1¾-ounce box regular powdered pectin
2 tablespoons lemon juice
1-2 drops oil of cinnamon

Use small pinches of ascorbic acid crystals on the pears to inhibit browning. Also use some ascorbic acid crystals in the prep water while peeling the pears. Mix the chopped pears with the pectin and lemon juice. After 10 minutes, boil for 1 minute. Add the sugar; boil for 1 minute. Add the oil of cinnamon; boil for 30 seconds. JSP/RWB10.

Variations: Pear Jam—Use the same recipe as above, but without the oil of cinnamon. **Pear 42 Jam**—*Add ¼ to ⅓ cup of Liqueur 43 to Pear Jam at the end; boil for 1 more minute. Check the set.*
Note: **JSP** *stands for jar, seal, and process.* **JSP/RWB10** *means jar, seal, and process in a rolling water bath for 10 minutes.* **JSR** *means jar, seal (by inversion or paraffin—or by just screwing on a lid), and refrigerate.*

Jamlady first encountered Liqueur 43 when a market patron, recently back from a trip to Spain, gave her a dozen sample bottles of *Cuarenta y Tres,* Liqueur 43. Jamlady has purchased Liqueur 43 over and over and has used it in many different jams.

Dried cranberries can be added to this same basic pear jam recipe for another effect. Jamlady has concocted several new jam recipes by experimenting with **contrasting jams** such as **Pear 'N Cranberry Jam, Violet 'Chojuro' Jam, Blueberries in the Snow,** and **Cranberries in the Snow.**

Pear 'N Cranberry Jam

The cranberries are added at the very end.

5 cups sugar
4 cups peeled, chopped pears
1¼ cups water
1 cup dried cranberries
2 tablespoons lemon juice
½ teaspoon cinnamon or oil of cinnamon to taste (optional)
True cinnamon sticks, 1 per jar (optional)
2 pinches ascorbic acid crystals
1 1¾-ounce box regular powdered pectin

Use a pinch of ascorbic acid crystals in the prep water and on the newly cut pears. Mix the chopped pears with the pectin, water, lemon juice, and ground cinnamon. Wait 10 minutes and boil for 1 minute. Add the sugar; boil 1 minute more. Add the cranberries, either into the hot jam or into the jars of hot jam after the jars have been filled. Place the cinnamon stick inside the jar. JSR or JSP/RWB10. If using oil of cinnamon, add it last into 1 cup of completed jam and add that jam slowly into the rest of the batch—to avoid getting too much oil of cinnamon.

Note: Different results are obtained if the cranberries are added in the beginning of the cooking process. The preferred, contrasting look is achieved when the cranberries do not intermix with or bleed into the pears, and the pristine-white pear jam is in direct contrast to the dried-red cranberries.

This next jam is inspired by classic Dutch Apple Pie and Dutch Pear Pie. Make this recipe with pears, apples, or Asian pears. Jamlady makes both sugar and "sugar-free" Dutch pear pie jams and pies.

Dutch Pear Pie Jam #2 or Dutch Apple Pie Jam #2

A "sugar-free" "jam."
Sweetened with aspartame.

4 cups peeled, chopped pears, apples, or Asian
  pears (or 6 cups with sugar)
¼ teaspoon or less ascorbic acid crystals
1 1¾-ounce box lite or "no-sugar" pectin
½ cup raisins or dried currants
2 tablespoons lemon juice
20 packets aspartame or alternate sweetener (or
  2-3 cups sugar)
1 teaspoon cinnamon
¼ teaspoon allspice or nutmeg

Wash the pears in water with a pinch of
ascorbic acid crystals. Peel the pears and rinse
them with water that has been laced with a little
pinch of ascorbic acid crystals. Chop the pears,
also using a pinch of ascorbic acid crystals. Let
the pectin sit with chopped pears, lemon juice,
raisins, and spices for 5-10 minutes. Stir and boil
for 1 minute. Add the aspartame or sugar; boil
for 1 minute more. JSP/RWB5(4OZ)10(8OZ).

This recipe was given to Jamlady as **Dutch
Pear Pie Jam** by a friend who told Jamlady his
mother had been making it for years. It works
just as well with **apples (Dutch Apple Pie Jam
#1)** or **Asian pears (Dutch Asian Pear Pie #1)**.
Jamlady makes this recipe with light-brown or
white sugar instead of dark-brown sugar, as the
latter darkens the jam too much.

Dutch Pear Pie Jam #1

Great on warm buttermilk biscuits!

4 cups peeled, sliced pears, apples, Asian pears,
  or perhaps quince
4 cups white sugar
1 cup light-brown sugar (or white sugar)
½ cup raisins or currants
1¼ cups water
1 1¾-ounce box powdered pectin
2 tablespoons lemon juice
1 teaspoon ground cinnamon
½ teaspoon butter
¼ teaspoon allspice or nutmeg
¼ teaspoon or less ascorbic acid crystals

Use ascorbic acid crystals in the prep water
and on the newly cut pears. Do not feel compelled to use all of the ascorbic acid. Use only
enough to prevent browning. Mix the pears,
pectin, water, lemon juice, raisins, butter, and
spices and let them sit for 10 minutes. Boil the
mixture for 1 minute. Add the sugar; boil for 1
minute more. JSP/RWB10.

*Jamlady Tip: If you need just a little more
jam to completely fill a jar, steal some jam
from the other jars and push a few additional
raisins in each. Don't overdo this, but it helps
the jars to come out evenly.*

Spiced Pear Marmalade with Grand Marnier

This is a scrumptious fall marmalade!

6 cups peeled, cored, chunked winter pears
5 cups sugar
3 cups water
2 lemons
¼ cup Grand Marnier
½ teaspoon cinnamon
¼ teaspoon ascorbic acid crystals
½ teaspoon ginger

Wash, peel, and core the pears. Put half the ascorbic acid in the prep water to cover the pears while peeling them. Combine the drained pears, water, other half of ascorbic acid crystals (or less), and the sugar. Let the mixture sit overnight in a cool place. Remove and finely chop the outer rind of the lemons. Discard the pith and seeds, and thinly slice the lemons' pulps. Add the spices and the prepared lemon parts. Cook the mixture to 105 degrees C. Add the Grand Marnier and cook the marmalade to achieve the proper set. JSP/RWB10(8OZ)15(16OZ).

Pear-Pineapple Colada Preserves or Pear-Pineapple Colada Jam can be made easily. This jam is sweeter than preserves. If the pears are very underripe, you may want to use 4 cups of pears with a ½ cup of water instead of 4½ cups of pears. Try not to use overripe pears without reducing some sugar (¼ to ½ cup) or compensating in some other way.

Pear-Pineapple Colada Jam

Appropriate for those with a sweet tooth!

9½ cups sugar
4-4½ cups peeled, finely chopped pears
1 20-ounce can crushed pineapple
¾ cup coconut-flavored rum
½ cup lemon juice
2 3-ounce pouches liquid pectin (6 ounces)
1 teaspoon butter
1 teaspoon freshly grated lemon rind
½ teaspoon or less ascorbic acid crystals

Use the ascorbic acid crystals sparingly in the prep water and as you work the pears. Boil all the ingredients, except the pectin and the rum, for 10 minutes. Add the pectin and boil for 1 minute. Add the rum and boil to 104-105 degrees C. Test the set. JSP/RWB5(4OZ)10(8OZ).

Note: Captain Morgan's Coconut Rum (good) or San Tropique (recommended, white-milk glass bottle, www.internetwines.com) can be put in regular pineapple preserves too. Jamlady can't seem to find San Tropique in the local stores anymore. Be brand conscious; some other brands do not work as well.

Jamlady has not always had good luck making pineapple preserves from fresh pineapples. Sometimes the pineapple does not become tender enough. Jamlady finds it is just easier to use canned pineapple in its own juice. This is the recipe that uses fresh pineapple. Jamlady has made it, but make sure you cook the pineapple until it is really tender. To be safe, make the recipe with canned pineapple in its own juice, as it is already tender. If you like challenges, make the pineapple preserves from scratch. Do not add the sugar until the pineapple is fully cooked and tender. The cultivar of pineapple used may affect the final outcome of these preserves.

PINEAPPLES

Pineapple Preserves

Excellent on warm bread, croissant, or biscuit!

3 pounds cubed, fresh pineapple (or 3 cans [16-20 ounces] crushed pineapple in its own juice)
4½ cups sugar
Water (for fresh pineapple only)

Pare the pineapple and cut out the eyes. Remove the core and cut the pineapple into cubes. Weigh the cubes and add water to half-cover. Cook covered until tender. Drain, reserving the liquid. Add the sugar to the liquid. Cook until the liquid coats the spoon. Add the pineapple and cook until clear. Refrigerate overnight to see if the preserves are thick enough. If not, cook more, stirring constantly. Be careful not to burn the preserves. Makes 3 pints or six 8-ounce jars. JSP/RWB10.

Variation: Pina Colada Pineapple Preserves—Add ¼ to ½ cup coconut-flavored rum and cook until thick enough.

Pina Colada Jam

A good beginner's jam.
A sweet jam.
For a less sweet product, make preserves!

7 cups sugar
2 20-ounce cans crushed pineapple in its own juice
¾ cup coconut-flavored rum
½ cup lemon juice
2 3-ounce pouches liquid pectin (6 ounces)
2 teaspoons grated lemon rind
1 teaspoon butter

Cook the pineapple, lemon juice, rind, and butter for about 5 minutes. Add the sugar and cook for about another 5 minutes. Pour in the pectin; cook for 1 minute. Pour in the coconut-flavored rum; cook to 104-105 degrees C. JSP/RWB10.

Homemade, small-batch, peach "jams" are extremely popular. This is probably because the oils in peaches are somewhat fragile, and the peach flavor is severely diminished in large-batch production. Small-batch "jams" are more flavorful. Jamlady's Hawaiian Peach Conserve is very refreshing, as it combines lots of different flavors. Try Hawaiian Peach Conserve with freshly baked scones and orange-flavored tea.

Hawaiian Peach Conserve

A lovely breakfast conserve for your English muffin!

5½ cups sugar
2 cups freshly peeled, chopped, slightly under-ripe peaches
1 cup crushed pineapple in its own juice
½ cup sliced, blanched almonds
½ cup diced, dried apricots
1 3-ounce pouch liquid pectin
3 tablespoons freshly squeezed lemon juice
2 tablespoons grated orange rind
½ teaspoon butter
¼ teaspoon ascorbic acid crystals or less

Use a pinch of ascorbic acid in the prep water and on the peaches, so they don't brown. Boil all the ingredients, except the nuts and pectin, for 10 minutes. Add the pectin; boil for two minutes. Check the set. Add the nuts. JSP/RWB5(4OZ)10(8OZ)15(16OZ).

❦

Aloha Peach Conserve

Tropical fruits with golden raisins and walnuts!

A preserve level of sugar.

6 cups sugar
3½ cups peeled, chopped peaches
1 20-ounce can crushed pineapple in its own juice
¾ cup golden raisins
¾ cup walnuts
2 Clementines
1 lemon
2 tablespoons lemon juice (in addition to the lemon above)
½ teaspoon butter (optional)

Cut the outer rind from the Clementines and lemon; chop and reserve. Discard the white pith and the seeds from both; reserve and chop the pulp. Cook all ingredients together, except the nuts. Add the walnuts when the conserve is thick enough. JSP/RWB10.

❦

Classic Pineapple Jam

**Quick, easy, and good!
A beginner's jam.**

3½ cups sugar
1 20-ounce can crushed pineapple in its own juice
1 3-ounce pouch liquid pectin
3 tablespoons freshly squeezed lemon juice
1 tablespoon freshly grated orange rind
½ teaspoon butter (optional)

Boil the pineapple, sugar, lemon juice, butter, and orange rind for 1 minute. Add the pectin and boil for 1 minute. Check the set with a frozen plate. JSP/RWB10.

*Variations: As a final step, add a liqueur to this jam for **Pineapple Jam with Liqueur** and boil for 1 more minute, or add thinly sliced almonds, or both. **Maraschino-Pineapple Jam**—At the beginning, substitute ¼ cup small pieces of maraschino cherries (no juice) for ¼ cup crushed pineapple. Jamlady has made variations of this jam with pear and coconut-flavored rum. (See pina colada jams.) For **Basil-Pineapple Jam:** Infuse some basil in the pineapple juice.*

French and Spanish words come in handy for Americans when we just don't have the right word for the expression, term, or product, or when the English word doesn't sound fancy enough. The French say *je ne sais quoi,* or literally

Mrs. Joan Anderson's Spiced Tomato-Pineapple Confiture or Spiced Tomato-Pineapple Samting

A jellied and spiced tomato-pineapple relish.

5½ cups sugar

2 cups prepared tomatoes (approximately 2 pounds fresh tomatoes)

1½ cups crushed pineapple in its own juice (canned or precooked)

1 1¾-ounce box regular powdered pectin

2 tablespoons red wine vinegar

2 teaspoons Worcestershire sauce, white or brown

½ teaspoon ground cinnamon

½ teaspoon ground allspice

¼ teaspoon ground cloves

"I don't know what!" That indefinable something, that recipe or taste with no good name or description can only be named something French, German, Spanish, or, perhaps, Pidgin. Maybe you're tired of "Fringlish" and "Spanlish." Perhaps, Pidgin cuisine could be stylish? Try out *wanpela samting* or *wanpela samting tomato painap* or *wanpela samting tomato ananas* or, literally, "something tomato pineapple." How about just *samting*?

This next recipe was given to Jamlady by Mrs. Joan Anderson, owner of a brickyard in Crystal Lake. She calls this condiment **Tomato-Pineapple Relish,** even though it really is a "jam" or a "jellied relish." So Jamlady decided to substitute the French word for *jam* or the Pidgin term *samting* for jam because the word *relish* just didn't fit. *Samting* is just as versatile a word as *je ne sais quoi* is. Use Spiced Tomato-Pineapple Samting as you would any other herb jelly. Try samting on a biscuit, with meat or cottage cheese, or with cream cheese and crackers. Samting would improve New Guinea's sun-dried sago bread, but then, what wouldn't? Just so you know, **sago** is a thickener for puddings or jams made from the dried pith of the **sago palm tree, Metroxylon sagu.** In New Guinea a sun-dried bread is made from sago pith.

Remove the tomatoes' skins by first plunging the tomatoes in boiling water for 1 minute; peel. Remove all tomato seeds and cook down only the tomato meats for 10 minutes. Measure out 2 cups cooked-down tomato meats. Add the pineapple to the prepared tomato meats, along with the vinegar, spices, and Worcestershire sauce. Add the pectin; boil 1 minute. Add the sugar; boil for another minute. JSP/RWB10.

SEEDED AND SEEDLESS BERRIES

There are more people asking for no-seed or semi-seedless jams or preserves than there are asking for jams with seeds, but believe it or not, there are many people who prefer seeds, or jam with seeds. The seeds, to these people, are like nuts in the jam and are part of the textural sensation that they like about raspberry, blackberry, or other berry jams with seeds. Berry plants, like raspberries, are loved for their fruits, but the raspberry plant is also liked for its leaves. **Raspberry leaves, *Rubus idaeus* Linn.,** are often used in teas and tea blends. Unlike the raspberry fruit, raspberry leaves do not taste very good and are usually combined with a more flavorful tea. The *fragarine* in raspberry tea stimulates and relaxes the uterine muscle tissue and helps soothe morning sickness, but pregnant women are advised to not drink it.

Raspberry fruits have intense flavor and are good combined with other fruits. Jams and preserves of seedless raspberry and rhubarb stalks cannot be beaten for flavor. Raspberry-Rhubarb Preserves or jams are the best of the best! Jamlady once saw a published recipe that won a ribbon at the Sioux Empire Fair and the Minnehaha County Fair. This recipe used rhubarb, sugar, and a brand-name box of raspberry gelatin. Jamlady has made the county-fair recipe, which has more sugar than rhubarb by almost half, excluding the gelatin with its sugar. Well, these ribbon-winning gelatin recipes are just not up to the standard of a real-fruit, all-fruit jam or preserve. Set up side-by-side for folks to taste, no one wants to eat the ribbon-winning, rhubarb-gelatin jam when they can dine on the real McCoy! You might say, "How could this be so?" It is so because, without a benchmark, a jam may seem to be great until something greater comes along. Further, Jamlady believes many judges at these state fairs give extra points for the creative use of unique ingredients like brand-name gelatin, but at the end of the day, who cares? We just want the best-tasting stuff, don't we?

❦❦

Seedless Raspberry and Rhubarb Jam

The best of both worlds!

5¾ cups sugar
2½ cups seedless raspberry pulp (see note below)
2¼ cups cooked rhubarb
1 1¾-ounce box regular powdered pectin
¼ teaspoon or less ascorbic acid crystal
½ teaspoon butter

If you don't have a juicing machine, then remove the seeds from the raspberries by sieving the chopped berries. You will need more berries if you do not have the machine. Use the leftover purée plain or cook it with a little sugar for a dessert sauce. Use a pinch of ascorbic acid crystals on the fruit in preparation, to prevent oxidation. Cook the rhubarb with a little water and repeatedly juice the raspberries to obtain the needed pulp (10-12 times through the machine). Mix the fruit with the pectin; wait 5 minutes. Add the butter; boil for 1 minute. Then add the sugar; boil for 1 minute more. JSP/RWB10.

***Variations: Seedless Raspberry and Rhubarb Preserves**—Use ½ fruit, ½ sugar, some finely grated lemon rind or juice, and no added pectin. (See rhubarb preserves.) Use a seedless raspberry purée for* *a seedless version and 1-2 ounces peeled and minced gingerroot for Jamlady's* **Seedless Raspberry-Rhubarb Ragtime Preserves.**

Note: It is difficult to estimate how many pounds or cartons of raspberries to buy to make purée, semi-seedless, or chopped-berry jam or preserves. There are many variables affecting the resulting measure of purée: the ripeness of the fruit, the seediness of the fruit, the number of times the berries are run through the juicing machine and if a manual method of seed removal is used, and the variety of berry that is actually used. So, just plan to buy enough, figuring you need twice the measure of whole berries for purée, maybe a little more, and eat the extras fresh or freeze for pie. Another estimate—figure 3½ cups of whole raspberries to the pound.

The ratios of the raspberry to rhubarb can be altered, and gingerroot can be added to make Raspberry Ragtime Jam.

the pulp, or use an alternative method of seed removal. Cook the rhubarb with a little water. Cook the gingerroot in a little water and retain the water. Mix the pectin with the raspberry pulp, cooked rhubarb, cooked ginger/water, and butter. Boil 1 minute. Add the sugar; boil 1 minute more. JSP/RWB10.

Variation: "No-Sugar" Raspberry Ragtime Jam—Use 4 cups total fruit (raspberry and rhubarb), 1 box lite or "no-sugar" pectin, along with the cooked gingerroot and 35 packets aspartame; or for **Low-Sugar Raspberry Ragtime Jam,** *use 5 cups total fruit, cooked gingerroot, and 1-3 cups of sugar with the "no-sugar" pectin. Put the fruits and gingerroot with the pectin, boil 1 minute. Add the sweetener and boil one more minute. JSP/RWB10.*

This next jam, a standard deluxe raspberry jam, can be made with no seeds, some seeds, or all seeds (use whole raspberries). As you can see from some of the recipes presented already, you can add a liqueur; halve it and combine it with one-half of a strawberry recipe; divide the berries into several types (see Triple-Berry Jam below); or add nuts, raisins, spices, dried fruits, grated citrus rind, or a cinnamon stick (see mango jam with cinnamon stick) to make a conserve. There is no end to the number of different combinations you can try.

☙❧

Raspberry Ragtime Jam

An old-fashioned taste to put a smile on your face!

7 cups sugar

4 cups seedless raspberry, wineberry, or thimbleberry pulp

1 cup cooked rhubarb

1½ ounces peeled, finely chopped, and cooked gingerroot

1 1¾-ounce box regular powdered pectin

½ teaspoon butter

¼ cup water (or more, if needed)

Juice the whole berries many, many times through a Champion juicing machine to obtain

Deluxe Raspberry Jam

Made with powdered pectin and some or all seeds removed.

> 7 cups sugar
> 5 cups crushed raspberries with some or all seeds removed
> ¼ teaspoon or less ascorbic acid crystals
> 1 1¾-ounce box powdered pectin
> ½ teaspoon butter

Chop the raspberries in a food processor, adding a pinch of ascorbic acid crystals. Repeatedly juice the raspberries to remove the seeds or strain out some of the seeds manually. Add the pectin with the fruit and butter in a pan. Wait 10 minutes; boil 1 minute. Add the sugar; boil 1 minute more. JSP/RWB5(4OZ)10(8OZ).

Variation: Seedless Raspberry Marnier Jam—Follow the recipe above. Remove all the seeds, and at the end, add ¼ to ½ cup of Grand Marnier or alternate liqueur. Cook for 1 minute more; check the set. Makes approximately eight 8-ounce jars.

The flavor of oranges goes extremely well with raspberries. Besides achieving an orange flavor with an orange liqueur, one can also do so by making a **Raspberry Marmalade**. The recipe in this chapter for raspberry preserves could have some orange or lemon rind grated into the preserves (prior to cooking it down), or a half recipe of orange marmalade could be combined with a half-raspberry-preserve recipe (shown here). Likewise, for recipes with pectin, use one-half of each recipe, or make whole recipes of both types in separate pans and combine them together at the end. **Grated rind added into preserves recipes helps to cook down the preserves a little faster.** Do not use the whole rind with the white part or pith, just use the outer rind, and grate it finely. If using slivers of citrus peels, it would probably be best to first parboil the outer peels in water alone, or in water with a pinch of baking soda (to remove some of the bitterness—American style), and to make sure the slivers get fully cooked. Discard the water used to parboil the peels.

Strawberry Marmalade could be made from a standard strawberry preserves recipe. Just grate some rind into the no-pectin-added, strawberry preserves, or use a half-marmalade recipe with a half-strawberry-jam recipe. Nuts could be added to a strawberry marmalade, and the product would then be called a **Strawberry Conserve** or, perhaps, a nutty, strawberry marmalade. **Strawberry Preserves with Apples** can be made with very finely chopped tart apples, strawberries, sugar or honey, and lemon juice (Andrea Chesman, *Summer in a Jar: Making Pickles, Jams & More* [Charlotte, VT: Williamson Publishing, 1985], 117). Various combinations of these ingredients will produce serviceable preserves.

୨୧

Semi-seedless Raspberry Genie Jam

Another one of the Jamlady's own original Genie Jams!

Made with semi-seedless raspberries and oil of cinnamon.

> 7 cups sugar
> 5 cups crushed raspberries (2 cups unseeded and 3 cups seedless)
> ¼ teaspoon or less ascorbic acid crystals
> 1 1¾-ounce box regular powdered pectin
> 2-3 drops oil of cinnamon (See note below.)
> ½ teaspoon butter

Chop the raspberries in the food processor, with a pinch of ascorbic acid crystals. Strain out some of the seeds, if you like, or put the whole raspberries through a Champion juicing machine, many times, to obtain the seedless purée. Add the pectin with the fruit and butter in a pan. Wait 10 minutes; boil 1 minute. Add the sugar, and boil 1 minute more. Add the oil of cinnamon and boil 1-2 minutes or until the jam sets on a frozen plate. JSP/RWB5(4OZ)10(8OZ).

Variation: Make raspberry jam with all seeds removed, no seeds removed, or as a semi-seedless jam (shown above). Check the set for each. The seedless version may take longer to cook down. The jam's cooking time will be determined by the ripeness of the raspberries and thickness of the purée. Review the "Quick Reference to Spirits and Liqueurs" section for information on liqueurs that may be used to flavor raspberry jam.

Note: There are approximately 60 drops to a teaspoon, so when using oil of cinnamon, 1-2 drops is equal to $1/60$ to $1/30$ of a teaspoon.

Jamlady Tip: Raspberry seeds are easily removed by a Champion juicing machine. Run the raspberries through repeatedly, until only seeds are ejected from the pulp ejector and all the raspberry pulp is in the juice section.

છેલ્

Red, Golden, or Black Raspberry Preserves

The seedless version of this preserves makes raspberry butter.
No added pectin.

> 4 pounds freshly picked, red, golden, or black raspberries
> 2 pounds sugar (about 4 cups)
> 1 tablespoon fresh lemon juice
> 1 pinch ascorbic acid crystals

Start with freshly picked, clean raspberries, as you will not wash the berries. Pick over the berries to remove any stem part or other leaf pieces. If the berries are old or moldy, the jam will not be topnotch. The sooner you make the jam after picking the berries, the better. In a bowl, mix 1 pinch of ascorbic acid crystals with the sugar. In a pan, sprinkle some of the sugar-and-ascorbic-acid mixture on the bottom of the pan, then a layer of berries, then another layer of the mixture, and so forth until all the sugar and berries are alternately layered. Leave the pan sit overnight or for at least 10 hours. Strain the juice that has wept from the berries and boil it down for a few minutes. Add the raspberries and lemon juice and boil the mixture until jell point is achieved. JSP/RWB10. Makes 8 cups.

If you prefer a seedless product, juice the berries in a Champion juicing machine prior to the first step. You will need to run the pulp through the machine as many as 10-12 times to get all the pulp from the seeds. If you do not cook this seedless mixture to jell point, you will have nice a **raspberry syrup or sauce** for cheesecake, chocolate cake, pancakes, trifles, or ice cream. Or, if the jam does not jell, do not despair; you still have incredible raspberry sauce.

*Variations: Raspberry Butter—Use 4 pounds, or about 7-8 cups, seedless raspberry purée. You will need a juicing machine like a Champion juicing machine to get all of the pulp off the seeds. Run the pulp through many times to get all the pulp from the seeds. When the seeds run hot out of the machine, you will have gotten all of the pulp that is possible to get off the seeds. Add 4 cups sugar (2 pounds), 1 pinch ascorbic acid crystals (vitamin C crystals and not powder), and 2 tablespoons freshly squeezed lemon juice. For a **Marmaladed Raspberry Butter,** use 1-2 tablespoons very finely grated lemon rind. Add the rind in after or before juicing the raspberries, depending on the texture desired. Allow a lot of time to "cook down" this butter. Jamlady heats the butter and then refrigerates it to reduce the volume.*

Seedless Raspberry Genie Jam—Genie jams, preserves, or butters have oil of cinnamon for that extraspecial, tongue-tingling pizazz! This jam is a favorite with Jamlady's children, who have tried them all. To see how to showplace your special jams and preserves in spritz or thumbprint cookies, see chapter 4.

Use the Switch Method. Repeat the evaporation process as many times as necessary. Additionally, this method allows you to see the thickness of the completed product. **This butter is a must for a true raspberry lover who desires a less sweet product!** *This is not a recipe for the beginner, as it will seem like it will never get done. If you do not boil this butter all the way down, you will have a wonderful* **Lemony Raspberry Sauce** *for trifles, ice cream, or other desserts like chocolate cake. Plan on taking your time, and refrigerate between checks for set. It is not unusual for this process to take two days to complete, depending on the size of the batch. Of course, you can cut this batch size down by ¼ or ⅛ if you like. Just use a proportionally smaller pan with a proportionally smaller surface area or maybe just a little larger surface area for speedier results.*

Mixed-fruit preserves can be made by halving original recipes and cooking both halved recipes together. The recipe above for raspberry preserves without added pectin could be combined with a strawberry preserves recipe for strawberry-raspberry preserves. **Strawberry-Raspberry Preserves**—2 pounds raspberries, 1½ pounds strawberries, 5 cups sugar, ½ tablespoon lemon juice, and about ¹⁄₁₆ to ⅛ teaspoon ascorbic acid crystals. The ascorbic acid is used to inhibit oxidation while preparing the strawberries and raspberries. **Blackberry Preserves** (including **Marionberry Preserves**), **Loganberry Preserves, Tayberry Preserves,** and **Thimbleberry Preserves** can all be made from the same preserves or jam recipes as are used for raspberries.

There are many cultivars and crosses of blackberries, such as **'Loganberry,'** *Rubus loganobaccus,* **'Tayberry,'** and **'Marion'** trailing blackberry or "Marionberry." The **'Marion'** cultivar is a cross between the **'Chehalem'** and the **'Olallieberry'** blackberry. The cultivar of blackberry or cross that one would select to grow or buy will depend on the zone in which the berries are grown, the time of the year that they fruit, or the grower's desire for thorned or thornless cultivars. Do not prune thornless cultivars, or they may develop thorned shoots. Other good cultivars of blackberries are **'Arapahoe'** Thornless (zone 3-8), **'Navaho'** Thornless, **'Apache'** Thornless, or **'Chickasaw'** Thorny.

Strawberry Preserves can be made with sliced strawberries, quartered strawberries, or whole strawberries. If they are made with whole berries, it is best to use the **French Plunge Method.** For this method, the berries are taken in and out of the hot syrup, so they do not get broken down by the cooking process. The syrup is brought up to boiling and simmered for a while to reduce the syrup, which makes it thicker, and then the berries are put back into the hot syrup, and the preserves are allowed to cool or evaporate. This step is repeated several times until the preserves are thick enough. The first recipe, shown below, is less sweet than the second. Some people call this type of whole-berry preserves "Strawberry Jewels" or "Strawberry Gems."

Blackberry Preserves—Large blackberries or blackcaps can be made into dark, glossy, blackberry preserves for use on thumbprint cookies. Recipes for red or black raspberries are usually interchangeable with similar berry cultivars like 'Loganberry,' 'Tayberry,' 'Marion' blackberry, and 'Thimbleberry.'

Strawberry Preserves or Strawberry Ice Cream Sauce

Cook down partially for ice cream sauce or all the way for preserves.

Two different formulations with varying sweetness.

No pectin added.

5 pounds washed, hulled strawberries
5 cups sugar
¼ cup lemon juice

or

3 pounds washed, hulled strawberries
6 cups sugar

Layer the strawberries, lemon juice, and sugar and let them sit overnight. If starting with sliced berries, you need only weep the berries for a couple of hours or overnight and then cook them down some. Let the preserves cool (SM). Repeat heating and cooling several times until the preserves are thick enough, as demonstrated on a frozen plate. For whole-berry preserves, use the French Plunge Method. Separate the berries from the syrup by straining. Cook down the syrup and add the berries back in; cool and repeat. If using sliced berries or quartered berries, cook down the preserves until thick (SM). You can refrigerate the preserves overnight to make sure they are thick enough. JSP/RWB10.

Variations: Grand Marnier (or some other liqueur—see list of liqueurs) may be added to these preserves to make **Marnier's Strawberry Preserves.** *Strawberry* **Genie Preserves** *are made with the addition of a few drops of oil of cinnamon.* **Spiced Strawberry Preserves** *can be made by adding a ½ to 1 teaspoon ground cinnamon, nutmeg, or other spices. Jamlady makes* **Strawberry-**

Banana Gems *or Jewels by adding 1 teaspoon banana extract or liqueur.* **Strawberry-Banana Preserves** *can also be made with mostly strawberries, a few slices of bananas, and some lemon or grated lemon rind. Jamlady has combined strawberries and bananas in a "sugar-free" jam. (See Spiced Fruit Cup Jam.)* **Strawberry Mint Preserves** *can be made by adding mint extract or mint liqueur to strawberry preserves, or some fresh mint can be cooked in the fruit-sugar syrup to infuse some mint flavor in the preserves. Remove the mint sprigs after infusing the flavor.*

Raspberry-Strawberry Jam

Choice of sweetener—aspartame, alternate sweetener, or sugar.

2 cups washed, hulled, processor-sliced strawberries (3 cups strawberries with 2 cups sugar or 2½ cups strawberries with 1 cup of sugar)
2 cups crushed raspberries (2½ cups raspberries with 1 or 2 cups of sugar)
1 1¾-ounce box lite or "no-sugar" powdered pectin
30 packets aspartame (or 1-2 cups sugar)

Mix the pectin with the fruit; wait 5 minutes. Boil 1 minute. Add the aspartame or sugar; boil 1 minute more. JSP/RWB10.

MULTIFRUIT COMBINATIONS

Strawberries, Cherries, and Pineapple Preserves

A versatile preserve for cake fillings, toast, or ice cream!

> 3 pounds sugar
> 1 pound pitted sour cherries
> 1 pound washed, hulled, sliced strawberries
> 1 pound shredded fresh pineapple or canned crushed pineapple in its own juice

If using fresh pineapple, precook it in a little water until tender. Cook all ingredients slowly until a set is achieved. JSP/RWB10 (Taken from Mrs. Cornelia E. DuBois's recipe in *De New Paltz Keuken Boek* [New Paltz, NY: Committee of the Ladies of the Reformed Church, 1909], 58).

Variation: Strawberry and Pineapple Preserves—3 cups sugar, 2 cups strawberries, and 1 cup pineapple (Mrs. C. H. Woosley, De New Paltz Keuken Boek *[New Paltz, NY: Committee of the Ladies of the Reformed Church, 1909]).*

Triple-Berry Jam

A trio of red raspberries, strawberries, and wild black raspberries.

> 7 cups sugar
> 1½ cups seedless red raspberry purée
> 1 cup crushed red raspberry pulp with seeds
> 1½ cups washed, sliced, hulled strawberries
> 1 cup crushed wild black raspberries
> 1 1¾-ounce box powdered pectin
> ¹⁄₁₆ cup water
> ½ teaspoon butter

Mix all ingredients together, except the sugar, and boil 1 minute. Boil the mixture 2-3 minutes if the fruits were ripe and less if the fruits were underripe. Add the sugar, and boil to set point. JSP/RWB5(4OZ)10(8OZ).

Fruit jams can be made with many different fruits together. Do not assume that combinations not ordinarily seen will not work well. Many fruits have not been combined before because they normally are not indigenous to the same area or have different growing seasons. Jamlady's Tango Jam is such a combination. Cranberries cooked in water can be combined with a lesser quantity of bananas, a little lemon juice or other citrus juice, and sugar equaling the fruit to make a nice **Nanaberry Preserves.** Four cups of cooked rhubarb can be combined with 2 bananas and 6 cups of sugar for **Rhubarb-Banana Jam.** In Guinea, West Africa, bananas (about 50 percent of the recipe) are combined with oranges, lemons, a grapefruit, and sugar for a four-fruit jam (Vera Gewanter and Dorothy Parker, Home Preserving Made Easy [New York: Sterling Publishing Co., Inc., 1975] 196). Jamlady has made this **West African Four-Fruit**

Jam for market, and while it was acceptable, it was not received as well as Banana Jam or other four-fruit jams.

German Four-Fruit Preserves, with equal parts gooseberries, raspberries, cherries, and currants, is a real winner and is often used to fill pastries, tarts, and thumbprint cookies. **These fruits can be mixed in most any combination using preserve ratios of sugar: ¾ pound of sugar or 1¾ cups sugar to each pound of fruit.** The Alfeld family uses 1 cup stoned sour cherries to ½ cup each of red currants, gooseberries, and raspberries for **Berry-Tart Preserves.**

JSP/RWB5(4OZ)10(8OZ).

ⓈⒼⓈ

Seedless Raspberry-Strawberry Jam or Double-Berry Jam

7 cups sugar
2½ cups juiced, seedless strawberry purée
2 ½ cups juiced, seedless red or black raspberry purée
¼ cup water
1 1¾-ounce box regular powdered pectin
½ teaspoon butter

Mix all ingredients together except the sugar; boil for 1 minute. Boil 2-3 minutes if fruits were ripe and less if underripe. Add the sugar, and boil to set point. Any combination of blackberries, strawberries, black raspberries, and red raspberries can be used in this recipe, so long as you have a total of 5 cups berry purée. A liqueur could be added to make a special jam. If adding a liqueur, add ¼-⅓ cup at the end, and boil for 1 more minute. Then check the set with a frozen plate. JSP/RWB5(4OZ)10(8OZ).

Classic Strawberry-Rhubarb Preserves

A market favorite!

4 cups sugar
3 cups processor-sliced rhubarb
3 cups whole, quartered, or processor-sliced strawberries
1 pinch ascorbic acid crystals

Use 1 pinch of ascorbic acid crystals on the fruits while working them and in the prep water. Mix the strawberries with 2 cups sugar and let the mixture sit overnight. Mix the rhubarb with 2 cups of sugar and let it sit overnight. The strawberry mixture and the rhubarb mixture can be cooked down separately and mixed together at the end, or the two mixtures can be cooked down together. The together method will take longer. Another advantage to cooking them separately is that the strawberries can be taken out and put back in the hot syrup several times (using the French Plunge Method). With this method, the strawberries will remain whole. If you are not seeking "jewels" (whole strawberries) in the finished product, then quarter the strawberries when mixing them with the sugar for overnight weeping. Further, you could actually jar up three or more products, the two separate preserves, and the two mixed together. Then you could make ⅔ of one and ⅓ of the other and so on, or layer the two preserves alternatively in the jar. (See recipe for Authentic Strawberry Rhubarb Preserves.)

This pineapple-and-rhubarb conserve recipe is an example of a marmalade that has been made into a conserve. Because 10-11 cups of fruits are sweetened with only 5 cups of sugar, this conserve's level of sugar equals that of a butter or of preserves. Considering the 1½ cups of almonds, the starting formula has twice the fruit (fruit and nuts) to sugar, making this a very low-sugar formulation. This pineapple-and-rhubarb conserve is easy to make and difficult to ruin, unless you burn it. Stir often and thoroughly.

ᏸᏩ

Jamlady's Pineapple and Rhubarb Conserve

The lovely orange flavor shines through! No added pectin.

5 cups processor-chopped, fresh pineapple
5 cups sugar
4 cups sliced rhubarb*
2 oranges
1½ cups sliced, peeled almonds

Slice and chop the rind of an orange. Add the rind to the pineapple, rhubarb, and sugar; let the mixture sit for 4 hours. Add the orange juice (juice only) and cook until the conserve becomes thick. Add the almonds. JSP/RWB10. Makes ten 8-ounce jars.

* Not all rhubarb is pink in color. Some cultivars are green. Try to use a pink-colored cultivar of rhubarb for "jam" recipes.

Note: Jamlady first saw this recipe as "4 cups pineapple, 1 cup water, 8 cups rhubarb, 2 oranges, 7 cups sugar, and 1 cup almonds," but she made the above recipe instead, as she did not have enough rhubarb for the first recipe.

ᏸᏩ

MULBERRIES AND APPLES

Mulberries come in various colors: black, red, or white. The **white mulberry, silkworm mulberry,** or **Russian mulberry,** *Morus alba* Linn., is native to China and was naturalized in the East and Pacific States. *Morus alba* is the mulberry tree, whose leaves were used to feed silkworms. Mulberry trees were planted in the United States early to support a growing silkworm industry, but due to disease and hardiness problems, the silkworm industry failed in its infancy. Furthermore, cotton was found to be more profitable in the South. The **black mulberry,** *Morus nigra,* is grown for its fruits and is commonly found in Europe and some parts of the United States.

The **Texas Mulberry, Mexican Mulberry,** or **Mountain Mulberry,** *Morus microphylla* Buckl., is a small tree or clump-forming shrub with edible mulberries. The Texas Mulberry is found in southern Oklahoma and Texas, west to Arizona. The fruits of the Texas Mulberry are small but are eaten by wildlife and, according to Albert Little in *The Audubon Society Field Guide to Northern American Trees* ([New York: Alfred A. Knopf, 1980], 425), were used by Native American tribes such as the **Havasupai.** The **red mulberry,** *Morus rubra,* is a medium-sized tree (60') with a short trunk and cylindrical fruits that are about 1" to 1¼" long, red to dark purple, bead-like, sweet and juicy, edible, and have a central stem that goes through each individual fruit.

Jamlady collects mulberry fruits in late spring for mulberry jam, wine, or syrup and usually comes home with purple hands and clothes, as mulberries stain like crazy. Mulberries are not the easiest fruit to pick, and often times, it works to leave an old sheet on the ground and collect the berries after shaking the tree branches. Anyway you do it, it is a messy job. On the upside, the fruits are wonderful in preserves, wines, and syrups.

Seedless Mulberry Preserves

What could be better on whole wheat toast?

3 pounds red mulberries
1 cup water
Juice of 3 lemons
6 cups sugar

Cook the mulberries with the water and lemon juice. Either push the berries through a sieve or juice the berries through a Champion juicing machine, many times, to obtain the mulberry pulp. Cook the pulp with the sugar until set is achieved. Check the set with a frozen plate. JSP/RWB5(4OZ)10(8OZ).

Note: If you don't have enough mulberries, use some red raspberries, black raspberries, or blackberries instead. Whole red raspberries, black raspberries, or blackberries can be combined with the stick-less mulberry purée in other recipes too.

Note: If you do not cook this recipe down all the way, you will have Seedless Mulberry Syrup for pancakes or desserts.

Seedless Mulberry-Apple Preserves

Mulberries are not really berries but collective or multiple fruits.

7 cups sugar
4 cups stemless mulberry purée
4 cups thinly sliced apples
2 cups water
Juice of 2 lemons

If you don't have enough mulberries, use some seedless raspberry purée or black raspberry purée along with the apples. Cook the mulberries in the water. Sieve or juice the mulberries in a Champion juicing machine or similar machine to obtain a smooth purée. Cook all ingredients until the preserves reach jell point.
JSP/RWB5(4OZ)10(8OZ).

Pippinberry Jam

A cost-saving, two-fruit jam with a beautiful color!

$5\frac{2}{5}$ cups sugar
$3\frac{1}{4}$ cups peeled, thinly sliced, tart green apples
1 cup seedless raspberry pulp
1 cup water
1 $1\frac{3}{4}$-ounce box regular powdered pectin
$1\frac{3}{4}$ tablespoons lemon juice
$\frac{1}{2}$ teaspoon ground cinnamon
$\frac{1}{2}$ teaspoon butter (optional)

Mix the raspberry pulp, apples, pectin, water, lemon juice, butter, and cinnamon. Wait 10 minutes. Boil the mixture for 1 minute. Add the sugar and boil for 1 minute more. Check for set. JSP/RWB5(4OZ)10(8OZ).

Jamlady Tip: If you don't have a lot of fresh raspberries, but still want to make raspberry jam, then try Jamlady's Pippinberry Jam recipe, as you only need 1 cup of raspberry purée to make this jam. Or try the Raspberry-Apple Jam, which requires only 2 cups of raspberry purée.

Raspberry-Apple Jam

You can juice the raspberries or use crushed raspberries with their seeds.

$7\frac{1}{4}$ cups sugar
2 cups juiced, puréed, or crushed fresh raspberries
2 cups freshly extracted apple juice (Use a juicing machine.)
2 3-ounce pouches liquid pectin (6 ounces)
1 tablespoon freshly squeezed lemon juice
$\frac{1}{2}$ teaspoon butter

Boil the raspberry purée or crushed raspberries with the freshly extracted apple juice, lemon juice, and sugar for 1 minute. Add the pectin and boil for a minute. Check for set on a frozen plate. JSP/RWB5(4OZ)10(8OZ).

Jamlady usually makes these spectacular-tasting, apple-and-maple preserves in October, when the fresh apples are being harvested. Use Apple and Maple Preserves on muffins, dark or whole wheat breads, pancakes, rice pudding, ice cream, oatmeal, yogurt, or with cottage-cheese-topped salad plates.

Apple and Maple Preserves

A good beginner's recipe.

12 cups finely peeled, cored, and chopped tart apples (about 6 pounds)

6 cups sugar

1 cup grade A, light or medium, amber maple syrup

1-1½ teaspoons ground cinnamon

½ teaspoon ground allspice

½ teaspoon ground nutmeg (optional)

¼ teaspoon ground cloves

Cook all ingredients together until they thicken. Stir well so the jam does not burn. JSP/RWB10.

Note: This Apple and Maple Preserves recipe was given to Jamlady by Farmer Martin, an old-timer from Tennessee. Athough Jamlady has not yet tried it, she thinks this recipe might be made with birch syrup, molasses, or sorghum instead of maple syrup. Check the pH before canning, or refrigerate.

Jamlady has made tart apple, pear, and orange jelly scented with **scented geraniums,** specifically **'Attar of Roses,'** *Pelargonium capitatum,* and other scented leaves like **lemon verbena,** *Aloysia triphylla* (syn. *Lippia citriodora*). The *Pelargonium* species is native to South Africa and is so popular that several Pelargonium clubs can be found in England, the United States, and elsewhere. Check the Internet for these clubs and companies selling at least 84 (Jamlady stopped counting there) different, scented geraniums. Not all cultivars of scented geraniums are useful for cooking, but many are and can be used in lemonade, tea, cocktails, sugar bowls, bathtubs, "jams," syrups, pies, and sauces. Other herbs—such as mint, rosemary, basil, sage, and parsley—can be used to flavor these apple or pear jellies too. Apple jelly can be jazzed up with 1-2 drops of oil of cinnamon, for an **Apple Genie Jelly,** or flavored with liqueurs.

Jamlady Tip: If you want to flavor jelly with scented leaves or flavorings, but do not want to make the jelly, just melt some commercial apple jelly in the microwave or in a double boiler, drop in a scented leaf or a few drops of oil of cinnamon, and who will know your jelly isn't totally from scratch?

Apple Jelly with Rose Geranium Leaves

Pelargonium capitatum.

5 pounds unpeeled, sliced tart apples

5 cups water

¾ cup sugar to each cup extracted apple juice

Before you can begin to make the apple jelly, you must extract the apple juice from the apples. You may use a press or a juicing machine to obtain the apple juice, or you may follow these instructions. Slice the apples in the food processor without peeling or coring. The peels, cores, and apples contain the pectin necessary for the jelling process. Cook the apples in the water until tender. Put the apples and juice in a jelly bag and drip the juice out overnight or in about 12 hours' time. Do not squeeze the jelly bag, or the jelly will be cloudy. Heat the extracted apple juice and drop in a rose geranium leaf or two and taste for flavor. Remove the leaves and add ¾ cup microwaved-warmed sugar to each cup of warm apple juice. Boil until the liquid sheets or to 104-105 degrees C. Place a new leaf in each jar of hot jelly. JSP/RWB10. Do not cook a batch larger than 4 cups of juice at one time.

Note: Remove the geranium leaf from the jelly prior to eating.

Note: Some people are allergic to cochineal or some food colorings.

Variations: Use **lemon verbena leaves,** Aloysia triphylla *or* Lippia citriodora, *instead of rose geranium leaves in apple or pear jelly for* **Apple Jelly with Lemon Verbena Leaves** *or* **Pear Jelly with Lemon Verbena Leaves. Wild Rose Jelly** *can be made by steeping rose petals in the hot apple juice prior to boiling down the jelly. Wild Rose Jelly can be colored with carmine (a coloring material found in cochineal) or other kinds of red food coloring (see note above). Jamlady steeps about a quart of fresh, unsprayed, wild or domestic rose petals to about 2-3 cups of extracted or commercial apple juice. Similar jellies can be made with extracted pear juice, but Jamlady recommends peeling the pears first and then juicing them to extract the juice. Asian pears and crab apples will also work. There is no need to use pectin for* **Crab Apple Jelly,** *but if you do, you will be extending the juice with extra sugar. Using commercial pectin is faster and simpler, but not necessarily better. Five pounds of crab apples cooked in 5 cups of water and hung in a jelly bag will give about 7 cups of juice, which then can be processed into jelly with 9 cups sugar and 1 box powdered pectin. The same extracted juice can be processed into jelly without pectin by using less sugar.* **When using powdered pectin, always remember to boil the pectin with the juice and then add the sugar.** *Jelly can also be made with juicing-machine-juiced juice or with commercial apple juice. Read the pectin insert sheet for specifics on using bottled juices.*

One trendy recipe called for hot, red, cinnamon candies to be added to apple jelly, but Jamlady thinks it is a waste of money to buy the cinnamon candies when the flavor that is obtained is basically oil of cinnamon and the color, coloring. Both can be purchased separately. Other **trendy recipes,** which fail to impress Jamlady, are the various recipes made with flavored gelatin. One recipe called for zucchini and gelatin. Jamlady made the recipe, and it sold at market, but no one ever came back asking to buy that jam again. Why? Because it sounded good, looked good, and was average. At best, it was a good way to use up zucchini, but Jamlady thinks zucchini are better used up for relishes or pickles.

This case is just like that of the state-fair recipe calling for rhubarb, sugar, and raspberry or strawberry gelatin. It tastes fine, until it is placed side by side with real strawberry rhubarb or raspberry-rhubarb preserves. Many trendy recipes have won blue ribbons, but Jamlady says: **"Good is only good until you've had better."** For this reason, Jamlady has attempted to personally make everything that she possibly could over a 15-year period of time. Unless you have "tried it all" in any given category, how could you know if you had the best there was to have? Where's the benchmark?

VEGETABLES IN PRESERVES

Jamlady does think that vegetables can be made into good preserves, jams, or marmalades. The Shakers thought up carrot marmalade years ago and also created horseradish jelly and its many variations. The Russian Jewish tradition is credited with the invention of beet preserves and black radish preserves.

The Shakers originally made **Carrot Marmalade** or **Carrot Conserve** with carrots and optional almonds, using 8 cups sugar, 6 cups shredded carrots, 4 shredded lemons, 2 oranges, ½-1 cup slivered and blanched almonds, and 2 tablespoons cinnamon. This is Jamlady's version of this old classic. Jamlady has made it with macadamia nuts or almonds and brandy. Both are excellent. Jamlady has been thinking about trying it with other nuts, maybe pine nuts, but has not gotten around to it yet.

Brandied Carrot Marmalade with Macadamia Nuts

This marmalade is technically a conserve. No added pectin.

12 cups sugar
8 cups peeled, grated, and cooked carrots (5 pounds)
2¼ cups freshly squeezed lemon juice
1 cup chopped macadamia nuts or 2 cups sliced skinless almonds
1 cup grated outer lemon rind with no pith attached
½ cup fine brandy (with macadamia nuts) or Grand Marnier liqueur (with almonds)
1 tablespoon almond extract (optional—especially if using almonds)

Cook (steam) the carrots and grated lemon rind in a little water in the microwave for about 8-10 minutes. Cook all the ingredients until thick and jell point is reached. Check with a frozen plate. Add the nuts and the brandy at the end. Other citrus can be used for variation—consider oranges, kumquats, calamondins, grapefruits, or limes. Check the completed pH. Hazelnuts might be tried with hazelnut liqueur. JSP/RWB5(4OZ)10(8OZ).

Horseradish Jelly

Horseradish is a herbaceous perennial. *Armoracia rusticana* Gaertn., Mey., Scherb. Use this Shaker jelly as a condiment for meats.

4⅞ cups sugar
1½ cups peeled, grated horseradish
1½ cups red wine vinegar (or any 5 percent acidity vinegar)
½-1 teaspoon minced fresh sage
2 3-ounce pouches liquid pectin (6 ounces)

Boil the sugar, horseradish, red wine vinegar, and sage for 1 minute. Add the pectin; boil for another minute. JSP/RWB10.

Variations: Instead of sage, use thyme, basil, parsley, or juniper berries. Read about other spices and find a spice that would go well with the other ingredients. Some of the horseradish could be substituted with a little garlic or garlic juice for a **Horseradish and Garlic Jelly.** *Interesting variations can be made with different types of vinegar or flavored vinegar. Make sure the vinegar's acidity is at least 5 percent. A tablespoon of* **balsamic vinegar,** *for example, changes the entire flavor of this*

Apple and Carrot Conserve—Myriad healthy flavors for the morning brunch. This conserve is inexpensive to make and utilizes apples, carrots, oranges, lemons, a little sugar, and a tad of salt. Great with an assortment of scones!

jelly. **Red Onion Jam** *is another jam made from a vegetable and fruit combination. This jam is lovely for a dinner party where party participants do not know each other very well. Red Onion Jam is something to start talking about. An unusual food helps to break the ice.* **Red Onion Jam Appetizer** *can be made by layering whipped cream cheese and Red Onion Jam between uniform deli meat slices or sandwiches. Cut the appetizer into cubes and serve with decorative toothpicks as an attractive, cocktail-party finger food.*

છ∞

Pear and Red Onion Jelly

Use as you would any herbal jelly—with assorted meats and crackers or celery and cream cheese.

5 cups sugar

3 cups prepared, red onion pieces or thin slices

1 1/2 cups freshly extracted pear juice (Use a juicing machine.)

3/4 cup red wine vinegar (5 percent acidity or higher)

1/2 cup light-brown sugar

1 3-ounce pouch liquid pectin

20 fresh sage leaves

1/2 teaspoon ground black pepper

1/2 teaspoon butter or margarine (optional)

"Blenderize" the sage leaves with the vinegar. Boil everything together except the pectin. Add the pectin and boil at least 5 minutes to 104-105

degrees C. If fresh juice is used, there will be more pectin and a faster set will occur. Jamlady does not recommend making this recipe with bottled juices. Experiment with different herbs and different kinds and flavors of 5 percent acidity vinegar.

Variations: **Apple and Red Onion Jam, Asian Pear and Red Onion Jam,** *or* **Garlicky Pear and Onion Jam**—*Apple juice or Asian pear juice can be substituted for regular pear juice. Try substituting shallots, other types of onions, or some garlic for some of the onions.*

Note: Butter or margarine is optional in most preserve and jam recipes. It is used to reduce the surface tension, thereby reducing the foam that forms on the top of the "jams." Butter or margarine is listed in "jam" recipes where foaming can be a problem.

Caution: Make sure you check the pH of these new creations. Shallots, onions, and garlic have a pH range around 5.3-5.8 or possibly higher. Remember: If the jam is to be canned, the product's pH may need to be lowered with further acidification. Test fully the ground-up jam product with your pH meter or refrigerate your "jams"!

Black radish preserve is not a canning recipe because the pH is not low enough or acidic enough to be canned, but the creation of black radish preserves does illustrate what can evolve out of scarcity with a little creativity. In years past, what else could a Jewish cook make in the Siberian winter besides love? **The lesson to be learned is limitations do not necessarily hinder innovation!** Out of scarcity came something sweet and crunchy to nosh on: black radish preserves!

Black Radish Preserves

Eastern Europeans made sweet vegetable preserves or *eingemachts*.

4 cups thinly sliced black radishes
1 ounce finely minced gingerroot
4 cups honey
Thinly sliced blanched almonds without skins

Cook the radishes in water for a few minutes. Drain and dry the radishes between layers of paper towels. Add the radishes to the honey and gingerroot and cook until thick. Add the almonds when serving.

The pH of black radishes are maximally around 6.05, and honey is maximally around 4.20. If you have equal parts of each, it appears clear to some that the completed preserve would be around 5.12? Right? Well, no! You see, it doesn't work like that. There are all sorts of things to consider, like **buffering capacities, molarity!** So, use your pH meter to check for pHs above 4.6. Make this preserve and just refrigerate it or make it for a party where it will all be consumed. The beet preserves below may be canned, as they have sufficient lemons to bring the pH down (increases the acid) so that the preserves can be canned safely in a RWB.

Caution: Do not can the Black Radish Preserves recipe shown above. Store it in the refrigerator (JSR)!

Russian beet preserves are a good example of innovation improvised out of scarcity. In the cold climates where fruits for jams are not plentiful, inhabitants devised unique preserve recipes using two root crops. Jamlady has spent considerable time researching beet preserves with lemons and almonds and found this preserve to far exceed any expectation regarding beet preserves. Once market beet-lovers got a taste of this preserve, it was requested over and over.

Jamlady thanks her Wilmette market patrons for recommending and requesting that Jamlady experiment with different root-crop recipes. Jamlady had passed them over for years, and it was a mistake. Not only are beet preserves good, but they are also economical. Most home gardeners can easily grow their own beets. This preserve is a great icebreaker at parties and wonderful for fall picnics and the Thanksgiving table. Try some on Jewish Challah (Egg Bread) or on a sliced French baguette.

To make **Challah Egg Bread:** Use 1 cake of yeast, 2 teaspoons sugar, 1¼ cups of lukewarm water, 4½ cups sifted flour, 1½ teaspoons salt, 2 eggs, 2 tablespoons olive oil, 1 egg yolk, 3 tablespoons poppy seeds or finely sliced, blanched almonds. Mix the yeast with ½ cup lukewarm water. Wait 7 minutes. Sift the flour and salt and mix the whole eggs, olive oil, remaining water, and dissolved yeast mixture into the flour. Knead it on a floured tabletop. Put in a greased bowl and paint the top with olive oil. Cover and let rise for 1 hour in a warm location. Punch the dough down and let rise until it doubles. Divide the dough into thirds and roll it out to make strands for a braided loaf. Braid the dough pieces, paint them with egg yolk and sprinkle with almonds or poppy seeds. Cover and let rise again to twice its original size. Bake in a 375 degree F oven for 45-55 minutes or until golden brown.

For the creative chef, consider dissolving spices in the water or steeping spices in the water for additional color or flavor. Spices that might be tried are saffron, turmeric, annatto, vanilla pod, rose geranium leaves, sage, and rosemary. This idea is not limited to this bread recipe but can be done with most any bread recipe. Flavored sugars can also be used in baking. For **Rose Geranium Sugar,** place scented geranium leaves in a closed container of sugar and wait.

Note: Annatto, Bixa orellana, is a plant producing seeds that are used for food coloring and dye. Rose geraniums or Pelargoniums—

like *'Attar of Roses,'* P. *capitatum;* *Old Fashioned 'Rose,'* P *graveolens,* *and 'Lemon Rose,'* P. *graveolens* x P. *tomentosum* (lemon-rose scent)—*can be found on the Internet and at some regular nurseries.*

Jamlady has been given many recipes for beet preserves by Jewish patrons who have family recipes for this wonderful preserve. Some recipes use cooked and canned beets, honey instead of sugar, but the best recipe Jamlady has tried is this one, made with fresh, young beets that are peeled then grated in the food processor and cooked on the range with just enough water to cover the grated beets.

ॐ

Russian Beet Preserves

A most unusual and delicious recipe!

> 4 pounds peeled, processor-grated, fresh young beets
> 3 pounds sugar
> 3 lemons
> 1/4 pound thinly sliced blanched almonds
> 2-3 ounces finely grated, fresh gingerroot

Cover the beets with water and cook. When the beets are tender, add the sugar, gingerroot, lemon juice, and very finely chopped lemon rind with the thick white sections removed. The rind is best chopped in the blender, even though it is difficult to get out when it's completely chopped. Cook the preserves about 1 hour or until it is thick and clear. When done, stir in the almonds. JSP/RWB10.

Note: The key to a successful beet preserve is to remove the bitter white portion from the rind and to very finely chop the lemon itself and the outer rind. Many recipes just state to chop up the lemon, but a better preserve is made with more care.

Variations: An interesting variation of this old recipe of beet preserves is an **Apple and Beet Conserve,** *made with 1 cup apples, 1 cup cooked beets, 1⅓ cup sugar, and 1 grated lemon rind and juice. This recipe was seen in an old* Cornell Bulletin for Homemakers (Extension Bulletin 88, *July 1924). The same bulletin shows* **Apple and Plum Conserve with Almonds** *(2 cups each, fruit plus 2⅔ cups sugar and ½ cup almonds),* **Apple and Carrot Conserve** *(2 cups of each fruit, 1 orange minus its pith or 1 peeled, diced peach—plumped in ½ cup water, 1-2 lemons [use slivered rind and pulp and no pith, or juice only], ½ teaspoon salt, and 2⅔-3 cups sugar),* **Apple and Tomato Conserve** *(2 cups each fruit, 1 lemon rind and juice, 2⅔ cups sugar, ½ teaspoon salt and ½ cup walnuts), and* **Apple and Peach Conserve** *(2 cups each fruit, ½ cup water, 1 orange rind and juice, 2⅔ cups sugar, and ¼ cup walnuts). As you can see, apples go well with most any combination and provide additional pectin to set the conserve. Another beet variation can be seen in* Mrs. Beeton's Household Management *([London: Ward, Lock & Co. Limited, n.d.], 1100), with* **Carrot and Beetroot Jam,** *using equal weights of carrots, beetroot, sugar, and lemons.*

Red peppers are a very versatile garden vegetable—well, fruit, really! The evolution of the *Capsicum* is still somewhat disputed. The not-hot bell pepper, *Capsicum annuum* var. *annuum,* can be made into gorgeous marmalade. Jamlady does not know where you can find a more vibrant and contrasting marmalade than this delicious offering from ripe, red bell peppers. Jamlady suggests that you finely chop or grind the red peppers instead of thinly slicing them or, to avoid the tough-skin problem, peel them. While appearing easy to make, this pepper marmalade really falls into the medium-to-difficult category. The variety of pepper can make a difference too, so try to select a thin-skinned variety of peppers if they

Russian Beet Preserves on French Baguettes—
A wonderful beet preserves with lemons,
sliced almonds, and gingerroot. Try
serving this preserves on homemade Challah Egg Bread or
warm croissants.

will not be peeled. For more information on peppers, consult *Peppers* by Jean Andrew.

A customer at the Palatine Farmers' Market requested **Red Pepper Marmalade.** Jamlady had not made Red Pepper Marmalade in years, and she didn't know why, because it is really something special! It's not too sweet and is similar to orange marmalade but distinctive in flavor due to the sweet red peppers. Red Pepper marmalade is lower in sugar than most "jams" and has no added pectin, so the fruits are not stretched out with too much sugar. The citrus provides enough natural pectin for the preserve to jell.

ꙮ

Red Pepper Marmalade

Good with hot pork medallions or cold meats!

6 seeded, peeled red peppers
6 Valencia oranges
4½ cups sugar
1 lemon
2 cups water

Peel the red pepper for the best results. Cut the oranges, lemon, and red peppers into thin slices and cover with enough water to barely cover. Simmer until the fruits are tender. Add ¾ pound sugar for each pint of fruits. Cook until thick enough. JSP/RWB10.

Note: The red pepper skins can separate from the fruit and present a less-than-perfect textual quality in the preserve. Peeling the peppers is one solution to the problem. Some thin-skinned varieties of peppers may be less troublesome than others are. Do not make with unpeeled, waxed peppers.

Another so-called "vegetable" easily grown to profusion in a home garden is the summer squash, **zucchini,** *Cucurbita pepo melopepo,* or **marrow,** *Cucurbita pepo pepo.* **Summer squash are fruits of the Cucurbitaceae family.** They are, with any luck, used when immature and while their rind is still soft and their seeds immature. A bumper crop of squash can be utilized and transformed by the artful canner into many jars of impressive pickles, relishes, chutneys, jams, preserves, and marmalades.

The zucchini and marrow squashes are best used small. The larger zucchini and marrow have tougher skins and keep better, but the smaller zucchini are the best for eating. **Most smart gardeners pick their zucchini fruits 4"-8" in length.** Most market vendors sell zucchini from 5"-10" long. Jamlady puts larger zucchini through the juicing machine for juice or soup stock. Larger zucchini can be used for quick bread, if the exterior is not too tough and the seeds are removed. **The *Cucurbita pepo* classification includes crookneck squash, straightneck squash, scallop squash, zucchini, and vegetable marrow.** Winter squashes have hard exteriors and store well.

As in the debate regarding pepper, scientists are still discussing, deciding, and mapping the origins of *Cucurita pepo* and the **Texan wild marrow, *Cucurbita texana.*** Jamlady suggests those interested in this topic check out both Latin classifications on the Internet. The Texan wild marrow is now being viewed as an ancestor of the garden marrow, which brings Jamlady to the topic of marrow or zucchini jam or marmalade.

Jamlady has seen recipes in at least 10 different published sources for summer squash marmalade, preserves, or jam, with or without pectin, and combined with pineapple and/or lemon, and sometimes gingerroot. A recipe in Maria Polushkin Robbins' *Blue Ribbon Pickles and Preserves* ([New York: St. Martin's Press n.d.], 108) calls for cooked zucchini (to remove the excess water), lemon juice, pineapple, pectin, sugar, and apricot gelatin. Clearly, in these types of gelatin recipes, the squash does not impart very much flavor but provides a certain consistency to the marmalade, jam, or preserve. Jamlady is not awed by the various gelatin recipes that she has tried, because the gelatin flavors, in Jamlady's and many market patrons' opinions, tastes artificial in comparison to real fruits. Jamlady believes that while we may want to find ways to eat lovely summer squash in preserves the best way to do that is with fresh and natural ingredients.

Jamlady suggests that other recipes can be developed with marrow or zucchini, but as with many recipes in some canning books, little deviation from the basic recipe is noted. Surely there are other combinations of fruits that would taste well with zucchini, but Jamlady has not sufficiently investigated this topic—and not for the lack of marrow or zucchini. Should some readers get interested in this topic, Jamlady would be very interested to discuss the topic with them. Jamlady thinks a great place to start is with all the different citrus fruits (like calamondins) that are available in some geographic locations. And when and if Jamlady finds the time, she herself will be delving into alternate formulations for zucchini or marrow preserves.

A likely variation could be to combine zucchini with a carrot, almond, and lemon marmalade or an apple marmalade. Perhaps a good **zucchini jam or preserve** can be made by not trying to make zucchini into a fruity solution and go the way of an **herbal-flavored cucumber preserves**, noted in Robin Howe's *Making Your Own Preserves* ([Pudsey, York, England: Magna Print Books, 1974], 78). **Keep in mind what a preserve is and you do not need a recipe. Just mix the sugar with the namesake and pH-adjust with vinegar, citrus, or another acid.**

Jamlady likes to name her "jams" and offers the name **Marrow Medley** for a gingered squash-pineapple preserves. One friendly proofreader disagreed about the use of the word *medley,* expressing it should only be used to name musical scores. Jamlady thinks pineapple and ginger evoke musical connotations, and *medley* can also mean a mixture, so Jamlady will call this gingered squash-pineapple preserve **Marrow Medley.**

⟳⟲

Marrow Medley

Peeled squash can be cooked with pineapple, sugar, and gingerroot to make preserves. Add equal parts of squash fruits to sugar plus about 2 cups of fresh or canned pineapple in its juice per gallon of prepared squash and 1 cup of fresh gingerroot or prepared ginger. This "no-can" version of squash preserves, **Marrow Medley,** has no lemon, and of course, as with many preserves, the fruits should be layered with the sugar for 8-12 hours to weep out the juices prior to cooking. Jamlady often makes this recipe and gives some away, "uncanned," as a compliment for cottage cheese or yogurt. **Store this completed preserve in the refrigerator (JSR).**

Caution: Do not can this Marrow Medley recipe unless you check the pH prior to canning and find it to be well under 4.3. Grated lemon peel or citric acid could be added to the recipe if it is to be canned or less squash can be used with more pineapple. Use your trusty pH meter to check each batch. A specific recipe is very difficult to give because the pH of squash is variable between 5.10-6.20. The zucchini marmalade recipe below has a lot more acid in the formulation, so it may be canned. If you have a pH meter, Jamlady recommends you test your batches, so you can learn firsthand how much lemon or other acidifier must be used for proper recipe formulation. This may be even easier with the advent of the new stainless-steel pH probe with ISFET silicon chip pH sensor. These are brand-new. Jamlady is still using a traditional glass pH electrode, which can break more easily. For sure, Jamlady and others should check out this new pH meter, because it stores dry, is easy to clean, and supposedly lasts longer.

Recipes also vary regarding the peeling of the squash. Most all zucchini preserves or marmalade recipes recommend peeling, but Marion Brown's *Pickles and Preserves* ([New York: Wilfred Funk, Inc., 1955], 171) does not mention peeling, and Jamlady remembers eating some zucchini jam at an American Field Service party years ago and the zucchini was not peeled. If very small zucchini with tender skins are used, Jamlady sees no reason why the zucchini would have to be peeled. Jamlady has made zucchini preserves with the skins, and it was fine. As a point of comparison, Howe's cucumber conserve in *Making Your Own Preserves* uses unpeeled cucumbers.

Grow some **marrow** this year as they do in England. Maybe the neighbors will be more receptive to marrow as something newer than those baseball bats that grow ahiding under big leaves! When your neighbors say, "Oh no, not another zucchini!" you can say, "It's not a zucchini. It's a marrow!" And, hopefully that difference will mean they will take some marrows off your hands. If not, convert the bloomin' *Cucurbita pepos* into marmalade, relish, chutney, casserole, and soup base.

Jamlady noticed an old recipe for **Vegetable Marrow Jam**—in *Good Cookery* by Francillon, W. G. R., and G. T. C. D. S. (1920; reprint, London: J. M. Dent & Sons, Ltd., 1948)— using, by weight, 4 parts sugar, 3 parts marrow, 2 parts apple, juice of 2 lemons and the rind of 1 lemon for every 3 pounds of marrow, and ¼ part

gingerroot or preserved ginger. As is done with many preserves, weep the marrow for 12-24 hours (depending on the size of the marrow pieces) with part of the sugar. Weep long enough that the juices are sufficiently out of the marrow. Refrigerate or check and adjust the pH before canning.

৩৫

Marrow or Zucchini Marmalade

Serve with thinly sliced ham, crusty bread, and cottage cheese!

8 cups peeled, processor-shredded (or small cubes—½" ½") marrow or zucchini

Grated zest or rind of 3 lemons

Lemon pulp of 3 lemons (without seeds, pith, and core)

Pip bag with all citrus seeds (optional)

Grated zest or rind of 4 Clementines or 2 oranges

Clementine or orange pulp of 4 Clementines or 2 oranges (without seeds, pith, and core)

2 cups crushed pineapple in its own juice (optional with 1 cup of sugar more)

4 tablespoons peeled, grated gingerroot or substitute spice (optional)

½ cup nuts (optional)

¼ to ⅓ cup liqueur of choice (optional)

½ to ¾ cups sugar for each pound of fruit mixture

In this recipe the citrus can be juiced, and both the juice and the pulp extract can be added back into the weeping pot. Measure the rind, marrow or zucchini, citrus juice and pulp, and add ½ to ¾ cup sugar for each pound of fruit mixture. Layer the sugar and fruit and let the mixture sit overnight in the "weeping pot."

Cook down the wept mixture with the ginger-root or substitute spice. Jamlady is speculating here—perhaps the substitute spice could be whole or ground cloves. If you don't like ginger-root, skip the gingerroot and mix in nuts—like almonds or macadamia nuts—at the end. No doubt Grand Marnier would go well with any number of combinations, including the recipe with no lemon or no ginger. Test and adjust the pH of your product, if necessary, and JSP/RWB10 or JSR.

Note: Jamlady still has ideas of a marrow or zucchini jam for meats or cottage cheese, made with some of the following ingredients: sage, rosemary, tarragon, white pepper, grapefruit (instead of oranges and maybe reduce or eliminate the lemons), balsamic vinegar, sherry, garlic, malt vinegar, cucumbers, onion, chives, Campari . . . but Jamlady's mother says, "No more cooking. Just finish writing the book." Maybe the grated marrow should be cooked with freshly juiced apple or pear juice, maple syrup, and vinegar to make an herbal jam! Jamlady has seen even rutabaga and grated parsnips tossed into a basic marmalade. Jamlady hopes she has given some of you creative types some ideas! Just make sure your jam is sufficiently acidic.

Check all new-and-unproven recipes with a pH meter or refrigerate the product. If you don't use lemon juice or lemons, you could use vinegar instead, and—quiz time—if we do this do we have a "jam" or a chutney? Then think about why hot pepper jelly is a jelly and not a chutney. It has vinegar! As you can see, there are gray areas. Just be careful of your acid levels with these low-acid root crops, and at some point, you have to ask yourself, "If I am not a parsnip farmer, why use this vegetable if regular marmalade tastes better?" Do you do it to be different, to survive, or to make great product? While Jamlady likes unique, she doesn't want to sacrifice quality just to be different.

To digress for a moment, and to further Jamlady's point, Jamlady was told once by a family friend who was so poor while growing up that he had to take lard sandwiches to school—or not eat—that he became a good salesman because he was able to convince other students to trade sandwiches. His sales pitch was "Even if you do not like the lard sandwich, at least you will know what it tastes like." **The lesson: Trying new things always comes with a few risks . . . and different doesn't necessarily mean good.**

For those cooks seeking a quicker solution, try this marrow recipe with added pectin. Keep in mind that even "added-pectin" recipes can be halved or quartered. There are approximately 18 teaspoons of pectin to the 1¾ ounce box of powdered pectin. This is an approximate number of teaspoons, and Jamlady has had boxes with more and less. You can measure out a box to see what you get, but an exact measurement is not necessary, as the product will be boiled to set point anyway. Of course, if you have an accurate scales like a postal scales, then measure out the needed pectin by weight. Just use a pan with a proportionally smaller surface area, and use ½ or ¼ of the pectin required for a recipe cut by ½ or ¼ respectively. Jam making need not be a long and involved project, and "jams" need not be canned. Consider making just one or two cups of "jams" for a layer cake or cookie batch, and use the jam immediately.

Gingered Marrow Jam

Made with added pectin.

6 cups peeled, processor-grated or thinly sliced
  chips of marrow or zucchini (about 2 pounds)
5 cups sugar
Juice from 2 lemons
1 teaspoon grated lemon peel
13-14 ounces drained pineapple from a 20-
  ounce can of pineapple in its own juice
1 1¾-ounce package regular powdered pectin
2-3 tablespoons peeled and finely grated fresh
  gingerroot.

Boil the following ingredients, uncovered, for 15 minutes: chipped or grated squash, lemon juice and peel, gingerroot, and drained pineapple. Add the pectin; boil for 1 minute. Stir in the sugar; boil for 1 minute. Check the set. JSP/RWB10.

Mr. Ovid Shifras is a friend of the Schoonmaker and Alfeld families. Ovid is a squash expert who worked for quite a few years in research and development for Burpee Seed Company. Ovid is never without a greenhouse. Even at ninety-plus years, he is still working on his squash experiments in Indiana. One day while touring Ovid's tagged squash displays in Naples, Florida, at Northrup, Jamlady asked Ovid what he was doing. He said, "Oh, I'm trying to take the wrinkles or ripples out of the squash's surface, so they will be easier to peel." To which Jamlady asked, "Ovid, how long will that take?" "Oh, only about a hundred years." "Ovid," said Jamlady, "I don't think you're going to make it."

Ovid sent Jamlady some seed so she could try to grow these experimental squash in Illinois. While they were the sweetest squash Jamlady has ever tasted, the cucumber beetles thought so too, and it was very difficult to keep the plants alive.

Jamlady had to germinate the seeds three times, use caps, and chemical sprays to keep the beetles from devouring the small seedlings.

Every year there are pumpkins left over after Halloween. Most of the farmers dump the leftover pumpkins. Jamlady always sees this as a shame and wonders when and if Americans will ever realize that pumpkins are great to eat in dishes besides pumpkin pie, which they more than likely make from canned pumpkin. Jamlady always puts pumpkin in stir-fry, and it is well received. Just don't overcook the pumpkin, as it is best somewhat crunchy. Pumpkin soup and, indeed, mashed pumpkin are good, fall recipes that put pumpkins back on the menu.

Pumpkins and squash are in the *Cucurbita* species. *Cucurbita pepo* Linn. are pumpkins. Even the little pumpkins that are painted with the little funny cartoon faces for the holidays can be eaten and, additionally, make a nice container in which to serve a small portion of pumpkin soup, baked custard (baked in pumpkin), or baked apples. Just steam them and fill them with the soup and serve, or stuff them with mushroom-and-sausage dressing and bake. If you cut the tops carefully, you can even put on a lid.

To make **Curried Pumpkin-Apple Soup,** use ¼ cup butter, 1 garlic clove, 1 chopped onion or 5 shallots, 1 chopped leek (white part only), 1 large cooking apple (peeled and chopped), 1 tablespoon curry powder, 2 cups peeled and cubed pumpkin or 1 can of pumpkin purée, 4 cups chicken or turkey stock, 1 cup of whipping cream, salt and pepper, and apple wedges or green onion strips. In a saucepan, heat the butter. Add the garlic, onion, leek, and apple. Sauté until softened. Stir in the curry powder and cook for 1 minute. Add the pumpkin and stock. Bring to a boil, stirring occasionally; reduce the heat and simmer for 20 minutes or until vegetables are tender. When cooled, "blenderize" the mixture for a smooth soup. Refrigerate the soup until it is time to serve. To serve the soup, heat it up again and slowly add the cream, stirring constantly. If you have a large batch of soup, reheat it in a double boiler to avoid burning the soup on the edges and bottom of the pan. Put the soup into serving dishes and decorate with apple wedges or green onion strips, salt, and pepper. For other versions, use olive oil instead of butter, and milk instead of cream.

One of Jamlady's original preserves recipes is this wonderful preserve made with uncooked pumpkins that are peeled and cut into slices. If you love pumpkins, you are going to really enjoy these classy preserves. Market patrons give Jamlady frequent accolades for this special pumpkin creation, and at least one Internet site for pumpkin lovers has had Jamlady's recipe posted for several years. Some smart and frugal cooks choose to paint their pumpkins for Halloween and then convert their smaller decorative pumpkins into Sliced Pumpkin Preserves with Grand Marnier.

ꙮ

Sliced Pumpkin Preserves with Grand Marnier

Great on buttermilk biscuits or inside a flaky tart!

9 cups sliced pumpkin (2 six- to eight-inch-diameter pumpkins)

2$\frac{1}{8}$ cups sugar (add in steps)

1 cup water (add in steps)

$\frac{1}{4}$ cup Grand Marnier (optional but recommended)

Grated rind from 2 lemons

$\frac{1}{4}$ cup chopped macadamia nuts or pistachio nuts (optional, often instead of the liqueur)

Grate the outer rinds of lemon. Peel, seed, and processor-slice the pumpkin. Mix the two with

1$\frac{1}{8}$ cups sugar. Cook very, very slowly, stirring constantly—until all the sugar is melted and the pumpkin is mostly cooked. If the preserves get too dry, add in steps—$\frac{1}{4}$ cup sugar and $\frac{1}{4}$ cup water—until the extra cup of sugar and 1 cup of water is used up. This should take about 1$\frac{1}{2}$-2 hours. At the end, add the Grand Marnier and/or the nuts. JSP/RWB10.

Note: Any extra or leftover raw pumpkin can be used in stir-frys or can be steamed as a side dish with butter and seasoning.

Caution: Be careful not to leave out the grated lemon rind. Safe canning requires a pH of under 4.6, and pumpkins are 5.0, as are carrots. For this reason, lemon, lemon rinds, or lime and lime rinds, which have a pH of 2.2 and 2.0 respectively, are usually added to bring the combined pH into the safety zone. Do not alter recipes unless you understand the significance of pH in a safely canned product.

Note: If you think the recipe for pumpkin preserves is a new recipe, think again. Jamlady found directions for pumpkin preserves made with "diamonds, hearts, or any other fancy shape you desire," in Mrs. M. E. Peterson's Preserving, Pickling & Canning—Fruit Manual ([Philadelphia, PA: G. Peterson and Company, 1869], 11), but there wasn't any mention of adding liquor or brandy like Jamlady does. Why not try both variations together? Who is worthy to eat such a labor of love? See Bar-le-Duc.

RHUBARB

Rhubarb, *Rheum rhaponticum,* is extremely popular at farmers' markets. Jamlady has decided that this is because a lot of people like rhubarb, and very few processed rhubarb products are available in the regular grocery store. This marmalade is tops. Jamlady has made variations with Clementines and other citrus with good results. Lemons work well too, as they provide the necessary pectin to set the marmalade. This marmalade can be made in larger batches, but it will take longer to cook down than if you make two pans side-by-side.

ᏨᏨ

Rhubarb and Orange Marmalade

Good on toast, ice cream, or cheesecake!
No added pectin, just rhubarb, 'Valencia' oranges, and sugar.

1 pound rhubarb
2½ cups sugar
1 juicy 'Valencia' orange

Processor-slice the rhubarb without peeling. Wash the orange; cut off the outer rind and finely chop the peel or rind. Discard all pith. Combine the sugar, chopped orange rind, and rhubarb. Allow the mixture to weep overnight in a cool place. Remove the rest of the pith from the orange, and juice the orange in a juicing machine. Add the orange juice to the rhubarb mixture and cook the marmalade until thick. JSP/RWB10.

Variation: Rhubarb and Orange Conserve—3 pints rhubarb or any tart fruit, 1 pound raisins, 4 oranges with no pith and some grated rind, 8 cups sugar, ½ pint water. Cook all for 15 minutes; add ½ pound nuts (Recipe of Mrs. John Osterhoudt, Warwarsing, New York. The Light of the Kitchen, *Kerhonkson, NY: Willing Workers Society of the Methodist Episcopal Church, n.d. 64).*

Rhubarb Marmalade

A classic marmalade for a toasted English muffin or scone!
No pectin, just rhubarb, lemons, and sugar.

1 pound rhubarb
2½ cups sugar
1 lemon
1 ounce preserved angelica (optional)

Thinly slice the rhubarb without peeling. Wash the lemon, cut off the yellow outer rind, and chop it. Combine the sugar, rind, and rhubarb. Weep the mixture overnight. Add the lemon juice and angelica in the morning and cook until thick. JSP/RWB10.

If you do not want the lemon flavor in rhubarb preserves, try a combination of 4 pounds processor-sliced rhubarb, 6 cups sugar, and ½ teaspoon citric acid for Rhubarb Preserves with Citric Acid. Layer the sugar and rhubarb and let the mixture sit overnight in a cool location before cooking down the preserve. To get more creative, add candied citron, nuts, or a liqueur—maybe a liqueur flavored with angelica. **Rhubarb-Kiwi Preserves** could be made as well. Use ½ the recipe for rhubarb preserves and ½ the recipe for kiwi preserves.

*Variation: Jamlady noted a similar recipe, called **Preserved Rhubarb,** in Mrs. M. E. Peterson's Preserving, Pickling and Canning— Fruit Manual ([Philadelphia, PA: G. Peterson and Company, 1869], 15): 1 pound rhubarb, ¾ pound sugar, juice of 1 lemon, and narrow strips of rind.*

*Note: Angelica, **Angelica archangelica Linn.,** is a three-year "biennial herb" or wild celery. This slightly licorice-flavored plant can be candied, made into jam, or mixed into jam. See Rombauer and Becker's* **The Joy of Cooking** *(page 743) or Leyel's* **Herbal Delights** *(page 17) for more information. Angelica seeds are sold as Persian "golpar," powdered, and used as a natural Beano®. See the liqueur section of this book for more on angelica.*

ဢ

Authentic Rhubarb Preserves

No added pectin.

1 quart sliced rhubarb (2 pounds)
3 cups sugar
1 tablespoon lime or lemon juice
¼ cup water

Mix the rhubarb and sugar in a stainless-steel pan. Cover the mixture and let it sit for 6-8 hours at room temperature. Then mix the lime or lemon juice and water with the mixture and bring it to a boil, stirring frequently. Boil for 30-40 minutes, or to 219-221 degrees F or to 104-105 degrees C, or until you have about 32-36 ounces of preserves. JSP/RWB5(4OZ)10(8OZ). Food coloring may be added if a pure red color is desired. Jamlady prefers this preserve with its natural color.

Note: Most jams or preserves will set when the temperature of the "jam" reaches, or is just approaching, 104-105 degrees C or 219-221 degrees F.

ဢ

Authentic Strawberry-Rhubarb Preserves

No added pectin.

1 quart processor-sliced rhubarb
6 cups sugar
1 quart washed, hulled, processor-sliced strawberries (2 quarts before slicing)
¼ cup freshly squeezed lemon juice

Let the sliced rhubarb and sugar weep in a stainless-steel pan overnight. On the next day, add the strawberries with the lemon juice. Wait 30 minutes and then cook until thick enough. JSP/RWB10. (See the recipe for Classic Strawberry-Rhubarb Preserves.)

Classic Strawberry-Rhubarb Jam

Most everyone loves strawberry-rhubarb jam!

Made with added pectin.

5½ cups sugar
2 cups hulled, processor-sliced strawberries
2 cups very finely processor-chopped rhubarb
1 1¾-ounce box regular powdered pectin
¼ cup lemon juice
¼ teaspoon ascorbic acid crystals

Use half the ascorbic acid crystals in the wash or prep water and the rest on the strawberries while slicing them. Boil the rhubarb, strawberries, lemon juice, and pectin for 1 minute. Add the sugar. Boil for 1 minute.
JSP/RWB5(4 OZ)10(8OZ).

Rhubarb Jelly can be made with liquid pectin or powdered pectin, but it may also be made as a marmalade, with citrus juice instead of pectin. (See Rhubarb Marmalade.) The problem with using the citrus is that it tastes like lemons and rhubarb or oranges and rhubarb. Those who want only the rhubarb taste can use this recipe or the rhubarb preserves recipe.

Rhubarb Jelly

Made with liquid pectin.
Rhubarb is low in natural pectin.

3½ cups sugar
1¾ cups rhubarb juice
¼ teaspoon butter
1 3-ounce pouch liquid pectin
½ cup water

Cook the pieces of rhubarb in the water until soft. Hang the rhubarb mixture in a jelly bag or run it through a Champion juicing machine to extract the juice. Cook the juice, sugar, and butter for 3 minutes. Add the pectin and boil for 1 minute. JSP/RWB10. Appropximate pH = 3.57.

Note: Rhubarb juice can also be extracted from raw rhubarb, but cut the pieces crosswise into small pieces or you may damage your juicing machine with the long fibrous strings.

Variation: Spiced Rhubarb Jelly—The rhubarb jelly recipe above is not spiced or flavored, but it could be. Try nutmeg, vanilla, or mint extract in the rhubarb juice. Fresh-cut mint stems with leaves may also be put in hot rhubarb juice to infuse the mint flavor into the rhubarb juice. Remove the mint stems after the mint flavor has been imparted to the rhubarb juice. Jamlady's inspiration can be traced to a recipe on the Internet for fresh Rhubarb Mint Chutney, intended to compliment roast leg of lamb. Jamlady says creative chefs are always thinking about what will go with what and looking to other recipes, even recipes of a different category, for inspiration.

Jamlady has included this rhubarb-nutmeg recipe to illustrate rhubarb jam made with powdered pectin. While the flavor of the rhubarb does not have lemon or orange in it, Jamlady would never select this rhubarb jam, made with added pectin, over the rhubarb marmalades given above. Yet, there are people who do select this recipe over the others.

Rhubarb-Nutmeg Jam

Rhubarb with nutmeg is absolutely great!

8 cups chopped rhubarb (4½ cups cooked-down rhubarb)
2 cups water
6½ cups sugar
1 1¾-ounce box powdered pectin
1 teaspoon nutmeg (optional)
½ teaspoon butter

Cook the rhubarb and water in the microwave or on the stove until most of the water is gone. Measure out 4½ cups of cooked rhubarb. Boil the rhubarb and pectin for 1 minute. Add the sugar, butter, and nutmeg; boil for 1 more minute. Check the set. JSP/RWB10.

Variation: Rhubarb Conserve—Add raisins, nuts, or both to equal 1 cup.

TOMATO JAMS AND PRESERVES

One of the most popular categories of old-timer preserves is tomato preserves. Jamlady has made easily over a hundred different jellies, jams, preserves, conserves, or butters from tomatoes: green, yellow, orange, and red. This versatile tomato-citron conserve with pecan halves is an original Jamlady formulation. Any citrus, such as Clementines, calamondins, or kumquats, can be used instead of the orange or lemon.

Tomato-Citron Conserve with Pecan Halves

Serve as a "jam" or use on ice cream, cottage cheese, or cheesecake!

4 pounds tomato meats
6 cups sugar
1 orange
1 lemon
3 ounces candied citron
4 ounces raisins
4 ounces pecan halves

Weep the tomato meats in the sugar overnight. Strain and cook the liquid with the lemon, orange, and citron until the liquid spins a thread. The oranges and lemons may be sliced whole or equivalent measures of orange and lemon peels and pulp may be used without the pith. Discard all seeds. Add in the tomato meats, cook down a little more, add the raisins and nuts, and check set. JSP/RWB10.

Another variation of the same tomato conserve uses English and black walnuts for a more earthy and full-bodied flavor. No added pectin is necessary to affect a set in this jam, as the natural pectin in the citrus fruits does the job perfectly.

Tomato Conserve with English and Black Walnuts

Use on bread, ice cream, crackers, pancakes, French toast, or cheesecake.

4 pounds skinless, seedless tomato meats
6 cups sugar
1 1/4 cups dark raisins
1 lemon
1 orange
1/4 cup black walnuts
1/4 cup English walnuts
1/2 teaspoon ground cinnamon

Plunge the tomatoes in boiling hot water for 1 minute and then into cold water. Remove the skins and seeds and reserve the meats. Layer the sugar and tomato meats and let them sit overnight. Using the French Plunge Method, strain out the meats and cook down the juice until it reaches 105 degrees C. To prepare the citrus fruits, either slice the fruits whole and remove the seeds or remove all outer citrus rinds by grating or cutting them into slivered pieces. Then remove the seeds and pith from the citrus fruits and slice the remaining fruits or run these fruits (without pith or seeds) through a juicing machine and use the outputs from both hoppers. Discard all citrus seeds or boil them in a pip bag with the rest of the mixture. Add the prepared citrus fruits and peels, and boil for 10 minutes. Add in the tomato meats and the cinnamon and cook down. Add in the dark raisins and cook to jell point. Add the nuts, cool, and check for appropriate thickness on a frozen plate. JSP/RWB10.

This plainer, but no less impressive, recipe uses golden raisins and nutmeg. Technically a conserve, this marmalade and preserves combines citrus fruits, tomatoes, and golden raisins

for a delightful country accompaniment for bread, ice cream, crackers, pancakes, or cheesecake. All of these tomato preserves recipes can be made with different types and colors of tomatoes, adding to the many more exciting combinations that could be made.

🙰🙰

Tomato Marmalade with Golden or Dark Raisins

Tomatoes are fruits and make great preserves.

4 pounds skinless, seedless tomato meats
6 cups sugar
1 cup golden or dark raisins (about 1/3 pound)
1 lemon
1 orange
1/2 teaspoon ground cinnamon
1/4 teaspoon ground or freshly grated nutmeg

Plunge the tomatoes in boiling hot water to remove the skins and seeds. Layer the sugar and tomato meats overnight. Strain out the meats and cook down the juice until it reaches 105 degrees C. To prepare the citrus fruits, either slice the fruits whole and remove the seeds or remove all outer citrus rinds by grating or cutting them into slivered pieces. Then remove the seeds and pith from the citrus fruits and slice the remaining fruits or run these fruits (without pith or seeds) through a juicing machine and use the outputs from both hoppers. Discard all citrus seeds or boil them in a pip bag with the rest of the mixture. Add the prepared or sliced citrus fruits and boil for 10 minutes. Add back in the previously plunged tomato meats with the spices

Tomato Marmalade with Golden or Dark Raisins is made with seedless, skinless, tomato meats, sliced lemons and oranges, cinnamon, freshly grated nutmeg, sugar, and raisins. This versatile preserve can be served on bread, cottage cheese, yogurt, or even ice cream. As shown, this marmalade can be served directly in a slightly hollowed-out fresh tomato for that special brunch or luncheon.

and cook everything down. Add in the raisins and cook the mixture to jell point. JSP/RWB10.

Spicing up the basic recipe with allspice makes for an interesting variation, as does adding candied citron and lemon peel. The number of variations on this basic tomato marmalade theme is endless. The type of nuts, candied peels, spices, cultivar of tomato, cultivar of orange or other citrus used (such as Clementines, kumquats, and blood oranges) allows for hundreds of variations just on this one basic recipe. **Tomatillos, *Physalis ixocarpa*, might well be used in this type of recipe instead of tomatoes, as could tamarillos, tree tomatoes, *Solanum betaceum*, or ground cherries, *Physalis alkekengi* Linn.**

*Note: Blood oranges, **Citrus sinensis**, of various cultivars are available in some grocery stores now. There are four fairly well-known cultivars: 'Moro Blood,' 'Toracco,' 'Sanguinelli,' and the famous 'Maltese'. The 'Maltese' blood orange, **Citrus sinensis 'Maltese'**, is used with hollandaise sauce to make Maltese or Maltaise Sauce (**Malteser Sosse**), which is used with asparagus, green beans, and broiled meats and fish. Blood oranges contain vitamin C and **bioflavonoids** (vitamin P—not really a vitamin), the latter enhancing the absorption of the former. Try some blood oranges in a marmalade.*

Spiced Tomato Marmalade with Raisins

Something special for the tomato and marmalade lover!

16 cups tomato meats
20 cups sugar
4 cups cooked-down tomato sauce or purée
28 ounces candied lemon peel
1 pound raisins
6 oranges
6 lemons
½ pound candied citron
1 tablespoon cinnamon
1 teaspoon allspice
½ teaspoon salt

Tomatoes may be juiced to obtain the juice, which is cooked down to purée. Use enough water to cover the peels. Cook the outer lemon and orange peels in water for 10 minutes. Discard the water; reserve the peels and sliver them. Remove all pith and slice the oranges and lemons. Discard the seeds or put them in a pip bag and cook them along with the mixture. Add the cooked peels to the rest of the ingredients—minus the raisins. Cook the mixture down until thick. Add the raisins near the end. JSP/RWB10. This recipe may be halved, quartered, or subdivided further.

Spiced Tomato-Lemon Peel Conserve

Great on bread, crackers, vanilla ice cream, pound cake, or cheesecake!
Good in thumbprint cookies!

6½ cups sugar

4 cups chopped, seeded, and peeled tomato meats

4 cups cooked-down tomato purée

2 cups raisins

10 ounces candied lemon peel

3 ounces chopped, fresh gingerroot

1 3-ounce pouch liquid pectin

2 tablespoons lemon juice

1 teaspoon ground cinnamon

1 teaspoon ground mace

Tomatoes may be juiced to obtain the juice, which is cooked down to purée. The size of the batch will determine how long it takes to cook down the purée (sauce). Plunge the tomatoes in hot water for 60 seconds to peel them easily and obtain the tomato meats. Cook down all of the ingredients except the pectin for about 30 minutes. Add the pectin and cook for another 20 to 30 minutes or to set point. Refrigerate, if necessary, to check the cooled thickness. A soft-side set is preferable to overcooking. JSP/RWB10.

Of course, green tomatoes—as well as yellow, orange, and red tomatoes—can be used to make marmalade. The only difference is that most green-tomato recipes call for the green tomatoes, like strawberry "gems" and Bing cherry preserves, to be wept with the sugar overnight. Jamlady has made green-tomato preserves with low-sugar pectin and did not like how it turned out, despite the fact that the recipe was published in a well-distributed cookbook. Jamlady deemed the texture grainy, dry, and unacceptable. Of the green-tomato jam or preserve recipes that Jamlady has tried, she much prefers the recipes with ginger or cinnamon to those without spice.

While the various green-tomato recipes in most books contain essentially the same ingredients, the methods do vary slightly, and the sugar ratios to green tomatoes vary quite a bit. Many cookbooks treat **green-tomato jam** as preserves and allow equal sugar to sliced green tomatoes; they then add 1-3 lemons or other citrus for every 4 cups of sugar and green tomatoes plus a spice, such as a cinnamon stick, ground ginger, fresh ginger, or both. Other ratios with less sugar are 4 pounds green tomatoes, 3 pounds sugar, 3 lemons, ½ tablespoon fresh or preserved ginger; or 2 pounds green tomatoes, 1 cup water, 3 cups sugar, and 1 lemon. Some cook the green tomatoes in water before adding the sugar or at least pour hot water over the tomatoes and let them stand for a few minutes before draining the water off and slicing the green tomatoes. This makes sense, because it might help to tenderize the tomato skins. Some people peel the skins from the green tomatoes before proceeding. Essentially, these green-tomato preserves are marmalades. If the green tomatoes are not boiled in water, then they usually are allowed to weep with the sugar overnight before the mixture is boiled down into preserves. Try the different methods explained and vary the sugar as you like.

This next recipe is a good way to use up those end-of-the season green tomatoes or pick green tomatoes early in the season so more actual tomatoes will grow on the tomato plants—or so they say!

Green Tomato Preserves with Ginger

Good on cottage cheese or toasted whole-wheat bagel!

4 pounds green plum tomatoes ('Roma')
3 pounds sugar
3 large lemons
1-2 tablespoons grated orange or Clementine peel (optional)
1 tablespoon freshly grated gingerroot or cinnamon stick

Wash the tomatoes. Boil a large pot of water on the stove. Plunge the tomatoes into the boiling water and cover the pot for 5 minutes. Remove the tomatoes and plunge them into cold water. Thinly slice the tomatoes to make 2-3" circle slices and layer them with sugar. Add very thinly sliced lemons (minus the pits) and the orange peel. Let the mixture weep for at least 8 hours. Drain the syrup and add the grated ginger or cinnamon stick. Boil for 6-8 minutes. Add the tomato and lemon mixture and boil rapidly until the fruits become somewhat transparent. Check the set. JSP/RWB10.

Variation: Gingered Red Tomato Marmalade—Make this recipe with red or yellow tomatoes. Plunge the tomatoes in hot boiling water for 1 minute and then plunge them into cold water. Remove the skins and seeds and work with the tomato meats.

Tomato Jelly

Very good with cream cheese and crackers!

10 cups sugar
4 cups freshly extracted tomato juice, cooked down some
1½ cups lemon juice
2 3-ounce pouches liquid pectin (6 ounces)
6 drops Louisiana hot sauce or Tabascö

Juice the tomatoes; cook the juice for 15 minutes. Measure out 4 cups of juice. Add the lemon juice, hot sauce, and sugar; boil for 1 minute. Add the pectin and boil for 1 minute. Check for set with a frozen plate or boil the mixture until the thermometer reaches or almost reaches 105 degrees C. Measure carefully.
JSP/RWB5(4OZ)10(8OZ).

Note: The amount of tomato juice in tomatoes can vary by cultivar. 'Roma' tomatoes will have more meat and less juice than a slicer. If you are juicing tomatoes by hand, you will need more tomatoes than you would if you are using a Champion juicing machine to obtain the tomato juice. Allow a minimum of 3¼ pound of tomatoes for each quart of juice.

If you have a pulp-extraction juicing machine, such as a Champion, the whole tomato can be washed and juiced and the purée cooked down some. Use the juice or purée for these jelly recipes. If you don't have a juicing machine, scald the tomatoes, remove the seeds and skins, and "blenderize" the meats to make the juice.

This tomato-lemon jelly can be made with mint extracts, or it can be made by using very aromatic mint that is first cooked in the tomato juice and then strained out completely, or almost completely, except for a very few small chopped pieces of mint. As with basil, there are many different cultivars of mint, and many are not very aromatic. See the tomato-basil recipe.

Tomato Mint Jelly

Great with lamb!

10 cups sugar
4 cups freshly extracted tomato juice
1½ cups lemon juice
2 3-ounce pouches liquid pectin (6 ounces)
1 tablespoon mint extract
½ tablespoon peppermint extract

Boil the tomato juice, lemon juice, and sugar. Add the pectin; boil 1 minute. Add the extracts; stir well. Check for set; boil longer if necessary to achieve a set. JSP/RWB5(4OZ)10(8OZ).

Jamlady has made umpteen variations of tomato jelly, flavoring it with gingerroot, powdered cinnamon, oil of cinnamon, nutmeg, basil, hot pepper, dill, and mint to name but a few. Jamlady has made tomato-cilantro and tomato-fennel jelly and did not like either combination—just in case you thought those might be a good idea. Specious recipes are always a problem. When attempting to flavor basic recipes with spices or liqueurs, be careful not to assume too much. Most experimental recipes should be tried in a small way and then modified to get them just right.

This tomato jelly recipe can be made with basil, and hotness can be added by cooking habanero peppers in the tomato purée or juice before the straining step. Remove the peppers with the straining step. Not all basil is really aromatic. Find the strongest-flavored and most aromatic basil possible. Jamlady had the best results with basil called 'Mammoth' basil, *Ocimum bacilicum.* 'Mammoth' was sold by a farmers' market vendor named Mike. Unfortunately, Mike is no longer vending basil, and Jamlady has not found the time to buy the seed and grow it herself. The large, aromatic, basil leaves tasted of licorice and mint and were wonderful in salads and "jams."

Tomato-Basil Jelly

A good jelly for meat sandwiches and hamburgers!

10 cups sugar
4 cups freshly extracted tomato juice
1½ cups lemon juice
2 3-ounce pouches liquid pectin (6 ounces)
6 drops Louisiana hot sauce or Tabascö
6 tablespoons finely chopped basil leaves

Cook the basil leaves with the tomato juice. Strain out most all of the basil. Measure out 4 cups of juice. Add the lemon juice, hot sauce, and sugar; boil for 1 minute. Add the pectin; boil for 1 minute. Check the set; boil longer if necessary. JSP/RWB5(4OZ)10(8OZ).

Of course, Jamlady would not want the "sugar watchers" to be denied tomato "jam." The "No-Sugar" Tomato-Basil Jam recipe that follows, along with the "jams"-with-molasses recipes is a Jamlady original and can be made with all of the same herbal variations—basil, dill, and mint—as the original sugar-based jelly. If a low-sugar jam is desired, make the "no-sugar" tomato-basil jam with 1-3 cups sugar, 1 cup honey, or maybe even try maple syrup or a little molasses. **But, remember, if using maple syrup or molasses, always measure the pH or keep the product refrigerated at all times.** "No-sugar" jams are best kept refrigerated anyway!

Since molasses tastes good in bean and tomato recipes, it would be interesting to see what it would be like in tomato jam, with or without the basil or another herb. Try using some (a little, not a lot) molasses in place of some of the sugar, instead of using only molasses, as molasses is pretty strong tasting. **Remember, molasses is not very successful in most jam recipes due to its strong flavor, and it does have a high pH, which would need to be lowered through** acidification, if canned. Most molasses recipes, like the two that follow, cannot be canned and need to be refrigerated (*150 Practical and Tasty Recipes,* a publication of Grandma's Molasses/Mott's Inc., 26).

Prune Conserve: 3 cups cooked, chopped prunes (stoned); 1 cup seeded, chopped raisins; 2 oranges (juice, pulp, and grated rind); 1½ cups sugar; 1½ cups water; ½ cup Grandma's Molasses. JSR.

Fruit Conserve: 3 cups cherries, 2 cups grated pineapple, 2 oranges and grated rind, 1 lemon and grated rind, 2 cups sugar, 1 cup Grandma's Molasses, and ¾ cup walnut meats. When using less sugar or an alternate sugar, such as molasses or honey, it may be necessary to use a "no-sugar" pectin to achieve a set, and then the product, depending on the final pH, will probably be a "refrigerate only" product. JSR.

☙❧

"No-Sugar" Tomato-Basil Jam

Sweetened with aspartame.

3 cups freshly extracted, basil-flavored tomato juice
1 cup lemon juice
1 1¾-ounce box "no-sugar" powdered pectin
30 packets aspartame or other "no-sugar" substitute
8 tablespoons chopped basil leaves
6 drops Louisana hot sauce

Cook some tomato juice with the basil for 10 minutes. Strain out the basil. Mix the pectin with the tomato juice, lemon juice, hot sauce, and a little new, chopped basil. Wait 10 minutes; boil 1 minute. Add the sweetener and boil 1 minute more. JSP/RWB5(4OZ)10(8OZ).

Note: As with other sugar-free recipes, 1-3 cups of sugar can be used when the amount of juice or fruit is increased. Jamlady has not made this jam in "low sugar," so you will just have to try 1-2 cups sugar to 4 cups tomato juice and 1 cup lemon juice as a test batch.

☙❧

Tomato Ginger Jelly

10 cups sugar
4 cups freshly juiced tomato juice
1½ cups lemon juice
2 3-ounce pouches liquid pectin (6 ounces)
Several small gingerroot pieces

Juice the tomatoes and cook the juice for 15 minutes with the gingerroot, to taste. Measure out 4 cups of juice. Add the lemon juice and sugar; boil for 1 minute. Add the pectin; boil for 1 minute. Check the set; boil more if necessary. JSP/RWB5(4OZ)10(8OZ).

Ginger with tomatoes is spectacular! Jam can be made by adding pectin, and preserves can be made with no added pectin. Jamlady always makes her tomato preserves by scalding the tomatoes in hot water, removing the skins and seeds, and using only the tomato meats. Some people do comment that their family jam makers leave the seeds in and that their family prefers tomato preserves with seeds. Jamlady prefers tomato preserves without the seeds. As with the two schools of seeded or unseeded raspberry jam, differences in preferences and opinions regarding seeds in jams occur over and over.

Few preserves are as beautiful and tasty as tomato-ginger preserves. This preserve is also wonderful when made with the small yellow pear tomatoes or the larger 'Lemon Boy' tomatoes (yellow "slicers"). Interesting preserves can be made from half-red and half-yellow preserves. Sometimes Jamlady makes two differently colored batches and alternates the preserves in the jar for a nice visual effect. When doing this, it is best to quickly lid the jars and not use a rolling water bath (JSR). If Jamlady chooses not to seal a canning jar in a rolling water bath, she always keeps the product in the refrigerator.

Caution: Just because a jar's lid appears to seal in the refrigerator does not mean that you can take it out and rely on the seal. The seal will probably break with the warmer room temperature. An alternate method of sealing is to use melted paraffin as a seal, and then refrigerate the product. If not refrigerating a wax-sealed jam, at least, always top a wax seal with brown paper, a traditional lid and ring, or cotton fabric tied with a string so that bees and other insects cannot access the wax and eat holes in the wax seal. Jamlady does not recommend storing jams or preserves at room temperature if they have been sealed with melted wax or by the inversion method.

The only time Jamlady recommends not using a rolling water bath (RWB) to seal a jar is when reheating the product will cause intermixing of areas intended to be separated for visual effect or because the pH is over 4.3. If a RWB or the pressure-cooker method of sealing at 10-15 PSI for a specified number of minutes is not used, Jamlady recommends that the product remain refrigerated at all times—JSR. **Blueberries in the Snow** is another jam best sealed by the JSR Method—quickly applying the lid while the product is very hot, inverting the jar, and refrigerating the jar at all times or sealing the jar with paraffin and refrigerating it at all times. Jamlady does seal this jam by the RWB for market because continual refrigeration is impractical, but then there is some bleeding of the blueberries into the white jam. When the RWB is used, some of the intended color separations may be destroyed. The "jam" will still taste the same.

Tomato-Ginger Preserves

The beautiful color of this tomato, ginger, and lemon preserves makes it taste even better!

2 pounds red or yellow tomatoes (or both)
3 cups sugar
1 lemon
2 ounces grated fresh gingerroot

Plunge the ripe tomatoes in boiling water for 1 minute and then in cold water. Remove the tomato skins and seeds, or leave the seeds in. Layer the tomatoes and sugar in a crock and leave overnight. Drain off the juice and boil the juice to 221 degrees F or 105 degrees C, or until it spins a thread. Add the lemons, thinly sliced and minus the seeds. The pips can be discarded or put into a pip or pippen bag and cooked with the juice. Add the gingerroot and cook for about 5 minutes to give the lemons a head start. Put in the tomatoes. You may use the French Plunge Method of putting the tomatoes in and taking them out, if you want the tomato meats to remain large and whole. (See Strawberry Preserves.) Cook the preserves down until clear and thick. Check the set. JSP/RWB5(4OZ)10(8OZ).

Tomato-Ginger Jam

This jam can be made with fresh ginger-root, candied ginger, or powdered ginger. Made with added pectin.

4½ cups sugar
2½ cups fresh tomato purée or purée and some small tomato meat pieces
½ cup lemon juice
1 1¾-ounce box regular powdered pectin
2 tablespoons diced candied ginger
2 tablespoons peeled, grated, fresh gingerroot (or substitute ¼ teaspoon powdered ginger)
1 teaspoon grated lemon rind
½ teaspoon butter

Cook the gingerroot, candied ginger or powdered ginger, lemon juice and rind, tomato purée, and butter. Add the pectin to the mixture and boil for 1 minute; skim the foam. Add the sugar and boil 1-3 minutes to 105 degrees C. Check the set. JSP/RWB5(4OZ)10(8OZ).

Jamlady has made tomato preserves like her grandmother's for years, as did her grandmother's grandmother. It is Jamlady's opinion that the classic plain tomato preserves, shown below, is not as tasty as some of the variations with nuts and oranges. Yet, if you were raised on plain tomato preserves, as many of Jamlady's customer's obviously have been, then you probably are going to prefer the plain tomato preserves. Jamlady's grandmother preferred the spiced variation with oranges and lemons. Jamlady likes the nuts and raisins thrown in as well.

Jamlady Tip: *If you aren't inclined to make several batches, Jamlady recommends cooking down a batch of tomato preserves and doctoring each jar differently for variation. One jar might have raisins, nuts, or candied orange peel added, and another could have additional spices. By experimenting, you can see how you would like the taste of these additional items without making an entire batch with the new additions. Don't overdo your additions of high pH ingredients.*

ॐ

Tomato Preserves Spiced with Cinnamon

From Mrs. Clara Pine, Stone Ridge, New York.
Picture-perfect color!

2 pounds red or yellow tomatoes
3 cups sugar
1 lemon
¼ teaspoon cinnamon

Plunge the tomatoes in boiling water for 1 minute and then in the cold water. Remove the tomato skins and, optionally, the seeds. Layer the tomatoes and sugar in a crock. Leave overnight. Drain off the juice and boil the juice to 221 degrees F or around 105 degrees C. Add the lemon, thinly sliced and minus the pips. Cook for about 5 minutes to give the lemons a head start. Put in the tomatoes. You may remove some tomatoes and add them again at the end if you wish to have larger pieces in the completed preserves—the French Plunge Method. Add the cinnamon and cook the preserves until clear and thick. JSP/RWB10.

Variation: Add in different kinds of nuts, raisins, currants, and spices, and use a different citrus fruit or a combination of different citrus fruits. For example, try 3 kumquats or calamondins and 1 lemon.

BANANAS

Common Banana, *Musa sapientum* Linn. (subspecies), is a large, fruit-bearing, herbaceous plant with over a hundred different varieties, such as **Golden Early Banana,** *Musa sapientum* L. var. *champa* Baker, which is hardy in cooler climates and grown in Florida and the West Indies. Known to the Greeks, Arabs, and Romans, this fruit has been grown in many tropical regions, such as Guam, the Philippines, India, Egypt, Malaysia, and the West Indies. The **Red Jamaica** or **Red Spanish Banana,** *Musa sapientum* var. *rubra* (Firm.) Baker, is the red banana of commerce.

Jamlady's father planted several banana plants on his lot at Chokoloskee Island, Florida, where Jamlady has had the opportunity to watch his bananas grow and to experiment with the bananas leaves and their culinary applications. Try cutting banana leaves into 6" square appetizer plates for crab-stuffed peapods and bacon-wrapped jumbo shrimp and, of course, accent them with local red hibiscus and bougainvillea flowers. Banana leaves can be used to make pouches for steaming foods and the fruits themselves. Bananas are high in vitamins A, B, C, and B_2 and are wonderful fresh or cooked. The fruit of the banana makes first-class preserves and Jamlady's clan, especially the children, have enjoyed these banana "jam" recipes.

Chokoloskee Island is known for its tropical fruits, beautiful vegetation, fish, and **blue crabs,** which fishermen either trap or fish for with poles. If you have never fished for crabs, it's an interesting sport. The crabs actually hang on while they are eating the fish part that is attached to the hook. As your line starts to walk upstream, you carefully pull in the line by hand. Another helper puts a net in the water, downstream. As the crab is pulled to the surface, it drops off and floats back into the net. After cleaning, the blue crabs are steamed, and the meat is picked out by hand. The crabmeat is then ready for appetizers, salads, crab cakes, or whatever.

For appetizer plates, Jamlady likes to use well-washed and water-misted banana leaves that are cold-stored between moist paper towels until serving time. Take a 6" square out, mist it with water to make it shiny, and set appetizers on a natural plate atop a smaller serving plate. Decorate with local flowers and minted melon balls. Thin strips of melon, especially tropical varieties like casaba or canary, can be added, along with small thin wedges of lemon or lime and some melon jams on rice crackers.

Chokoloskee Island, Florida, is not spoiled and is on Route 29, 3 miles from Everglades City and the National Everglades Park Headquarters. If you do visit Chokoloskee, don't miss the spectacular sunsets and wildlife at early morning sunrise out on Route 41 between Everglades City and Naples, the Fakahatchee Strand Boardwalk along the same stretch of Route 41, the Smallwood Museum, the museum in Everglades City, and the wonderful citrus orchard just off 951 on Sabal Palm Road in Naples, where Jamlady has purchased calamondins.

This next banana jam recipe won a ribbon at the Minnesota State Fair in 1994 and appears in many old-timers' cookbooks and notes. Africans also make many jams with combinations of bananas and other fruits. This recipe, perhaps, should be listed with the preserves or butters because it has low added sugar, but because the bananas are sweet themselves, the sugar level is actually higher, and it is, therefore, usually called a jam. If it is well "blenderized" at the end of the cooking time, it has a buttery consistency and is a butter. Otherwise, according to Jamlady's definitions, it is technically a preserve or a chunky butter.

Banana Jam or Preserves

A favorite with children and banana lovers!

3½ pounds bananas without skins
3 cups sugar
1½ cups lemon juice
1 teaspoon butter
¼ teaspoon cinnamon

Mash the bananas and cook them with the rest of the ingredients for about 20 minutes. Stir a lot, or the banana jam may burn. Use a very heavy-bottomed pan with even heat distribution for making this jam. Jamlady uses a heavy stainless-steel pan with a thick bottom specifically made for cooking sauces and preserves. Jamlady actually cooks this jam some and then lets it cool down and then heats it some and lets it cool down—the **Switch Method** (SM or CD/SM = cook down, switch method). In this way, the jam evaporates down, and one does not have to stand over it the entire time, stirring it. Sometimes, Jamlady transfers the ingredients into a large glass bowl and microwaves it to heat it some and then lets it cool down. If you use this method, be forewarned that if you microwave it too much, making it too hot, it will caramelize and ruin the entire batch. Only heat the jam up to warm and then let it cool down; it does not need to boil or bubble. "Blenderize" and JSP/RWB10.

Variations: *Vary the spices or add liqueurs such as hazelnut, melon, peach, or orange.*

Jamlady's Original Spiced Fruit Cup Jam

May be made with aspartame or 1 cup of sugar or honey.

2½ cups processor-sliced strawberries
2 cups peeled, processor-sliced peaches
½ cup processor-sliced banana
¼ cup lemon juice
1 1¾-ounce box lite or "no-sugar" pectin
25 packets of aspartame (Equal® or other brand) or 1 cup sugar or honey
¼ to ½ teaspoon or less ascorbic acid crystals
¾ teaspoon ground cinnamon

Use a pinch of ascorbic acid crystals in the fruit prep water and on the fruit to inhibit oxidation. Processor-slice the hulled strawberries or, for a seedless jam, run the strawberries through the juicing machine about 10 times to collect all of the pulp. Mix the fruits and juices with the pectin, add the cinnamon, and wait 10 minutes. Boil for several minutes, add the aspartame (or sugar or honey), and cook for 1 minute more. JSP/RWB10.

Variation: Fruit Cup Preserves—*Make as preserves with 5 cups fruits (similar to those listed above), ½ cup freshly squeezed lemon juice, grated rind of 1 lemon (optional), cinnamon (optional), and 5¼ cups sugar.*

KIWIS

The **kiwifruit** or **Chinese gooseberry,** *Actinidia chinensis,* is a perennial, climbing plant that produces fruits about 2⅝" long, 2⅛" wide, and 6¼" in circumference. A kiwifruit weighs about 4 ounces and contains about 61 calories. These fruits have a green flesh and a thin brown skin that is hairy. Besides *Actinidia chinensis,* which is sold in China and some American markets, there is another plant known as **bower actinidia, tara vine,** and **yagtao,** *Actinidia arguta,* that also produces fruits, but they are much smaller and weigh about ¹/₁₅ the weight of an *Actinidia chinensis,* kiwifruit.

According to the new crop page of Purdue University, the **kiwifruit,** *Actinidia deliciosa* (A. Chev.) C. F. Liang and A. R. Ferguson, has been domesticated during this century. Almost all the kiwifruit cultivars grown in commercial orchards outside China descended from two female plants and one male plant brought to New Zealand in 1904 (I. J. Ferguson and G.C. Bollard, "Domestication of the Kiwifruit," in *Kiwifruit: Science and Management* eds. L. J. Warrington and G. C. Weston [Auckland, New Zealand: Ray Richards Publisher, 1990]). The 'Hayward' was selected from descendants of these original plants and has become the kiwifruit of choice. Other cultivars have been grown, but customers seem to prefer the 'Hayward,' and now the **'Hayward' cultivar is the most represented in the marketplace.** The 'Hayward' cultivar has an excellent shelf life, making it an excellent export for distant countries.

Of the various *Actinidia* species, which number about 60, *A. chinensis* is most similar to *A. deliciosa* 'Hayward.' *A. chinensis* is grown in China and most recently, since 1995, has been grown in California, where it is seen in the Los Angeles market. The first release of *A. chinensis* grown in New Zealand was released in 1999. A new yellow-fleshed kiwi, with hairs that rub off the fruits, is now being grown in New Zealand and will carry the commercial name of **Zespri Gold Kiwifruit.** Small plantings of the smooth-skinned *A. arguta* have been planted in Canada, France, Germany, Italy, New Zealand, and the United States, and it remains to be seen what new kiwis will be available for jam makers and creative chefs in the years to come.

For more information on this exciting kiwi topic, go to Purdue University's new crop page. Jamlady has noticed that Stark Brothers Nurseries has a cultivar called 'Issai' that is self-fruitful, removing the necessity of a plant of each sex for fruit production. Some of these new kiwi cultivars are hardy and can be grown in northern climates. Jamlady was amazed at all the different sizes and shapes of kiwifruits illustrated on the new crop page and cannot wait to see some of these new cultivars in the United States marketplace.

Caution: Jamlady noticed two reports by scientists alerting the public to a possible reaction or contact dermatitis from eating the Chinese gooseberry or kiwifruit, **Actinidia chinensis.** *Reported reactions consisted of marked swelling and itching of the lips and tongue that occurred within minutes of eating the fruits and continued with stomach pain* (Zina and Bundino, "Contact urticaria to *Actinidia chinensis.* Contact Dermatitits 9:85, 1983).

Jamlady recommends you take advantage of the various kiwifruit sales during the summer months and make some kiwifruit preserves. Jamlady first created this recipe in 1995 and has been making it ever since.

Grand Kiwi Preserves

Kiwifruit preserves with wonderful orange-flavored Grand Marnier.

In fifteen minutes, you can make this preserve with $\frac{1}{12}$ of this recipe.

Made with no added pectin.

6 cups sugar

2 dozen peeled and finely chopped kiwis (approximately 4 pounds)

$\frac{1}{2}$ cup Grand Marnier liqueur (or less, as budget allows—$\frac{1}{4}$ cup or $\frac{1}{3}$ cup)

1 teaspoon citric acid*

Cook the kiwis and the citric acid until soft. Add the sugar and cook to 105 degrees C. Add $\frac{1}{2}$ cup Grand Marnier and cook to 105 degrees C. Test the set with a frozen plate. JSP/RWB5(4OZ)10(8OZ).

* $\frac{1}{8}$ teaspoon crystalline citric acid is the equivalent of 1 tablespoon of lemon juice.

Note: For $\frac{1}{12}$ batch sizes, use a very small saucepan (4"-5" in diameter).

*Variation: Kiwi Marmalade—Add the grated rind of 1 lemon and 1 orange and the chopped citrus pulp (**without the white pith and seeds = "seed and pith"**) to the original kiwi recipe. **Add sugar equal to the measure of citrus fruit pulp. Cook the entire mixture down until thick.***

Variation: Jamlady's Original Kiwi Genie Preserves—Use 1-2 drops oil of cinnamon instead of the Grand Marnier.

MELONS

Jamlady had the good fortune of having the melon man right next to her market stand. Any melons that did not sell he would give to Jamlady. This situation forced Jamlady to find a way to use all of those melons. Some were made into pickles and others were made into chutney and jam. Little did Jamlady imagine that melon conserve would become one of her most favorite preserves!

Jamlady loves this conserve, as do many market patrons. Most people are not enthusiastic about the idea of a melon conserve until they taste it. This conserve is not too sweet, and its mellowness is contrasted with a slightly bitter citrus flavor, making it a great breakfast treat! The types of nuts and the amounts of each nut type can be varied. This next recipe contains pecans, walnuts, and apricot liqueur.

Cantaloupe Conserve

A threesome of cantaloupe, apricots, and lemons with some liqueur and nuts.

12 cups peeled, diced cantaloupe
9 cups sugar
2 cups chopped, dried apricots
2 cups chopped pecans
7 lemons
1 cup chopped walnuts
½ cup apricot liqueur

Cut the outer rinds from the lemons. Discard the pith or white parts. Finely chop the rinds in a blender. Slice the lemons, seed them, and juice them in a Champion juicing machine or similar machine. Reserve the lemon juice. Dice the peeled cantaloupe; add the sugar, reserved lemon juice, and finely chopped lemon rinds. Cook this mixture for about 15 minutes. Add the dried apricots; simmer very slowly, stirring frequently, until the conserve thickens. Add the liqueur and cook until the correct thickness is achieved. Add the nuts. JSP/RWB10.

Variation: Marnier's Gold Conserve—Substitute Grand Marnier for the apricot liqueur and use 3 cups of walnuts instead of walnuts and pecans.

Jamlady's Original Tropical Conserve

Tastes like a melon marmalade with macadamia nuts!

8 cups sugar
4 cups peeled, diced cantaloupe
6 cups peeled, diced casaba melon
6 lemons
2 cups dried, diced papaya (See "Buyer's Guide.")
2 cups pecans, walnuts, or macadamia nuts

Use the exterior peels from the lemons without the white pith and the inner fruit without the seeds. Run the outer peel and the seedless pulp through a Champion juicing machine and use both outputs. Cook all ingredients together except the nuts. Stir the conserve frequently until thickened. Add the nuts last. JSP/RWB10.

Jamlady is always looking for something to do with the whole watermelon. **This recipe for Watermelon Rind Preserves uses the watermelon's rind, as does Pickled Watermelon Rinds and Chokoloskee Island Chutney. Melon Preserves and Watermelon Molasses use the meat of the watermelon.** Jamlady says it's time to make these recipes when watermelons are on sale. Look for the Pickled Watermelon Rind recipe and the Chokoloskee Island Chutney in future Jamlady cookbooks.

This recipe is an old classic. **Preserved Melon Rind,** published in *What to Cook and How to Cook It* (Author unknown, book given as a complimentary copy by the bank to customers [Kingston, NY: The Kingston Savings Bank, 273 Wall Street, circa 1900], 50), calls for the rind to be soaked in 2 teaspoons of alum per quart of water, then cooked in the solution for 10 minutes, drained, and then boiled in equal sugar to rind, with half as much water, plus 2 lemons.

The church ladies in Accord, New York, were making rind preserves before Jamlady was born. This is the recipe from her church-lady friends, which Jamlady has had for years. Alum is not used in this Watermelon Rind Preserves recipe. **Besides, most canners try to avoid alum anyway, because it can cause stomach distress in some people.** If you have enough time, salt the rind as shown in the variation below.

ॐ

Watermelon Rind Preserves

Use both the meat and the rinds of the watermelon.

4 cups peeled rind
3 cups sugar
3 sliced, seeded lemons (or, preferably, 2 oranges and 1 lemon)
1 cup grated pineapple (optional)

Select a watermelon that is not too ripe. Peel the rind from the watermelon and cut the watermelon rind in ½"cubes or strips, leaving some firm pink flesh attached. Cook the ingredients for about 2 hours or until done. JSP/RWB10.

Variation with salting: "*Peel off outside and cut off red part of inside of watermelon rind. Cut in pieces. Sprinkle with salt (⅓ c. to 8 qts. rind). Let stand 6 hours, drain. Sprinkle with a little salt, let stand overnight. Squeeze well, rinse. To each gal. add juice of 2 lemons, peel of ½ lemon and as much sugar as rind. Boil until syrup is thick*" (Mrs. Gladys D. B. Glanz, De New Paltz Keuken Boek, #2 [New Paltz, NY: Committee of the Ladies of the Reformed Church, 1923], 60).

Jamlady has made many variations of watermelon and melon jams with peaches, nectarines, apricots, and mangoes. The peaches, apricots, nectarines, and mangoes can be interchanged for one another in most "jam" recipes.

Melon and Peach Conserve

A wonderful tropical combination! Make with most any variety of melon.

3 cups sugar
2 cups coarsely chopped peaches
2 cup diced cantaloupe, watermelon, canary melon, or other melon
1 whole, seeded lemon, shredded (or 2 lemons, no pith)
¼ cup reconstituted lemon juice or fresh lemon juice
1 cup broken nut meats (pecans, almonds, macadamia, hazelnuts, Brazil nuts)
¼ cup golden raisins (optional)
¼ cup liqueur like Grand Marnier® (optional)

Cut and seed the lemon. Shred the lemon rind and chop the lemon pulp. Optionally, and preferably, discard the bitter pith and add a second pithed lemon. Cook all ingredients, except the nuts and liqueur, until thick. Add the nuts and liqueur at the end. Check the set and JSP/RWB10. For this conserve, Jamlady prefers cantaloupe or muskmelon to other kinds of melon, but watermelon is also very interesting.

Variation: Nectarine-Cantaloupe Conserve—Not only can the type of melon be varied, but the peaches can be changed to nectarines, mangoes, or apricots and different types of nuts can be stirred into the conserve.

PERSIMMONS

Persimmon or **Oriental persimmon,** *Diospyros kaki,* is a fruit with yellow to deep-orange color and is soft when ripe. Persimmons can be used to make tea, marmalade, pudding, syrup, cookies, and pies. The **American persimmon,** *Diospyros virginiana,* is grown in cooler climates, zones 5-9, while the *D. kaki* is grown in zones 7-10. The *D. kaki,* when ripe, produces more juice than the *D. virginiana.* Usually, these fruits are picked after the first frost, when their quality is considered by some people to be the best, but this is not an absolute requirement, as there are some fruits that ripen prior to the first frost. The quality of the flavor and size will vary from tree to tree, and tree-ripened persimmons are considered the best.

Raw persimmons should be soft to the touch and can be cut in half and eaten with a spoon. The scooped-out pulp can be mixed with lemon juice and spooned over pudding, fresh fruit cocktail, or ice cream. Persimmon leaves are used for tea. Persimmon fruits are eaten plain, on salads, or are made into beer, jam, ice cream, bread, sauce, marmalade, pudding, pie, frosting, candy, griddle cakes, soup, sherbet, fudge, cookies, and cakes. Persimmons can be stuffed with nut meats and rolled in granulated sugar, as can dates. The common persimmon tree is often used as base stock, and branches of other varieties are then grafted onto the tree. Medicinally, persimmons are an excellent astringent and can be used for dysentery, kidney stones (decoction of the seed), wounds, hemorrhage (as a styptic), thrush, expelling worms in children, and intestinal complaints.

Freezer Persimmon Jam—$1\frac{1}{2}$ pounds soft 'Fuyu'-type persimmons or $1\frac{1}{2}$ pounds soft, ripe 'Hachiya'-type persimmons; 3 cups of sugar; 1 pouch (3 ounces) liquid pectin; and $\frac{1}{4}$ cup lemon juice. Peel or scoop out the persimmons, discarding any seeds and skin. Mash the fruit or cut into $\frac{1}{2}$-inch chunks. Mix the fruit and sugar; wait 10 minutes. Mix the pectin with the lemon juice; stir gently. Add the lemon and pectin to the fruit; stir. Vigorous stirring creates too many air bubbles. Fill freezer containers with jam, leaving a $\frac{1}{2}$" head space. Leave the jam at room temperature for 12-16 hours. Then refrigerate or freeze (Source: Mrs. Tara Danae Rhodes, Fresno, California).

Persimmon Marmalade: Blend enough persimmons to make 2 quarts. Cook for 15 minutes, add 1 cup pure orange juice and 1 cup crushed pineapple. To each cup of mixture, add $\frac{3}{4}$ cup sugar. Boil, stirring often, until thick. Pour into jars, lid, and **do not seal in a RWB without pH testing first.** Add more acidic fruits or citric acid if the pH is not well under 4.3. Refrigeration is recommended (Source: Rhodes: CA). Unless you have a persimmon tree, Jamlady recommends making this recipe in smaller batches, perhaps $\frac{1}{4}$ or $\frac{1}{2}$ of the recipe. JSR.

An annual persimmon festival is held in Mitchell, Indiana, in September. The Greater Mitchell Chamber of Commerce gave Jamlady more than 65 persimmon recipes that they have collected, so evidently, a lot of Indiana women are cooking with persimmons. Here are a few of these recipes:

Persimmon Sauce: 1 cup persimmon pulp, 1 cup sugar, 4 tablespoons honey, and 4 tablespoons orange pulp or juice. Heat to boiling, cool, and serve over pound cake or ice cream.

Persimmon Frosting: Use a cup of mashed persimmons with $\frac{1}{3}$ cup butter, a tad of vanilla, and 3 cups powdered sugar.

Candied Persimmons: Make by alternating persimmon and sugar layers in a jar. **Fit the jar with a closed, but not sealed, lid.** Store the jar in a cool location until the persimmons become candied. **Keep the fruit pushed down under the syrup.** This recipe is sometimes called

Preserved Whole Persimmons and is an appropriate **recipe for a child chef** to try. Serve as a dessert confection.

Persimmon Pie: 2 cups persimmon pulp, 1 egg (beaten), 1 cup milk, ½ cup sugar, ⅛ teaspoon salt, 1 tablespoon cornstarch, and 1 uncooked 9" pastry shell. Mix the persimmons pulp, egg, and milk. Mix the sugar, salt, and cornstarch and add it to the first mixture. Pour the filling in the pastry shell and bake at 450 degrees F for 10 minutes. Reduce the temperature to 350 degrees F and bake for 50-60 minutes.

❧❧

SWEET CHESTNUTS

Jamlady likes working with **sweet chestnuts,** *Castanea vesca* or *Fagus castanea,* but she does not have a chestnut tree. Luckily, she has relatives and friends who are willing to share their crops. Jamlady was awakened to the wide range of uses of chestnuts when she met a lovely older lady from Vienna, Austria, one sunny, Florida day in a swimming pool. The lady talked on for over an hour just on the topic of chestnuts—which made Jamlady realize she was missing something, having come from New York State, where cooks mostly roast the chestnuts, while ice skating outside during the cold Christmas season, or put them in turkey stuffing.

In Vienna, they make puddings, jams, frozen desserts, and all sorts of lovely foods with chestnuts. Jamlady's Viennese friend said to use canned, unsweetened chestnut purée to make jam, sauces for pasta, soups, croquettes, and desserts like torte, puddings, and tarts. This nice lady told Jamlady to cook a pound of chestnuts in water until tender, then drain and peel, and add 6 tablespoons of sugar, 4 tablespoons of cocoa, and 4 tablespoons of liqueur like Amaretto. Grind all of this mixture in a food processor. Whip 8 ounces of heavy cream; fold in the puréed mixture and chill. Serve this **chestnut mousse** with chocolate curls on top. She said canned chestnut purée could be used as well. Chestnuts can be frozen as a block or paving stones, ***Pavé aux marrons,*** after mixing a thick sugar syrup with canned, unsweetened chestnut purée and butter, and then topping it with a chocolate frosting of unsweetened chocolate, sugar, water, and butter (I. Kirshman, ed., *French Cooking* [New York: 'Round the World Books Inc., 1972], 84).

The Von Welanetz Guide lists about 6 canned chestnut products (including Purre de Marrons Naturel, an unsweetened chestnut puree in a 15-ounce cans—under the Clement Faugier label [French]). Jamlady's Viennese friend recommended cooking jam with a can of chestnut purée and about ¾ cup of sugar and excellent French Cognac. **Refrigerate the chestnut jam (JSR). Do not can!**

Jamlady has not fully investigated chestnut jams or chestnuts preserved in alcohol, as she cannot can chestnut jam in a RWB so that it can be sold at market and she has no liquor license to sell alcoholic products at market. Nevertheless, Jamlady has made chestnut jam for personal consumption. Jamlady has noticed this simple two- or three-ingredient chestnut jam with other variations and another chestnut jam from scratch in Lesem's *Preserving Today.* Brown's *Pickles and Preserves* has a recipe for French Preserved Chestnuts (Marrons Glacés), which can be made by preserving the chestnuts in French brandy.

Kander's *The Settlement Cookbook, 28th ed.* has recipes for chestnut ice cream, chestnut vegetable, chestnuts in prunes, chestnut soufflé, and chestnut torte. Jamlady has noticed chestnuts are now available at her local grocery stores, so check your local market and see what you can find both in fresh and canned chestnut products. Chestnut jam can be put into a flaky tart shell and then topped with whipped cream or used as a sauce with cheese, like in tiramisus, and then drizzled with chocolate, or used between the layers of a chocolate cake. Chestnut flour is gluten free and is often used in baking.

Caution: Not that you would try, but don't eat uncooked or raw sweet chestnuts. They're toxic!

☙ ❧

CACTI

Jamlady grew up in the era of the B. F. Woolworth and W. T. Grant stores, with their small houseplants in 2½" and 3" pots, especially succulents and cacti. Jamlady was accustomed to picking out the infested cacti hairs, minutely barbed glochids, from her fingers, a hazard of planting these cacti. Jamlady's parents' business sold many succulents and cacti to various chain stores.

Prickly pear, *Opuntia* spp., was well known to Jamlady's family as the genus consisting of about 200 species of cacti, many of them small enough to be potted and sold to plant enthusiasts. Jamlady learned, early on, that a cactus pad could be removed and grafted onto another cactus or rooted to make a new plant, but she didn't know that cactus pads could be eaten, or that the fruits of cacti could be made into jelly, marmalade, or syrup.

Prickly pear *Opuntia macrorhiza* Engelmann, 1850, is classified as an evergreen perennial, and it likes to grow in a well-drained, gravelly, or sandy soil. *Opuntia* spp. needs lots of sun, and the state of Texas as well as Arizona and Mexico have optimum conditions for growing the prickly pear plant. In 1995, the state of Texas embraced the prickly pear as its state plant. Prickly pear's classification name can vary depending on the naming scientist. *Opuntia compressa* MacBride, 1922; *Opuntia plumbea* Rose, 1908; *Opuntia mesacantha* var. *macrorhiza* Coulter, 1896; and *Opuntia fusiformis* Engelmann & Bigelow, 1856, is commonly known as **tuberous-rooted prickly pear** and is known for its spines, yellow flowers with a red center, and red-purple to purple fruits (mature) that contain "prickers."

The pads of the prickly pear cactus are known as *nopales* and can be eaten as vegetables after removing their pesky hairs. Removal of the hairs can be done by holding the pad with a towel and using a knife to cut off the hairs. For eating as a vegetable, select the thicker deep-green pads, as they are the most tender. Pads are nutritional; they contain large amounts of vitamins A and C and fair amounts of B vitamins and iron. Some stores, even in Crystal Lake, Illinois, have cut up, prepared *nopales* for sale. So, what are you waiting for?

When young Jamlady was a foreign-exchange student in Guadalajara, Mexico, she had opportunities aplenty to see native women sitting in the marketplace cleaning off the hairs from the cacti pads. Even today this image is clear in Jamlady's mind, as it triggers Jamlady's memory back to childhood experiences of planting those little "sticker plants" in small terracotta pots. Jamlady has been served Mexican breakfasts of scrambled eggs with cactus leaves, with or without hot peppers. Try sautéing the cut-up *nopales* in butter or olive oil. Toss in some scrambled eggs, some tofu or cheese, and you have made a *nopales* omelet. *Nopales* can also be made into a nopalitos-potato frittata. See where this all leads us? *Nopales* can go in stew, chicken-vegetable soup, or stir-fry. How about cactus pads in chutneys, marmalades, or preserves like zucchini or cucumbers? Whoever tries this, just remember to check the pH of the finished product or always refrigerate the product—JSR.

In Crystal Lake, Illinois, prickly pear fruits, or "tunas", are available at the little Mexican store on Route 14. When selecting prickly pears, try to get fruits that are soft but not too ripe. The tunas' colors may vary from greenish-yellow to red. Try to get fruits that are just turning toward red to bright red. If only green fruits are available, simply let them sit at room temperature until they ripen to red.

To prepare the prickly pear fruits, make sure the "prickers" have been removed first. Wash the fruits under cold water and cut off the ends and cut them in half, lengthwise. Chop the bright-red prickly pear fruit in a food processor and press the pulp through a fine sieve, using a wooden spoon to remove the seeds. A juicing machine can be handy to use with prickly pear fruits too. All parts of the prickly pear are edible; indeed the seeds can be roasted and ground into flour (www.survivaliq.com). Some recipes state to peel the prickly pears first, and others simply leaving the skin on. Jamlady sees no difference, so why peel? Some recipes call for cooking the whole fruits and removing only the juice with a jelly bag. Use the extracted juice for your recipes and discard the seeds. **Twelve prickly pears should net about 1 cup of prickly pear juice.**

Consider mixing prickly pear juice with a little vinegar and making it into **Prickly Pear Vinaigrette,** especially with any interesting herbal vinegar you have made. Try making **Red Wine and Tarragon Vinegar-Prickly Pear Vinaigrette**

to use with a salmagundi of greens, chilled seafood pieces, hard-boiled eggs, slices of Clementines, melon balls, and mint leaves. Jamlady is going to try uncooked, seeded, prickly pear pulp in freezer jam someday, or in some of that CLEARJEL® starch. Jamlady has seen several recipes for prickly pear and cranberry sorbet on the Internet, so why not ½ cranberry preserves with ½ prickly pear-lemon jelly? She wishes to do all of these things prior to publication, but there simply isn't enough time, for when one idea has been tested, another one comes to the fore. Jamlady hopes some of you will try these things and let her know how they turn out.

In Mexico, red "tunas" are used to make a **Cured Prickly Pear Pulque.** The red prickly pears are peeled, mashed, and mixed with the pulque and strained through cheesecloth. Sugar, cinnamon, clove, and black pepper are used to flavor and sweeten this concoction (J. Velazquez de Leon, *Mexican Cookbook for American Homes,* 6th ed. [Mexico City: Culinary Arts Institute, 1967], 206). Jamlady takes note when she sees a certain spice used with an underresearched fruit, such as prickly pear. **Pulque** is a mildly intoxicating drink made from fermented maguey juice. Perhaps the drink makers should take note. **What can be done with fresh, strained, prickly pear juice and other types of alcoholic ingredients?** Given the time to tinker, the answer to this question is a whole weekend project for Jamlady and some of her friends. Jamlady has more ideas than time. Perhaps, someone out there would like to experiment with this idea and get back to Jamlady? It is frustrating to have the desire to know the answers to questions and no time to do the research because Jamlady is researching in a different direction. Jamlady has seen an iced drink called Miss Blyden that is made with prickly pear juice, rum, and sugar (E. Dooley, *Puerto Rican Cookbook* [1950], 19). Also check out Sabra liqueur in the liqueur section of this book.

Many recipes for cactus jelly have been floating

around, and they vary in the ratios of sugar to lemon to pectin. Different methods for getting the juice have been used (without documentation in many recipes); some leave the skin on, cooked and strained; some chop, cook, and strain; others peel, chop, cook, and sieve. Such variables may affect the amount of pectin needed. Another variable is the ripeness of the fruit. Select slightly underripe fruits (just beginning to turn red) for a better and surer set. Make sure you cook the jelly or marmalade down enough; check the set with a frozen plate.

Prickly Pear-Lemon Jelly

The prickly pear is also called a tuna.

2½ cups extracted prickly pear juice (2½ pounds cactus fruit)
½ cup lemon juice (8 tablespoons)
5 cups sugar
1 box regular powdered pectin (approximately 18 teaspoons to a box)

Remove the thorns from the fruits (some underripe); cut up and cook the cactus fruit for 10 minutes with enough water to cover. Strain and measure out 2½ cups of cactus juice. Add the lemon juice and regular powdered pectin. Hard boil for 3 minutes. Add the sugar and boil 2 minutes or until jell point is reached. JSP/RWB5(4OZ)10(8OZ).

Variation: A Small Batch of Prickly Pear-Lemon Jelly—This can be made with approximately ¾ cup of extracted prickly pear juice, 3⅓-4 tablespoons lemon or lime juice, 6 teaspoons powdered pectin, and 1½ cups sugar. Cook in a 6½"-diameter pan. This cactus jelly tastes tutti-frutti. These measures are not exactly ¼ of the recipe above, but ¼ of the above recipe could also be made. Sometimes it is easier to make the measurements an even number of this or that. The ingredients just need to be somewhat close, as you will boil it to set point anyway. JSP/RWB10.

Note: Different boxes of pectin can measure differently. To be very accurate, you might measure out the exact number of teaspoons in your brand of pectin's box and then figure recipes accordingly. In any account, you will boil the jelly to set point. Liquid pectin could also be used and would allow for a little pectin to be added gradually. However, saving the leftover liquid pectin is more difficult than saving an open package of powdered pectin.

Several other recipes for cactus are seen in Lesem's *Preserving Today* and the Caloosa Rare Fruit Exchange's *Tropical Fruit Cookbook* (Fort Meyers, FL, 1991), but Jamlady thinks there may be more options out there than just putting cactus pear into an orange, lemon, or lime marmalade. Clearly this fruit is a good candidate for a cook who has time to experiment. Why not prickly pears (tunas) with mangoes, peaches, apples, cranberries, pineapple, or ruby grapes? You'll just have to try it or wait until Jamlady gets around to it. For starters try ½ of a fruit preserve recipe combined with ½ of a cactus-lemon recipe. Or mix some completed fruit jam or preserve with a completed cactus-lemon jelly. Melt them together in a saucepan or in the microwave and then taste! Experiment!

Besides the prickly pear cactus, there are other cactus fruits from **epiphytic cactus** that are truly amazing (search on the Internet). The **Dragon Fruit,** *Pitahaya* **(Spanish),** or **Orchid Cactus,** *Hylocereus undatus,* is from South America but is now grown in Indonesia. These fruits are edible, and their beautiful blooms open only during the late afternoon and evening. When traveling to Indonesia, keep an eye out for this gorgeous flower and fruit as well as the fruit from a small, spiny palm tree, *Salacca zalacca,* that produces **Snake Fruit.** Maybe you enthusiastic "jammers" need to bring along a small hot plate, an adapter, a 6" saucepan, two 4-ounce canning jars, 2 lids, a small strainer, and some pectin and make some **Dragon Fruit Jam** to bring home.

⚭

HERBAL JELLIES

Jellies can be made from herbal infusions, the base liquid being water, fruit juice, or wine. If you have good mint, then you can make the following recipe. If your mint, due to its poor gene pool, is not very flavorful, you might as well give up before you try and use an apple or pear base with mint extract.

This infusion can be made with just mint, or it may contain orange zest and a cinnamon stick. Or it may contain mint, lemon grass, blue hyssop flowers, and/or lemon balm (to taste). Alternately, cardamom and mint could be used for the infusion. For those who like to experiment, here is your chance to try adaptogenic herbs—like Suma or Cat's Claw tea—and spices in these infusions! You too can make **medicinal jellies.**

⚭

Mint Jelly or Herbed-Mint Jelly

Serve with roasted leg of lamb.

5 cups water
4 cups chopped, fresh mint leaves
4 cups sugar
3 cups mint infusion
1 1¾-ounce box regular powdered pectin
A couple drops green food coloring (optional)
¼ teaspoon butter

Boil the mint leaves in the water, uncovered, for 30 minutes to make the mint infusion. Strain and measure out 3 cups. Boil 3 cups infusion, food coloring, butter, and pectin to a rolling boil for 1 minute. Add in the sugar and raise to a boil that cannot be stirred down. Check the set. JSP/RWB5(4 OZ)10(8OZ).

Note: Cat's Claw or **Uña de Gato, Uncaria tomentosa,** *or other spp. is a thorny, liana vine (surely not the liana vine on which Tarzan would choose to swing) or Amazonian herb that has* **quinovic acid glycosides** *that show systemic antiviral, antitumor, and anti-inflammatory activity. This herb acts as an antioxidant and anti-inflammatory. It boosts the immune system and cleanses the intestinal tract. Cat's Claw is recommended for people* with AIDS, systemic candidiasis, genital herpes, arthritis, cancer, tumors, and ulcers. This herb appears to provide some relief from the side effects of chemotherapy treatments.

Although there are approximately forty different varieties of parsley, there are three basic cultivated varieties of parsley that are grown in the United States: the plain, Italian, or flat-leaf type, **Petroselinum crispum var. neapolitanum Danert.;** the **common or curly leaf type, Petroselinum crispum var. crispum;** and the **turnip-rooted parsley** or **Hamburg type, Petroselinum crispum (Mill.) Nyman ex A.W. Hill var. tuberosum (Bernh.) Crov.,** which is grown for its root. There are many cultivars for these types of parsleys. Parsley leaves contain the essential oils *myristicin, limonene,* and others. Because of the flavor from these oils, parsley can be made into good-tasting jelly.

Caution: Do not take Cat's Claw if pregnant (R. Moss, "Cat's Claw *[Uncaria tomentosa]*: New Treatment from the Amazon," *The Cancer Chronicles* 30 [1995]; J. A. Duke, *The Green Pharmacy* [Emmaus, PA: Rodale Press, 1997]).

Variation: Mint Jelly #2—Slice a ½ peck of tart apples and cook with a little water until soft. Strain the apple mixture through cheesecloth. Boil the juices for 15 minutes before adding in the sugar. Add 1 pound sugar. Add the juice of ½ lemon to every pint of extracted juice. Add 4 drops peppermint oil and 4 drops spearmint oil. Color the jelly with food coloring (optional). Boil to set point. JSP/RWB5(4OZ)10(8OZ).

Parsley Jelly

Here is a jam you can make any time of the year!

4 cups chopped parsley
3 cups water
3 cups prepared parsley infusion
2 tablespoons lemon juice, herbal vinegar, or balsamic vinegar
4½ cups sugar
1 1¾-ounce box regular powdered pectin
Green food coloring (optional)

Cook the chopped parsley in the water for two minutes. Steep the mixture for 20 minutes; strain the infusion through a jelly bag or very fine mesh strainer. In a pan, mix the pectin with the parsley infusion, lemon juice, herbal vinegar, or balsamic vinegar. Boil for 1 minute. Add the sugar and boil for 1 more minute. Add the food coloring, if used. JSP/RWB5(4OZ)10(8OZ).

Variation: Chervil Jelly—Chervil or French Parsley, Anthriscus cerefolium *(L.) Hoffm., is a licorice-flavored, leafy plant resembling parsley. Chervil is often in "Fines Herbes," which contain at least 3 of the following: parsley, tarragon, chives, sage, savory, basil, and chervil. Some cooks make this jelly recipe with chervil instead of parsley. The taste of chervil is a very delicate, short-lived flavor, but you can try it, or try a* **Fines Herbes Jelly.**

Jamlady Tip: If you do not own a fine strainer, maybe you have one of those gold mesh filter inserts for coffee makers. It works pretty well as a fill-in strainer.

WINE JELLIES

Wine jellies are easy to make, especially if you have made your own wine. Jamlady has made wine jelly from her sour cherry wine, elderberry wine, and mulberry wine. It is especially good to make the wine jelly from mulberry, because you do not have to deal with the stems to make the jelly. Commercial wines work just as well, and herbs can be placed in these wines too. Either infuse the herbs or add small amounts of them in the wine. Mint is a common herb that is infused into wine jelly. Wine jellies are very good from ruby port, zinfandel, or Merlot. Rose and Riesling will yield a fruitier jelly.

Try making this jelly with sherry, claret, port, sauterne, muscatel, or other interesting homemade fruit wines. Do not boil this wine, or the alcohol will be lost. Seal the jar with melted paraffin or seal using the inversion method. JSR.

Basic Wine Jelly

Make with a variety of different wines!

3 cups sugar
1¾ cups wine
3 ounces liquid pectin
Food coloring (optional)

Cook the jelly in a stainless-steel pan with a thick aluminum or copper core in the bottom and sides or in a double boiler. Cook the sugar with the wine until it is dissolved. Remove the pan from the stove and stir in the pectin. If using herbs, heat them with just a little of the wine, remove them, add the sugar, and complete the recipe or soak the wine with the herb for several hours prior to making the jelly. Experiment with different combinations of wines. Put your **hangover jelly herbs** of thyme, rosemary, and spearmint directly in the wine jelly. Why wait?

Note: Do not boil or seal by RWB, or the concentration of alcohol will be diminished from the wine. If you do not care if the alcohol is diminished, then seal by the RWB method.

Variation: Hot Wine Jelly—Use wine that has been sitting in a bottle with dried hot peppers and/or other herbs or add them when making the jelly.

BRAMBLES AND OTHER UNUSUAL PLANTS

Creative cooks can make "jam" from fruits, flowers, or edible storage roots. In apples, pears, quince, pear apples (pome fruit of the Rose Family), and rose hips (**aggregate fruit** or **etaerio** of the Rose Family), the **hypanthium**—as opposed to the core—is eaten. In other fruits, the actual **ovary** is eaten.

Here are a few more plants, fruits, berries, and vegetables of interest.

Agar-agar, or **Japanese isinglass,** is a white gelatinous substance obtained from sea vegetables—*Gelidium corneum* Lam.; *G. cartilagineum* Gaill.; and *Sphaerococcus compressus* Ag.; and other algae. It is available in bars, flakes, and powder and is used to make jams, kanten, and vegetable aspics. Birdnest soup is made from the dried nests of the Salangane swallow. This swallow feeds on very gelatinous seaweed like agar-agar or goémon, which the swallow regurgitates to make its nest. These dried nests are used to make soup, especially beef consommé flavored with basil and Madeira wine.

Barberry, betberry, European barberry, jaundice berry, or **common barberry,** *Berberis vulgaris L.,* is a bushy, deciduous shrub with small, yellow flowers that bloom from May to June and clusters of oval, reddish fruits. Barberries can be made into tea or **Barberry Jelly.** Gather barberries just before the first frost; remove any stems, and wash the berries. Cook 2 quarts of berries with 2 cups of water. Remove the stones, measure the juice, and cook to set using equal sugar and juice. Barberries have a high acid content and barberry tea or jelly is an excellent antidiarrheal.

Caution: Do not use barberry if pregnant.

Black sapote, or **chocolate pudding fruit,** *Diospyros digyna,* is a tropical fruit with a chocolate-colored, soft, sweet pulp that is used in desserts and breads, but normally not in jam or jelly.

Buffaloberry (Sakakawea buffaloberry), *Shepherdia argentea* 'Sakakawea', is a tall, thorny, thicket-forming shrub that produces a round, one-seed berry, 1/8-1/4 inch wide, which is scarlet to yellow when ripe and positioned in groups along its stem. For **Buffaloberry Jam:** Cook 16 cups washed buffaloberries with 2 cups water; mash and strain. Buffaloberry juice will appear milky. Cook the jelly with equal parts juice to sugar. After a frost, you may need to add some liquid pectin to achieve a set. Try variations with orange juice, cinnamon, or cloves. Buffaloberries taste something like grapes and red currants.

Canistel, or **eggfruit,** *Pouteria campechiana,* is a tropical fruit with an orange skin and dry flesh that looks like a cooked egg yolk. Canistel is used to make pies, custards, and ice cream but is not usually used to make jelly or jam.

Carambola, or **star fruit,** *Averrhoa carambola,* is a tropical fruit. When crosscut, star fruits are star shaped. Carambola can be used to make leather, preserves, jelly, marmalade, and chutney. **Carambola Marmalade or Preserves:** Melt 1/2 box powdered pectin in 2 cups water and boil. Add 3¾ cups sugar and then 3¾ cups unpeeled,

Back row (left to right): Starfruit, or carambola (_Averrhoa carambola_ Linn.); tuna, or prickly pear (_Opuntia_ spp.); quince (_Cydonia oblonga_); Asian pear apple, apple pear, sand pear, water pear, or nashi (_Pyrus pyrifolia_ or _Pyrus ussuriensis_); and sweet potato (the sweet orange-fleshed South American _Ipomoea batatas_, not the starchy West African or Asian yam, _Dioscorea_ species). Front row (left to right): Dried roselle, or Jamaica (Spanish name for hibiscus, _Hibiscus sabdariffa_); rose hips (_Rosa_); vanilla fruit pods (_Vanilla planifolia_— incorrectly, but commonly, referred to as "vanilla bean").

seeded, crosscut carambolas. Boil until thick. Half or quarter this recipe to make a small amount of preserves to use star pieces as decorative accents on cakes, puddings, or tiramisu desserts.

Note: The pH of this fruit can vary significantly depending on the variety, which ranges from tart cultivars at 2.2-2.6 to sweet cultivars at 3.8-4.1.

Carissa, or **Natal plum,** *Carissa grandiflora* (E. H. Mey.) A. DC., is a glossy, red tropical fruit that is used to make jelly and preserves. **Carissa Jelly:** Use ¾ cup sugar to each cup carissa juice. Cook down to set point. **Carissa Preserves:** Peel and pit a quart of fruit. Cook a wedge of peeled lemon with the prepared fruits in a simple syrup (heated together, half water and half sugar). Use ¼ more fruit than sugar. Some say carissa tastes like raspberries. The jelly is a beautiful color, but only after the sugar is added. Cook down to achieve a set.

Chicle, ciku, naseberry, or **sapodilla,** *Manilkara zapota* (L.) van Royen (formerly *Achras zapota* L.), is a tropical American tree that can be found in India, Africa, the West Indies, the Philippines, Malaysia, and South Florida. Supposedly, maximum-size fruits can be picked and allowed to ripen. Jamlady has tried to pick large sapodilla fruit in Florida in April, prior to ripening, and has brought them back to Crystal Lake, but alas, the very hard fruits never ripened. When ripe, this fruit's inner flesh is yellowish to pinkish-brown, soft and quite unlike the hard and astringent unripe fruit. The ripe fruit is tomato-sized and will shed brown powder from its skin. This low-acid fruit is called a sapodilla (in the Florida Keys) or a naseberry (in the British West Indies). Ciku's trunk is tapped for chicle, which is used to make chewing gum. This fruit is good fresh or in sherbet, leather, and pancake batter. **Sapodilla Leather:** Cook 1 cup fruit purée with ⅔ cup sugar until thick enough to spread and sun-dry on foil. Cut, dust with powdered sugar, and store in a closed container. Sapodilla fruit may be "cooked into jam or preserves, if the gummy sap is skimmed off during cooking" (dessertagriculture.org).

Clove-pink, also **carnation, grenadine,** or **gillyflower,** *Dianthus caryophyllus* Linn., is a plant with edible pink flowers. For **Clove-Pink Syrup,** combine an infusion of clove-pink petals with sugar and lemon rind. Use this syrup in preserves (**Gillyflower-Apple Preserves** or **Gillyflower-Pear Preserves**), canned pears or apples, fresh fruit cups, or medicinal ratafias for flatulence and indigestion. Combine 12 ounces fresh clove-pink petals in 2 cups spirits of alcohol for 10 days for **Clove-Pink Cordial;** strain and sweeten. As with violets (**Violet Jam**) and rose petals (**Rose Petal Jam**), **Gillyflower Jam** can be made from clove-pink using equal parts simple syrup or, preferably, lemon-rind or lemon-juice-spiked simple syrup, to clove-pink petals. All of these petal jams, as well as wild strawberry preserves, can be made under glass on a hot, sunny, full, eight-hour day. **Clove-Pink Sorbet** can be made with 2 cups water, ¼ cup sugar, and ½ cup petals.

Dovyalis, tropical apricot, or **Florida apricot,** *Dovyalis abyssinica* x *Dovyalis hebecarpa,* is a tropical fruit with reddish-purple color and fuzz. The fruit's inside flesh is golden-orange and is used in jams, jellies, punch, and cakes. For **Dovyalis Preserves,** cook down equal parts purée and sugar and check and/or adjust the pH prior to canning. **Ketembilla** or **Ceylon gooseberry,** *Dovyalis hebecarpa,* and **kei apple/*umokokolo*** (Africa), or ***umkolo*** (Philippines), *Dovyalis caffra* Warb., are both very acidic fruits that can be used for jelly.

Grumichama, *Eugenia brasiliensis,* is a tropical bush with purple-black, sweet fruits that are about ½ inch in diameter and look like small cherries in clusters. Good wine-colored jelly or pie can be made from this fruit. **Grumichama Jam:** Cook down 4 cups fruit pulp, 4 cups sugar, and 2 tablespoons lime or lemon juice. Cook the berries in water and sieve out the seeds to obtain the pulp. **Cook down the "jam" or preserves until set point is reached.** Look to buy this jam in Captain Cook, Hawaii. The **Australian brush cherry,** *Eugenia myrtifolia* Sims., often seen as a bonsai tree, is used to make jam, as is the **rose apple, jamrosade,** or **jambos,** *Eugenia jambos* Linn. *syn. Syzygium jambos* (L.) Alston, and the **Surinam cherry,** *Eugenia uniflora* Linn. *Eugenia aromatica* Baill. is the tropical clove tree.

Hawthorn, may, quickset, or **whitethorn,** *Crataegus oxyacantha*— The flowers of the hawthorn bloom in May—thus the name—and ripen in September. Red berries called 'haws' are used for tea and Mayhaw jelly. Because hawthorn affects the heart, Jamlady doesn't advise anyone to consume an entire jar in a day, as some people are capable of doing. Limit jam intake to 3 normal servings a day. Hawthorn contains *oligomeric pro-cyanidins* (OPCs) and flavonoids that are dialators of coronary artery tissues. Commission E of the German government has approved hawthorn's use for some heart problems.

Indian jujube, *Zizyphus Mauritiana,* is a tropical, glossy, yellow to reddish fruit with whitish flesh and a single stone. It is used for preserves and butters. One source says cook halved fruits in water and work with pulp, sugar, ginger, and cinnamon to make a butter or preserve, but Jamlady is worried about the pH and has not had an opportunity to test jujube. The USDA Web site shows the pH of jujube as 5.20, so if you make this preserve, refrigerate it (JSR) or, if canning it, properly acidify it first (probably with citric acid or lemon juice). In Venezuela, a jujube liqueur is sold as Crema de Ponsigue.

Jaboticaba, or **Brazilian grape,** *Myrciaria cauliflora* Berg, is a small, round, grapelike fruit that grows from the trunk of the tree in "onesies," "twosies," or "threesies." **Jaboticaba Jam:** Remove the seeds, chop the skins, and cook together equal parts of chopped fruit and sugar, with a tablespoon of lime juice to every 3 cups of fruit and sugar. For **Jaboticaba Jelly,** use 7 cups sugar, 4 cups jaboticaba juice, ½ cup lime juice, and 3 ounces of liquid pectin. Again, check the pH before canning. A related plant, **guavaberry,** or **rumberry,** *Myrciaria floribunda,* is used to make **Guavaberry Liqueur.** (See Folk Jam.)

Kiwano, African horned cucumber, African horned melon, English tomato, hedged gourd, hedged melon, jelly melon, melano, or **metulon,** *Cucumis metuliferus* E. Mey. ex Naud or ex Schad., is a spiny-looking, oval, orange fruit with the subtle taste of bananas, limes, and passionfruit. The interior pulp is green, and it grows like a cucumber. Use kiwanos in smoothie or lassi recipes. Try "blenderizing" the pulp of 1 kiwano with 1 cup plain yogurt and ½ cup ice cream; add honey to desired sweetness. Kiwanos are high in potassium and low in sodium. One might try to make a freezer jam of kiwano or kiwano with some other fruit. The kiwano fruit is very watery, and the flavor is quite delicate, so it is not an ideal fruit for traditional preserves.

Langsat, *Lansium domesticum,* is a slender tree that occurs in four cultivated forms: *duku, langsat* (lansone), *duku langsat,* and *dokong.* The genetic relatedness of this species is still being studied. The tree's edible, sweet-sour arils cover the fruits and are consumed fresh. This tree is found in southern Florida, Puerto Rico, Indonesia, Cambodia, China, Vietnam, Malaysia, the Philippines, and Australia. The arils of langsat are sometimes canned in a syrup, as are lychee fruit, *Litchi chinensis* Sonn.

'Loganberry,' *Rubus loganobaccus,* is similar to a 'Tayberry,' but not identical. A 'Loganberry' is a cross between a raspberry and a blackberry. 'Loganberries' make excellent preserves. Follow red raspberry recipes for making other *Rubus* genus berry preserves. There are many brambles or briar plants that produce edible berries. Do not mistakenly assume these berries are unrelated to raspberries or blackberries. If their name is

Rubus-something, they are related and are in the same genus as red raspberries. For example, **'Marion' blackberries,** or **Pacific blackberries,** *Rubus ursinus,* are Marionberries. *Rubus,* Latin for "bramble or briar," is a genus of the order of Rosales (the Roses). The **'Boysenberry,'** *Rubus ursinus* x *idaeus;* **evergreen blackberry,** *Rubus lacianatus;* **'Loganberry,'** *Rubus loganobaccus;* **western dewberry,** *Rubus ursinus loganobaccus;* **black raspberry,** *Rubus occidentalis;* **'Tayberry,'** *Rubus loganobaccus 'Tayberry';* **cloudberry** (bakeapple, baked-apple berry, or dwarf mulberry), *Rubus chamaemorus;* **thimbleberry** (white flowering raspberry, western thimble raspberry, or mountain sorrel), *Rubus parviflorus* Nutt.; **American dewberry** (smooth blackberry, Canadian blackberry, or running blackberry), *Rubus canadensis;* **Youngberry,** *Rubus ursinus* var. *loganobaccus* 'Young' or *Rubus ursinus* 'Young' (tasty dark-purple fruit, similar to the 'Boysenberry' but matures 2 weeks earlier); **salmonberry,** *Rubus spectabilis;* or **wineberry** or **wine raspberry,** *Rubus phoenicolasius* are all brambles or in the *Rubus* genus. There are many, many more brambles with more or similar common names. To differentiate between them, get the full Latin and cultivar name.

Loquat, or **Japanese plum,** *Eriobotrya japonica* (Thunb.) Lindl., is a small, oblong, tropical fruit with one or two large seeds. Loquats can be canned and are also used to make wine, jam, syrup, soup, pie, cake, pudding, and liqueur. For **Loquat Preserves,** use 4 cups loquats to 3 cups simple syrup and cook until fruits are transparent. For **Loquat Jam,** use 1 pound chopped loquats, 1½ cups sugar, and 1 cup water. Loquats are acidic, having a pH of around 2.8-4.0. You might want to add lemon juice to very sweet loquats or combine the loquats with citrus fruits for a marmalade (basic preserve recipe). (See www.tytyga.com.)

Mangosteen, *Garcinia mangostana* Linn., is an evergreen tree that grows primarily in humid, tropical rainforest areas such as can be found in Malaysia. The Rare Fruit and Vegetable Council of Broward County, Florida, has this tree on their plant list. Considered an exceptionally good-tasting fruit, this juicy, creamy-pulped, acidic fruit can be eaten out of hand or made into juice or jam. The edible sections or segments, numbering four to eight, are actually soft arils.

Maple tree and **maple syrup**—A sweet syrup or sugar, mainly sucrose, is made from the juice or tap of the sugar-maple ("rock-maple" or "hard-maple") tree, *Acer saccharum.* Maple syrup is graded, with grade A being the best and usually preferred. **Tapping the maple tree for its sap is called sugaring. Sugaring was learned from Native Americans and was clearly documented from the 1720s forward.** Maple syrup can be made into **maple jelly** with ½ gallon grade A, medium-amber syrup; 3 cups of cold water; and 2 teaspoons of Genugel, as pectin does not work with maple syrup (www.massmaple.org/recipe.html).

Mastic gum comes from the tree *Pistacia lentiscus* of the Greek Islands. The tree is grown for its resin or gum. Powdered mastic is used to flavor puddings, liqueurs, and other sweet dishes.

Monstera, ceriman, Mexican breadfruit, or **swiss-cheese plant,** *Monstera deliciosa* Liebm., is a shrublike vine in the philodendron family. Its ripe fruits are edible and can be used to make preserves. The fruits are conelike, sweet, and taste of banana and pineapple, and its leaves have holes. The fruits of this vine ripen from the bottom up, and the outer peel is not eaten. The inside segments of the fruit are used for **Monstera Jam.** Sugar and lime juice are cooked with the fruit to make jam. Cook together (parts) 96:24:48:1, segments: water: sugar: lime juice. Check the pH of the jam prior to canning or JSR. Do not eat unripened fruit.

Nutmeg, *Myristica fragrans* Houtt., is the kernel of an apricot-like fruit. It has a yellow, fleshy, outside covering on the nutmeg that is called the pericarp. Delicious jam can be made from this fiberous and sour pericarp. Jamlady has purchased jam made from nutmeg pericarps and found it to be delicious, but she has no nutmeg pericarps. This type of jam is sold in Grenada and on line. Jamlady does have a recipe for **Nutmeg Pericarp Jam:** 1 kg. (2.2 lbs.) outer cover of nutmeg, ¼ teaspoon crushed nutmeg, and 2 kg. (4.4 lbs.) sugar. Cook the cut-up pericarp (outer covering of the nutmeg) and nutmeg in water to cover. Mash or blend the mixture; strain through a jelly bag or cloth. Boil the solution with the sugar to jell point. Definitely test the pH. Do not can, but refrigerate until you can establish the pH of the completed product. Jamlady has never made this jam but got the recipe from those who have. Similar jams are made in Indonesia and India.

Passionfruit, or **granadilla,** *Passiflora edulis,* is a perennial vine with large glossy leaves that are heart shaped and a flower that is very unusual looking. The fruits are yellow and then purple and are ready to eat when dry and wrinkled. Use this fruit for syrups and jellies. **Passionfruit Jelly:** Boil the seed and pulp for 15 minutes; strain. Combine equal juice and sugar; boil 25-30 minutes or until it sets. For **Passionfruit Syrup:** Cook 4 cups water, 6 cups sugar, and 2 cups extracted juice together. Use extracted passionfruit juice in gelatins, preserves, or punches.

Pindo palm or **jelly palm,** *Butia capitata,* is an orange-colored, apricot-sized fruit with a sweet flesh that is used to make jam. For **Pindo-Palm Fruit Jam,** boil down equal parts sugar to fruit or use 2 cups extracted juice to 3¼ cups sugar with ½ cup liquid pectin (Mickler article [August 3, 1997], newsherald.com). JSR. Jamlady has been unable to find the pH of these palm fruits in any article or from any expert consulted prior to publication of this book, and she could not obtain the fruits in time to test them. The pH of the hearts of palm is 6.7. Do not can

any jam without knowing the pH of the product. These fruits are excellent out-of-hand fruits and produce two crops a year, spring and summer.

Rambutan, *Nephelium lappaceum* Linn., is a fruit tree indigenous to the Malay Archipelago and now grown in Thailand, South Vietnam, Indonesia, the Philippines, India, and Sri Lanka. Rambutan's red or yellow fruits are translucent and sweet, their shape is oval, and their skins have hairs or tubercles. Rambutans are usually eaten raw and out of hand.

Roselle, sorrel, Jamaica sorrel, Indian sorrel, sour-sour, Queensland jelly plant, jelly okra, lemon bush, or Florida cranberry, Jamaica, *Hibiscus sabdariffa* Linn., is native to India and Malaysia but is also grown in Africa and throughout the West Indies, Central America, Florida, and other tropical or subtropical areas. The fresh calyx of the roselle plant is harvested for use in salads or is pulverized with peanuts for a side dish. When heated or cooked, it can be made into drinks, sauces, "jams," and chutneys. Cooked and sweetened roselle calyces taste very similar to cranberry sauce. Fresh roselle calyces contain about 3.19 percent pectin (www.hort.purdue.edu) and do not need additional pectin to be cooked into a firm jelly. **Roselle Jelly** can be made with 2 cups of extracted roselle juice, 2 teaspoons freshly squeezed lemon juice, and 1½ cups sugar. Cook the jelly until it sheets or sets on a frozen plate. JSP/RWB10. **Jamaica concentrate** can be purchased in Mexican stores, and the creative jam maker might try some roselle infusion or roselle concentrate in jams or marmalade like lemon marmalade. Some of the Jamaica or roselle concentrates contain a lot of dyes and preservatives. **Dried Jamaica** can also be found for making drinks or infusions.

Roundleaf serviceberry, *Amelanchier sanguinea* (Pursh) DC, is a plant producing small to medium-sized dark-blue pomes. For

Serviceberry Jam, cook 5 cups berries in ¼ cup water. Cook ¾ cup sugar per cup of pulp and add in 3 ounces of liquid pectin (more or less). Boil; check the set and the pH. For jam without pectin, combine with high-pectin fruits and check the pH prior to canning or JSR only. **Saskatoon,** or **Western serviceberry,** *Amelanchier sanguinea* var. *alnifolia,* also has a dark-blue pome; **Bartram juneberry,** or **oblong fruit serviceberry,** is *Amelanchier bartramiana.*

Sea grape, *Coccoloba uvifera,* is an August fruit that grows 20 fruits per cluster, with each fruit measuring about ½ to ¾ inch in diameter. **Sea Grape Jelly:** Cook equal amounts of juice and sugar; some citrus such as lime juice can be added to hasten the set and assure proper acidification. Prior to canning, adjust the pH to under 4.3 or JSR only.

Soursop, or **guanabana,** *Annona muricata,* is a deciduous tree bearing 6-9"-long fruits weighing up to 5 pounds. The fruit's flesh is white and juicy, tastes similar to a mango, and is used to make sherbet, ice cream, jelly, and cold drinks.

Sugar apple, custard apple, or **sweetsop,** *Annona squamosa,* is a tropical dessert fruit with a white, buttery-textured flesh. Several related fruits include the **cherimoya** (*A. cherimola* Mill.) and **soursop** *(A. muricata).*

Sumac, lemonade berry, or **smooth sumac,** *Rhus glabra* Linn., is a cluster of berries that can be soaked in water overnight or boiled in water, strained, and used immediately. Sumac juice does not store well. A jam can be made of ground **squawberry,** *Rhus trilobata* Nutt. (Carolyn Niethammer, *American Indian Food and Lore* [New York: Macmillan Publishing Company, Inc., 1974], 80). **Sumac Jelly:** Boil, for only 10 minutes, 4 bunches red sumac in 6 cups water; strain and reserve the juice. To 5½ cups infusion, add the juice of 1 lime and 1 box pectin; boil. Add 6½ cups sugar and boil about 1 minute. Check the set.

Chapter 4
&
Baking with "Jams"

Throughout the years of Jamlady's childhood, Jamlady watched her grand-mother Clara Pine, called "Gammy," make wonderful thumbprint cookies. Jamlady never got Clara Pine's thumbprint recipe and attempted to get the recipe from Clara when she was in a nursing home, but Clara could not remember the recipe correctly, and Jamlady's attempts at duplicating the thumbprint cookies did not turn out the same.

Many years after her grandmother passed away, Jamlady's Aunt Gladys Carle found Clara's thumbprint cookie recipe in a letter addressed to her Aunt Gladys Decker, who had also passed away. This is a quote from the letter written by Mrs. Clara Pine of Cottekill Road, Stone Ridge, New York, to Miss Gladys Decker of Center Street, Ellenville, New York.

"I did not delay writing because my cookie receipt was a secret, I just forgot and was careless." Jamlady believes Clara would have given Gladys the recipe will-ingly, but Jamlady also knows that just listing the ingredients would not tell every-one exactly how Clara made the recipe. Jamlady remembers Clara telling her the extra secret as they were making the cookies one time—Clara was poetically com-menting on how she always put in "a little Spry by eye." Jamlady was always told that, as far as her grandmother was concerned, nothing but Spry would do. Clara's comments in her letter: "¾ **pound butter—I use some Spry.**" So, you see, we still do not know the exact recipe. Jamlady has tried ¾ butter, ½ butter, and ¾ Spry, but she believes ¼ Spry is a close approximation of the original recipe. The high baking temperature and/or refrigerated condition of the cookies prior to baking makes a difference in the outcome of these cookies. One thing—family and friends agreed—Clara Pine made the best thumbprint cookies around her parts.

The bright, warm, yellow color of these mango preserves is hard to resist. This preserve can be made plain or laced with Grand Marnier or another liqueur, or this recipe may be made with peaches, nectarines, apricots, or a mixture of any of these fruits for a tropical preserve. How about a spoonful in a thumbprint cookie?

Clara Pine's "Spry-by-Eye" Cookies

A jam-filled thumbprint cookie.

¾ pounds of butter ("I use some Spry"* = 18 tablespoons butter [2¼ sticks] and 6 tablespoons vegetable shortening [Crisco®])
2 egg yolks
1 cup sugar
3 cups flour

Cream the butter and vegetable shortening. Add, as you mix, yolks first, sugar second, and flour last. Chill the dough thoroughly in the refrigerator. Roll the dough in a small ball in the palm of your hand and make a little indention with your finger (or some other appropriately shaped tool) deep enough to hold a dot of jelly, jam, preserves, or butter. If you cut a ball in half, it should measure 1-1¼" across, no larger. Set the cookies on an ungreased cookie sheet (or on no-stick foil) with adequate space between them, as they may spread out a little during cooking. Chill a tray of 6 to 8 cookies. Bake the thoroughly chilled cookies between 425-450 degrees F—until light brown. Reduce the temperature to 350 degrees F after adding the "jam" in each cookie's indention. Bake just long enough to slightly melt the "jam" and to complete the cookies.

Spry and Fluffo are no longer manufactured, so you will have to substitute another vegetable shortening. For a list of other discontinued food products, go to hometownfavorites.com and see "Boy They Were Good but . . ." As old products get discontinued, new products emerge. Try Crisco® or a similar shortening as a substitute for Spry.

Jamlady believes her grandmother always put the jam on the cookies near the very end of the baking, and her mother puts the jam on after the cookies are done, but still hot. Anyway, Jamlady puts the jam on for only the last few minutes. For this reason, Jamlady uses several small baking sheets—as opposed to using a great, big one—so the cookies can receive the jam quickly and go right back into the oven. Also, be sure to refrigerate the cookie dough prior to baking. Jamlady's modern version of this thumbprint cookie incorporates some unusual preserves and even some hot jellies—to spice things up a bit.

Jamlady has compared various "church lady" thumbprint cookies from Clara Pine's local area, the Rondout Valley near Stone Ridge, New York, and found the closest recipe to be **Thumbprint Cookies:** ¾ pound of oleo, 1 cup sugar, 3 egg yolks, 3 cups flour, a dash of salt, and 1 teaspoon vanilla. Bake for 10 minutes at 350 degrees F (J. Countryman and L. Martin, eds., *275 Years Cookbook* [Accord, NY: Rochester Reformed Church, 1976], 164). The *275 Years Cookbook* is recommended by Jamlady.

Some of the butter cookie recipes in Simon Kander's *The Settlement Cookbook* use only yolks in the cookie batter and brush the egg whites on top of the cookies, but none use more flour than the egg and butter/Spry combination, and none bake at a temperature higher than 350 degrees F. Also, all recipes have flavoring or lemon rind in their formulations. Most of the spritz cookies, which are excellent for sandwiching jam between them, use whole eggs with butter, sugar, and flour. Rombauer and Becker (*The Joy of Cooking* [Indianapolis, IN: Bobbs-Merrill Company,

Inc., 1974], 663) comment on "Yolk Cookies" as being a good way to use up leftover yolks, "having good tensile strength" and "making an excellent base for filled nut or jam tarts," but their recipe uses a 2:1 ratio of yolks to cups of flour, and Clara's recipe uses 2:3.

Another thumbprint recipe is located in Barbara Ohrbach's *Merry Christmas,* a little book given by a relative to Jamlady's daughter. This recipe uses the same amount of butter and yolk, but it uses more sugar. Additionally, it uses items not found in Clara's recipe: vanilla, baking powder, salt, and grated orange peel. The orange peel is a nice touch when filling the cookies with the recommended raspberry jam. The Ohrbach recipe's baking temperature is 350 degrees, 75 to 100 degrees lower than Clara's cookies' baking temperature. Jamlady likes the idea of the orange peel in the cookie and will try orange peel with her grandmother's recipe, filling the cookies with Seedless Raspberry Marnier Jam.

Another great cookie to use with jelly, jam, or preserves is the spritz cookie. These cookies are made using a cookie press or a pastry bag. Jamlady's spritz cookies are extruded with a template in the cookie press that produces a ridged-wafer cookie. There are other shaped templates that can be used for cookies.

The whole concept of cookie making is old, dating back to at least the Persian Empire in the seventh century A.D. Wafer-filled cookies, like spritz cookies, were sold in Paris during the 1500s. The first cookies are thought to have been little test cakes, probably created when bakers were trying to test the temperature of their ovens before placing an entire cake in the oven.

Note: *In German, the word* spritzen *means to squirt, as from a syringe or cookie press. The Dutch word* koekjo *means little cake (cookie).*

Large-Batch Spritz Cookies

Form these cookies with a cookie press or a pastry bag.

4 cups flour
1⅓ cups sugar
½ teaspoon baking powder (scant)
¾ teaspoon salt
1¾ cups butter
2 medium eggs
1½ teaspoons flavoring of choice

Cream the butter and sugar; add the eggs and the rest of the ingredients. Chill and bake the extruded, flat cookies at 350 degrees F for about 11 minutes. Allow the cookies to cool before filling them with "jam."

Plain or Almond Spritz Cookies

Almond spritz cookies are good filled with sour cherry jam!

2½ cups flour (or 2¼ cups with cocoa)
¾ cup sugar
½ teaspoon baking powder
1 cup butter
A pinch of salt
1 large egg
¼ cup cocoa or 2 ounces of melted chocolate (optional)
1 teaspoon pure vanilla, almond extract, lemon extract, rum flavoring, or a couple drops of anise oil or very finely ground coffee beans with vanilla (recipegoldmine.com)

Cream the butter and sugar. Add the eggs and the rest of the ingredients. Chill the dough and bake the extruded, flat cookies at 375 degrees F for about 10-15 minutes. If cocoa or melted chocolate is added for **Chocolate Spritz Cookies,** adjust the flour, if necessary.

With spritz cookies, the "jam" is added, after baking, to each cooled wafer cookie; the two wafers are then put together like a sandwich. These cookies make wonderful gifts for the holidays. Jamlady likes to make spritz cookies with ridges, because they hold the jam well and are a bit more attractive than smooth and flat cookies.

Jamlady's mother, Doris Pine Schoonmaker, makes Italian Holiday Cookies that are actually coconut thumbprints with preserves in the centers.

Italian Holiday Cookies

Coconut thumbprint cookies to delight young and old!

½ cup butter (1 stick)
⅓ cup sugar
1 egg yolk
¼ teaspoon vanilla
1¼ cups flour
½ teaspoon salt
1 egg white, slightly beaten
1 cup flaked coconut
Assorted preserves

Cream the butter; add the sugar. Add the egg yolk and vanilla. Beat. Gradually add the salt and flour. Chill the dough for ease in handling. Preheat the oven to 300 degrees F. Make 1" balls, dip them in egg white, and roll them in coconut. Place the dough balls on an ungreased baking sheet, or on no-stick foil on a cookie sheet, and press a thumbprint in each cookie. Bake for 20-25 minutes. Add the preserves for the last 5 minutes of baking.

There are many other different recipes for jam-filled cookies, but one famous one is the **Hamantaschen** or **"Haman's Hats,"** a cookie that commemorates a time when the Jewish people living in Persia were saved from extermination (Esther 9:32) (Purim holiday or Festival of Lots). These jam-filled pastries look like triangles, symbolic of the **evil Haman's three-sided hat (Haman's pockets**—full of money— **Haman's ears** or **Haman's nose,** depending on the storyteller). Use the flaky tart dough recipe below and make triangle cookies from cutout circles that are then filled with preserves before or after baking, or try this next dough recipe.

This dough recipe is intended specifically for **Haman's Hats.** Use ⅔ cup butter or margarine, ½ cup sugar, 1 egg, ¼ cup no-pulp orange juice or

Italian Holiday Cookies with Grand Kiwi Preserves, Bing Cherry Preserves, and Raspberry Preserves—Very small batches of different preserves can be made for immediate use in cookies. Enough Grand Kiwi Preserves to fill an entire batch of these cookies can be made in 15 minutes with just two kiwis, sugar, citric acid, and Grand Marnier.

other juice—like fresh lemon juice, 1 cup white flour, 1 cup whole wheat flour (recommended, or use white flour), and preserves to fill the triangles. Cream the butter and sugar, add the other ingredients (alternating wet and dry), chill the dough, roll out the dough on a floured surface, cut the 3-4" circles (a wide-mouth canning ring cuts a good size), fill the cookie with preserves by folding up the sides to form a triangle, and bake at 375 degrees F for 10-15 minutes. Haman's Hats can be filled with apricot or prune preserves/butter, apple butter, maple and apple preserves, poppy-seed filling, or any other preserves or butter that you might like to try. **Prune Butter** can be made quickly in the food processor by processing 12 ounces of pitted prunes or dried plums with ½ cup (or more) of hot water or fruit juice. JSR or use prune butter directly in Haman Hat's. For baking, you might want to add 2 teaspoons or more of corn syrup, sugar, molasses, or honey in the mixture. Alter the liquid in prune butter, if necessary, to make the correct consistency. For two other Hamantaschen recipes, one a yeast dough and the other a honey dough, see Jennie Grossinger's *The Art of Jewish Cooking* ([New York: Bantam Books, 1958], 172-73) or search the topic on the Internet, where you will find a dozen or more similar recipes.

Note: *Please be aware that there are many variations in the spelling of* Hamantaschen, *such as* Hamenstaschen. *These spellings are not considered incorrect spellings, since foreign-language sounds do not always translate into English well. Often, different translators will spell the same word differently.*

Besides using cookies to receive jam or preserves, Jamlady's Aunt Frances was well known for her strawberry tarts. As a child, Jamlady would do most anything she asked—in the line of small jobs—so that Aunt Frances would have less work to do and could make strawberry tarts. The specialness of these tarts is in the crust, which also can be used to make very **flaky pie crust, miniature thumbprint cookies** (¾" in diameter with ¼" indentions), **Haman's Hats,** and **snowballs.** Mrs. Frances Basten of Stone Ridge, New York, received this recipe from Mrs. Margaret Cahill, also of Stone Ridge, New York, and passed it along to Jamlady, who continues to impress children with these treats. It is not that adults do not appreciate these treats—they do—but these tarts just are special favorites of many children.

Tarts with flaky pastry can be constructed using a rolling pin, cookie cutters, a pastry brush, muffin pans, and slightly beaten egg whites. The small tartlets with Folk Jam and macadamia-nut centers were made with Christmas-tree star cutters and mini-muffin pans, and the larger stars were made with a variety of different-sized star cutters. The other shaped tarts were made with identically shaped cutters of different sizes.

Flaky Strawberry Genie and Peach Butter Tarts—Each tart was brushed with frothy egg whites prior to baking, and the different pieces of each tart are held together with a paint brush full of slightly beaten egg white. Some tarts have macadamia-nut centers.

Flaky Strawberry Tarts

Mrs. Margaret Cahill to Mrs. Frances Basten to Jamlady to you!

4 cups flour
1 tablespoon sugar
2 teaspoons salt
1¾ cups shortening (Spry is no longer manufactured, Crisco® recommended)
½ cup water
1 tablespoon vinegar
1 egg

Mix the water, vinegar, and egg. Set aside. Cut the shortening into the flour, sugar, and salt and then mix in the water, vinegar, and egg mixture. Roll it out as with any tart and fill with strawberry jam or strawberry preserves. An alternate filling can be used instead of strawberry preserves. Jamlady highly recommends gooseberry preserves, strawberry-rhubarb jam or preserves, raspberry or strawberry genie jam, triple- or double-berry jam, kiwi preserves, peach butter, sour cherry preserves, and blueberry almond jam. For constructed tarts made with several cutout parts, use beaten egg whites to cement the parts together and to give the entire tart color. The Wilton's Cookie Tree Kit's star cookie cutters make excellent tarts. Push the cutout stars into mini-muffin tins or cut out a larger star and brush one with beaten egg white (cement). Then cut the center from a second star so that only an edging is left. Apply the edging and brush the tart with egg white. Bake and add preserves near the end of the baking process.

Jamlady Tip: Use those runny or "not quite set up enough" jams or preserves in tarts. Tarts made with "underset" preserves often turn out better than those with properly set preserve or jam, as the excess water evaporates during the baking process, resulting in a perfect consistency for the jam or preserve.

Jamlady Tip: Use the flaky tart pastry to make snowballs. Peel and core a tart apple. Cover the peeled apple with a paste made from flour and water. Fill the apple's center hole with marmalade or other preserves and cover the entire apple with tart pastry. Use slightly beaten egg whites to cement the dough together and brush the entire snowball with egg white. Leave a vent hole on the top. Bake as apple pie and cool; dust with powdered sugar or glaze with **White Butter Cream Icing:** *1 tablespoon butter; 1 tablespoon cream, milk, water, or brandy; ¼ teaspoon vanilla (optional); and ½ cup confectioners' or powdered sugar. (See the snowball photo in the orange marmalade section of chapter 3.)*

Jams or preserves can be put into prebaked shells or initially baked in the shells. Otherwise, put the preserves in three-quarters of the way through the baking process. Jamlady bakes runny preserves in unbaked tart shells at 350 degrees F but gauges when to place normally set preserves in the tart shells based on the consistency of the preserves to be used. Jamlady's mother usually starts her pies and tarts at 425 degrees F for a few minutes and then turns the temperature down to 350 degrees F. Some people fill the tart shells with dry beans and bake them and then fill the shells with preserves, custards, puddings, and toppings. Use a fork to prick indentions in the tart crust before baking. Turgeon's *The Encyclopedia of Creative Cooking* presents a basic custard filling baked on top of raspberry jam and later topped with a baked meringue topping. Similar recipes using custard on top of jam can be found on the Internet. But Jamlady prefers what she was raised on: classic preserve tarts made with homemade preserves or jams and no frills!

If you want old-fashioned tarts, make small circles or ovals with finger-crimped, raised edges to hold the jam. For neatnik tarts, buy specially designed tart pans to help you construct the tarts. Or, cut 4-inch squares, put the preserves in the center of each square, bring all four corners together, pinch so an enclosed tart is constructed, and bake until golden brown. See Haman's Hats.

Often at market, patrons tell Jamlady that they start consuming a jar of jam and then they tire of eating jam and the jar just sits in the refrigerator. For this reason, patrons often prefer to buy smaller jars of jam, even though they are more expensive per ounce. Jamlady has a suggestion. Buy the more economical jar of jam and use any leftover jam to make a jam cake, coffeecake, cookies, or tarts.

In Kentucky, holiday jam cakes are classically made with blackberry or strawberry jam or preserves, and they are sometimes made with a combination of blackberry and strawberry jam. Jamlady has seen recipes using peach preserves (Lyn Stallworth and Rod Kennedy, *The County Fair Cookbook* [New York: Hyperion, 1994]), strawberry preserves, and blackberry jam. Some jam cake recipes call for orange marmalade instead of the traditional blackberry or strawberry jam. Also noted in *The County Fair Cookbook* and the Rochester Reformed Church's *275 Years Cookbook* (but not on the topic of jam cakes—Jamlady wanted to fit this recipe in somewhere) is an interesting recipe for **potato candy,** with ratios like 6:1:1 of confectionary sugar: mashed potatoes: coconut, respectively, plus a dab of butter and vanilla. Frost with bitter chocolate if you like, or use no coconut. Anybody tried sweet potato candy? Sweet potato butter is delicious! Check the Internet and you will see some.

Jamlady has made wonderful jam cakes using as many as 4 or 5 leftover jams or preserves. The last jam cake Jamlady made from leftover jam included strawberry preserves, strawberry jam, black raspberry jam, red raspberry-cherry jam, and cherry jam. No blackberry was used, and the cake was absolutely delicious.

Jamlady's Kentucky Jam Cake*

This cake is rich, relatively easy to make, solid like pound cake or fruit cake, and freezes well.

1 cup butter
1½ cups blackberry jam or 4-5 assorted jams or preserves
1½ cups sugar
3 cups flour
1 teaspoon baking soda
¼ teaspoon salt
1 cup buttermilk
1 teaspoon ground cloves
1 teaspoon ground nutmeg
1 teaspoon ground cinnamon
3 large eggs

Mix the butter, sugar, eggs, and jam until creamed. Sift the flour. Add the flour, baking soda, salt, and spices (alternately with the milk) to the creamed mixture. Grease a Bundt pan or two layer pans and flour. Add the mixture and bake at 350 degrees F for about 55-65 minutes. When done, the cake tester comes out clean.

Caramel Frosting: ½ cup butter, ½ cup brown sugar, 1¾-2 cups sifted powdered sugar, and ½ cup milk. Melt the butter and brown sugar. Boil for two minutes. Add the milk and keep stirring until it boils. Wait until the frosting mixture cools. Add the powdered sugar. Wait until the cake cools before frosting. A butter cream icing or other icing can be used alternately on this jam cake.

There are many different recipes for jam cake. Check around in other books and on the Internet. Some jam cake recipes include rum-soaked raisins, nuts, baking powder, sour milk, dates, crushed pineapple, cocoa powder, coconut, and/or as many as 5-6 eggs. Some jam cakes are frosted *with icings using corn syrup, cream, and vanilla, and others are boiled icings with sugar, water, egg whites, cream of tartar, and vanilla. Some jam cakes are made into two layers and have a date-filled center. Both seeded and seedless jams and preserves can be used for jam cakes.*

Jamlady Tip: Use leftover "jams" between the layers of a cake, in thumbprint cookies, in coffeecakes, and in jam breads or to make a famous Kentucky Jam Cake.

❦❧

Jamlady's Preserve-Filled Coffeecake

A quick coffeecake recipe to dress up any brunch table!

¾ cup sugar
½ cup butter
¾ teaspoon baking powder
½ teaspoon vanilla or other flavoring
2 eggs
1½ cups sifted, unbleached flour
8- or 12-ounce jar of fruit butter or preserves
Powdered sugar for dusting

Cream the butter and sugar. Add the eggs, baking powder, and vanilla or other flavoring; stir in the flour slowly while mixing. Grease and flour a pie or cake pan (64 square inches). Add ½ to ⅔ of the batter. You may need to flour your fingers to spread out the sticky dough. Add the fruit butter or preserves and top with the rest of the batter. Bake at 350 degrees F for 35-45 minutes. Dust with powdered sugar.

Jam or Marmalade Bars

Delicious cookies in record time!

Bar cookies can be made very quickly with **Accordion Cookie Dough #1 or #2** (see "Figs and Strawberries" section in chapter 3) or with ¾ cup of butter cut into 1½ cups flour, 1½ cups rolled or quick oats, 1 cup brown sugar, 1 teaspoon baking powder, and ¼ teaspoon salt. Pat ⅔ of the crumbly mixture in a greased or "no-stick-foil"-lined, 11" x 7" pan; add a layer of 1½ cups of fruit preserves; and add the remaining ⅓ of the mixture for the top. Bake at 350 degrees F for 35 minutes. Alternately, a few finely chopped nuts can be used in place of some oats. Another good recipe for jam bars can be found in *The Fanny Farmer Cookbook,* and understandably, the same recipe is found in many places on the Internet.

Sour Cherry Jam Kugel sided with sour cream and sour cherry preserves. Jams and preserves are not just for the morning toast. Bake with jams and preserves and make interesting desserts, like layered noodle kugel. Sour cherry vinegar with whole sour cherries is shown in the background.

Jam Kugels

A noodle dessert with an interesting history!

"Jams" are often served with sour cream on plain noodle kugels, but this recipe bakes the jam or preserves in the center of two noodle layers. Grease a 7" x 8" oval dish. Cook and drain 8 ounces of wide egg noodles and mix with ¼ cup melted butter. Add to the noodle mixture 2 large beaten eggs, 2-3 tablespoons sugar (or reduce further to be less sweet), 1 teaspoon vanilla (or other flavoring), and 8-10 ounces semidrained pineapple. Fill the baking dish with half of the noodle mixture, add 6-8 ounces jam or preserves, and add the rest of the noodle mixture. Top with 1 cup semicrushed Total® (whole-grain wheat and brown-rice flakes), 1 tablespoon sugar, and 1 teaspoon cinnamon or other spice. Construct this basic kugel with your choice of preserves—cherry, apricot, or apple, etc.

Jamlady Tip: Consider using several leftover preserves in Jam Kugels; place cherry preserves on left side of the kugel and apricot preserves on the right.

The next recipe, for strawberry jam bread, comes from an old newspaper clipping.

Strawberry Jam Bread

Good texture, easy slicing, and excellent fruit flavor!

1 cup butter
1½ cup sugar
1 teaspoon vanilla extract
¼ teaspoon lemon extract
4 eggs
3 cups sifted flour
1 teaspoon salt
¾ teaspoon cream of tartar
½ teaspoon soda
1 cup strawberry preserves (or other "jams" like raspberry preserves or apricot butter)
½ cup sour cream or fresh whipping cream
½-1 cup nuts

Cream the butter, sugar, eggs, vanilla extract, and lemon extract. Alternately, add the dry ingredients, sour cream and preserves, and finally the nuts. Top the unbaked bread with some decorative nut pieces. Bake at 350 degrees F for 50 minutes (2 loaves). A recipe for peach jam bread can be found in Stallworth and Kennedy's *The Country Fair Cookbook*.

Since Jamlady is on the topic of strawberry bread, Jamlady feels compelled to include the best recipe for it, even though it has absolutely no jam in the ingredients. It seems like everybody who tastes this bread asks for the recipe, including Jamlady, who got the recipe from her Florida "snowbird" neighbor, Mrs. Thomas Howard of Tennessee.

Strawberry Bread

A perfectly wonderful bread recipe.

3 cups flour
2 cups sugar
2 cups thawed, sliced strawberries, drained
1¼ cups vegetable oil
1¼ cups chopped pecans
4 beaten eggs
1-2 tablespoons ground cinnamon
1 teaspoon baking soda
1 teaspoon salt

Combine the dry ingredients. Stir in well the remaining ingredients. Bake in two greased and floured loaf pans at 350 degrees F for 60-70 minutes.

Note: If you do not drain the frozen strawberries, the completed bread will be very moist, and the baking time will need to be increased.

Variation: Strawberry Bread with Fresh Strawberries—You may use fresh strawberries instead of frozen strawberries. A different and equally good-tasting bread results.

A quick-to-make recipe for the "jam" lover is the jelly roll. **Although this rolled cake has always been called a "jelly roll," it can be filled with most any preserve, butter, jam, or jelly.** Rolling the jelly roll cake in a roll used to be tricky, but using the no-stick foil makes it easy. Some people line the jelly roll pan with floured waxed paper, but Jamlady recommends using a no-stick foil (Release™) that has been sprayed with aerosol baking oil (like PAM®) and then dusting it lightly with flour. If you don't want to roll the jelly roll, then just make it as two layers.

Sponge cake recipes with separated eggs, the whites whipped, are often a little tenderer than recipes that use the whole, unseparated egg. They also take longer to make. Sometimes, due to time constraints, the whole-egg recipes are just as good—the difference in quality is so little. All of these recipes can be made with the egg whites whipped. Jamlady has seen many different recipes for the sponge cakes that are used to make jelly rolls. Recipe #1 is probably the best of the bunch, but you decide.

Note: For those of you with fat-restricted diets, there is no butter or margarine in this dessert.

Jamlady Tip: Mix some cocoa powder into some of the sponge-cake batter and bake as a marbleized sponge cake. Alternatively, make one side plain and the other side chocolate, creating a finished and rolled-up jelly roll cake that is chocolate on the inside and vanilla on the outside, vanilla on the inside and chocolate on the outside, or all chocolate on one end and all vanilla on the other.

Jelly Roll Cake #1: 5 eggs; 1 teaspoon fresh lemon juice or other flavoring, such as pure almond extract or coconut extract; ½ teaspoon salt; 5 tablespoons sugar; 5 tablespoons cornstarch; and 5 tablespoons flour. Separate the eggs, reserve the yolks, and whip the egg whites until they almost peak. Add the salt and beat until the whites peak. Add the sugar and beat until stiff. In another bowl, beat the yolks and flavoring; fold in the whites, cornstarch, and sifted flour. Bake at 375 degrees F for about 11-12 minutes or until cake tester comes out clean. Put the preserves on the sponge cake, and if using "no-stick" foil, it will be possible to roll directly from the baking pan. Roll the cake up and dust the jelly roll with confectioners' sugar. During the baking test, this jelly roll recipe rolled beautifully, without cracking.

*Variations: Sour cherry preserves are recommended for the **almond-flavored sponge-cake roll,** and pineapple preserves are good in the **coconut-flavored sponge-cake roll.** Jamlady has* *thought about using ½ mashed banana in this sponge-cake recipe, adding 1 additional tablespoon of cornstarch and flour for a* **banana sponge cake,** *but she did not have time to try it. Banana extract works fine. The perfect filling for the banana sponge-cake roll, strawberry preserves. Rum extract or regular rum may also be used as a flavoring for* **rum-flavored sponge cake.**

Jelly Roll Cake #2: 3 eggs, 1 cup white sugar, ⅓ cup water, 1 teaspoon vanilla, 1 cup cake flour, 1 teaspoon baking powder, and ¼ teaspoon salt. Optional: 2 tablespoons cocoa, for a chocolate jelly roll, or 1 teaspoon vanilla. Cream eggs and sugar and add the rest of the ingredients. Bake at 375 degrees F. The exact number of minutes will be determined by the thickness of the batter in the pan. Use a cake tester to check and refer to the other sponge-cake recipes as a guide.

Jelly Roll Cake #3: 4 eggs, ¾ cup flour, ¾ cup sugar, ¾ teaspoon baking powder, and ¼ teaspoon salt. Cream eggs and sugar and add the rest of the ingredients. Bake in a 375-400 degree F oven until a toothpick comes out clean. During the baking test, this sponge cake rolled without any cracking.

Jelly Roll Cake #4: Cream 4 egg yolks, ¼ cup sugar, and ½ teaspoon flavoring such as pure vanilla or pure almond extract. Mix in ¾ cup cake flour, ¼ teaspoon salt, and 1 teaspoon baking powder. Fold in a mixture of 4 stiffly beaten egg whites with ½ cup sugar that was beaten in when the whites were peaking. In a 10" x 15" pan, bake in a 375 degree F oven. Do not overbake; 10-13 minutes is recommended. Remove the cake from the oven, spread the jelly, jam, preserve, or butter, and roll right away. Roll and sprinkle with confectioners' sugar. This recipe rolls very easily.

These next three recipes are not baked, but they are a good way to use jam or preserves. Jam can be used to make a sweet sauce to go on rice. This practical and easy recipe was noted in *Mrs. Winslow's Domestic Receipt Book for 1877* ([NewYork: Jeremiah Curtis and Sons and John I. Brown and Sons, 1876], 9) and could be used for steamed rice just as well as boiled rice.

⚭

Sweet Sauce for Boiled or Steamed Rice

Try a recipe from the olden days.

"Mix a tablespoonful of flour quite smooth in four tablespoonfuls of water; then stir into it half a pint of boiling water; sugar or syrup to taste; stir over the fire until the sauce boils, when, if allowed, an ounce of butter may be added, with a tablespoon of lemon juice. When sweetened with sugar, a little nutmeg or ground cinnamon may be used, instead of lemon juice, if preferred, a tablespoonful of raspberry jam, or any fruit syrup, may be used to flavor the sauce and is generally much liked."

In the good old days, jams were used often. These two old recipes (the one above and the one below) from Miss E. Neil's *The Everyday CookBook and Encyclopedia of Practial Recipes* ([Chicago, IL: Merchant's Specialty Co. 1892], 219-20) are both are easy to make, but Jamlady cautions readers about using raw eggs in the "snowwhipped cream." (See the following recipe.) From a historical aspect, both of these Neil recipes are interesting.

Dish of Snowwhipped Cream

An old recipe to try anew.

"To the whites of three eggs beaten to a froth, add a pint of cream and four tablepoonsfuls [*sic*] of sweet wine, with three of fine white sugar and a teaspoonful of extract of lemon or vanilla; whip it to a froth and serve in a glass dish; serve jelly or jam with it. Or lay ladyfingers or sliced sponge cake in a glass dish, put spoonfuls of jelly or jam over and heap the snow upon it."

Caution: Please inform yourself about the risks of salmonella inside raw eggs and, perhaps, use pasteurized eggs-in-shell or pasteurized egg whites, adding a smidgen of cream of tartar to keep the whites peaking.

Neil's fritter recipe (below) turns out like little, thin fritters, blini, or pancakes and tastes somewhat bland. Of course, flavors can be added—a smidgen of sugar or honey—but these fritters are supposed to have a plain taste to contrast with the preserves that will be placed upon them. Jamlady likes to add a few dashes of ground cinnamon and an extra tablespoon or two of flour to the batter for the perfect fritter to accept preserves. These fritters are very popular with children who are often overwhelmed with the size of regular pancakes. These little fritters can also be used with caviar or smoked salmon with sour cream. The creative chef might consider modifying this fritter recipe to include some of the new types of flours on store shelves, like gram, amaranth, and banana. Top these newly formulated fritters with jam or preserves!

Jelly Fritters

Small little fritters—plates to hold jams, caviar, or strawberry gems!

"Make a batter of two eggs, a pint of milk, a pint bowl of wheat flour or more, beat it light; put a tablespoonful lard or beef fat in a frying or omelet-pan, add a saltpoonfuls [*sic*] of salt, make it boiling hot, put in the batter by the large spoonful, not too close; when one side is a delicate brown, turn the other; when done, take them on to a dish with a doily over it, put a dessert-spoonful of firm jelly on each and serve."

One of Jamlady's favorite cookbooks, *The Encyclopedia of Creative Cooking* by Charlotte Turgeon ([New York: Weathervane Books, 1985], 402), shows a **fried cheese fritter** made with a little milk, Worcestershire sauce, hot pepper sauce, egg, biscuit mix, and American cheese. The dipping sauce used—a dish of jelly or jam. Some other fritter batters use baking powder as an ingredient, like the old Danish recipe for **Peach Fritters,** in which the peach halves are dipped in the batter and then fried: 1 cup flour, 1½ teaspoons baking powder, a pinch or two of salt, 2 tablespoons sugar, 1 egg, ⅓ cup milk, 1 tablespoon melted shortening or oil. **Apple Fritters,** pieces of apple or whole apple sections that are dipped in fritter batter and then fried, are old-time favorites. The taste of apple fritters can also be achieved with plain fritters topped with Apple and Maple Preserves (shown in chapter 3).

Chapter 5

&c.

Butters

Butters are fruit pulps cooked with sugar until they are thick. Butters have less sugar than most preserves, jams, or jellies. The sugar contained in a butter is usually approximately half that of the pulp measure at the onset of cooking. Most preserves, jams, and jellies have as much or more sugar than the fruit measure and, therefore, have more sugar than butters do. Some butters have fruit juice in their recipes. This juice adds flavor, sometimes acidity, and sometimes sweetness. Butters can be cooked in a Crockpot, on the stove, or in a microwave oven. **Since butters can scorch or burn easily, some cooks prefer to alternate cooking with cooling.** Jamlady calls this method of cooking the "On-Off Method" or "Switch Method" (SM). This method allows for a lot of evaporation without burning the butter, and when the butter is cool, the method allows the cook to determine the butter's true thickness. Butters can be cooled overnight in the refrigerator to check their true thickness.

Caution: Be very careful of reheating cooled butters that are thick and stick to the bottom of the pan. Try a double-boiler setup or stir constantly to avoid scorching the butter. When heating butters in the microwave or on the stove, do not superheat them and do not boil the mixture. It is not necessary to boil the mixture to start the process of evaporation. Just heat it enough to make the mixture reasonably warm. Look for the steam to rise when the heat is turned off.

An older cookbook might describe the process of making butter differently than the recipes of today, for we now have blenders, food processors, juicing machines, and packaged pectins. Historically, a butter was made by cooking the fruit until soft, pressing the fruit through a sieve, and then adding sugar and other ingredients. As you will see as you read through these recipes, many fruits can simply be juiced and then cooked with sugar and other ingredients.

Most any fruit can be made into a butter, but the most likely candidates are fruits with more bulk and less water. Watermelon, for example, is not a likely candidate to make into a butter, but it does cook down into a "**molasses.**" Butters are usually made from fruits such as apples, apricots, bananas, cherries, blueberries, grapes, guavas, mangoes, nectarines, pears, plums, quince, and tomatoes. Tamarillos and many other exotic fruits can be made into butters, if you have a good supply of them.

Jamlady has developed some new types of butter recipes, butters that do not caramelize or turn dark when cooked down because they are not cooked down

Flaky Strawberry Genie and Peach Butter Tarts—
Each tart was brushed with some frothy egg white
prior to baking, and the different pieces of each tart
are held together with a paintbrush full of slightly
beaten egg white. Some tarts have macadamia-nut
centers.

that much. Jamlady's butters, or **Heavenly Butters,** utilize the newer pectin, referred to as lite, LM pectin, or "no-sugar" pectin. The recipes offered by most LM pectin manufacturers, on their insert sheets, are jam recipes. Most of these jam recipes with LM pectin call for less fruit than Jamlady uses for her Heavenly Butter recipes. The benefits of "the Jamlady Method," or "the Heavenly Butter Method" (using LM pectins for butters—"stretched fruit to sugar ratios"), are a shorter cooking time, better color, better consistency, more nutrition, and less sugar per tablespoon of completed product. Jamlady has coined the term "Heavenly Butters" for butters made using "the Jamlady Method," or the practice of using approximately twice as much fruit to sugar as pectin manufacturers suggest in their directions for making "no-sugar" jams.

While butters start out with less sugar than fruit, as they cook down, some of the water evaporates, and the actual sugar content increases in comparison to the volume of butter or fruit solids remaining. With LM pectin, since you are not cooking the product down for hours, you are not increasing the sugar to fruit ratio that much either. The best results using LM pectin can be seen with peaches, mangoes, apricots, and other fruits that tend to get dark when being cooked down by traditional butter methods.

Butters made using both the new and old methods of butter-making are produced for market, but Jamlady rarely makes traditional peach, mango, or tropical butter anymore, as most people do not like the dark, caramelized flavor obtained when no additional powdered pectin or liquid, pouch pectin is used. Using traditional methods for peach or mango butter makes the butter either too runny or too dark. Of course, liquid pectin can be added to a traditional, peach butter recipe, and a few people do use this method to achieve a lighter color and quicker set, but using LM pectin in this fashion allows for much less sugar to be used. (See peach preserves made with pectin in chapter 3.)

Apple butters and tomato butters are old-time classics. Apple butter can be made alone or with spices, mixed with other butters, spiked with ginger, or sweetened or flavored with different liquids or choices of sweeteners. Many Amish apple butters, for example, are cooked with apple cider and/or apple cider concentrate, but apple butter can also be made tart and flavorful with lemon, orange juice, or citrus rind. Spices can vary, but the commonly used spices are cinnamon, ginger, cardamom, and nutmeg. The spice nutmeg, *Myristica fragrans,* is from a tropical tree and is a stimulant that should not be used to excess.

Maple syrup or honey may be substituted for part of the sugar in a butter recipe.

ⱷⱻ

Maple or Honey Apple Butter

Classic flavors in a traditional butter!

14 cups apple purée (from cubed tart apples)
6 cups sugar
1 cup maple syrup or honey (or sugar for plain apple butter)
1 teaspoon cinnamon
½ teaspoon allspice
¼ teaspoon cloves
¼ teaspoon ascorbic acid crystals (only a pinch or two in the recipes, the rest for the prep water)

Use ascorbic acid crystals in the water when peeling the apples. Totally peel and core the tart apples. Cube the apples, add a pinch of ascorbic acid, and cook a cup of water with each pound of apples. When soft, run the fruit through a Foley food mill to obtain the purée. Cook all of the ingredients together and finish off using the

"Switch Method." Be patient; take your time. Stir and scrape the bottom and sides of the pot well. Do not cook with high heat. A completed butter is thick when cold.
JSP/RWB5(4OZ)10(8OZ)15(16OZ).

Variations: Spices can be varied. Try cardamom, nutmeg, ginger, oil of cinnamon **(Jamlady's Apple Genie Butter),** *or grated lemon rind. Lemon rind will hasten the thickening process.*

To make mixed butters like **Plum-Apple Butter,** you can either mix the plum pulp and the apple pulp together and use half as much sugar as pulp and cook down the batch, or make a batch of each separate butter and, when both batches are fully cooked, mix the two together in differing ratios. For some fruits, equal parts of each butter do not make the best-tasting combination. As an **experiment,** Jamlady encourages cooks in training to make a batch of plum butter and apple butter separately and mix each individual jar differently and with differing spices. One jar can be ¾ plum and ¼ apple, and another can be ½ and ½, and another ¾ apple and ¼ plum. This method serves several purposes. **First,** each batch will cook down more quickly. **Secondly,** several different products can be made from the two batches, making for a variety of choices when selecting a butter to eat during the winter months. **Thirdly,** jars of plain apple butter and plain plum butter have been made. **Fourthly,** if you burn one batch, you might not burn the other. This fourth comment was intended as a joke, but it won't be a joke if it happens to you.

Jamlady Tip: Cook butters slowly, stir constantly, and scrape the pan bottom and sides as you stir. If you cannot watch over the butter, turn it off and let it evaporate some and return when you can watch over it constantly.

Applesauces, like butters, can be flavored with various other fruits. **Applesauces have less sugar than butters do, and they require a shorter cooking time.**

Apple-Raspberry Sauce

This sauce is special!
Use plain on pork chops or as a dessert sauce.

- 7 pounds peeled, cubed, tart apples
- 7 cups water
- 6 small boxes (pints) fresh raspberries (4 cups seedless raspberry purée)
- 2¾ cups sugar
- ½ teaspoon or less ascorbic acid crystals

Put some ascorbic acid crystals in the water used to wash the apples and dunk the apples while peeling them. Totally peel and core the apples. Measure out 7 pounds of cubed apples and cook them with 7 cups of water and a couple of pinches or more of ascorbic acid crystals. Do not use too much ascorbic acid crystals, or the applesauce will be too tart; use just enough to deter oxidation/browning. When cooked enough to be soft, put the apple mixture through a Foley food mill. Add 4 cups of seedless raspberry purée, made by juicing the raspberries (many times—10-15 times—or until the seeds run hot) through a Champion juicing machine or by pushing the raspberries through a sieve. Add the sugar and cook for 10 minutes or until the proper thickness is achieved. A little more or less sugar may be used, depending on your taste buds. JSP/RWB10(8OZ)15(16OZ).

Variation: Apple-Elderberry Sauce or Elderberry-Apple Sauce—Make with 5 pounds apples, 2 cups extracted elderberry juice (or juiced, seedless pulp), and 1½ cups sugar. This sauce can be made with juiced elderberries that have been run through a Champion juicing machine, but the flavor will not be quite as clear or as bright as the flavor of a sauce using extracted juice. Still, why throw out the elderberry pulp if you have a juicing machine? The ratio of elderberries to applesauce

Elderberry-Apple Sauce—A combination of apples and elderberries can be made as a sauce or as a butter. A butter will have more sugar than a sauce will, and a butter will be glossier looking. If more elderberries than apples are used, then the product would be called Elderberry-Apple sauce or Elderberry-Apple Butter.

could be increased. If there are more apples than elderberries, this sauce should probably be called Apple-Elderberry Sauce and not Elderberry-Apple Sauce, but most people call it Elderberry-Apple Sauce either way, as Elderberry-Apple Sauce sounds better. Either way, this sauce is great on pork chops, grilled venison, cottage cheese, fritters (see Neil's recipe for jelly fritters in chapter 4), pancakes, blini, French toast, or even cheese blintzes.

Tomato-apple butter can be made together or separately. Many people consider **Tomato-Apple Butter** superior to regular apple butter. In New York State, where Jamlady was born and raised, **New York-Style Tomato-Apple Butter** is often made with twice as many apples as tomatoes and is combined with orange juice, grated rind of orange, sugar, and cinnamon. Cook 5 cups peeled, chopped tart apples with 2½ cups skinless, seedless, chopped tomato meats, and the grated outer rind of 1 large orange. "Blenderize" the mixture until smooth. Add the juice from the orange, 3 to 3½ cups sugar, and some optional cinnamon sticks. Some cooks add a little vinegar (1-2 tablespoons) to increase the tartness of the butter. A pinch of ascorbic acid crystals will accomplish the same tartness. Cook the butter until thick. JSP/RWB10. Some cooks make a **50-50 Tomato-Apple Butter** with 4 cups apples and 4 cups tomato meats, 1½ pounds (2¾-3 cups) brown sugar, and ½ cup red or white wine vinegar. Cook the mixture with a spice bag of cinnamon sticks, whole allspice, gingerroot slices, and whole cloves, or add ½ teaspoon of the ground spice of each. Blueberries and apples can be combined to make **Blueberry-Apple Butter.**

Blueberry-Apple Butter

Wonderful on whole-wheat toast!

4 cups washed, destemmed, fresh blueberries
4 large, peeled, sliced, green tart apples
4 cups sugar or alternate sweetener
1½ teaspoons total spice (select from allspice, cinnamon, mace, nutmeg, pure almond extract, and grated lemon peel)

Totally peel and core the apples. Cube the apples and cook them with 1 cup of water per pound of apples. Add in the blueberries while the apples are cooking. When soft, run the fruit through a Foley food mill to obtain a purée. Add the sugar and spices and cook down (SM) the butter to the correct consistency.
JSP/RWB5(4OZ)10(8OZ).

Variation: Blueberry-Apple Sauce—Follow the recipe above, but do not cook the mixture down as far and sweeten it to taste, using less sugar.

Tomato Butter (Two Basic Recipes)

Tomato Butter with two oils.
Wake up your taste buds!

7 pounds skinless, seedless tomato meats
6⅓ cups sugar
1 cup red wine vinegar or cider vinegar
1-2 drops oil of cloves and oil of cinnamon

Cook all ingredients until thick. Add the drops of oil of cloves and oil of cinnamon to a cup of the tomato butter; mix and add part of the cup of flavored butter to the whole batch. This method should prevent unintended over-spicing of the entire batch. One would do this step at the very end. The flavoring would be the last thing in, to prevent cooking the flavors away. This oil is so strong that you must add it in this way so as not to get too much. You cannot always pour out just a drop or a half of a drop. JSP/RWB10.

Variation: Tomato Genie Butter—Use oil of cinnamon only, or for **Gingered Tomato Butter,** *see the next recipe.*

Gingered Tomato Butter

So good on warm biscuits!

5 pounds tomato meats
1 cup vinegar
3 cups sugar
1 cinnamon stick
1 tablespoon finely minced gingerroot
2 teaspoons cloves in a spice bag with the cinnamon stick

Cook all ingredients together until thick. JSP/RWB10.

There are many combination of butters that can be made with herbs, spices, and teas. Rose hips can be cooked with apple juice, and that flavored juice can be cooked into the apple butter or applesauce. Consider freshly juiced cranberry juice with a pH of 2.7 in recipes that require a lowering of the pH. Cranberries have about the same pH as apple juice: 2.7. Look through your list of herbs and spices and design your own, special, apple-butter combination. Here is one of Jamlady's special apple butters.

Minty Apple-Ginger Butter

A "blenderized" apple butter.

4 cups extracted apple juice from peeled, cored apples (5 pounds or less)
1 ounce fresh mint
10 cups peeled, sliced tart apples (3½ to 4 pounds)
2 tablespoons peeled, grated gingerroot
6 cups sugar
Green food coloring (optional)
Mint extract (optional)

Juice the peeled, cored, tart apples with mint to net 4 cups of juice. Cook 10 cups peeled, sliced apples in the mint-apple juice until soft and then blend the mixture in a blender with the grated ginger. Cook the apple-mint-ginger pulp (about 14 cups) in a heavy-bottomed pan with the sugar until thick (SM), or, in a Crockpot, cook the entire batch until thick. A double-boiler setup may be used if no heavy-bottom pan is available. Add a very small drop of mint extract if your mint is not flavorful enough. Be careful! It is easy to get too much (see tip below). Add food coloring. JSP/RWB10.

Jamlady Tip: Add the mint extract to just 1 cup of the apple butter and then slowly add that minted apple butter to the main batch, a little at a time.

Variations: Deluxe Apple Butter—Use no mint or ginger, but instead, spice with cardamom, or try cinnamon, nutmeg, cloves, or a combination of all three. For **Ginger Apple Butter,** *spice with ginger.*

Most recipes that will work for apples will work for pears or Asian pear apples. Here is a traditional pear butter. Jamlady's Amish friends, the Millers, in Nappanee, Indiana, make their pear butter in a large steam-jacketed cooker, with apple cider and/or juice concentrate. You can make your own pear butter too!

Deluxe Pear Butter

Pears, apple cider, nutmeg, and allspice!

20 peeled, chopped pears
3 cups sugar or 2½ cups sugar and ½ cup honey
1½ cups apple cider
1 cup light-brown sugar
½ teaspoon pickling salt
¼ cup fresh lemon juice
½ teaspoon nutmeg
½ teaspoon allspice

Cook all ingredients until thick. The spicing can be changed to include cinnamon or other spices like cardamom. A half or quarter recipe will cook down faster. JSP/RWB10.

Grape butter has the concentrated flavor of grapes and tastes similar to wild grape jam. Each 8-ounce jar contains almost a pound of grapes that have been cooked down! This labor-intensive butter can be used as any jelly or jam and is especially good on hot biscuits with a dinner meal like roast beef or roast pork! You'll never want grape jelly again after lip-smacking over this butter!

Grape Butter

Rich, thick, and luscious!

4 pounds destemmed grapes
2 cups sugar
1 cup water

Wash and remove all stems from the grapes. Add the water to the grapes and cook until the grapes are tender. Put the grapes through a Foley food mill or sieve to remove all of the seeds. Add the sugar and CD/SM. Some cooks prefer to bake down the grape butter in a 200 degree F oven, which takes 5-8 hours; stir at least hourly (Andrea Chesman, *Summer in a Jar: Making Pickles, Jams & More* [Charlotte, VT: Williamson Publishing, 1985]). Makes 3-5½ 8-ounce jars, depending on how well you sieve the product and how much you cook down the butter. Grape butter can be spiced with thyme, basil, or other herbs. JSP/RWB10.

Pumpkin butter is well known in Amish country. It is relatively easy to make but more dangerous to can than high-acid fruit products. Pumpkin butter can be made from fresh pumpkin or canned pumpkin. No better pumpkins, or other vegetables for that matter, can be obtained than those from Tammy and Rich Partsch of Hawthorn Farms in Harvard, Illinois. Both Hawthorn Farms and Jamlady have had vendor spaces at the Thursday-afternoon Lindenhurst Farmer's Market, Lindenhurst, Illinois; the Saturday Palatine Farmers' Market, Palatine, Illinois; and the Friday Gurnee Farmers' Market, Viking Park, Gurnee, Illinois. There is also a good farmer's market Thursday morning in front of village hall in LaGrange, Illinois.

You might be surprised to know that many so-called homemade and commercial butters are made from canned pumpkin rather than directly from fresh pumpkins. No doubt safety, as well as convenience, weighs into the decision to use canned pumpkin, which has already been processed at a high temperature, in lieu of fresh pumpkin.

Pumpkin has a pH of 4.9-5.5. Any pumpkin butter processed in a RWB must have a final pH of around 4.0 or lower to be safely processed. While the water activity of pumpkin butter is lower, and there is sugar in pumpkin butter, it still is necessary to have a pH in a safe range, where botulinus cannot grow.

Jamlady has e-mailed several Webmasters on Internet Web sites out of concern for improperly formulated pumpkin butter, peach salsa, and onion chutney recipes displayed on their sites. Some of these posted pumpkin recipes have no added acidification of any kind, yet would-be canners are instructed to can them in a RWB. Some acidic ingredients, like apple cider, vinegar, citric acid, lemon rind, lemon juice, or lime juice, must be added to pumpkin if you are to can it in a rolling water bath (RWB). Likewise, onion or garlic chutneys or spreads must be appropriately acidified to assure a safe canning process, and placing too many peppers in salsa that is not properly acidified is also asking for trouble. Refer to the pH charts at the end of this book for more information.

If you have a pH meter, pumpkin season is the time to use it. Anyone with a pH meter can cook pumpkin with apples, apple juice, lemon juice, orange juice, lemon rind, citric acid, or other fruits and test the pH of the completed product. Do not RWB can any product that has a pH in excess of 4.2 or 4.3.

If you do not have a pH meter, consider the dollars spent on other hobbies. If your hobby is creative canning, buy yourself a pH meter. Far too many recipes for pumpkin butter are being distributed that are intended for the refrigerator and not the canning jar. Not only can you be a watchdog who identifies these dangerous recipes, you also won't have to think too hard for a science project for your daughter or son. Turn pH testing into a family activity and dispel the notion that the average housewife or cook is incapable of applying scientific methods to the art of canning. Jamlady believes in educating cooks, as they are not going to stop creating canning recipes, whether they have or don't have the necessary knowledge and equipment.

Caution: Rule of thumb—If there is little or no added acid or acidic ingredients in any given pumpkin butter recipe, be wary of canning it in a rolling water bath (RWB). It probably cannot be safely canned without further acidification.

Pumpkin butter can be made by CDSM 1 16-ounce can of pumpkin purée or the equivalent in fresh pumpkin purée, 1 cup of freshly extracted apple juice, ½ cup brown sugar, and assorted spices. The typical spices for pumpkin butter are ⅛ teaspoon cinnamon and ⅛ teaspoon allspice or ½ teaspoon cinnamon and ¼ teaspoon nutmeg. Also consider adding ¼ teaspoon ginger and ¼-½ teaspoon salt for added flavor and safety. Some of the recipe's apple juice may be reduced if fresh lemon juice is substituted. Some recipes use honey as a sweetener, and some are made with equal quantities of apple and pumpkin purée. For such recipes, try to use a tart variety of apple, which has a lower pH reading (higher acid). Check the pH of the completed butter with a pH meter, or at the very least, use pH papers or refrigerate the product and do not can it. For butters under 4.2., JSP/RWB10(8OZ)15(16OZ).

When referencing the pH tables at the end of this book, you can see the variance in the pHs of different varieties of apples. To be safe, you may want to add the grated rind of a lemon to your pumpkin butter. Refer to Jamlady's recipe for **Sliced Pumpkin Preserves with Grand Marnier** (in chapter 3) for further ideas regarding the pH issue and the use of citrus to reduce pH readings.

Pumpkin Butter d'Orange

Serve on warm bread or French toast.

4 cups pumpkin pulp
2 cups light brown sugar
½ cup orange-blossom honey
½ cup orange juice or other citrus juice of equivalent pH, such as Clementines or lemons
Grated rind of an orange or Clementine
1 teaspoon cinnamon
½ teaspoon nutmeg
½ teaspoon salt

Cook all ingredients together until thick. JSP/RWB10(8OZ)15(16OZ).

Jamlady has not tried sorghum or maple syrup (higher pH than other standard sweeteners) in pumpkin butter, but they probably would be good in a pumpkin and apple combination. Replace only some of the sugar with sorghum, as sorghum has a stronger flavor. If you do not have a pH meter to check your new formulation, do not can it, but refrigerate it instead. Sorghum is good in Sweet Potato Sorghum Pie (J. S. Collester, *Old-Fashioned Honey Maple Syrup Sorghum Recipes* [Nashville, IN: Bear Wallow Books, 1991]), and creative cooks might try sorghum in pumpkin pie too.

In Argentina, the **sweet potato,** *Ipomoea batatas,* is grown for its large, edible root-tubers, which are used to make **sweet potato paste** or **Dulce de Batata.** (See the photograph in the "Brambles and Other Unusual Plants" section of chapter 3.) **The sweet potato, the root of a vine in the morning-glory family, is not related to the true yam.** The **yam,** a tropical vine, *Dioscorea batatas,* can reach 7 feet in length and is usually much larger than a sweet potato. The sweet potato, probably originating in tropical America, produces root-tubers in several colors. **The flesh of the sweet potato's root-tuber can be white, yellow, or orange.** According to Jamlady's South American e-mail buddy, "Batatas are yellow sweet potatoes. You steam them, peel them, mash them, add sugar and cloves, and stir forever. It is so thick and it takes forever. *Dulce* means sweet; it also means candy or jam. *Dulce de leche* is milk jam."

Caution: This recipe is a refrigerate-only recipe (JSR). Even if you increase the acidity of this product, it is still quite starchy and thick and is probably best kept in the refrigerator.

This recipe for **Sweet Potato Butter** is of Caribbean origin and is made with sugar, lemon, and spices. **Keep Sweet Potato Butter in the refrigerator!**

Sweet Potato Butter

This recipe is indicative of Caribbean cookery at its best!

1½ pounds peeled, ½" x ½" cubed sweet potatoes
4 cups water
2 cups sugar
Juice of 1 lemon with juiced zest (6 strips, no pith)
Spice bag (5 cloves, 1 cinnamon stick, and ½ length-cut vanilla pod)
½ teaspoon freshly grated nutmeg

Cook all ingredients and mash into a smooth butter. **JSR.**

Caution: Do not seal and process in a RWB.
Variation: Jamlady found this old recipe in an 1894 cookbook: "Sweet Potato Preserves—Make syrup as for peaches. Parboil the potatoes, first cutting in round slices, and boil in the syrup until clear" (Mrs. M. Palmer, The Woman's Exchange CookBook *[Chicago, IL: Monarch Book Company, 1894], 52).*

Jamlady usually cooks the peeled and cut-up sweet potatoes in water, puts the mixture through a food mill, adds the lemon, sugar, and spices, like cloves, and cooks it until it is thick enough. This unappreciated recipe is so easy and the taste is terrific. **You do not need to make a large batch; one potato will make a small jar** of sweet potato butter. The clove spice is from dried flower buds of the tropical evergreen tree *Syzygium aromaticum.* The *eugenol* in cloves has anesthetic and antiseptic properties, and oil of clove is often used for toothaches.

Caution: Jamlady cautions readers that the pH of sweet potatoes is 5.3-5.6 and that the pH of any sweet potato product should be checked carefully with a pH meter before canning. The sweet potato's pH is even higher than that of the pumpkin: 4.9-5.5. As an extra precaution, if canning a properly acidified batch or sealing it with wax, refrigerate the sweet potato butter jars at all times.

Guavas are an important jelly, butter, or "cheese" fruit. Many Northerners are not familiar with the 25'-30' guava tree, *Psidium* spp., but guavas are quite common in Florida, California, and other tropical regions. The common guava of the tropics, *Psidium guajava* Linn., is eaten out of hand, sliced with cream, stewed, and preserved, and it is made into jams and jellies. Guavas can even be made into **Guava Brown Betty** (E. Dooley, *Puerto Rican Cook Book* [Richmond, VA: Dietz Press, Inc., 1950], 120). Dooley's book also shows a recipe for **Gooseberry Brown Betty**.

Jamlady was first introduced to **guava jelly** and **guava paste** when she was 9 years old and visiting her grandparents who lived in Davie, Florida, near Miami. Her grandparents served **guava paste** with aged, sharp-cheddar cheese and apple pie. The paste was thick as fudge, deep pink in color, clear, and quite firm. In Brazil, *goiabada,* a thick guava jam or paste, is also made. In the West Indies and in Florida, a similar product, called **guava cheese,** is manufactured. There appear to be many names for these different guava products.

Jamlady has noticed that grocery stores in Florida and Mexico sell fresh guavas and guava products, and recently Jamlady has seen both fresh guavas and guava products in Northern, ethnically orientated grocery stores. The **Cattley** or **strawberry guava,** *Psidium cattleianum,* of California is hardy to 22 degrees F, unlike **common guava,** *Psidium guajava.* The strawberry guava produces smaller, less flavorful fruits than does the common guava, whose fruits are as large as 4" long. The guava fruit is distinguished by its thin skin, which encases a soft, seeded, granular pulp. Some describe the aroma of the guava as musky.

To make **guava jelly,** wash ripe, green fruit under water and slice. Cover the sliced guavas with barely enough water to cover and cook until the fruit is soft. Hang the guava pulp in a jelly bag. Do not attempt to make large batches. Cook 4 cups to a batch. Boil the juice for 30 minutes and then, boil the juice again, with equal amounts of sugar to juice, until the jelly passes the sheet test or sets up on a frozen plate.

To make **guava butter or paste,** cut the guavas into pieces and cook as for the guava jelly. Run the soft and cooked pulp through a food mill to remove the seeds. Put the pulp in a double boiler and make a syrup by adding ¾ cup of sugar for each 1 cup of fruit pulp. Boil the mixture over a double boiler until it forms a soft ball in cold water. Pour the mixture into a mold lined with waxed paper. Dust the top of the butter with powdered sugar to inhibit molding.

Note: If using ripe fruits, you may need to add lemon or lime juice.

Nora Carey's *Perfect Preserves* ([New York: Stewart, Tabori and Chang, Inc., 1990], 114) calls for mixing a cooked-down and strained, guava pulp-lime juice mixture with honey for **guava honey.** Fresh, peeled, and seeded guavas can be eaten raw on a bed of greens. Peel, slice, and seed the fruit first. Raw guava flesh can be mixed with slivered blanched almonds, grated coconut, and topped with whipped cream for a **tropical guava dessert.**

A large, red, porcupined, 'Rome' apple holds a tasty trio of thick and luscious guava paste, 'Granny Smith' apple slices, and Vermont, white, sharp-cheddar cheese. Guava jelly is shown on crackers with cream cheese.

Strawberry Butter

Traditional method.

8 cups washed, hulled, and chopped strawberries
2 cups white sugar
2 tablespoons lemon juice

Simmer chopped strawberries and push them through a food mill or easier yet, just juice them until all the pulp is retrieved from the seeds and only seeds are coming out. Cook the strawberry purée or pulp with the sugar and lemon until it becomes thick. JSP/RWB10.

Spiced Plum Butter

Traditional recipe, unique method.

8 cups plum pulp and juice
6 cups sugar
1 teaspoon cinnamon
½ teaspoon allspice

Run the pitted plum flesh with skins through a Champion juicing machine. Reserve the outputs from each spout, juice and pulp. Mix both the juice and the pulp with the sugar and spices; cook them down until thick. Finish off the cooking in a microwave, scraping the sides of the bowl often (SM). Do not superheat.
JSP/RWB10(8OZ)15(16OZ).

The **mamey** or **mammee Apple,** *Mammea americana,* is sometimes called the **Santo**

Domingo apricot. This grapefruit-sized fruit is used in the Caribbean Islands for **mamey butter** (Dooley, *Puerto Rican Cook Book*), preserved mamey, mamey sherbet, and other sweet dishes. Mamey fruit tastes like an apricot or raspberry. Some island people have reported to Jamlady that mamey can cause stomach distress in some individuals. The **rose apple** or **Pomarrosa,** *Eugenia jambos,* is another tropical fruit. It is normally ornamental but is used in Puerto Rico and Florida for preserves (Dooley, *Puerto Rican Cook Book*, 127). **Barbados cherry** or **acerola,** *Malpighia punicifolia* Linn., is a twelve-foot-high tropical bush that produces a red to scarlet berry about ¾" to 1" across. Barbados cherry fruits are used in jellies, jams, and punches and are eaten out of hand. **Barbados Cherry Jelly:** Use equal parts prepared juice to sugar. Refrigerate or check the pH prior to canning. For more information, see Purdue University's New Crop Page on the Internet.

The calyx of the **roselle, Jamaica,** or **red sorrel of Guinea,** *Hibiscus sabdariffa,* is used to make jelly and preserves in Florida (see the photograph in the "Brambles and Other Unusual Plants" section of chapter 3) and Puerto Rico, as are the grapelike fruits of the **sea grape,** *Coccoloba uvifera* (see the end of chapter 3). If you are ever in Trinidad and Tobago, have a **gua-nabana** or **soursop,** *Annona muricata,* sherbet, or try a **custard apple,** *Annona reticulate,* ice cream. Don't miss seeing Tobago's Pigeon Point, or staying at the Asa Wright Nature Center in Trinidad—where many unique vegetables and fruits are served daily—amidst spikes of local ginger and feeding hummingbirds. To try guanabana in the United States, look for guanabana yogurt drinks at the grocery under the brand name of Yonique®. Just in case some of you might want to try to grow an exotic fruit tree, and do live in a geographical area where you might try, Jamlady noticed the California Rare Fruit Growers, Inc., at http://www.crfg.org. Their site lists many pages of such trees, from *Abelmoschus manihot,* **edible hibiscus** (edible leaves) to *Zizyphus jujube,* **common jujube** or **Chinese date.** Another site of interest is Edible Landscaping & Gardening by Ben Sharvy, at http://members.efn.org/~bsharvy/edible.html. Jamlady supports the philosophy of increased self-sufficiency. Why not landscape with useful trees and plants?

The **sugar apple** or **sweetsop,** *Annona squamosa,* of the West Indies, is often eaten plain. Jamlady points out these possibly unfamiliar fruits to cooks to illustrate the benefits of travel and exposure to different cultures, flora, and foods. There is always something new to try! And remember, if making jellies, jams, preserves, or butters from new fruits, test the pH and adjust the pH prior to canning or refrigerate the product.

⊗

BUTTERS USING LM PECTIN

Ascorbic acid crystals or vitamin C crystals are very tart to the taste. **Do not mistake vitamin C powder for the crystals. They are not interchangeable in these recipes.** Ascorbic acid crystals increase the acidity of a product and retard the oxidation that causes discoloration in fruits. No more dramatic illustration of this principal of oxidation can be seen than with apricots.

If you juice apricots without a pinch of ascorbic acid crystals, they will immediately begin to turn brown. **Use as little ascorbic acid crystals as necessary to prevent the darkening of the fruits.** Too much ascorbic acid crystals will make an overly tart product. Many old-time recipes use lemon juice to retard oxidation, but then you have a lemon flavor. Jamlady has found that using ascorbic acid crystals is a convenient way to inhibit browning, even in fruit cups. Lemon juice may still be used with the ascorbic acid crystals where the lemon flavor is desired. Many traditional butters turn to an unappetizing dark-brown color because of oxidation.

Quick and Zesty Apricot Butter

Use that trusty juicing machine instead of peeling.

Use LM pectin for a smooth Heavenly Butter!

8 cups juiced apricot purée
4 cups sugar
1 1¾-ounce box "no-sugar" pectin (LM)
Peel of 1 lemon
½ teaspoon cinnamon
Several pinches of ascorbic acid crystals

Wash the apricots. Juice the pitted, unpeeled apricots with a pinch of ascorbic acid crystals. Put the extracted pulp and skins through the juicing machine many times until only the skins are leaving the pulp ejector spout. For those cooks without a juicing machine, peel the apricots and processor-chop them to get the necessary pulp. The cooking time may be longer for apricot butter made with peeled apricots. Mix the purée (with the ascorbic acid already in it) with 1 lemon peel. "Blenderize" the mixture until the peel is no longer visible in the purée. Add the pectin and wait 5 minutes. Boil for 5 minutes, stirring constantly. Add the sugar and cinnamon and boil for 10 minutes or until the butter sets up on a frozen plate. JSP/RWB10.

Angel Food

An original Heavenly Butter of mangoes and apricots.

4 cups juiced apricots, skins discarded
4 cups peeled, chopped mangoes (about 6)
3 cups sugar
1 1¾-ounce box "no-sugar" pectin (LM)
½ teaspoon or less ascorbic acid crystals (use by the pinch)
½ teaspoon citric acid

Run the apricot pieces through a Champion juicing machine about 10 times with a pinch or two of the ascorbic acid crystals to prevent discoloration. When all the pulp has been extracted from the skins, only a small amount of skin will be coming from the pulp ejector. Mix the pectin and citric acid with the apricot and mango pulp and wait 5 minutes. Boil for 1 minute; add the sugar. Cook until the butter sets on a frozen plate. JSP/RWB5(4OZ)10(8OZ).

Mango Butter

For the true mango lover!
A quicker recipe with good color and flavor.

8 cups peeled, pitted, and chopped mango (12)
3 cups sugar
1 1¾-ounce "no-sugar" pectin (LM)
¼-½ teaspoon or less ascorbic acid crystals
½ teaspoon citric acid

Use the ascorbic acid crystals sparingly with the fruit during preparation. Mix the fruit with the pectin and citric acid; wait 5-10 minutes. Boil for 1 minute; add the sugar. Stir well and frequently. Cook to set point. JSP/RWB10.

Note: Do not use lemon instead of citric and ascorbic acid, or the flavor will be altered! Also, ⅛ teaspoon crystalline citric acid is the equivalent of 1 tablespoon of lemon juice; they cannot be exchanged 1 for 1.

Chunky Tropical Fruit Butter

Quicker than old-fashioned methods.
A tropical trio—mangoes, apricots, and nectarines!

4 cups purée of juiced apricots (8) and nectarines (8)
4 cups peeled, chopped mangoes (about 6)
3 cups sugar
1 1¾-ounce box "no-sugar" pectin (LM)
¼-½ teaspoon or less ascorbic acid crystals
½ teaspoon citric acid

Use a pinch of ascorbic acid crystals on the fruit during preparation, one very small pinch at a time. Mix the pectin and citric acid with the fruit; let sit for 5 minutes. Boil the mixture for 1 minute; add the sugar and cook for 10 minutes or to set point. JSP/RWB5(4OZ)10(8OZ).

☙❧

Nectarine Butter

Juicing the skins makes this butter tasty!

8 cups pitted, juiced nectarines with skins
3 cups sugar
1 1¾-ounce box "no-sugar" pectin
¼-½ teaspoon or less ascorbic acid crystals
½ teaspoon citric acid crystals

Use a pinch of ascorbic acid crystals on the fruit during preparation. Mix the fruit pulp only or pulp and skin with the pectin; wait 5 minutes and boil for 1 minute. Add the sugar and cook for 10 minutes or until a set is achieved. JSP/RWB10.

Peach Butter

**Taste and soar on angel wings!
Smooth perfection for the peach lover!**

8 cups peeled, pitted, and chopped peaches
3 cups sugar
1 1¾-ounce box "no-sugar" pectin (LM)
¼-½ teaspoon or less ascorbic acid crystals
½ teaspoon citric acid

Use the ascorbic acid crystals sparingly with the fruit in preparation. Mix the fruit with the pectin and citric acid; wait 5 minutes and boil for 1 minute. Add the sugar and cook to jell point. JSP/RWB5(8OZ)10(16OZ).

ᘙᘚ

Spiced Italian Prune-Plum Butter

A rich plum experience, with hints of cinnamon and allspice!
Only 3 cups of sugar to 10 cups plums.

10 cups pitted, unpeeled, chopped plums
1 1¾-ounce box "no-sugar" pectin
3 cups sugar
1 tablespoon cinnamon
1 teaspoon ground allspice

Cook down the pitted, unpeeled, chopped plums with skins for 30 minutes. Add the pectin and boil for 2 minutes. Add the sugar, cinnamon, and allspice. Cook for 25 minutes or to jell point. Check for a set on a frozen plate. JSP/RWB5(4OZ)10(8OZ).

Spiced Strawberry-Banana Butter

Lower sugar without sacrificing taste!

5 cups washed, hulled, sliced, ripe strawberries
3¾ cups sugar
1 cup peeled, sliced bananas
1 1¾-ounce box "no-sugar" pectin (LM)
⅛ cup lemon juice
1 teaspoon butter
½ teaspoon ground cinnamon
¼-½ teaspoon or less ascorbic acid

Drop a pinch of ascorbic acid crystals on the strawberries and bananas. Slice the fruit in the food processor. Mix the sliced fruit, lemon juice, butter, and pectin together. Wait 10 minutes; boil for 1 minute. Add the sugar and cinnamon; boil 1 minute and skim.
JSP/RWB5(4OZ)10(8OZ).

Variation: Strawberry Butter—Use 6 cups of strawberries and no bananas; cook down. Alternately, use no bananas and add banana extract to the strawberry butter.

Appendix A

ꙮ

Approximate pH of Foods and pH Measurements

The pH numbers shown on this chart are approximate figures. **The term "pH" means potential of hydrogen. It is a measure of acidity.** Special pH papers can be ordered from a druggist or scientific supply house. They are similar to litmus paper, but more refined. The papers can read acids from 3.0 to 5.5, but not as accurately as a pH meter. While Jamlady recommends a pH meter, pH papers are better than nothing and are a good teaching tool. The ½"-wide papers are easier to read than the thinner pH papers.

Foods with a pH of 4.6 or lower are classified as high-acid canning, while foods with a pH of 4.6 or higher are classified as low-acid canning. Many factors—such as growing conditions, varieties, diseases, and others—can affect the pH value of any given food. A 'Delicious' apple, for example, has an approximate pH of around 3.90, whereas a 'Golden Delicious' apple has a 3.60, a 'Jonathan' a 3.33, a 'Macintosh' a 3.34, and a 'Winesap' a 3.47. Information for the "Relationship of pH, Hydrogen Ion Concentration, and Foods Commonly Used in Food Processing" table in this chapter is taken from pH testing by Jamlady and various other sources:

1. U.S. Food and Drug Administration Center for Food Safety and Applied Nutrition, *Approximate pH of Foods and Food Products* (http://vm.cfsan.fda.gov/~comm/lacf-phs.html, June 2000 [cited February 2, 2004]), 1-11.
2. David R. Lide, ed., *Handbook of Chemistry & Physics,* 81st ed. (New York: CRC Press, LLC, 2000-2001).
3. M. A. Bridges and M. R. Mattice, "Over Two Thousand Estimations of the pH of Representative Foods," *American Journal of Digestive Diseases 9* (1939): 440-49.

Low-acid vegetables, such as green beans, can be canned, but if they are canned in a RWB, rolling water bath, they need to be acidified. Canners use the terminology of **"high-acid canning"** and **"low-acid canning"**; the latter requires using higher temperatures for processing or using a pressure cooker/retort. In the case of dilly beans, the addition of vinegar lowers the pH of the product and increases its overall acidity; salt lowers the water activity. **An "acidified food" is a low-acid food that has been modified by the addition of an acid(s) or an acid food(s),**

Relationship of pH, Hydrogen Ion Concentration, and Foods Commonly Used in Food Processing

	pH	Food or Other Substance (pH)	Hydrogen Ion Concentration, Gram Mols Per Liter	
Acid Range (0-6.9)	0	Hydrochloric N Acid (0.1)	1.0	10^0
	1	Sulfuric 0.1N] Acid (1.2)	0.1	10^{-1}
Process pH 4.6 or lower at 212 degrees F in boiling water bath	2	Lemons (2.2-2.8)	0.01	10^{-2}
	3	Grapefruit (3.0-3.7)	0.001	10^{-3}
Process pH 4.6 or higher at 240 degrees F in steam pressure canner	4	Bananas (4.5-5.0), Tomatoes (4.42-4.65)	0.000,1	10^{-4}
	5	Beans (5.60-6.50), Figs (5.0-6.0)	0.000,01	10^{-5}
	6	Dates (6.2-6.4)	0.000,001	10^{-6}
Neutral (7.0)	7	Fresh White Eggs (7.6-8.0)	0.000,000,1	10^{-7}
	8	Hominy (Lye) (6.8-8.0)	0.000,000,01	10^{-8}
	9	Borax (9.2)	0.000,000,001	10^{-9}
Alkaline Range (8.0-14.0)	10	Ammonia 0.01N (10.6)	0.000,000,000,1	10^{-10}
	1	Ammonia N (11.6)	0.000,000,000,01	10^{-11}
	2	Trisodium Phosphate, 0.1N (12.0)	0.000,000,000,001	10^{-12}
	3	Sodium Hydroxide, 0.1N (13.0)	0.000,000,000,000,1	10^{-13}

whereby the resulting product has a pH of 4.6 or less and a water activity greater than 0.85. This process of adding acid to a low-acid food is also called "pickling."

In 1916, **G. N. Lewis** formuated a theory that classified all acid and bases in terms of electron-pair donors and electron-pair acceptors, that **"an acid is a substance that accepts an electron pair, and a base is a substance that donates an electron pair"** (James Quaglino, *Chemistry* [Englewood Cliffs, NJ: Prentice-Hall, Inc., 1964], 480). Pure water, considered a neutral, consists of a very small but detectable number of H+ ions and OH- ions in equal amounts in equilibrium with H_2O molecules. The more hydrogen ions (H+) in a solution, the more acidic the solution, and if the number of hydroxyl ions (HO-) exceeds

that of the hydrogen ions, the solutions is basic. An equal amount of the two ions creates a neutral aqueous solution, such as water, with a respective pH of 7.0 on a scale ranging from zero to fourteen. A neutral, such as pure water, with a pH of 7.0, has a hydrogen ion concentration of 0.0000001 grams per liter (10^{-7}gr./1). Dealing with such small numbers is unwieldy, so a pH scale was adopted.

❦

Jamlady's pH meter is a Digital pH/Temperature/mV/ORP Meter with Automatic Temperature Compensation #5938-10 pHW/ATC, which is sold by Cole-Parmer Instrument Company (625 E. Bunker Ct., Vernon Hills, IL 60061) (800-323-4340). It is important to purchase a high-temperature, double-junction electrode for jam making, as the other types of electrodes are not made for highly viscous substances and high heat. A single-junction electrode will more than likely clog in highly viscous jams. The high-temperature, double-junction electrode that Jamlady currently uses is a 5998-30 HH5 made by Cole-Parmer Instrument Company. For this meter, you will also need a temperature probe, as temperature affects pH and the probe will compensate for temperature variations. Other companies making meters are VWR Scientific, Fisher Scientific, and Omego. Also, there appears to be a new type of nonglass, more durable, stainless-steel pH probe with ISFET (Ion Specific Field Effect Transistor) silicon chip pH sensor. This new technology promises to make pH

testing simple and easy for the home canner. Check out these new products before you buy a pH meter, temperature probe, and electrode. Search pH meters online. Contact Cole-Palmer or the other scientific supply companies listed above.

Any food processor to altering a recipe in any way should check the final product with a pH meter. For a partly liquid and partly chunky product, remember to blend the product into one consistency and test carefully to avoid an inaccurate reading. Electrodes should be rinsed between samples with distilled water to prevent cross-contamination. Another alternate method is to rinse the electrode with part of the next sample, if the sample is not too thick. Make sure to throw away the sample used to rinse the electrode. This alternate method, of course, would not work well on many jellies or jams, as these products are too thick. For these thicker products, rinse the electrode with distilled water and blot off (not wipe) the excess water. Also, electrodes may become clogged.

If your electrode gives either unstable or

erroneous readings, it may be clogged. Contact the manufacture of your pH meter for directions regarding all aspects of use and care of your equipment. Directions will vary for different models and manufacturers.

Besides a pH meter, it is recommended that you have a **temperature probe,** as **temperature affects pH measurement.** A temperature probe is especially necessary with warm, cooked samples (like jam) that must be measured for pH before they cool and jell. The closer the temperature of the sample to the buffer solution used when setting the standard, the more accurate the reading will be. Remember, if the pH of a product is not under the pH of 4.6, and therefore not acceptable for canning, you can always refrigerate it instead. It does not need to be discarded if kept under refrigeration at all times. **Further, test only small amounts of product, and do not eat a product that has been tested with a probe, since small amounts of "stuff" is actually coming out of the end of the electrode while you are measuring—or so Jamlady has been told. If purchasing a newer-design pH meter and probe, be sure to ask about the differences in operation and care of the unit.**

The temperature of the product you are testing is important because the pH reading will not be the same at different temperatures. When an ATC probe is connected to your pH meter, the temperature compensation is automatic from 0 degrees to 100 degrees C. Wherever you purchase your pH unit, please make sure you speak to a technician capable of matching your needs to the appropriate equipment. If you are making jams, make sure you purchase a probe that is appropriate for high heat and thick product. Make sure you carefully read the correct way to store your electrode, as the tip may need to be kept wet at all times. The newer metal probes store dry.

Standardization is a necessary step to an accurate pH reading. Turn on your unit and allow it to warm up. Standardization checks the accuracy of your unit's readings against two buffer solu-

tions of known pH, usually buffer 4.01 and 7.0. **Do not fail to standardize your pH meter before measuring samples.**

Acidification procedures vary according to the product being made. For antipasto, some recipes recommend boiling the vegetables in water-vinegar brine for 10 minutes, draining, and allowing the vegetables to stand overnight. A recipe for **Peter Piper Pickled Pepper** (from an agriculture extension office) says layer the pepper and onions in a crock and cover with 5 percent apple-cider vinegar and let stand at room temperature for 24 hours. Some recipes recommend the vegetables be steamed and then placed in a vinegar solution to soak, and other recipes combine high- and low-acid foods together to affect the pH. Commercial packers often use acid pellets that are placed directly into each jar to increase product acidity. **The most common method of acidification is probably direct batch acidification, where the acid is added directly to the batch in the kettle and cooked on the stove. Whatever method you use, make sure to follow tested recipes and keep written records of the steps you take in making your product.** Home food preservers often skip record keeping, but like a diary, one learns from his mistakes and observations, so keep records. Spiral notebooks are inexpensive!

For those interested in selling their canned products, please contact the FDA, the USDA, and your local and state health departments for copies of current rules and regulation. **In recent news, at least one extension office is warning canners who use the RWB method of canning against canning with oil in the product. The reason given is that the oil can make a hospitable environment where the dangerous *Clostridium botulinum* can thrive and produce poisonous toxins.** Another useful source of information is the Food Processors Institute or a Better Process School. Contact one of the Better Process Schools, like Chapman University, Cornell University, or Purdue University, for more information.

List of pHs

Apples 2.90-4.00	Boysenberries 3.00-3.30
Apricots 3.30-4.80	Bread, white 5.00-6.00
Artichokes 5.60	Broccoli, cooked 6.30-6.52
Asparagus 5.00-6.70	Brussels sprouts 6.00-6.30
Avocados 6.27-6.58	Butter (melted) 5.70-6.80
Bananas, red 4.50-4.75	Cabbage 5.20-6.80
Bananas, yellow 5.00-5.29	Cactus, pear cactus (tuna) 5.30-7.10
Beans 5.60-6.50	Cantaloupe 6.13-6.58
Beers 4.00-5.00	Carrots 4.90-5.30
Beets 4.90-6.60	Cauliflower 5.60-6.00
Bilberry 2.80-3.70	Celery 5.70-6.00
Blackberries 3.20-4.50	Cheese 4.10-7.44
Blueberries, Maine 3.12-3.33	Cherries 3.20-4.20

Cherries, maraschino	3.47-3.52	Jellies, fruit	2.80-3.40
Cherries, 'Royal Anne'	3.80-3.83	Ketchup	3.89-3.92
Chicory	5.90-6.05	Kiwano fruit	4.40 (single test)
Chives	5.20-6.35	Kiwi fruit	3.10-3.50
Cider	2.90-3.30	Kumquat, Florida	3.64-4.25
Coconut, fresh	5.52-6.18	Leeks	5.52-6.17
Corn	5.90-7.30	Lemons	2.20-3.20
Corn syrup, Karo Light	4.60 maximum	Lettuce	5.80-6.15
Corn syrup, Karo Dark	5.00 maximum	Limes	1.80-2.35
Cranberries	2.30-2.70	Loganberries	2.70-3.50
Cream of coconut, canned	5.51-5.87	Loquats	2.80-4.00
Cucumbers	5.12-5.78	Mangoes, Florida	3.40-4.63
Cucumbers, dilled pickles	3.20-3.60	Maple syrup	6.50-7.00
Cucumbers, sour pickles	3.00-3.40	Melba toast	5.08-5.30
Currants, red	2.90	Melons, casaba	5.78-6.00
Dates, canned	6.20-6.40	Melons, honeydew	6.00-6.67
Dates, Deglet Noor (Sun Fresh)	5.50-6.00	Melons, Persians	5.90-6.38
Eggplant	4.75-5.50	Milk, acidophilus	4.90-4.25
Eggs, newly laid	6.58 (as CO_2 in egg decreases with time, the albumen pH rises)	Milk, condensed	6.33
		Milk, cow	6.30-6.80
		Milk, evaporated	5.90-6.30
Eggs, white	7.96	Milk, goat	6.48
Eggs, yolk	6.80	Milk, human	6.60-7.60
Elderberries	3.60-3.80	Molasses	4.90-5.40
Fennel, Anise	5.48-5.88	Mushrooms	6.00-6.70
Figs	5.05-5.98	Nectarines	3.92-4.18
Flour, wheat	7.60-8.00	Okra	5.50-6.60
Gelatin dessert	2.60	Olives, green fermented	3.60-4.60
Gelatin, plain jell	6.08	Olives, ripe	6.00-7.30
Gooseberries	2.80-3.30	Onions, red	5.30-5.80
Grapefruit	3.00-3.75	Onions, white	5.40-5.80
Grapes, 'Concord'	2.80-3.00	Onions, yellow	5.32-5.60
Grapes, 'Niagara'	2.80-3.27	Oranges	3.00-4.35
Grapes, seedless or seeded	2.90-4.50	Oysters	6.10-6.60
Grapes, wild	3.14 (single test, Illinois)	Palm, heart of	6.70
		Papaya	5.10-5.72
Ground cherries	4.25-4.35	Parsley	5.70-6.03
Guava	4.60	Parsnips	5.30-5.70
Guava, canned	3.70-4.00	Peaches	3.30-4.05
Honey	3.70-4.20	Peanut butter	6.28
Horseradish, freshly ground	5.35	Pears, 'Bartlett'	3.50-4.60
Jackfruit	4.8-6.80	Peas, chick, Garbanzo	6.48-6.80
Jams	3.50-4.50	Peas, cooked	6.22-6.88

Peas, dried (split gr.), cooked 6.45-6.80
Peas, dried (split yell.), cooked 6.43-6.62
Peppers 4.65-5.45
Peppers, green 5.20-5.93
Persimmons 4.42-5.80
Pickles, dill 3.20-3.60
Pickles, sour 3.00-3.40
Pimiento 4.40-4.90
Pineapple 3.20-4.10
Plums 2.80-4.00
Plums, blue 2.80-3.40
Plums, 'Damson' 2.90-3.10
Plums, 'Green Gage' 3.60-4.30
Plums, red 3.60-4.30
Plums, yellow 3.90-4.45
Pomegranate 2.93-3.10
Potato 5.40-5.90
Potato, sweet 5.30-5.60
Prunes, dried, stewed 3.63-3.92
Prunes, puréed 3.30-4.30
Pumpkins 4.80-5.50
Quince, freshly cooked 3.12-3.40
Radishes, red 5.85-6.05
Radishes, white 5.52-5.69
Raisins, seedless 3.80-4.10
Raspberries 2.80-3.60
Red pepper relish 3.10-3.62
Rhubarb 3.10-3.40
Rice, white, cooked 6.00-6.68
Romaine 5.78-6.06
Rose hips 3.70
Rowanberry 3.70
Salmon 6.10-6.35
Sauerkraut 3.30-3.60
Shallots 5.30-5.70
Shrimp 6.80-7.00
Sorrel 2.90-3.70
Soursop, fresh 5.00
Soursop, pulp (for sale) . . . . 3.70 (Some pulps
. . . . .are acidified prior
. . . . .to shipping.)
Soy sauce 4.40-5.40
Spinach 5.10-6.80

Squash 5.00-6.20
Starfruit (Carambola) 2.20-4.10
Strawberries 3.00-4.30
Swiss chard, cooked 6.17-6.78
Tamarillos or tree tomatoes 4.21-4.30
. . . .(changes with
. . . . .storage)
Tangerine 3.32-4.48
Tomatoes, vine ripened 4.42-4.65
. . . .(safety level = 4.60)
Tomato puree 4.30-4.47
Tuna 5.90-6.10
Turnip 5.29-5.90
Vinegar 2.40-3.40
Vinegar, cider 3.10
Walnuts, English 5.42
Water chestnut 6.20
Watercress 5.88-6.18
Watermelon 5.18-5.60
Water, tap 6.50-8.00
Wines 2.80-3.80
Worcestershire sauce 3.63-3.67
Yams, cooked 5.79-6.81
Yeast 5.65
Zucchini, cooked 5.69-6.10
Zwieback 4.84-4.94

Note: This page attempts to get the pH numbers correct, but finding all the values has proven to be a challenging task. Please report any errors in this list, and Jamlady will post corrections on her Web site (jamlady.com) or make changes in any subsequent reprints of this book. This is all the more reason to have your own pH meter, so you can check fresh fruit pulps and completed products yourself. Some frozen fruit products may have been acidified by the food processor and may not reflect the true pH of the natural food.

Appendix B
ꝏ
Buyer's Guide

This buyer's guide has been provided so that consumers might have at least one source for some of the ingredients or equipment that are mentioned in this book.

Bronson Laboratories
350 South 400 West #102
Lindon, UT 84042
800/235-3200
Pure ascorbic acid crystals and other supplements.

California Rare Fruit Growers, Inc.
www.crfg.org
A long list of exotic fruit trees, with their common and Latin names. CRFG's own magazine is called the *Fruit Gardener* and features reviews of books on topics related to horticulture.

Champion Juicing Machines
Plastaket Company
www.championjuicers.com
Jamlady recommends Champion's commercial-model juicing machine.

Healthnut Alternatives
P.O. Box 264
New Fairfield, CT 06812
800/728-1238
www.ezjuicers.com

Cole-Parmer Instrument Co.
625 E. Bunker Court
Vernon Hills, IL 60061
800/323-4340 or 847/549-7600 or 847/549-7676
Sells pH meters, standard buffer solutions, probes, and large stainless-steel trays.

Chop-Rite Two, Inc.
531 Old Skippack Road
Harleysville, PA 19438
800/683-5858
info@chop-rite.com
www.chop-rite.com (for a list of retail locations)
#16T cherry stoner

Cook, Seal, and Process
Box 874
Crystal Lake, IL 60014
815/459-9518
Canned jellies, jams, preserves, butter, relishes, pickles, chutneys, and other food products for sale.
or
Jamlady.com
3202 Northwest Highway, J
Cary, IL 60013
www.jamlady.com
Homemade jellies, jams, preserves, chutneys, relishes, pickles, and other condiments. Small-batch products have the recipe attached to the jar. Canning equipment, canning supplies, group and individual instruction, and books.

Cumberland General Store
#1 Highway 68
Crossville, TN 38555
800/334-4640
Food mills, food grinders, cherry pitters, and canning equipment.

CutleryAndMore.com
Elk Grove, IL 60007
800/650-9866
Jamlady recommends All-Clad's 8 quart, 10 ¼" x 5⁵⁄₁₆", stainless stock pot with lid and heavy bottom for making jam, and a tall stainless stock pot, 13"x13", with core bottom and ¾" high rack for the bottom, for processing jars. Commercial stock pots, canning pots, racks, knives, strainers, steam juicers, and stainless ladles.

E.C. Kraus Home Wine Making Supplies
733 South Northern Boulevard
Independence, MO 64053
816/254-7448 or 800/353-1906
Sells pH papers and other wine-making supplies.

Eurofresh Market
130 W. Northwest Highway
Palatine, IL 60067
847/202-0333
www.eurofreshmarket.com
Bulk spices, unusual vegetables, inexpensive wine vinegar in gallon containers.

Let's Spice It Up
105 Washington Ave.
Highwood, IL 60040
800/659-6302
www.letsspiceitup.com
All sorts of spices. Spicelady Jane is a vendor at many Chicagoland markets.

Lorann Oils, Inc.
4518 Aurelius Rd.
Lansing, MI 48910
800/862-8620
www.lorannoils.com (to find a retailer)
Oils and flavorings are available where many cake decorating supplies are sold and at some pharmacies.

Micro Essential Laboratory, Inc.
P.O. Box 100824
Brooklyn, NY 11210
718/338-3618
custserv@microessentialab.com
Sells pH test papers.

Miller Orchards
501 W. Randolph St.
Nappanee, IN 46550
574/773-3923
Visit the Amish and buy fresh apples, canned meats, apple butter, and other homemade products. Ask about homemade cider vinegar.

Precision Foods, Inc.
11457 Olde Cabin Road
St. Louis, MO 63141
800/647-8170
Pickling lime, pickling salt, citric acid, Home Jell and Home Jell Lite (LM) pectins.

The Home Economist
906 S. Northwest Highway
Barrington, IL 60010
847/382-4202
Bulk spices, teas, nuts, dried papaya, and other dried fruits.

Walton Feed
135 North 10th
P.O. 307
Montpelier, ID 832354
800/847-0465
www.waltonfeed.com
Modified food starch (CLEARJEL®), grains, bulk food for co-ops.

We Are Beer & Winemaking Supplies, Inc.
154 King St.
Northampton, MA 01060
413/ 586-0150
www.beer-winemaking.com
Supplies for small-batch wine making, citric acid, and vinegar cultures.

Bibliography

The books listed in this reading section include some books or handbooks that may be difficult or nearly impossible to locate, as they are housed in private collections, small libraries with unshared catalogs, or at libraries restricting the use and circulation of antiquarian books. While some specific books may not be available to you through regular libraries, there are collectors and sellers on the Internet that may be able to provide you with the same book or handbook, or with a similar publication. Many of these older cookbooks were printed for years with many versions and only minor changes in the titles. Although Isabella Beeton, for example, only lived for twenty-eight years, her name continued to be seen in print for 125 years, as publishers Ward, Lock & Co. continued to produce revisions of her *House Management* book. The first Beadle Dime Books was published on April 19, 1859. It was a songbook. Quickly after this song handbook came out *The Dime Cook Book* and *The Dime Recipe Book* were published. These small-sized handbooks continued to be published until 1880—with few published during the last ten years (from 1870-80). While you may not be able to access the exact handbook Jamlady cites here, you still can find handbooks like these around. As for other older books, do not give up on the book if you cannot find it on World Cat. Sleuth around small-town libraries, estate sales, and other places where these books might be found.

Alltrista Corporation and Ball. *The Ball Blue Book, Vol. 1.* Muncie, Ind.: Alltrista Corporation and Ball, 1995.

Anderson, Jean. *The Green Thumb Preserving Guide.* New York: William Morrow and Company, Inc., 1976.

Andrews, Jean. *Peppers-The Domesticated Capsicums, New Edition.* Austin, Tex.: University of Texas Press, 1995.

Archdeacon, William. *Archdeacon's Kitchen Cabinet.* Chicago, Ill.: William Archdeacon, 1876.

Bailey, L. H. *The Standard Cyclopedia of Horticulture,* 3 vols. New York: Macmillan Publishing Co., 1930.

Bailey, Liberty Hyde, and Ethel Zoe Bailey. *Hortus Third.* New York: Macmillan Publishing Co., 1976.

Balch, Phillis, and James Balch. *Prescription for Nutritional Healing.* New York: Penguin Putnam, Inc., 2000.

Barash, Cathy Wilkinson. *Edible Flowers.* Golden, Colo.: Fulcrum Publishing, 1993.

Beckett, Barbara. *Chutneys & Pickles (The Country Kitchen Series).* Willoughby, Australia: Weldon Publishing, 1992.

Beeton, Isabella. *Household Management,* new ed. London: Ward, Lock & Co., n.d.

Beeton, Isabella. *Mrs. Beeton's All About Cookery.* London: Ward, Lock & Co., n.d.

Beeton, Isabella. *Mrs. Beeton's Hors d'Oeuvres & Savories.* London: Ward, Lock & Co., n.d.

Belsinger, Susan. *Flowers in the Kitchen.* Loveland, Colo.: Interweave Press, 1991.

Benson, Evelyn Abraham, ed. *Penn Family Recipes, Cooking Recipes of Wm. Penn's Wife, GULIELMA with an account of the life of Gulielma Maria Springett Penn., 1644-1694.* York, Pa.: George Shumway, Publisher, 1966.

Berto, Hazel. *Cooking with Honey.* New York: Crown Publishing Co., 1972.

Blits, Prof. H. *Methods of Canning Fruits and Vegetables by Hot Air and Steam, and Berries by Compounding of Syrups, and the Crystallizing and Candying of Fruits, Etc., Etc.* Brooklyn, N.Y.: H. I. Blits, 1890.

Bosland, P. W., and E. J. Votava. *Peppers: Vegetable and Spice Capsicums.* New York: CABI Publishing, 2000.

Boyd, Polly [Jill Norman]. *Cooking with Spices.* New York: DK Publishing, Inc., 1998.

Brannt, William T. *A Practical Treatise on the Manufacture of Vinegar and Acetates, Cider, and Fruit-Wines; Preservation of Fruits and Vegetables by Canning and Evaporation; Preparation of Fruit-Butters, Jellies, Marmalades, Catchups, Pickles, Mustards, etc.* Philadelphia, Pa.: Henry Carey Baird & Co., 1890.

Bremness, Lesley. *Herbs.* London: Dorling Kindersley, 1994.

Brown, Marion. *Pickles and Preserves.* New York: Wilfred Funk, Inc., 1955.

Caloosa Rare Fruit Exchange, Inc. *Tropical Fruit Cookbook,* 2nd ed. Fort Meyers, Fla.: Caloosa Rare Fruit Exchange, Inc., 1991.

Carey, Nora. *Perfect Preserves.* New York: Stewart, Tabo ri & Chang, Inc., 1990.

Cookery and Domestic Economy for Young Housewives, 26th ed., London and Edinburgh: William and Robert Chambers, 1876.

Chesman, Andrea. *Summer in a Jar: Making Pickles, Jams & More.* Charlotte, Vt.: Williamson Publishing, 1985.

Chevallier, Andrew. *The Encyclopedia of Medicinal Plants.* London: Dorling Kindersley Ltd., 1996.

Choate, Judith. *Gourmet Preserves.* New York: Weidenfeld & Nicholson, 1987.

Claiborne, Craig. *The New York Times Food Encyclopedia.* New York: New York Times Company, 1985.

Cooking with the Horse & Buggy People, A Collection of Over 600 Favorite Amish Recipes from the Heart of Holmes County. Sugar Creek, Ohio: Carlisle Press, 1994.

De Brevan, J. *The Manufacture of Liquors and Preserves — History of Technology Vol. No. 3.* Park Ridge, N.J.: Noyes Press, 1972.

De Leon, Josefina Velazquez. *Mexican Cook Book for American Homes,* 6th ed. Mexico City: Culinary Arts Institute, 1967.

Dick, William B. *Encyclopedia of Practical Receipts and Processes. Containing over 6400 Receipts Embracing through Information, in Plain Language, Applicable to Almost Every Possible Industrial and Domestic Requirement.* New York: Dick & Fitzgerald, Publishers, 1872.

Doerfer, Jane. *The Pantry Gourmet.* Emmaus, Pa.: Rodale Press, 1984.

Domine, Andre. *Culinaria France.* Cologne: Könemann, 1998.

Downing, Donald, ed. *The Complete Course in Canning and Related Processes,* 13th ed. 3 vols. Baltimore, Md.: CTI Publications, 1996.

Dragan, Mary Anne. *Well Preserved.* Vancouver and Toronto: Whitecap Books, 1998.

Duke, James A. *The Green Pharmacy.* Emmaus, Pa.: Rodale Press, 1997.

Elliott, Sarah A. *Mrs. Elliott's Housewife.* New York: Hurd and Houghton, 1890.

Ewell, Alice Priest. *The Crystal Cook Book.* New York: Warner Baking Powder Company, 1905.

Experienced Preservers. *A Treatise on the Art of Preserving Fruits and Vegetables Hermetically in the Gem and Hero Jars.* N.p., n.d.

Farmer, Fannie Merritt. *The Fannie Farmer Cookbook,* 12th ed. New York: Knopf Publishing Co., 1979.

Ferber, Christine. *Mes Confitures.* Translated by Virginia R. Phillips. East Lansing, Mich.: Michigan State University Press, 2002.

Fitzgibbon, Theodora. *The Food of the Western World.* New York: New York Times Book Co., 1976.

Forsell, Mary. *Berries.* New York: Bantam Books, 1989.

Francatelli, Charles Elmé. *The Modern Cook; Practical Guide to the Culinary Art in All Its Branches.* Philadelphia, Pa.: T. B. Peterson and Brothers, 1876.

Francillon, W. G. R., and G. T. C. D. S. *Good Cookery.* 1920. Reprint, London: J. M. Dent & Sons, Ltd., 1948.

Gewanter, Vera, and Dorothy Parker. *Home Preserving Made Easy.* New York: Sterling Publishing Co., Inc., 1975.

Gillette, F. L., and Hugo Ziemann. *The White House Cookbook.* Edited by Frances R. Grossman. New York: David McKay Company, Inc., 1976.

Grimes, Lulu. *The Food of Thailand.* Murdock Books: Sydney, Australia, 2003.

Grossinger, Jennie. *The Art of Jewish Cooking.* New York: Bantam Books, 1958.

Gunst, Kathy. *Condiments.* New York: G. P. Putnam's Sons, 1984.

Hallgarten, Peter A. *Spirits and Liqueurs.* London: Faber & Faber, 1979.

Hanle, Zack. *Cooking with Flowers.* Los Angeles, Calif.: Price/Stern/Sloan Publishers, 1971.

Hayes, S. C.. *Mackenzie's Five Thousand Receipts.* Philadelphia, Pa.: T. Ellwood Zell, Publisher, 1860.

Heaton, Donald D. *A Produce Reference Guide to Fruits and Vegetables from Around the World.* New York: Food Products Press, 1997.

Hertzberg, Ruth, Beatrice Vaughan, and Janet Greene. *Putting Food By,* 2nd ed. New York: Bantam Books, Inc., 1976.

Hobbs, Christopher. *Herbal Remedies for Dummies.* New York: IDG Books Worldwide, Inc., 1998.

Hoffman, David. *The New Holistic Herbal,* 3rd ed. Rockport, Mass.: Element Books Ltd., 1990.

Hogan, Elizabeth, ed. *Home Canning,* 3rd ed. Menlo Park, Calif.: Sunset Publishing Corporation, 1993.

Holland, Mary. *The Complete Economical Cook and Frugal Housewife.* London: Thomas Tegg, 1830.

Housekeeper's Friend, - Containing Valuable Receipts for Those Who Regard Economy as Well as Excellence, Synonyms and Homonyms, Almanac 1883. Keene, N.H.: M. V. B. Clark & Co., 1883.

Howe, Robin. *Making Your Own Preserves.* Pudsey, York, England: Magna Print Books, 1974

Hume, Rosemary, and Muriel Downes. *Jams, Preserves & Pickles.* Chicago, Ill.: Henry Regnery Company, 1972.

Junior League of Charleston. *Charleston Receipts,* 23rd ed. Charleston, S.C.: The Junior League of Charleston, 1981.

Kluger, Marilyn. *Preserving Summer's Bounty.* New York: M. Evan and Company, Inc. 1979.

Ladies Aid Society. *The Cook's Manual.* Esopus, N.Y.: The Ladies Aid Society, Esopus Methodist Episcopal Church, 1891.

Ladies Aid Society of the Methodist Episcopal Church. *"Tried and True" Cook Book of Domestic Receipts.* Ellenville, N.Y.: The Ladies Aid Society of the Methodist Episcopal Church, n.d.

Lady of Philadelphia. *The National Cook Book.* Philadelphia, Pa.: Robert E. Peterson, 1850.

Lemcke, Gesine. *Preserving and Pickling.* New York: D. Appleton and Company, 1899.

Lesem, Jeanne. *The Pleasures of Preserving and Pickling.* New York: Knopf Publishing Co., 1975.

Leslie, Eliza. *Miss Leslie's New Cookery Book.* Philadelphia, Pa.: T. B. Peterson and Brothers, 1857.

Leyel, C. F. *Herbal Delights.* London: Faber & Faber, 1947.

Lincoln, D. A. *Boston Cook Book.* Boston: Roberts Brothers, 1891.

Marquart, John. *600 Miscellaneous Valuable Receipts Worth Their Weight in Gold - A Thirty Years' Collection.* Lebanon, Pa.: Christian Henry, 1860.

Morton, Julia F. *Fruits of Warm Climates.* Miami, Fla.: Julia F. Morton, 1987.

Mrs. Winslow's Domestic Receipt Book for 1871. New York: Jeremiah Curtis & Sons and John I. Brown & Sons, 1870.

Mrs. Winslow's Domestic Receipt Book for 1876. New York: Jeremiah Curtis & Sons and John I. Brown & Sons, 1875.

Mrs. Winslow's Domestic Receipt Book for 1877. New York: Jeremiah Curtis & Sons and John I. Brown & Sons, 1876.

Naj, Amal. *Peppers, A Story of Hot Pursuits.* New York: Knopf Publishing Co., 1992.

Neil, E. *The Every-Day Cook Book and Encyclopedia of Practical Recipes.* Chicago, Ill.: Merchants' Specialty Co. Publishers, 1892.

Niethammer, Carolyn. *American Indian Food and Lore.* New York: Macmillan Publishing Co., 1974.

Norman, Jill. *Spices.* London: Dorling Kindersley, 1990.

Norwalk, Mary. *The Book of Preserves.* Tucson, Ariz.: HP Books, 1986.

Ohrbach, Barbara Milo. *Merry Christmas.* New York: Clarkson Potter Publishers, 1992.

Pacult, F. Paul. *Kindred Spirits.* New York: Hyperion, 1997.

Palmer, Minne. *The Woman's Exchange Cook Book.* Chicago, Ill.: Monarch Book Company, 1894.

Pandya, Michael. *Indian Chutneys, Raitas, Pickles and Preserves.* New York: Thorson Publishing Company, 1986.

Perdue, Charles L., ed. *Pigsfoot Jelly & Persimmons Beer: Foodways from the Virginia Writers' Project.* N.p.: Virginia Writers' Project, 1993.

Peterson, M. E. *Peterson's Perserving, Pickling & Canning—Fruit Manual.* Philadelphia, Pa.: G. Peterson and Company, 1869.

Rich, Chris, and Lucy Clark Crawford. *The Food Lover's Guide to Canning.* Ashville, N.C.: Lark Books, 1997.

Richardson, Rosamond. *Harrods Book of Jams, Jellies & Chutneys.* New York: Arbor House Publishing, 1986.

Robbins, Maria Polushkin, ed. *Blue Ribbon Pickles and Preserves.* New York: St. Martin's Press, 1987.

Rombauer, Irma, and Marion Rombauer Becker. *The Joy of Cooking.* Indianapolis, Ind.: Bobbs-Merrill Company, Inc., 1974.

Rorer, S. T. *Canning and Preserving.* Philadelphia, Pa.: Arnold and Company, 1887.

Rosengarten, Frederic. *The Book of Edible Nuts.* New York: Walker Publishing Company, Inc., 1984.

Rosengarten, Frederic. *The Book of Spices.* Wynnewood, Pa.: Livingston Publishing Co., 1969.

Schwartz, Oded. *Preserving.* New York: DK Publishing, Inc., 1996.

Smith, E. *The Compleat Housewife: or Accomplish'd Gentlewoman's Companion.* 1753. Reprint, London: T. J. Press, 1968.

Stallworth, Lyn, and Rod Kennedy, Jr. *The Country Fair Cookbook,* New York: Hyperion, 1994.

Stewart, Hilary. *Wild Teas Coffees & Cordials,* Seattle, Wash.: University of Washington Press, 1981.

St. Luke's Aid Society. *Earnest Worker's Cook Book.* Chicago, Ill.: St. Luke's Aid Society, Trinity Church, 1886.

Street, Myra. *The Encyclopedia of Homemade Preserves.* London: Quintet Publishing, 1996.

Turgeon, Charlotte. *The Encyclopedia of Creative Cooking.* New York: Weathervane Books, 1985.

Tyler, Varrio E. *The Honest Herbal.* New York: Pharmaceutical Products Press, 1982.

Victor, Mrs. *The Dime Cookbook.* New York and Buffalo: Irwin P. Beadle Publishers, n.d. (Prince & Co. were selling Improved Melodeons with Divided Swell for $45-$350).

Willing Workers Society of the Methodist Episcopal Church. *The Light of the Kitchen.* Kerhonkson, N.Y.: Willing Workers Society of the Methodist Episcopal Church, n.d.

Index

BOTANICAL LATIN NAMES

GENERAL INDEX